The Christian Tradition

The Christian Tradition

Ralph Keen

University of Iowa

Prentice Hall, Inc., Upper Saddle River, NJ. 07458

Published 2004 by Prentice Hall Inc.
A Division of Pearson Education
Upper Saddle River, New Jersey 07458

10 9 8 7 6 5 4 3 2 1

ISBN 0-13-090461-9

This book was designed and produced by Laurence King Publishing Ltd, London
www.laurenceking.co.uk

Editors: Richard Mason, Melanie White
Development editor: Damian Thompson
Design concept: Melinda Welch
Typesetting and layout: Paul Barrett
Cover design: Price Watkins
Picture research: Peter Kent
Cartography: Andrea Fairbrass

Printed in Hong Kong

Front cover: Odilon Redon, *Sacred Heart*, c. 1906. Pastel. Musée d'Orsay, Paris.
Frontispiece: The Master of Santa Chiara, *St. Clare with Scenes from her Life*, 14th century. Tempera on panel. Bridgeman Art Library, London.

Contents

The Christian Religion in Late Antiquity 77

Timeline 400–800 C.E. 78

**From Medieval to Modern,
from One Church, Many** 201

Timeline 1500–1700 202

From Enlightenment to Modernity 275

Timeline 1700–1900 276

The Twentieth Century and Beyond 333

Preface

Traditions evolve, and the ways of interpreting them also evolve, sometimes quite quickly. The transformations that Christianity underwent in the twentieth century have been reflected by an ever-increasing pace of change in academic approaches. This book reflects the most recent research into its subject. As the pace of change seems likely to continue, any historian's version of the story of Christianity will necessarily invite radical reinterpretations. Therefore, it is important to concede that although today's textbook may serve for many tomorrows, it may not meet all the expectations of the next generation of readers. If in years to come writers choose to interpret the Christian tradition in radically new ways, they will inherit an onerous task, but they will also earn the sympathies and blessings of a host of predecessors.

This text aims to introduce students in a new millennium to a tradition that shaped two previous millennia whose onset coincided with the dawn of the Roman Empire. The church emerged at a time most unfavorable to its survival. It gradually found shape and momentum amidst incalculable political and cultural obstacles, and became in turn an obstacle to forces hostile to itself. Although the intention of nineteenth-century Christian missionaries was to standardize the ways in which the church provided meaning to various peoples, the global expansion of Christianity actually provided a diversity of such meanings. In recent decades the church has slowly come to recognize that it is just one cultural system among many, existing in a pluralistic world where the spread of civilization is no longer predominantly identified with the expansion of European culture. If the church of the first century recognized no differences between Jews and Greeks, East and West, so the church in the twenty-first century must struggle to eliminate differences between races and sexes, nations and classes. This narrative explains how some of the current problems confronted by the modern church came into being.

Thematically, this work aims to be as inclusive as possible. It begins by focusing on the Jewish roots of Christianity within the context of the Roman Empire, and Judaeo-Christian relations in general. It also covers the history of Christianity's relations with Islam, and the rivalry between the Holy Roman Empire in the West and the Byzantine Empire in the East that oversaw the spread of Orthodoxy continuing to this day. The book deals with the impact on Christianity of the pivotal change from a largely oral medieval Christian tradition to a written culture that flourished with Gutenberg's invention of moveable type and the first printing presses. The various roles played by women in the church is exemplified by Beguines, female medieval mystics, and contemporary feminist theologians. The book's subjects range from scholasticism, nominalism, Jansenism, and Pietism, to Enlightenment religions, social Christianity, and Liberation Theology. The additional coverage of artistic strains and popular religious movements is intended to point to a new direction in church history.

This book is meant to be as flexible as possible and is organized so that it can be read either continuously or selectively. Instructors who wish to omit periods of church history will be able to do so. The six parts represent conventional breaks in the history of the Christian tradition. A timeline at the beginning of each part gives an overview of some of the most important events within that period. Each chapter is an independent unit, although cross-references to other chapters offer extended explanations and discussions of points at issue.

Biographical Profiles highlight the lives and works of some of the most influential people in the history of Christianity, including Jesus himself, St. Augustine, St. Teresa of Ávila, St. Vincent de Paul, Søren Kierkegaard, and Paul Tillich. Extracts from the writings of religious figures—St. Benedict, Hildegard of Bingen, Margery Kempe, Jonathan Edwards, Karl Barth, Gustavo Gutiérrez, and many others—offer insights into the important issues of the day. Who's Who boxes summarize the leading figures within various religious movements, from the twelve apostles to current Liberation and feminist historians. Nine maps offer snapshots into areas such as the first Christian communities and the spread of Christianity compared with other religions.

With a view to objectivity, I have adopted as much as possible the stance of an outsider to the Christian tradition. If some observations appear challenging, they are offered in the interest of depicting Christianity as it might be viewed by today's non-Christians.

My thanks are extended to the following reviewers, whose comments helped me in preparing the final version of the manuscript: Greta Austin, Bucknell University; Lee Bailey, Ithaca College; and Joseph Currie, Fordham University.

This work has been a team effort, and it is a pleasure to recognize the help of my often indefatigable partners at Laurence King Publishing Ltd: my editors Richard Mason, Damian Thompson, Christine Davis, and Melanie White; copy-editor Eleanor van Zandt; picture editor Peter Kent; designer Melinda Welch; and typesetter and layout artist Paul Barrett.

Ralph Keen
University of Iowa
May, 2003

Introduction

On any given Sunday, and on numerous other days over the course of the year, a vast and diverse population assembles, in places ranging from cathedrals to storefronts, to affirm their faith in a particular view of a few events that took place in the Middle East during the first century of the common era (C.E)*. Rome was the dominant power of the time; the Judaism centered on the SECOND TEMPLE in Jerusalem was in its final decades; and among the colonized peoples of the Mediterranean, injustice, turmoil, and suffering were constants. Nothing would have been more common in such a world than to have a popular preacher, whose message implicitly challenged the established order, put to death. Many—we do not know how many—suffered that same fate. If all we could know about Jesus of Nazareth is that he was a preacher who extolled a different realm and attracted a wide following before being put to death as a troublemaker, there might be no reason to remember him any more than many other martyrs to tyrannical regimes.

As one observes the typical Christian service, however, it quickly becomes clear that there is much more than biographical fact to the popular understanding of Jesus. Biographical elements form only a small part of this understanding; rarely does one find references in the New Testament to Jesus' historical context or the circumstances in which the books themselves were written. Instead, the modern understanding of Jesus must be considered religious rather than historical. That is to say, what modern Christian communities celebrate is the shared understanding that resides in the realm of faith, rather than that of historical certainty. This understanding has changed over the centuries; as Albert Schweitzer recognized a century ago, each age looks to Jesus Christ and sees its own ideals reflected back.

---

* "C.E." for "Common Era" and "B.C.E." for "Before the Common Era" have proved more congenial for non-Christians in recent decades than the traditional "B.C." (for "before Christ") and "A.D." (Latin "Anno Domini," "in the year of the Lord").

What can be studied historically, therefore, is the way the picture of Jesus of Nazareth has been augmented by the ideals of each successive age of the Christian era—the course of this changing awareness of him. These shifting perceptions of Jesus can, in fact, be described far more accurately than Jesus' own life, since Christians have left a far richer record of their thoughts and practices than Jesus did of his. From the first proclamation after the original Easter to the latest service to have concluded, and from the earliest New Testament books to the latest statement issued by a church body, the Christian tradition has produced a wealth of material available for study. This tradition can rightly be considered a culture in its own right; and that is how the present survey approaches it.

To see Christianity as a culture is to recognize both complexity and change—indeed unwieldy complexity and constant change—so that any sequence of episodic or thematic "snapshots" will necessarily be incomplete in details and give a static picture of phenomena always in flux. The alternative being complete ignorance, we must proceed in an imperfect way. Training in an impossible range of disciplines would be required in order to deal proficiently with all the components of a culture—attitudes about government, artistic traditions, moral values, and the like. And of course, so broad an approach would blur the distinction between religious studies and other humanistic and social-scientific disciplines.

Nevertheless, we can discern certain cultural patterns over the larger course of the history of the Christian tradition. We can recognize, for example, that the Christian religion emerged out of one culture, the Judaism of the later Second Temple period, and developed within a different one, the Roman Empire in its centuries of ascent and eventual collapse. The community was, in differing ways, alien within each milieu, for the rest of the Jewish community rejected Christian claims of a realized redemption, and Roman polytheism and the cult of the emperor were unable to absorb the idea of the sole divinity of Jesus Christ. In both cases the purely religious elements in Christianity coexisted with secular aspects of the indigenous culture, until those aspects were replaced by Christian traditions (in terms of art, architecture, holiday customs, and so forth). This extended period of cultural transition, now generally referred to as Late Antiquity, should be seen as the time of Christianity's emergence as a fully formed religion with clearly defined beliefs and practices.

As Christianity went on to play an increasingly dominant role in culture during the period from about 600 to 1100, it faced a different kind of competition: the folk practices of the various non-Romanized European peoples. By around the year 400, when the Roman civilization was all but exhausted, the land north of the Alps had been populated by Lombards, Burgundians, Vandals, Goths, and Franks, peoples making the transition from a migratory to a more settled existence. Christianity, anchored in Roman antiquity, offered the stability and some of the social infrastructure needed for the formation of the fledgling states that took shape in northern Europe during this period—a period long known as the Dark Ages because of its relative absence of high culture.

The following two hundred years saw a maturing and flowering of European Christian culture which is sometimes called the "twelfth-century renaissance"; indeed, some scholars feel that this period has more claim to be called a renaissance than the movement of the fifteenth and sixteenth centuries generally known by that name. Monastic culture reached its apex in the twelfth century with the phenomenal burgeoning of the Cistercian Order; and in the following century the MENDICANT friars—the Franciscans and Dominicans—provided new forms of religious teaching for a still mostly illiterate laity.

Ritual dominated the life of the church, as it had since the time of the earliest Christians: practices, rather than written doctrines, were the principal means of communicating sacredness. Nevertheless, there was also an astonishing harvest of theological writings during this period, much of it explaining and defending the system of church practices.

With the invention of printing in the middle of the fifteenth century, the character of Christianity changed dramatically. This invention, which had first been put to use in printing Bibles and service books, soon became a means of attacking the system of authorities and practices that had developed during the Middle Ages. With increasing literacy and the proliferation of Bibles in vernacular languages, the extended Christian community became for the first time a "reading" church, with ritual in many cases becoming subordinate to intellectual understanding.

Historical Approaches

Christianity can be studied either SYNCHRONICALLY or DIACHRONICALLY. The synchronic approach examines a body of teachings and practices in a given period, with little attention to issues of historical development. The merit of this approach is that it allows the greatest appreciation of a religious tradition at the time of its flourishing, since one can then see the interconnected elements of a complex cultural system. As such, synchronic study of a religion provides a commentary on practices and doctrines that may not appear related. The diachronic approach, on the other hand, is more concerned with details of development over time, focusing inquiry on the contexts for each step in the course of a long history. Each of these approaches has a fairly obvious blind spot: the synchronic specialist may be oblivious to the original character and intention of an established religious phenomenon, while the historically oriented scholar might give no attention to contemporary perceptions, and thus fail to recognize the continuing evocative power of traditional religious elements. A full understanding of any religious tradition must include, in some proportion, both of these complementary approaches.

The historical approach has generated a formidable canon over the centuries, and histories of the church have become some of the classics of Christian thought and teaching. The Gospels themselves are historical records, accepted as fully factual by many believers; the Acts of the Apostles is their obvious continuation. Other gospels and "acts"-style histories from the time of the apostles reinforce the awareness that this is a tradition rooted in concrete events. Many of the dogmatic treatises of the early decades of Christian history (think of the Epistles preserved in the New Testament) are interpretations of historical events. Like Judaism, Christianity relates a story, placing narrative before theory. One must first know what happened and then discern within these events the meaning for faith.

This has been more easily said than done, of course, since beliefs about what actually did happen have colored the historical tradition—and not just with

Wheeled Ark of the Covenant, Dura-Europos, Syria, c. 245 C.E.

The tablets of Mosaic Law were thought to have been preserved in the sacred ark, one of the holiest relics of ancient Judaism.

respect to the life and teaching of Jesus. Beliefs about the sacredness of the church and its charismatic power find expression in such early Christian histories as those of Sozomen (c. 400–443) and Eusebius (c. 260–c. 339), the second regarded as the first great church historian. Hence, if historical narrative is traditionally considered to be concerned with facts, and religious faith with beliefs, we have in these early authors a combination of theoretically distinct strands of thought. Within Christian history, it is something of an article of faith that the life of the church is divinely guided. Hence the story of the church is believed to be the story of God's work in history.

The Anglo-Saxon historian Bede (c. 672–735), whose *Ecclesiastical History of the English People* is a treasure-house of early English history, saw the progress of the church as the evolution of a providential design; and the Carolingian chronicler Einhard (c. 770–840) depicted the reign of Charles the Great (742–814; r. [as emperor] 800–814) as the realization of a divine plan for a Christian empire. Not seeing history as the unfolding of a grand design would have been a denial that God acts in history, an assumption contrary to biblical revelation and the medieval religious mentality. Likewise, in the early-modern period (c. 1500–1700), historians both Catholic and Protestant composed narratives supporting the thesis that divine activity was on their side. Church history has thus been, until recently, a CONFESSIONAL genre—written by believers and apt to ignore or minimize contrary or embarrassing details.

The course of Christian history, from regional persecution, in Late Antiquity, to international dominance, has been such an unlikely and peculiar story that most historians of the tradition have attributed its success either partly or wholly to divine power, thus using the history of Christianity as evidence of the truth of Christianity. Such explanations are themselves part of the religious tradition, a fact of which not all historians are consciously aware. Much of the history of the Christian tradition, indeed even of Western civilization, has been marked by religious biases and been prone to the historical fallacy of TRIUMPHALISM: the tendency to see a tradition as being destined by divine will to dominance and to narrate its history as the unfolding of that destiny. The desire to incorporate religious beliefs in the explanation of their development is pronounced in Christianity, an essentially historical religion, for reasons already cited. However, it remains possible to describe the course of Christian history without engaging personal beliefs. It may, in fact, be argued that a history that does not attribute the success of Christianity to divine causation presents a more fascinating story; for if it is entirely the result of human effort and imagination, the phenomenon of Christianity shows humans at their most creative, confident, and energetic.

The story of Christianity, in all its complexity, is one of triumphs and defeats, conflicts and concords, and persecutions both suffered and perpetrated. It is one in which the church, the organized body of believers, has had to redefine itself in order to continue, and in which Christian thinkers have had continually to redefine doctrine in order to preserve a coherent body of beliefs.

It was only during the twentieth century that the study of religious traditions became in earnest a subject of critical academic inquiry. The history of Christianity became a branch of history, subject to the same standards as the history of anything else; but in the process a sensitivity to the religious element was diminished. The reductive tendencies of past generations of historians have seen religion as a form of some other aspect of human activity—economic, political, and the like; concomitantly, the notion that these diverse activities are driven by an irreducible religious element is seldom acknowledged. Put another way, in becoming a branch of secular history, rather than religious studies (where the irreducible character of the religious is recognized), the study of a religion's history broke away from the study of the religion itself. Confessional church history continued to be written, of course, but its biases were quickly identified and discounted by "secular" historians, who often thought they were free of such biases themselves.

The present survey steers a course between piety and positivism. It was not written from a confessional perspective but from the standpoint of a sympathetic observer. The author has striven to be aware of the distinctly religious element of a complex cultural tradition, and thus to avoid the reductionism of other historical approaches. Also central to this study is an emphasis on the changing character of Christianity's means of communicating its basic truths. From the church's inception until the invention of printing and the Reformation's "rediscovery" of the Bible, ritual was the primary channel of communication; thereafter, doctrines and ideas assumed the dominant role. Accordingly, our narrative shifts at around 1500 as the tradition, at least as seen by the laity, changes from one almost exclusively made up of life and practice to one in which thought and clarity of belief play an increasing role—even in the Roman Catholic and Orthodox Churches, which still remain highly liturgical. As we shall see, among the clergy, dogmatic systems were of paramount importance from the beginning; but a religious tradition, in all its varied manifestations, far exceeds the scholarly debates of theologians.

Key Terms

CONFESSIONAL   Approaching a religious tradition from the perspective of one of its branches, or confessions.

DIACHRONIC   Viewing a tradition as it develops over time.

MENDICANT   Literally, a beggar, and specifically, the religious who possessed no property and depended on others for sustenance.

SECOND TEMPLE   The period in Jewish history between the return from the Babylonian Exile and the destruction of the Temple in 70 C.E., when the Diaspora began.

SYNCHRONIC   Viewing a tradition at a particular period, without regard to earlier or later historical development.

TRIUMPHALISM   The belief that one religion is divinely destined to prevail over others.

Ercole de Roberti, *The Institution of the Eucharist*, c. 1490. Egg tempera on panel.
National Gallery, London.

The Emergence of Christianity

Christianity emerged from a tumultuous world in which empires rose and fell, and cultures struggled to retain autonomy. Amidst the confusion of conflicting Jewish sects awaiting deliverance from Roman dominion, Jesus and his followers emphasized the qualities of charity and devotion at a time when most religious leaders, by contrast, stressed rigor and ritual.

The disciples of Jesus interpreted the Roman destruction of the Second Temple (the ancient center of Jewish religious life) in 70 CE as a sign that God had transferred the ancient covenant from the earthly realm, and a geographical promised land, to a heavenly "kingdom." Ancient Jewish themes such as redemption were adopted and adapted by Jesus' followers. For example, they interpreted the historical event of the Exodus from Egypt as a worldly anticipation of the Christian "exodus" from this world to a greater—because everlasting—one. The Roman Empire's periodic campaigns of Christian persecution only served to enhance this otherworldly view. Christian martyrdom became an affirmation of faith in a greater reality; death was not a punishment to be avoided but instead a rebirth to be embraced. The consequences were that over time the Christian Church grew rather than declined.

The traditional Jewish structure of early Christianity did not resonate among Greeks and Romans; their cultures included neither an exodus nor a covenant, much less a single sovereign deity. In extending beyond the cultural boundaries of their Palestinian origins, Christian communities sought ways in which to convert other peoples through an appeal to a broader human experience. Thus theologians with philosophical leanings cast Christianity in the Platonic light of a supernatural and absolute "Word"—divine reason—taking on human form in the person of Jesus Christ. In the early fourth century a blend of elements from Jewish, Greek, and Roman cultural traditions took shape. With the reign of the emperor Constantine (312–337), an eclectic and autonomous system of ideas and practices known as the Christian liturgy emerged from the shadows of imperial persecution.

c. 1000 B.C.E.		
	c. 1000	King David rules Israel and Judah.
	586	Babylonians destroy the first Temple and deport the Jews to Babylon.
	538	Return to Jerusalem and rebuilding of the Temple.
	167	Led by the Maccabees, the Jews successfully revolt against Seleucid rule.
1 C.E.	37	The Romans help the Idumean chieftain Herod install himself as king of Judaea.
	c. 4	Birth of Jesus Christ.
	6	Judaea becomes a province of the Roman Empire, governed by a procurator.
	27	Herod Antipas, Tetrarch of Galilee, has John the Baptist imprisoned and executed.
	30	Jesus is believed to have been crucified and resurrected.
	33	Saul of Tarsus (later St. Paul) persecutes Christians but undergoes conversion on the road to Damascus.
	33	Stephen is stoned to death in Jerusalem, and becomes the first Christian martyr.
	46–48	First missionary trip of Paul and Barnabas to Cyprus.
	c. 49	Apostolic Council meets in Jerusalem.
	60–100	The four gospels are written, the gospel of Mark probably the first.
	64	Emperor Nero blames Christians for fire in Rome; they are severely persecuted.
	c. 64	The Acts of the Apostles are written.
100 C.E.	66–70	Jewish revolt against Roman rule ends in sack of Jerusalem by Emperor Titus.
	132–35	Abortive revolt by Bar Kochba and Jewish followers (Zealots) ends in ruin of Jerusalem.
	c. 141	Justin of Samaria writes his *Apologies*, claiming Christians are good citizens of the Roman Empire.
200 C.E.	c. 200	Clement of Alexandria in his writings tries to reconcile Christianity with Greek learning.
	c. 220	Death of Tertullian, regarded as the father of Latin theology.
	241	Persian mystic Mani declares himself the messiah, founds Manicheanism.
	252	Cyprian writes a plea for the unity of the church under the bishop of Rome.
	c. 254	Origen, the most learned of the early church fathers, dies after persecution under Emperor Decius.
	256	Emperor Valerian persecutes the Christians.
300 C.E.	275	St. Antony withdraws to a solitary life in the desert, taken as inaugurating the monastic tradition.
	303	Emperors Diocletian and Maximian initiate a systematic effort to suppress the Christian faith.
	313	By the Edict of Milan, Constantine grants tolerance to Christians in the Roman Empire.
	324	Eusebius of Caesarea writes his *Ecclesiastical History*.
	325	The first ecumenical council at Nicea adopts the Nicene Creed and condemns the Arian heresy.
	330	Constantine makes Constantinople his new capital.
	333	Christian Jews are ordered by Constantine to abandon all ties to Judaism or be killed.
	337	Death of Constantine; Christianity becomes the state religion of the Roman Empire.
	361–63	Emperor Julian "the Apostate" attempts to restore paganism, but fails.
	382	St. Jerome begins translating the Bible into Latin, the Vulgate version.
	391	Theodosius bans all pagan cults in the empire.
	397	St. Augustine of Hippo begins writing his *Confessions*.
	398	St. John Chrysostom, author of *Commentaries* on the Bible, is made archbishop of Constantinople.

CHAPTER 1

Judaism in Various Forms
An Ambivalent Inheritance

The phrase "Judeo-Christian tradition," so familiar to us today, is an affirmation of the organic and historic relationship between these two ancient faiths and of the many shared values they profess. The fact that it is of relatively recent coinage, reaching the height of currency in the second half of the twentieth century, reflects the strained relationship that has existed between the two religions throughout most of the past two thousand years. Indeed, most Jewish and Christian thinkers of previous times would have dismissed the term as incomprehensible.

In examining Christian traditions, however, it is necessary to recognize that the structure and conceptual "vocabulary" of Christianity—the shape and arrangement of its dominant ideas—are unmistakably Jewish. So we must first turn our attention to the Jewish matrix out of which Christianity grew.

For the area and age in which it emerged—the Middle East during the first century C.E.—Christianity presented little that was radically new. Judaism, which had grown and profoundly influenced the people of the eastern Mediterranean coast for the previous millennium, had also been divided by particularly sharp religious and political factions for almost two centuries, so a new sect was nothing revolutionary. As to the founder of the new community, Jesus of Nazareth appeared to some to be a healer, to others a PROPHET (an inspired teacher or interpreter of God's will), and to others the divinely promised MESSIAH, the king awaited by the Jews to deliver Israel from foreign rule. But similar miracle workers, prophets, and messianic figures had come and gone with predictable regularity. And under the domination of the Roman Empire, which demanded both absolute obedience and recognition of the divine status of its emperors, conditions for any new religion were so unfavorable that few contemporaries, among Jews and non-Jews alike, could have imagined that any band of believers would survive beyond the first generation. Yet over the next few centuries the followers of Jesus would overcome these obstacles and eventually transform themselves into the majority religion of the Roman Empire, the religious foundation of European culture for over a millennium, and the religion most widely diffused outside of Europe in the modern era.

Christian Beginnings

As a collection of beliefs and expectations, much of Christianity originated long before the birth of Jesus, but there is no shared sense of when recognizably "Christian" ideas began to take form. Where the beginnings of the Christian tradition are located is determined largely by what is identified as the defining characteristic of the religion. To define Christianity primarily as a "covenantal" religion is to give it affinities with the ancient covenants established between God and the patriarchs Noah and Abraham, with whom YHWH (or JHVH, the most sacred Hebrew name for God) sealed covenants, as recorded in Genesis 9 and 17. To identify Christianity as a "messianic" religion is to anchor the church in a tradition dating back to the prophets of the later books of the Old Testament, who warned the Jews of YHWH's coming. To see the followers of Jesus as one sect among the many varieties of Judaism existing in the first century C.E. sets the beginnings of the church much later, but still in a Jewish context—even though the followers of Jesus defined themselves in terms of their differences from some of these sects.

Even the original components of Christian teaching are best understood as explanations, expansions, and revisions of the body of traditional literature that the Jews saw as their "law." For example, the first and central rite of the Christian community, the communal meal called the EUCHARIST, also known as Holy Communion or the Lord's Supper, owes its place in part to the meaning attached, in the Jewish tradition, to the PASSOVER, the meal celebrating the liberation of the Jews from slavery in Egypt. Both liturgically and doctrinally, therefore, the early church was in many respects a form of Judaism. Unlike the branching off of Islam from the same trunk six centuries later, however, the emergence of Christianity does not begin simply with the lives of the founder and the first generation of followers, for they saw themselves as the heirs of an ancient tradition.

However, we can hardly begin the history of Christianity with the beginnings of Judaism. It is inaccurate to study one tradition merely as the forerunner of another. In order to find a middle ground between the greater, but inaccurate or misleading, simplicity of beginning the story of Christianity in the first decades after the birth of Christ and the more accurate but labyrinthine method of searching for the scattered origins of its parts in remote antiquity, we do well to recognize that the Christian tradition, like all religions, is a composite of intellectual, cultural, ritualistic, and social elements, each with its own origins and each adding an essential ingredient to the religious system as a whole. The history of Christianity serves as an excellent case study in the analysis of religion in all its complexity.

The Master and his Followers

The identity of Jesus can be found at the point where faith and history come together, not always harmoniously. Contemporaries saw him in a number of different lights: as an itinerant healer, as an interpreter of the law, as the leader of a sect, or as the long-awaited Messiah. There was no unanimity at the time, and there are surviving documents to support each of these views.

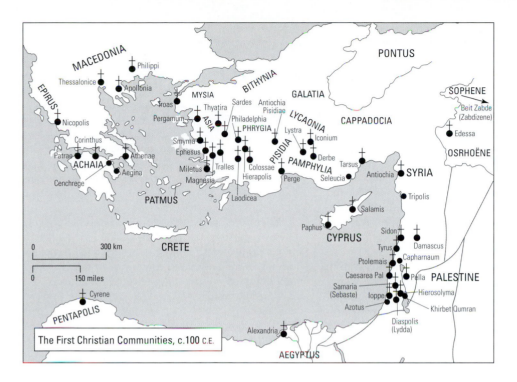

The First Christian Communities, c.100 C.E.

Jesus was a Jew and possibly of royal lineage (according to Matthew, he came from the Davidic line, which it was believed would produce the expected Messiah), the child of Mary and Joseph. The nativity narratives in the gospels of Matthew and Luke attribute Jesus' conception to the Holy Spirit, implicitly asserting that Mary was a virgin when she gave birth—in fulfillment of a prophecy in Isaiah (7:14). Stories about the young Jesus' precocious insight circulated among his followers and were later recorded in the first four books of the New Testament; however, we have no other texts with which to test whether the stories are true. His life from age twelve to this point is a mystery and an invitation to wild speculations. As a first-century Jew, he would have been thoroughly familiar with purity laws and customs governing sacrifice and Sabbath observance.

We do know from sources outside the New Testament that at about age thirty Jesus began to teach and heal, and that in this work he attracted followers. Jesus' teachings were interpretations of the Jewish law, and tended to recommend charity rather than severity in its application. He condemned haughtiness and advocated love of God and of neighbor above all other virtues. His healing work consisted mainly of restoring sight to the blind and mobility to the lame, but some accounts go further and credit him with raising the dead. During his active ministry he and his followers aroused suspicions among other Jews and the Roman authorities that they were advocating revolution. Jesus had already criticized and offended the priests and other leaders of the Temple in Jerusalem (the capital of Judaea) for their narrow interpretations of the Jewish law. Rebuilt after its destruction by the Babylonians in 586 B.C.E., the Temple was the central focus of Jewish ritual worship. Now the Temple leaders apparently sought to distance themselves from Jesus and his followers in the interest of peace with the Roman

BIOGRAPHICAL PROFILE

Jesus of Nazareth (c. 4 B.C.E–c. 30 C.E)

The son of Joseph and Mary, Jesus was born in Bethlehem in the final years of Herod's reign (c. 4 B.C.E), and when eight days old was entered into the Jewish covenant by means of circumcision. His childhood in Nazareth was probably typical for the time and place, though he showed unusual interest in his religion and surprised some of the authorities with his insights and claims.

Little is known about Jesus until he entered public life at about thirty years of age, though ungrounded specu-lation has put him in almost every corner of the inhabited world. His appearance on the historical scene was as an itinerant preacher and healer, one of many during the Roman occupation, a time of extreme anxiety for the Jewish inhabitants of Palestine—or Judaea, as it was known when it was a Roman province.

The teachings of Jesus were grounded in the dual law (10 written laws and 613 oral ones) of traditional Judaism, but offered comfort to those concerned about fulfilling the particular demands of the law. In his first recorded public presentation, known as the Sermon on the Mount, he interpreted a number of the Ten Commandments (the Decalogue) in a distinctive way, locating merit and demerit in the intention of the agent rather than in the actual deed performed. While this may have heightened anxieties about purity among some of his listeners, he offered consolation in the form of bless-ings to those who were humble, peace-seeking, and per-secuted. His followers regarded the Sermon on the Mount as a new revela-tion of the law, similar to the revelation to Moses on Sinai, and their identification of Jesus as a new Moses—or even a new divine lawgiver—may have begun at this particular point in his ministry.

Although Jesus attracted helpers and followers from all walks of life, there was little agreement about the kind of work in which he was engaged. His healing activities brought him a reputation as a wonder-worker among the sick and lame, while his pronouncements about the will of God and the character of the "heavenly kingdom" brought him many followers. This also encouraged the sceptics, who seemed to enjoy challenging him on points of doctrine.

He was a man of apparently inexhaustible patience with lowly persons, but regularly scolded the leaders of various Jewish sects for what he saw as their deviations from the divine law. Since conformity to the law was a matter of pride among these leaders, his rebukes were welcomed by his followers and rejected by the recipients of his criticism.

The enigmatic nature of Jesus' work was com-pounded by his teaching style. Whereas many of his con-temporaries preached in a literal and straightforward fashion, Jesus tended to convey his lessons in parables, likening something in the kingdom of heaven to some part of everyday experience. This pedagogical style had the advantage of bringing celestial phenomena within the conceptual grasp of ordinary persons, but the use of similes and metaphors also had the disadvantage of con-fusing his literal-minded listeners.

Jesus' final week on earth was spent in Jerusalem, where the enthusiastic reception he received from his followers aroused the suspicions of the Temple authori-ties and the Roman provincial government. One of his followers revealed his whereabouts; he was arrested and tried; and subjected to the standard form of capital pun-ishment, crucifixion, outside the city walls. His body was laid in a cave, which was then covered by a rock. What followed, in narrative and interpretation of the narrative, is the history of the Christian tradition.

Christ in Majesty, c. 1250–1260. Manuscript illumination, Rutland Psalter. British Library, London.

provincial government, and did nothing to protect him from persecution. The Roman officials, themselves unwilling to tolerate even potential revolutionaries, saw Jesus as someone seeking political leadership of the Jews, and condemned him to death by crucifixion. After the execution his body was placed in a tomb; but in three days' time it had disappeared. Shortly thereafter he reappeared to his followers, having presumably risen from the dead. He lived among them for another forty days and then (according to some gospel accounts) is said to have ascended to heaven.

Among the closest followers of Jesus were the APOSTLES, literally the "sent ones." They were twelve in number, like the original twelve tribes of Israel, and thus would have symbolized the totality of Judaism. These men, drawn from the ordinary Jewish populace, were attracted to the teachings of Jesus, who in turn called them to help him spread his message. Just as there can be no teacher without students, there can be no leader without followers, and the apostles served as a necessary entourage for the itinerant Jesus. The New Testament records of their activity suggest that they did not understand their leader very well. In numerous instances they have trouble believing his miracles or understanding his teachings. Although their portrayal as naive followers probably has some basis in fact, the image serves an important literary purpose, which is to contrast their imperfect knowledge of the work of Jesus while alive with their divinely illumined understanding of his work after his death and apparent resurrection. A theme that will recur throughout the history of Christianity is the belief, among its adherents, that one cannot understand the work of Jesus without believing in the resurrection, and that theme is sounded first and most clearly in the New Testament depiction of the apostles' spiritual enlightenment.

Two of the apostles need to be singled out as dominant figures in the life of the early church. The first of these, Peter, was a fisherman called by Jesus to be a "fisher of men"—that is, to attract followers. Peter was unique in believing, before the crucifixion and resurrection, that Jesus was the Messiah. Because of this insight, Jesus entrusts the "keys of the kingdom of Heaven" to Peter, whose

---

Peter and Jesus

Jesus' identity was a mystery even to his followers. In the following exchange, Peter is rewarded for his knowledge of Jesus' nature by being named the "rock" on which the church will be built. The passage has traditionally been used to support Peter's successors, the popes.

When he came to the territory of Caesarea Philippi, Jesus asked his disciples, "Who do men say that the Son of Man is?" They answered, "Some say John the Baptist, others Elijah, others Jeremiah, or one of the prophets." "And you," he asked, "who do you say that I am?" Simon Peter answered: "You are the Messiah, the Son of the living God." Then Jesus said: "Simon son of Jonah, you are favored indeed! You did not learn that from mortal man: it was revealed to you by my heavenly Father. And I say this to you: You are Peter, the Rock; and on this rock I will build my church, and the powers of death shall never conquer it. I will give you the keys of the kingdom of Heaven; what you forbid on earth shall be forbidden in heaven, and what you allow on earth shall be allowed in heaven." He then gave his disciples strict orders not to tell anyone that he was the Messiah.
(Matthew 16:13–20, *The New English Bible: New Testament*. Oxford: Oxford University Press, 1961.)

Christ in Majesty,
apse of Sant
Climent de Taüll,
Spain, c. 650.
Museum of Catalan
Art, Barcelona.

*The glory of the
risen Christ is
represented here
as a triumph over
all creation. Belief
in the resurrection
helped identify him
with the Godhead.*

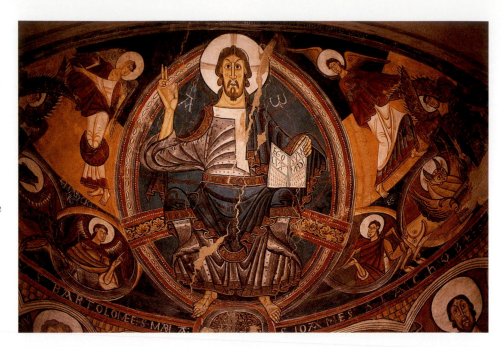

successors, the bishops of Rome (the popes), will use this passage from Matthew 16:13–20 to claim final accountability for the salvation of all the faithful. (See "Peter and Jesus.")

The other outstanding apostle, Paul, was also privileged with a unique insight, but was not one of the original twelve whom Jesus called before his death. It is questionable whether Paul, originally named Saul and one of the PHARISEES (a

---

Paul and the Risen Christ

Saul was a distinguished Jew and a persecutor of Christians who was confronted by Jesus and became a Christian, taking the name Paul. The fact that he encountered Jesus after the resurrection gave him a unique role among the followers of Jesus.

Meanwhile, Saul was still breathing murderous threats against the disciples of the Lord. He went to the High Priest and applied for letters to the synagogue at Damascus authorizing him to arrest anyone he found, men or women, who followed the new way, and bring them to Jerusalem. While he was still on the road and nearing Damascus, suddenly a light flashed from the sky all around him. He fell to the ground and heard a voice saying, "Saul, Saul, why do you persecute me?" "Tell me, Lord," he said, "who you are." The voice answered, "I am Jesus, whom you are persecuting. But get up and go into the city, and you will be told what you have to do." Meanwhile the men who were traveling with him stood speechless; they heard the voice but could see no one. Saul got up from the ground, but when he opened his eyes he could not see; so they led him by the hand and brought him into Damascus. He was blind for three days, and took no food or drink.

(Acts 9:1–9, *The New English Bible: New Testament.* Oxford: Oxford University Press, 1961.)

Jewish sect noted for their strict observance of the law), ever actually met Jesus while he was alive. Instead, Paul came to know Christ only after his death, and it was this experience that gave him his calling. In the biographical account that survives in the Acts of the Apostles, Paul was originally a determined opponent of Jesus' followers until he was confronted by Jesus while traveling toward Damascus. (See "Paul and the Risen Christ.") Becoming convinced that the stories of the resurrection were true, Paul became the most articulate and prolific interpreter of the new religion, a master at constructing a theological system able to affirm Christianity's origins in Judaism as well as its points of departure from it. We will consider Paul in greater detail in Chapter 4.

This brief cast of characters is incomplete without mentioning the role of women in the early community surrounding Jesus. In his ministry of compassion, Jesus sought to comfort the outcasts from and the subservient members of

Who's Who

The Twelve Apostles

The word "apostle" derives from the Greek *apostolos* ("person sent"). According to the Bible, these were the twelve disciples selected by Jesus to form his close circle of followers, and to undertake preaching and healing work. The number twelve probably had special significance, and may well refer to the twelve tribes of Israel. The list of apostles varies, but the following is commonly accepted:

St. Peter (d. 54–68 C.E.?), St. James (d. 44 C.E.; sometimes called "the Great"), and St. John These three formed an inner circle of apostles. Of all the disciples, only they were allowed to be present at special events such as Jesus's agony in the Garden of Gethsemane. Peter, a fisherman and brother of the apostle Andrew, is usually considered the unofficial leader of the apostles. He denied Christ three times and later repented. James and John were the sons of Zebedee. James was the elder brother, and the first apostle to be martyred; John is said to have written the Fourth Gospel.

St. Andrew (d. 60 C.E?) Brother of the apostle Peter. Peter and Andrew are said to have been called away from their fishing to follow Christ. Andrew may have been crucified at Patras, Greece.

St. Philip Possibly from Bethsaida in Galilee, he was said to have observed that there was not originally enough bread to go around at the feeding of the five thousand. He may have been crucified.

St. Bartholomew Sometimes called Nathaniel, he may have traveled to India, and some said that he was killed by flogging in Armenia.

St. Matthew He may have been a publican and legend has it that he made a collection of Christ's sayings. He is said to have written the Gospel of St. Matthew.

St. Thomas He is said to have doubted Jesus's resurrection at first, but he later swore his total faith. He may have visited India.

St. James Son of Alphaeus, he was sometimes known as "the less" to distinguish him from the other apostle James.

St. Jude, or Thaddaeus He was generally thought to have written the Epistle of Jude.

St. Simon, the Cananaean, or the Zealot He may have belonged to an extreme Jewish group called the Zealots.

Judas Iscariot He betrayed Christ and so delivered him into the hands of the Jewish authorities. Some reports say that he committed suicide.

St. Paul (Saul) (c. 10–67 C.E.) Others such as Paul have also been called apostles. A Pharisee, he converted to Christianity a few years after Jesus's death and considered himself an apostle because he had seen the risen Lord and received a mission directly from him.

The Women at the Resurrection

Women played a significant role in Jesus' circle and the early church: they had experiences and knowledge that the typically more worldly men couldn't fathom. In this passage, they are the first to learn the mystery of the resurrection.

The women who had accompanied him from Galilee followed; they took note of the tomb and observed how his body was laid…. Finding that the stone had been rolled away from the tomb, they went inside; but the body was not to be found. While they stood utterly at a loss, all of a sudden two men in dazzling garments were at their side. They were terrified, and stood with eyes cast down, but the men said, "Why search among the dead for one who lives? Remember what he told you while still in Galilee, about the Son of Man: how he must be given up into the power of sinful men and be crucified, and must rise up again on the third day." Then they recalled his words and, returning from the tomb, they reported all this to the Eleven and all the others. The women were Mary of Magdala, Joanna, and Mary the mother of James, and they, with the other women, told the apostles. But the story appeared to them to be nonsense, and they would not believe them.
(Luke 23:55; 24:2–11, *The New English Bible: New Testament*. Oxford: Oxford University Press, 1961.)

society, including women, and, unlike many other Jewish figures, to include them in his work to a remarkable degree. Poor widows and women of questionable morals figure prominently in the New Testament as recipients of his care and friendship: and the more unlikely the recipient, the greater the affection Jesus shows. Thus the women in Jesus' circle, including Mary Magdalene (who was alleged to have formerly been possessed by seven devils), and Joanna, the wife of a steward for Herod Antipas (one of several women who followed and supported Jesus in his preaching), are the first to learn of Jesus' resurrection. They, in turn, are instructed to convey this news to the apostles, who still do not believe or understand. (See "The Women at the Resurrection.") We will see in later chapters that women played a vital role in the survival of the church during its first three centuries.

The Social Context of Christianity

When we open the New Testament to find out about the beginnings of the church, we are confronted by an obvious but troublesome fact: the text cannot be understood without some knowledge of its context. Identifying some of the central and constant themes of Judaism, as we did above, provides some background but does not help us see the early Christians in their own world. Their world was still a Jewish one—marked by readings of the Hebrew Scriptures, observance of the law, and other Jewish customs—so the perennial themes were not foreign to them. However, the harmony and independence of this world had recently been disrupted by a number of circumstances.

By the end of the first century C.E., the Jewish world was in turmoil as a result of forces both within and without. Internally, the unity of the tradition was threatened by fragmentation into cultlike groups, or sects, while political domination by Rome undermined the freedom that the Jews felt had been divinely granted to them. Thus, we should take a brief look at these two pressures upon the Jewish community at the time of Jesus and his earliest followers.

Sectarian Judaism

Divisions over Jewish life and ritual probably began in the second century B.C.E., brought on by efforts on the part of some Jews to blend their religion with the Greek (Hellenistic) culture then dominant in the eastern Mediterranean. Although the Jewish people never allowed themselves to be completely assimilated into Hellenistic culture, there was no consensus on how much of the surrounding milieu they could themselves absorb while still retaining their Jewish identity. Suspicion of anything Greek made reading pagan literature questionable; and pagan political ideas and institutions were viewed with hostility.

The PHARISEES, who are thought to have dominated Temple life, were teachers and interpreters of the law. They adhered to the 613 precepts of the Oral Law, in contrast to the SADDUCEES who officiated in the Temple and who accepted only the written word of the Bible itself. Although we do not know for sure, the Pharisees may have been aware of and influenced by Greek currents of thought; nevertheless, they remained resistant to non-Jewish encroachments upon religious practice and to any softening of the demands of ritual observance. The conflicts between Jesus and the Pharisees in Matthew 12, Mark 2 and 3, and Luke 5 and 6 show the contrast of viewpoints clearly. The Pharisees, who in these versions are out to ensnare Jesus, watch what he does and then complain that it is not in accord with the law ("illegal") or is in violation of the Sabbath (the day set aside for rest and worship). Jesus rebukes them for paying more attention to the law than to the needs of their fellows. The episodes contrast Jesus' compassion and mercy with the Pharisees' scruples about whether one can do good deeds on the day of rest.

Often linked with the Pharisees by the gospel writers, but differing from them on several important issues, were the Sadducees, a group drawn mainly from the elite, in contrast to the rank and file Pharisees. Many Sadducees were descendants of the ancient priestly class; the family of one high priest, named Zadok, gave the group its name. Although lack of evidence prevents us from saying much about the Sadducees with any certainty, it appears that they adhered to a strict standard of ritual observance and purity at the Temple, though they may not have tried to impose their standards on the broad populace, as the Pharisees seem to have done. In the New Testament, the Sadducees figure most prominently for their denial of the doctrine of the resurrection of bodies, a doctrine that the Pharisees accepted.

Among the other influential Jewish sects, the ESSENES were a group that practiced a very strict self-discipline in anticipation of a coming kingdom, a reign of justice in place of the injustice of Roman rule. The Essenes lived in separated communities, to which they were admitted only after a year's initiation. The life of the community resembled that of a monastery, being focused on shared property, fixed times for worship, and labor. John the Baptist, a preacher who baptized Jesus in the river Jordan, and who regarded him as a true leader, was probably an Essene (and one can see his hostility to the Pharisees and Sadducees in Matthew 3:7); but there is no reason to think that Jesus himself belonged to this group,

The Sadducees and the Afterlife

Sectarian Judaism pitted one authority against another, with one man's followers always trying to trip up their master's opponents. Here some clever members of a sect that denied the possibility of an afterlife try to bait Jesus with a trick question.

The same day Sadducees came to him, maintaining that there is no resurrection. Their question was this: "Master, Moses said, 'If a man should die childless, his brother shall marry the widow and carry on his brother's family.' Now we knew of seven brothers. The first married and died, and as he was without issue his wife was left to his brother. The same thing happened with the second, and the third, and so on with all seven. Last of all the woman died. At the resurrection, then, whose wife will she be, for they had all married her?" Jesus answered: "You are mistaken, because you know neither the scriptures nor the power of God. At the resurrection men and women do not marry; they are like angels in heaven. But about the resurrection of the dead, have you never read what God himself said to you: 'I am the God of Abraham, the God of Isaac, and the God of Jacob'? He is not God of the dead, but of the living." The people heard what he said, and were astounded at his teaching.

(Matthew 22:23–33, *The New English Bible: New Testament*. Oxford: Oxford University Press, 1961.)

Model of the Temple in Jerusalem at the time of Herod the Great (detail), c. 20 B.C.E.

Herod, more an agent of Roman domination than a Jewish ruler, tried to synthesize Roman and Jewish cultures; yet his allegiance to Roman power is reflected in his choice of architectural styles.

even though he shared their belief in a coming kingdom of God and the immortality of the soul. We will encounter the Essenes again in Chapter 2, in connection with the Dead Sea Scrolls.

Christian Belief and the Destruction of Jerusalem

The most visible part of the Judaean political landscape in the first century C.E. was the Roman Empire. Since its conquest in 63 B.C.E. by the Roman general Pompey (106–48 B.C.E.), Judaea had been a province of an empire extending from the Iberian peninsula well into the Arabian. Under the reign of King Herod the Great (73–4 B.C.E; r. 40–4 B.C.E.), the land of the Jews became a province of the empire, with Herod himself responsible for its wholesale Romanization. Herod

himself could not have come to power, or kept it, without the help of the Roman army, and he showed his gratitude with building projects designed to make Judaea a miniature Rome. Temples to the Roman gods were built, as well as amphitheaters and a whole port city for Roman trade, named Caesarea in honor of the emperors. After Herod's death the territory was ruled by a succession of "procurators," or provincial administrators. All of these administrators were Romans who were unaware of, and unsympathetic to, local religious life, a fact that aggravated the Jews' resentment of foreign rule.

In retaliation for the Romans' insensitivity, some of the priests of the Temple withheld their tax contribution to the emperor. Such a subversive act aroused the Romans, who, in 67 C.E., conquered the area around Jerusalem; three years later, they attacked Jerusalem itself, destroying all of the ancient Temple except the Western Wall, which still stands today. After a bloody war lasting seven years, recounted in the seven books of the *History of the Jewish War*, written by the Jewish historian Josephus (c. 37–c. 100 C.E.), the Promised Land of the Jews was no longer theirs. In striking what it hoped would be a fatal blow to Judaism, the Roman Empire drove the Jewish people far and wide throughout the Mediterranean world, in what would later be called the SECOND EXILE, or, more commonly, the DIASPORA, or "dispersion." (In fact, the Diaspora had begun much earlier, in the sixth century B.C.E., when the Babylonians captured Jerusalem and drove thousands of Jews into exile in their own country; when the Jews achieved their freedom, with the Persian conquest of Babylonia, not all of them returned home. However, the term "Diaspora" is conventionally associated with the second exile, instigated by Rome.)

For Christianity, the destruction of the Temple had far-reaching theological significance. The first Christians did not see the Romans' siege of the Temple in political or "human" terms at all but, rather, viewed it as the divine act of closing one period of history and ushering in a new one.

Consistent with their Jewish convictions, these people believed that history was governed by divine providence, and thus they interpreted the destruction of the Temple as the divinely decreed end of Judaism. The destruction of the Temple marks a watershed (or a parting of the ways) in Jewish–Christian relations. It may have coincided with, or even prompted, the start of Christianity as a religion in its own right. Certainly, as far as mainstream Jews were concerned, the destruction shifted the focus from temple worship, sacrifices and ritual, to the law itself. The now-dominant Pharisees reconstructed Judaism around the Oral Law. They became RABBIS (teachers), and set up synagogues. Judaism lost its geographic focus, but it gained a new character, that of a "portable" faith.

Like their mainstream Jewish compatriots, the first Christians were also forced into exile. In their new homes, they won adherents among Jews and increasingly among Gentiles (non-Jews). But now Christianity was set on its own path: it began to establish its own institutions, collate its own scriptures, and develop its own concept of redemption through the Lordship of Jesus Christ. To Christians, the Risen Christ was an intercessor with God, or even a part of God himself—both of which were concepts most Jews could not accept.

Jews and Christians parted company, above all, in their diverging views of history and the nature of redemption. In the New Testament Jesus is recorded as saying that "not one stone [of the Temple] will be left upon another; all will be thrown down" (Matthew 24:2; cf. Mark 13:2). If Jesus said this, it was a remarkably accurate prediction; but the gospel itself may have been written after 70 C.E., and the author may have put those words in Jesus' mouth. Hence, although the early members of the Christian community retained the thoroughly Jewish belief in a providential ordering of history, their reading of such history was one that saw the end of Second Temple Judaism as a necessary step in the foundation of the church.

Judaism itself, of course, saw things differently. Because they expected their redemption to take place within the historical realm, the Jewish people rejected the Christians' otherworldly concept of redemption, and continued (as they still do) to await a restoration similar to those they had experienced in the liberation from Egypt and the restoration after the exile in Babylonia in the sixth century B.C.E. Thus the Jews' understanding of divine action remains consistent with their historical experience, whereas the Christian vision offers a redemption that has already taken place. As our narrative continues, we will see how this Christian vision is articulated and embodied by the believing community.

Defining a New Religion

As we have seen, the historical bonds between the Jews and the early Christians were extremely strong. Unfortunately, however, historical bonds do not lead naturally to strong and positive ties, and nowhere is this more true than in the history of the early church. Almost in reaction to its strongest influences, the early Christian community struggled to define itself as a new religion, rather than as another Jewish sect. In the following chapters we will see the church giving emphasis to those elements of its teaching and rites that were altogether new or that had replaced Jewish precedents.

Key Terms

APOSTLE One who is sent—specifically, one of the Twelve sent out by Jesus to continue his work.

DIASPORA The dispersion of the Jews, especially after 70 C.E.

ESSENE One of a separatist ancient Jewish group which practiced rigorous asceticism and held apocalyptic and dualistic beliefs.

EUCHARIST The ritual meal of bread and wine that unifies all believers in Jesus Christ; one of the sacraments.

MESSIAH The anointed one, the deliverer of the Jewish people, a unique instrument of God's redemptive work.

PASSOVER The annual Jewish festival commemorating redemption from servitude in Egypt.

PHARISEE A member of one of the branches of 1st-century Judaism, which consisted of separatists who emphasized ritual purity.

PROPHET A spokesperson for God, a voice of criticism and exhortation to a people that has gone astray.

RABBI A teacher of Jewish lore and observance.

SADDUCEE A member of one of the branches of 1st-century Judaism, which emphasized written law and denied resurrection.

SECOND EXILE The dispersion of the Jews after the Roman conquest and the destruction of the Temple in 70 C.E.

Literature of the Early Church
Texts as Preservers of Experience

The last chapter made use of the New Testament as a primary source for the history of the beginnings of Christianity. However, picking up a copy of the New Testament for insights into the creation of the early church is similar to looking at a finished work of art for clues to its composition, since these writings are an integral part of the institution itself. Any evidence that the finished product (in either case) might provide can be, at best, partial and inconclusive. This is especially true in the case of early Christian literature, which was condensed from draft material many times greater. Think of any given author's work: How well can you know that writer's creative and productive ability if you are limited to a selection of texts chosen by people with their own conceptions of the author's purpose? A similar situation applies to the "official" body of early Christian literature, for the collection of texts known as the New Testament is in reality a selection from an extensive and varied body of writings.

The early church bore little resemblance to the organized body it became in later centuries—run by a centralized government and a multilevel hierarchy. There are numerous reasons for this. The scattered congregations that formed throughout the Mediterranean world had, by virtue of their indigenous cultures, differing approaches to organization and politics. They also had a wide variety of texts which aimed to preserve and interpret the essential Christian message. Very likely no two of the early congregations possessed the same set of texts, and the ways in which these were understood would also have differed.

One reason why the Christian community was slow to achieve uniformity owed to the persecutions by the Romans, which forced the church to remain an underground movement. Another reason was that the idea of a rigid standard of doctrine was not foremost in their minds. Lack of consensus is understandable when one considers the fragmented nature of Judaism in the first century. One universal feature of Judaism, however, is its adherence to a fixed CANON, or authoritative collection, of texts; and in this respect the early Christian sect was no different from other branches of the Jewish tradition. But the set of texts they adopted, and the ways in which these texts were interpreted, set the early church apart from its Jewish origins. In its canonical literature, as in other respects, the early church tried to create and preserve a constructive balance between the ancient faith and the new interpretation of its convictions.

The Hebrew Bible: Christianity's Earliest Scriptures

The earliest sacred texts of the Christian tradition are the books of the Hebrew Bible. This collection of texts comprises three kinds of writings, known as the Law (often called the Torah—the first five books of the Bible, which tell the story of Creation and the early history of the Jewish people and which incorporate the essential laws governing Jewish society), the Prophets, and the Writings (the wisdom and historical works). These texts are not only the founding documents of Jewish life and faith; they provide a fixed reference point for continuing reflection. Together these writings bind the Jewish people to their past and to their God, who is understood as the revealer of the law. They also serve as the basis for a continuous stream of interpretations of possible, but not explicit, applications and adaptations of the law. And after a millennium of development, a broad range of approaches to Judaism had taken form. As we noted in Chapter 1, in the first century B.C.E., different schools had emerged, from the Temple-based Sadducees, with their rigid adherence to the Scriptures, to the Essenes, who had withdrawn to ascetic lives in the desert.

The Law

In the first century C.E. Judaism was focused on law as never before, since it was commonly felt that the miseries of the Jews at the time were the result of divine anger at earlier forms of disobedience. All the major forms of Judaism saw a return to purer observance of the law as the way to restore God's favor, which would be manifested in the expulsion of the Romans from the promised land and the restoration of Jewish autonomy. Thus any Jewish leader who claimed to know the way to God's good graces was given a serious hearing. One who, like Jesus, offered new insights into the law, as in the Sermon on the Mount (Matthew 5), would have been given a serious hearing indeed.

Some of the earliest Christian messages on record are adaptations of the law, the rules for conduct handed down on Mount Sinai by God to Moses in the form of ten written commandments and the 613 oral ones that finally took written form in the second century C.E. The Sermon on the Mount, in which Jesus states the relation of his own teachings to the Decalogue (the collective name for the Ten Commandments), shows that the earliest teachings to the followers of Jesus were refinements of the meaning of the law. In the Sermon, Jesus is not claiming that he is replacing the old law with a new one; rather, he says, at Matthew 5:17, that his teaching is the "completion" of the law, its final interpretation, and a guide to its perfect fulfilment. However, among the earliest texts of the Christian tradition, Paul's letters to various communities make the point that Christianity is a new law, one based in faith, intended to replace the old law, at least in part. Although scholars have come to realize that Paul's contrast of the two viewpoints may have been an exaggeration intended to contrast the inner life of faith with the outer one of "works," the fact that Christianity was understood in the beginning as a law—that is, as a claim upon people's obedience—is too significant to ignore.

The Prophets

Without the existence of a strong prophetic element in the Judaism of the last two centuries B.C.E., Jesus would not have drawn such a large following. While Jewish tradition looked back to God's deliverance of the Jews from Egypt—a redemptive act that revealed God's goodness and protection toward them—the Jewish view of history also looked to the future, to another act of redemption, from their present persecution at the hands of the Romans and from any later oppressors. At this future time—actually at the end of human history—their piety would receive its divine reward. Whether that was the near or distant future, no one knew; but all felt that a Messiah (literally, "anointed one") would appear and, like a second Moses, lead the faithful to a state of new peace and plenty. But such a leader would come only on condition that the people had merited that deliverance by their own actions and purity. Consequently, much prophetic literature expresses anger at the Jewish people for their religious infidelity, idolatry, or lack of trust in God. Although prophets such as Jeremiah and Isaiah come across as harsh, they are good indicators of how strongly the Jewish people believed in a coming messianic redemption. This expectation, which rose in proportion to the amount of suffering the people endured, reinforced their confidence in God's goodness and a sense of the duty to reform their lives.

Ever since the destruction of the First Temple by the Babylonians in 586 B.C.E., the Jewish community had been expecting a redeemer to release them from servitude to earthly powers. This attitude was intensified with the expansion of the Roman Empire into Palestine and the establishment of the province of Judaea in 63 B.C.E. Thus, when a figure came along who offered new insights about improving the faith, people paid attention to him. Such a person was seen as a prophet—but not as the Messiah.

It may seem simplistic to state that Jesus entered history as a prophet and left as the Messiah, but there is some truth to this. In the Sermon on the Mount, as we have seen, he expounds on the difficulties of the law, and throughout the Gospels he declares woe upon the faithless and blessedness upon the good. There are grounds for saying that before his crucifixion Jesus saw himself as a prophet, and that it was his followers, after the resurrection, who first saw him as the long-awaited Messiah, or redeemer. And it was as the Messiah that the followers' followers—the early church—interpreted him. Their conviction that Christ himself was the fulfillment of the ancient Jewish prophecies and promises was the crucial difference between the first Christians and other Jews. This conviction shaped the early church leaders' views of Christ's nature and the purpose of his crucifixion.

It is not surprising, then, that continuity with Jewish prophecy would be a theme in some New Testament books. The Pentecost event described in Acts 2—in which the Holy Spirit (see Chapter 3) descends on the apostles in the form of tongues of fire, causing them to speak in foreign languages, in order to spread Christ's teachings to other nations (Acts 2: 2–8)—has distinct echoes of the bestowal of spiritual power on the seventy elders with Moses (Numbers 11) and of other moments in the Bible when persons acquire a power beyond the merely human. The Gospels make frequent references to the prophets, such as Moses and Elijah, as forebears of Jesus, and even (Matthew 16:14) alludes to popular belief that he was actually one of these prophets, reborn. Hence his words were believed to have more than human authority behind them.

The Writings

The third category of scriptural texts in Judaism, known as the "Writings," comprises the historical and WISDOM (broadly speaking, practical and ethical)

The Gospel of Peter

Among the early Christian texts that were not included in the New Testament, the Gospel attributed to Peter offers a Passion narrative that corroborates the canonical versions and at the same time presents significant variations.

But of the Jews none washed his hands, neither Herod, nor any one of His judges; and since they did not choose to wash them, Pilate arose. And then Herod the king commandeth the Lord to be taken, saying unto them, What things soever I commanded you to do unto Him, do ye.

Now there stood there Joseph, the friend of Pilate and of the Lord; and knowing that they were about to crucify Him, he came to Pilate, and begged the body of the Lord for burial. And Pilate sent to Herod and begged His body; and Herod said, Brother Pilate, even if no man had begged Him, we should bury Him, inasmuch as the Sabbath draweth on; for it is written in the law that the sun set not on one that hath died by violence.

And he delivered Him to the people before the first day of unleavened bread, their feast. So they took the Lord and pushed Him as they ran, and said, Let us hale the Son of God, since we have gotten power over Him. And they clothed Him with purple, and set Him on a seat of judgment, saying, Judge righteously, O King of Israel. And one of them brought a crown of thorns and put it on the head of the Lord, and others stood and spat upon His eyes, and others smote His cheeks; others pierced Him with a reed, and some scourged Him saying, With this honour let us honour the Son of God....

Now it was midday, and darkness overspread all Judaea; and they were troubled and distressed lest the sun had set, inasmuch as He was yet alive; it is written for them that the sun set not on one that hath died by violence. And one of them said, Give Him gall to drink with vinegar; and they mixed and gave Him to drink. So they accomplished all things, and filled up their sins upon their head. And many went about with lamps, supposing that it was night; and some fell. And the Lord cried aloud, saying, My power, my power, thou hast left Me; and having said this He was taken up. And the same hour the veil of the temple of Jerusalem was torn in twain.

And then they drew the nails from the hands of the Lord, and laid Him upon the earth; and the whole earth was shaken, and great fear came upon them. Then the sun shone out, and it was found to be the ninth hour. But the Jews rejoiced, and they gave His body to Joseph to bury it, inasmuch as he beheld all the good things that He did. So he took the Lord and washed Him, and wrapped Him in linen and brought Him into his own tomb, called Joseph's Garden.

(*The Gospel of Peter: The Akhmîn Fragment*; in *Excluded Books of the New Testament*, trans. J.B. Lightfoot. New York: Harper & Bros., 1927.)

literature that gave the people a sense of community. Much of this literature depicts leadership, polity, and the people's faith in their protection by God. If one may roughly consider that the law describes the divine mission of the covenantal people, and the prophetic books its divine destiny, the Writings capture its human character and history. In the Jewish imagination, much of this material is an explanation of the divine care for Jews between the earthly redemption from Egypt and the anticipated heavenly redemption at the end of human history.

Of the three categories of Jewish Scripture, the Writings bear the closest resemblance to early Christian literature. Although we will evaluate the whole corpus of early Christian literature in the following pages, it is worth noting here that much of what would become the New Testament is devoted to explaining how the prophecies were fulfilled in the work of Jesus. The Passion narratives, which relate the traditions of Jesus' last days up to and including his crucifixion, are an example of the tendency to describe Christian events in Jewish terms. (See "The Gospel of Peter" and "The Gospel of Nicodemus.") Whatever actually happened on the cross, the surviving record has Jesus speaking the opening words of Psalm 22 ("My God, my God, why have you forsaken me?"). Like most of the Psalms, this one includes a declaration of loyalty to God in the face of persecution. The point of the psalmist is that no matter what happens to a person in this life, trust in God's redemptive power and goodness cannot be diminished.

Writings of the Early Christians: What Do We Know?

As we have just noted, the canonical writings of the first-generation followers of Jesus were the books of the Hebrew Bible. However, with the destruction of the Second Temple in Jerusalem in 70 C.E. and the self-conscious separation of the early Christians from their origins in sectarian Judaism, the believers of the second generation and beyond created their own body of writings; some of these were interpretations of the earlier Hebrew Scriptures, others were records of the actions and teachings of Jesus and the apostles. These writings form the New Testament and fall into three distinct sections—Gospels, Acts, and Epistles—each covering different historical periods, and each with its own unique purpose. A unique book, Revelation, concludes the text.

The Gospels

The Gospels attributed to Matthew, Mark, Luke, and John are perhaps the most distinctive genre of Christian literature. They record the many deeds and teachings of Jesus and were intended to make sure that the "good news" Jesus was credited with bringing would be obvious to the reader or hearer. Thus in a real way these texts continued the work of Jesus, and the apparent uniqueness of their content gave them a holy character almost from the beginning.

Paradoxically, we do not really know whether the gospels were written by the four evangelists to whom they are attributed. We can be fairly certain that Luke's

Gospel and Acts were written by the same person; and the author, possibly Luke himself, introduced both his books with a declaration of purpose. We are least sure of John's authorship—so unsure, in fact, that some scholars refer to this gospel simply as the "Fourth Gospel." The Gospels of Matthew and Mark bear some relation to what we know of those evangelists, but most scholars cannot with conviction give them complete "authorship" of those works. Instead, these two Gospels are often thought to be compilations from sources that originated with Matthew and Mark—much as one might attempt to reconstruct someone's teaching from notes taken by a listener to those teachings.

The most obvious feature of the Gospels is the differences among them. To be sure, the first three have much in common: they portray the life, teachings, and actions of Jesus as seen by members of the community he attracted. Because many passages in one of these Gospels will have echoes in others, they are called SYNOPTIC—that is, presenting a common view of these events. The fourth Gospel is in a class by itself, being an account of Jesus' work and teaching as seen from the perspective of a follower of the post-resurrection Christ. Thus the JOHANNINE (after "John") image of Jesus is one that anticipates the PASSION (suffering) and crucifixion of Jesus; and much that he says and does earlier is depicted as preparation for these events.

The literary origins of the gospel genre are somewhat more obscure than their purpose. In form, the gospel seems to follow the pattern of an ARETALOGY, a chron-

---

The Gospel of Nicodemus

The Gospel of Nicodemus, one of the early texts that tried to record and interpret Jesus' life, shows us a member of Jesus' circle defending him before Pilate. Here we see Jesus compared to Moses, and witness Jewish animosity in the wake of the comparison.

And one Nicodemus, a Jew, stood before the procurator, and said: I beseech your honour, let me say a few words. Pilate says: Say on. Nicodemus says: I said to the elders and the priests and Levites, and to all the multitude of the Jews in the synagogue, What do you seek to do with this man? This man does many miracles and strange things, which no one has done or will do. Let him go, and do not wish any evil against him. If the miracles which he does are of God, they will stand; but if of man, they will come to nothing. For assuredly Moses, being sent by God into Egypt, did many miracles, which the Lord commanded him to do before Pharaoh king of Egypt. And there were there Jannes and Jambres, servants of Pharaoh, and they also did not a few of the miracles which Moses did; and the Egyptians took them to be gods—this Jannes and this Jambres. But, since the miracles which they did were not of God, both they and those who believed in them were destroyed. And now release this man, for he is not deserving of death.

The Jews say to Nicodemus: Thou has become his disciple, and therefore thou defendest him. Nicodemus says to them: Perhaps, too, since he defends him, the procurator has become his disciple. Has the emperor not appointed him to this place of dignity? And the Jews were vehemently enraged, and gnashed their teeth against Nicodemus. Pilate says to them: Why do you gnash your teeth against him when you hear the truth? The Jews say to Nicodemus: Mayst thou receive his truth and his portion. Nicodemus says: Amen, amen; may I receive it, as you have said.
(*The Gospel of Nicodemus: Part I, The Acts of Pilate*; in *Excluded Books of the New Testament*, trans. J.B. Lightfoot. New York: Harper & Bros., 1927.)

icle of the virtues and teachings of sages of the Hellenistic world. By the first century B.C.E., the Greek philosophical tradition had divided into a number of rival schools, each with its own core doctrines. Besides adhering to these teachings, each of the schools venerated its founder and sought to preserve his memory by including a record of his work among their books. Because these works were meant to preserve only the praiseworthy aspects of their subject, they can hardly be called biographies in the strict sense. Instead, the term "aretalogy," meaning an account of a person's excellence or virtue (in Greek, *arete*), has been used to capture both the nature and purpose of these works. These philosophical schools had a cultic character, focusing as they did upon their founder, and had little in common with the more rigorously intellectual followers of the earlier philosophers Plato and Aristotle.

The philosophies embraced by the Hellenistic schools were, with some exceptions, mostly practical, so that their teachings were exemplified in their members' own lives. Stoicism, for example, held that the good life was one of complete tranquillity, and its practitioners thus sought to pare their emotional attachments to a minimum. The masters of the school not only presented its philosophical principles as doctrine but exemplified them in their own conduct. Their followers, in turn, strove to emulate the masters in their own lives. Thus aretalogies were guides to living the good life and complemented the more theoretical treatises produced by these schools, which we might consider their "philosophical" works.

The aretalogical character of the Gospels is readily apparent. One need only think of the parables—narratives embodying a moral truth or lesson—or such incidents as Jesus' pardoning the woman taken in adultery (John 8:3–11) and his walking on the water (Mark 7: 48–50). In line with the aretalogical pattern, Jesus is depicted in the Gospels as a sage, one who not only dispenses wise counsel but also embodies the virtues necessary for a good life. As such he comes across as the figure whom his followers most strive to emulate (especially in the synoptic Gospels). The Gospel authors tried to capture his qualities in such a way that readers, like the original followers, could follow his example.

Bishop Eadfrith, *Luke the Evangelist*, from the *Lindisfarne Gospels*, c. 700. Manuscript illumination. British Library, London.

This image was one of several rendered and illuminated by Bishop Eadfrith in Lindisfarne Monastery.

The Book of Acts

Whereas the Gospels tell of Jesus' life, ending with his crucifixion, the book of Acts sketches the history of Christianity from the time of his resurrection to the arrest of the apostle Paul. A sequel to the Gospel of Luke and addressed to the same person, "Theophilus," the book of Acts tries to set out the early history of Christianity in some sort of orderly way. While Acts does not in fact tell the story of all the apostles—although Peter and Paul are mentioned frequently—it does provide the earliest account of the massive conversions, the miraculous deeds performed by the apostles, the opposition and persecution by non-believers, and the dramatic spread of the Christian Church.

The book of Acts was written by the same person who wrote the Gospel of Luke, but its structure is quite different, having more similarities with other histories of the Hellenistic world. The historical genre during this period was dominated by chronological narratives, covering the ancient events in the memory of a nation. This genre is often referred to as "general history"; an example can be seen in *The Antiquities of the Jews* by Josephus, which was written at about the same time (c. 90 C.E.) as the book of Acts. Because Acts is concerned with the historical development of the Christian Church, with a chronologically organized narrative, some scholars have seen it as a work in the genre of general history and one that uses the devices and modes that were common features of popular literature of the late first and early second centuries C.E.

Letters and Other Documents

Letters, often known as the Epistles, from the Latin for "letter," *epistola*, are as diverse in purpose as the Gospels are specific. Originally meant as private communications, often from one apostolic leader to a community, the Epistles were probably not intended to carry the universal and binding authority that they were later to acquire. This later authority developed because of their authors' standing in the history of the church, and this determined in part which letters were to be included in the New Testament. Peter, to whom Jesus is thought to have entrusted his "flock," and Paul, who saw the risen Christ on the road to Damascus, were thought to have a greater authority and deeper understanding than the other apostles; and their personal prestige was, in turn, enhanced by the letters attributed to them.

Other documents—"Acts" of various apostles, and martyrologies—preserve the memory of other noteworthy early followers and, in particular, of martyrs, people who served as inspiration to the struggling early church. Unlike the Gospels, with their aretalogical approach, these records do not claim to be revelations of practical truths actualized in biographical form. They do, however, aim to portray the fidelity of the earliest believers to their master. The fact that Christianity was a persecuted sect, and that fidelity to Christ often led to death, gave special meaning to MARTYRDOM. Death for one's beliefs gave the martyr a bond with the crucified Christ that no other experience could; and the concept of "oneness" with Christ, which would become so important over the course of Christian history, may have originated with this ultimate form of sharing another's experience. The continuing persecution of Christians by the Roman government, on top of the crucifixion of Jesus, gave the church a sense of historical continuity. Contrary to its intended result, the persecution of the early church, by facilitating such a bond, helped strengthen the commitment to the faith on the part of the earliest believers.

These genres are but three—albeit the most important—of a range of literary forms produced by the early Christian community. During the first two centuries, many authors sought the ideal form in which to capture the meaning of their faith. Because the new religion had absorbed strands of different traditions, both pagan and Jewish (see Chapter 4), there was little consensus on how best to convey its truths. Among the Christian writings not found in the New Testament are numerous orations, poems, fables, and even satires whose authorship can be traced, with various degrees of accuracy, to the apostolic community itself.

Many of these works fall short of ordinary definitions of great literature; few would hold up well against the texts of the Greek golden age (fifth–fourth centuries B.C.E.), for example. (Neither would many non-Christian texts of the same period.) But aesthetic pleasure was not their purpose; this was, rather, to instruct the reader in the new religion. And the test of that instruction was its success in evoking the emotions, in particular that of reverence.

To a certain degree, the composition and purpose of early Christian texts is easy to account for. A more difficult task is to describe how a selection of this literature came to be seen as uniquely authoritative. How the New Testament was formed is one of the most complex and controversial problems in religious history. Why, and how, did the early church conclude that it needed a canon of texts at all? In what sense can the texts of the New Testament be considered unique—or are they merely representative? What weight did the early Christians themselves give to these works? These questions are fascinating but unanswerable—at least here. We can, however, describe the steps that led to the realization of the New Testament.

Many of the texts from the early church duplicate each other, and many others vary from each other in some way. Both duplication and variation are results of the lack of a centralized hierarchy, a body able to make authoritative statements for the whole church. Various communities, possessing copies of the different books, were aware of discrepancies but wanted to preserve only what was true and most reliable. They felt that texts with the closest connections with the original apostles were the most accurate records of the teachings of Jesus, and so they applied the criterion of APOSTOLICITY—that is, conformity with the teachings and experience of the apostles—to the various texts. A given text did not need to be directly from the hand of an apostle to be considered "apostolic" (although this clearly would be an advantage). The apostolicity of the Fourth Gospel has never been questioned, but whether John was its true author is a matter of ancient dispute. Similarly no one has ever been sure about the authorship of the Epistle to the Hebrews, another unquestionably "apostolic" book. The crucial test was whether a given text truly captured the teachings and experiences of the original apostles. Since a correct attribution of apostolicity obviously hinged on close familiarity with the apostles themselves, it was important that the canon be defined as early as possible.

The impulse to preserve as much as possible of the first generation's experience points to an important fact about the early church. Instead of being a body of concepts that could be refined and perfected, even completed, over the course of time, the core of early Christianity lay in a set of experiences, narrated in such a way that a believer a century later in a different part of the Roman world might get a sense of what it was like being

The sarcophagus of Giunius Bassus, Prefect of Rome, 359. Vatican Museum, Rome.

Christian communities wanted to preserve the bodies of their dead, as seen in catacombs and sarcophagi, sensing that they would be raised at the end of history.

with and learning from Jesus. Persecution (and sometimes martyrdom) gave many early Christians a keen sense of sharing in Christ's suffering. But later generations kept their faith alive mainly by participating in services and hearing about the deeds and words of Jesus and the first apostles. Thus, not only the apostles themselves but also the texts associated with them—the canonical books— perpetuated the work of Jesus. The intimate contact with Jesus and the apostles that these books were thought to provide became one of the factors in the sacred status that they would acquire during the Middle Ages.

As the apostolic group broke apart and each apostle became the starting-point for a new community, links with them provided a valuable connection to Jesus' own world. Thus the followers of Mark formed a nascent church, the Gospel attributed to him serving as a textual relic of sorts: a memoir that kept both Jesus and Mark alive in the memory of the group—in different ways, of course. Other church groups were recipients of epistles, and these too became points of contact with the first generation of followers. As time went on and texts were copied and circulated, communities gathered together more and more books, stimulating a desire to set a fixed canon. Thus, lists of approved and disapproved books were drawn up, and from these we get the first efforts to establish a canon of Christian writings: in other words, a Christian Bible.

The Bible and its Contexts: How Do We Know?

For centuries, historians and theologians saw the New Testament in relative isolation. They knew about the history of the early church from the historian Eusebius (see Introduction) and other early historians, but there were few complete texts with which these historians' works could be compared. Then in the eighteenth century an Italian priest and librarian named Lodovico Antonio Muratori (1672–1750) discovered a fragment that represents the earliest list of canonical New Testament writings. The list, known as the "Muratorian Canon," dates to the latter part of the second century C.E. and includes the books of the New Testament as well as some, like the "Apocalypse of Peter" and the "Wisdom of Solomon," that were not included in later canons. In the nineteenth century historians discovered—or, more accurately, rediscovered in manuscripts and early printed editions—texts such as the writings of the APOSTOLIC FATHERS, a small library of nine texts from the first two centuries, which included epistles to various communities and an allegorical text called *The Shepherd of Hermas*. Soon classical scholars began to explore early Christian texts, while theologians looked seriously at non-canonical works from the time of the New Testament. Thus in the nineteenth century, when biblical studies came into their own as an academic discipline, a bridge was built between classical studies and theology. To this day, any serious research into early Christian studies requires a knowledge of ancient Greek and familiarity with the body of non-canonical, or APOCRYPHAL (literally, "hidden") early Christian texts.

The middle of the twentieth century has so far been the most exciting—and potentially disruptive—period in the history of biblical scholarship. In 1945–46 archaeologists discovered, near the Egyptian town of Nag Hammadi, a number of texts that date to a Coptic-speaking sect of the third to fifth centuries known as

GNOSTICISM. Although a complex movement, Gnosticism essentially maintained that God revealed the origin and destiny of the world as a form of knowledge, or *gnosis* in Greek, and that salvation, which took the form of returning to a divine being, came from possessing this knowledge. Although there were elements of Gnosticism in some early Christian communities, many of the Fathers of the church were outspoken critics of its beliefs, and we know about the movement mainly from their attacks on it. With the discovery of the Gnostic collection at Nag Hammadi, we can now begin to understand Gnosticism on its own terms—and see some of its relations with Christianity.

The Dead Sea Scrolls

The most exciting discovery of ancient religious writings was made in 1947 in Jordan, in a series of caves along the Dead Sea, at a site called Qumran. Led there by bedouins who had discovered the caves by accident, scholars found more than 750 texts in Greek, Hebrew, and Aramaic, some fragmentary, some almost complete. The texts are the remnants of the library of a Jewish sect that apparently settled there in the first century B.C.E.—probably the Essenes (see Chapter 1), whose numbers may have included John the Baptist. From these "Dead Sea Scrolls," as they are called, we have discovered that messianic expectations, and the enthusiastic and radical practices that went with them (from initiation rites to feats of extreme asceticism), were widespread and detailed. These expectations involved a divine–human being, an "anointed" one, also referred to as the Teacher of Righteousness. The group lived a monastic life, organized around liturgy and a common meal, which seems to have resembled the Last Supper in some respects; for example, the use of bread and wine to represent the Messiah may derive partly from this sect.

It became obvious from the first inspection that these texts would profoundly change our understanding of Christian origins. What had been assumed to be original statements by Jesus have turned out to be the kind of doctrines expected from a so-called "Teacher of Righteousness." The doctrines that Christians assumed were unique now appear to have had counterparts at Qumran. And the teachings that the church has associated with a realm of peace and charity have turned out to be shared by an apparently warlike sect. Since the middle of the past century, Christianity has had to acknowledge that its origins may lie in a setting completely different from the one it had imagined over the previous centuries. In significant ways, the church has not been the same since 1947; and the mystery over the contents of the scrolls has been augmented by scandals, real and imagined, over suppression of certain documents and the very slow pace at which they have been edited and published. The last word on this early episode in Christian history is a long way away.

The Beginnings of Theology

As the canon of Christian scripture was taking shape, leaders within the church were interpreting the relevance of these writings amid the changes of the times. With the passing of the writers of the scriptural (and apocryphal) books, questions about the meaning of the texts and the significance of Jesus' life and death became all the more urgent. Was this worldly life the real one, or were the crucifixion and resurrection evidence that a realm beyond this one was humanity's true goal? Was Jesus a divine figure and, if so, in what way? Or was he merely a human agent of God? How was the church to relate to the secular world, and to the Roman Empire in particular? And how were the Christians to see themselves in relation to Judaism? We touch on some of these questions elsewhere, but they are crucial enough to deserve mention here as problems for the earliest Christian THEOLOGIANS.

The discipline of theology can be defined as discourse about God—a deceptively simple definition. Difficulties arise even in identifying the subject matter, since the early Christians' God was both the same as, and different from, the God of the Hebrew Bible. The Christian God was the same in that the sovereignty of the Hebrew God is affirmed in the New Testament, but different in that God came to be understood as a threefold unity, known as the TRINITY. Moreover, the scriptures themselves, both old and new, can be seen as discourse about God; so are they, too, part of theology?

The answer to this last question is "no." Scripture was understood by the early Christians as revelation, a message originating with God though transmitted in human terms—much the same way that the Jews regarded the Law as revealed by God to Moses on Mount Sinai. Theology was, accordingly, the human interpretation of that revelation—and, like the Jewish Talmud (the Oral Law and commentaries), the continuing explanation of its meaning and application.

Fathers of the Early Church

The period from c. 200 to c. 600 is known as the PATRISTIC era in Christian theology, the name being taken from the fact that these authors are considered the "fathers" (from the Latin *pater*) of the church, by virtue of their office (as in the case of bishops), their sanctity (as with martyrs), or the influence of their writings. This is the golden age of Christian thought.

The church fathers draw on Greek and Latin, as well as Jewish, theological traditions, each of these bearing the traits of their cultures. The philosophically inclined Greeks saw Christ as the incarnation of something they had recognized since the time of Plato: the LOGOS or divine reason, the absolute to which everything in the world of experience is relative (see Chapter 3). The idea that a god who existed beyond sensory experience could enter the material world was readily acknowledged. And the continuing presence of the deity in the form of the Holy Spirit reinforced this idea of God's connection with the material world. The development within the Orthodox branch of Christianity of the doctrine that icons are also manifestations of divinity, underscores the metaphysical stance of the early Greek theologians.

It was thus an imperative of the early Greek tradition that theology appear in a philosophical form. Since metaphysical reflection was as alien to most Jews in the first century as messianic hopes were to the Greeks, it took bold creativity to synthesize the Hebrew doctrine of redemption with the Greek philosophical concept of participation in some absolute essence. The coherence of the doctrines of the Incarnation and the Trinity (see Chapter 3) is due in large measure to these early Greek theologians.

The Latin theological tradition, like Roman culture generally, was more pragmatic, the work of a busy people whose destiny, to all appearances, was dominance of the Mediterranean world. With few exceptions, Roman philosophy never rose to the levels of its Greek sources. Roman theology, however, was less dependent upon Greek models, and this tradition reveals a high level of vitality and originality. Authors such as Tertullian (c. 155–222) and Cyprian (d. 258) were shaping Latin religious thought a century before the great generation of Greek

BIOGRAPHICAL PROFILE

Origen (c. 185–c. 254)

Through his voluminous scholarly output, Origen of Alexandria became known as one of the greatest thinkers of the early church. In the eyes of many he is the first truly systematic theologian of Christianity. Unlike many of the church fathers who preceded him, Origen did not convert to the faith as an adult but was raised in a Christian family. When he was a boy, his father was murdered by the authorities for his faith, and so martyred. Origen himself was so inspired by this event that he wanted to follow his father's example; his mother, however, managed to prevent him from turning himself over to the same authorities.

Origen further showed his zealousness when, following literally Jesus's comments about becoming eunuchs for the kingdom of heaven, he castrated himself. When he was about seventy, Origen suffered under the persecutions of the Emperor Decius. He was imprisoned and tortured. He died shortly after his release.

Origen's theological career began when he was still in his teens and the bishop of Alexandria gave him the responsibility of educating new converts to the faith. Following this assignment, Origen taught at, and served as director of, a Christian school of philosophy. His work here brought him respect from Christians and pagans alike. Even the Roman emperor's mother went to hear his lectures, as did Porphyry, a young pagan who would become an influential neo-Platonist philosopher.

Perhaps Origen's most famous work is *Against Celsus*, an apologetic treatise, or defense, which answers, point by point,

the accusations made against Christianity by the pagan philosopher Celsus. Origen's theological magnum opus, however, is *On First Principles*, which among other things serves as a guide to the allegorical method of interpretation for which he became famous. Besides these works, Origen wrote numerous biblical commentaries (many of which exemplify the allegorical method) and prepared the *Hexapla*, a version of the Hebrew Bible in six columns containing the Hebrew text, a Greek transliteration of the Hebrew, and four Greek translations.

Despite the enormous contributions that he made to Christian thought, Origen's thinking was questioned early on in church history, though not during his own lifetime. For example, Origen denied that hell is a place of eternal torment. He taught that God would save everyone in hell, even Satan and his demonic hordes. Moreover, Origen believed that all human souls existed before their earthly embodiment and that the reason for their "imprisonment" in the corporeal realm owed to their sin during their purely spiritual existence. Furthermore, while he did affirm the doctrine of the Trinity, Origen nevertheless argued that the Son was subordinate to the Father. One might well argue that, by promulgating such "heterodox" teachings at a time when there was no established "orthodoxy," Origen helped give shape to what would become orthodoxy at the hands of later Christian thinkers who responded to his work.

Origen, c. 185–254. Engraving.

fathers. Tertullian's writings consist of dogmatic treatises on such subjects as baptism, prayer, and repentance, on the one hand, and on the other, defenses and polemical works, in which he refutes various theological opponents. The bulk of Cyprian's writings is made up of letters to various churches and to his peers, some of which are carefully crafted treatises in their own right. However, in such treatises as *On the Lapsed* and *The Unity of the Catholic Church*, he sets out some of the terms according to which one could call oneself a Christian.

The towering figure in Latin Christianity is Augustine (354–430), Bishop of Hippo in North Africa, and the thinker whose works would serve as a standard of orthodoxy for over a millennium. Augustine was a many-sided figure, and a good part of his fascination for later ages has been his complex personality—which with subtle insight he shares with readers in his introspective *Confessions*

Who's Who

Fathers of the Early Church

LATIN:

Tertullian (Quintus Septimius Florens Tertullianus) (c. 155–c. 222) After a pagan upbringing in Carthage, North Africa, he went on to write many works, such as *Apologeticum* (c. 197), which supported Christianity. He may have practiced as a lawyer.

St. Cyprian (Thascius Caecilianus Cyprianus) (d. 258) Having converted from paganism to Christianity c. 246, he became Bishop of Carthage, North Africa, shortly afterward. A theologian of repute, his writings include *De Catholicae Ecclesiae Unitate*, which deals with unity in the church.

St. Ambrose (c. 339–397) As Bishop of Milan, he was a zealous preacher and a powerful, influential figure. He played a part in Augustine's conversion. His writings include Latin hymns, and he is responsible for the central role of hymns in Western church services.

St. Jerome (c. 345–420) Born in the cultured Adriatic city of Aquileia, he eventually settled in Bethlehem. Perhaps the greatest biblical scholar of his time, he is famed for translating much of the Bible from various languages into Latin.

St. Augustine of Hippo (354–430) Born to a Christian mother, he turned his back on the faith as a young man, but later underwent a religious conversion and was baptized by St. Ambrose in 386. He was appointed Bishop of Hippo Regius (now Annaba, Algeria) and went on to become a hugely influential figure in Western Christianity.

GREEK:

St. Gregory of Nazianzus (329/30–389/90) Son of the Bishop of Nazianzus (Cappadocia), he became a monk and was appointed Bishop of Sasiama (also in Cappadocia). Gregory helped to support the Nicene faith, and was briefly Bishop of Constantinople.

St. Basil, or Basil "the Great" (c. 330–379) Brother of St. Gregory of Nyssa, and once a hermit, he was made Bishop of Caesarea (Cappadocia) in 370. A talented organizer, he created a new framework for monasteries in the East that has lasted to this day.

St. Gregory of Nyssa (c. 330–c. 395) Brother of St. Basil, he became first a monk and then Bishop of Nyssa (in Cappadocia) around 371. His notable writings deal with the mysticism of scripture and with spiritual guidelines for monks.

St. John Chrysostom (c. 347–407) Before becoming Bishop of Constantinople in 398, he was a renowned preacher; Chrysostom translates as "golden-mouthed." After riots at Antioch during which imperial statues were attacked, he gave a particularly famous series of sermons entitled "On the Statues."

Saint Augustine (354–430)

Aurelius Augustinus was his Latin name; he is known as Augustine in English. In the Middle Ages he was referred to as the "Doctor of grace" because of the emphasis on grace in his teachings. He was born in North Africa in 354 to a pagan father and a Christian mother, of mixed race, too late to witness classical Rome at its peak and too far from Italy to regard himself as anything but an outsider. Augustine navigated a complex cultural milieu, aided by intellectual gifts and a tendency toward introspection. (One sees this in his *Confessions*, written c. 400.) He also went to Carthage to study for a while, and had a son by a mistress there.

Nurtured on the Roman classics, he rose to the top of his profession as a teacher of rhetoric, in the process taking in the best of pagan culture. He was looking for a fixed, permanent, and true set of beliefs, but failed to find them in the culture of the time. Instead, he recognized that his mother (who was later canonized as St. Monica) possessed what he was looking for: a Christian faith. Upon that realization he became a committed Christian. He was baptized by Saint Ambrose in 386.

His career proved meteoric. Ordained, and made a bishop shortly later, he devoted himself to church governance and the defense of still-maturing Catholic doctrine. Heretics demanded refutation: among them, the Donatists, an African sect that insisted that sacraments were effective only when administered by morally faultless clergy, and the Pelagians, who asserted that human nature was sufficiently good to merit salvation. Many of the works that Augustine composed in response to these and other heresies became standard systematic treatises that would shape the course of Western doctrine.

His greatest work was the *City of God* (413–26), an epic survey of the course of both pagan and Christian civilization. It was written while the Roman Empire was in the final stage of collapse. In this tome Augustine combines careful philosophical critique with a close awareness of the events around him to present a theological vision of history, possibly the first in that vein. The primacy of the spiritual over the physical, and of the Christian over the pagan, are the major themes of this grandest of narratives.

Augustine both shaped doctrine and laid the path upon which doctrines in the future might be shaped. In *De doctrina Christiana* (*On Christian Doctrine*), written between 397 and 427, he elucidates a method of biblical interpretation that remained largely unchallenged until the rise of the historical-critical method in the nineteenth century. For Augustine, all scripture is the revelation of the divine will, and is thus as coherent as the will it expresses is unified. Hence there is a single "message" to scripture, and it is love, *caritas*. To read the Bible faithfully is to read it in such a way that love—of God and neighbor—is ordered and strengthened. Love needs to be ordered because in the original fall from grace humanity's affection turned in upon itself, so that self-love seems the norm. In restored grace, love is directed first back to God, with affections for all worldly things deriving from that proper love. By this method of interpretation, one gained a true understanding of a biblical text if one's piety was augmented.

This teaching would also prove influential in monasticism, especially the Cistercian tradition of the twelfth century, a movement that saw the monastery as a "school of charity."

Augustine himself was a monk at heart. In 396 he created a small monastery at Hippo in what is now Algeria, wanting nothing more than the chance to devote himself to a life of prayer and contemplation. He composed a *Rule* for his monastic brothers and saw their life as an ideal one. However, whether Augustine was himself totally suited to the monastic life is questionable:

he certainly possessed the sense of religious devotion, but a life without the exercise of writing would surely have been a strained existence for him. On the one hand, he might have thrived in a life of silence and prayer. On the other hand, the Western Church would not have reaped the benefits of his imposing collection of classic texts, and moreover viewpoints such as those of the early heresies might have prevailed.

Simone Martini, *St. Augustine of Hippo*, c. 1320. Egg tempera on gold panel. Fitzwilliam Museum, Cambridge University, England.

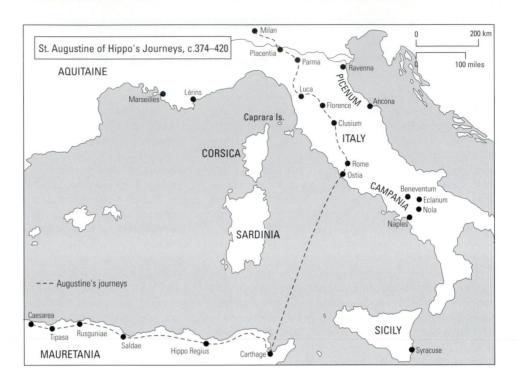

(c. 400). The son of a pagan father and a Christian mother, Augustine was also part of the mixed culture of North Africa: part Roman, part Carthaginian, the civilization conquered by the Romans in 146 B.C.E. after centuries of tense coexistence. Augustine himself witnessed the decline of the Roman Empire, a process that convinced him of the transient nature of all human civilizations.

Augustine became a member of the church; was ordained and made a bishop in short order; and devoted prodigious energy to writing theological works, including a guide to interpreting scripture (*On Christian Doctrine*: first three books, 397; fourth book, 427); a fifteen-book treatise, *On the Trinity* (399–419); and treatises defending Catholic teaching against various heretical opponents and a vast body of exegetical works. All of these, however, were eclipsed by the monumental *City of God* in twenty-two books (413–26), a history of pagan civilization, a Christian philosophy of history, and an explanation of the relation of the church to the heavenly realm that is the only true "city," or we might say the only true homeland, of the Christian believer. Augustine's greatest influence in Latin Christianity lies in his doctrine of GRACE: the concept that Christ's death on the cross—referred to by Christians as the ATONEMENT—reconciles God and humanity by nullifying the penalty of original sin. We will see this doctrine in closer detail in later chapters.

There were Latin Christian writers after Augustine's time, of course, the most prominent of whom was the pope and saint Gregory the Great (c. 540–604; r. 590–604). But with Augustine the Christian tradition reaches a point of maturity; and it is no exaggeration to call much of the later course of Christian thought in the West, both Catholic and Protestant, "Augustinian."

BIOGRAPHICAL PROFILE

Pelagius (c. 360–431)

While little is known of Pelagius's life, he is nevertheless one of the most important figures in the history of Christianity because of a dispute that developed between him and Augustine of Hippo. A British monk, Pelagius was an ascetic widely recognized for his virtuous character, who taught that God created humans in such a way that they may freely choose to live a good life and in fact live without sin. When two young Christians, Timasius and Jacobus, who knew Pelagius and had read his works, encountered some of Augustine's works on human nature, original sin, and grace, they immediately recognized that the views of the two men were incompatible. They therefore sent Augustine a copy of some of Pelagius's works and asked him for his opinion. Augustine, who had already dealt with the Pelagian controversy in *On the Spirit and the Letter*, was only too happy to reveal to these young men the truth as he saw it, and so in 415 he wrote *On Nature and Grace*.

On Nature and Grace clearly presents the opinions of both Augustine and Pelagius, but Augustine argues that Pelagius's teachings are incompatible with authentic Christianity. According to Pelagius, some people can achieve salvation if they simply lead good and virtuous lives, so that they have no need for Christ's atoning sacrifice. Thus, Christ did not really die for all humanity, but only for those who sin. Additionally, Pelagius taught that those who never have an opportunity to hear the gospel, and infants who die without being baptized, can attain salvation. For Augustine, such assertions were heretical because they diminished God's gift of grace. Grace, in Augustine's view, is necessary for everyone's salvation, and it is given completely freely (which is the reason that it is called grace) by God without regard to the merits of the recipient. Augustine repeatedly emphasized that if salvation were possible apart from faith in Christ, even for those ignorant of the gospel and unbaptized infants, then Christ's death would have to be considered as having no effect. Augustine therefore refused to compromise on the need for grace.

While Pelagius's views may seem more palatable to some modern Christians who do not subscribe to radical notions of original sin, his fifth-century contemporaries largely sided with Augustine. However, the publication of *On Nature and Grace* did not entirely settle the dispute between the two men. Augustine continued to write against Pelagianism for the rest of his life. He further expounded his views in *On the Grace of Christ and Original Sin* and in *On Grace and Free Will*.

While church Councils condemned Pelagius's work as heretical in 416, 418, and 431, and he was excommunicated and banished from Rome, the argument between Pelagius and Augustine was never really settled. Later in the Middle Ages, Catholicism rejected the extreme views of Augustine, embracing instead the "semi-Pelagian" view of humanity, according to which human nature is compromised but not destroyed by original sin. Before the Enlightenment, most Protestant theology, reflecting the views of Luther himself, was extremely anti-Pelagian, but much of modern Protestantism (with some exceptions, notably the Neo-Orthodox movement of Karl Barth and others) shares Pelagius's more optimistic view of the human capacity for good. Thus, those teachings of Pelagius that were once unquestionably heretical are now fairly widely accepted, by both Catholics and Protestants.

Pelagius was a thinker ahead of his time; without his seemingly innocuous teachings, orthodox Christian doctrine in the West regarding grace might never have assumed the form that it did. And it was only through his longstanding disagreements with Pelagius that Augustine was led to develop fully his own doctrine of grace.

Pelagius, 6th century. Engraving.

Key Terms

APOCRYPHAL Literally, "hidden"; concerning parts of the Bible not accepted as canonical, which have been kept from general access but not discarded.

APOSTOLIC FATHERS The authors of a set of early Christian writings said to originate in the community around Jesus.

APOSTOLICITY Authentic origins in the community of the first apostles.

ARETALOGY A chronicle of a leader's or teacher's excellent or unique qualities; literally, a record of a person's virtues.

ATONEMENT Reconciliation between God and humanity, restoring the relationship spoiled by original sin; understood by Christians to have been achieved by Christ on the cross.

CANON A fixed and authoritative set of writings.

GNOSTICISM A branch of early Christianity which held that God had revealed human destiny only to certain people, who shared it as a secret knowledge.

GRACE A gift bestowed by God on believers; usually understood as salvation.

JOHANNINE The texts (and the community) associated with the apostle John.

LOGOS Literally, "word"; the mind of God in tangible form in the Incarnation; also, in Stoic philosophy, the active principle determining the world.

MARTYRDOM Witnessing to one's beliefs by voluntarily enduring punishment or death.

PASSION The suffering of Jesus on the cross.

PATRISTIC Of the era or literature of Christianity from ca. 200 to ca. 600, the time of the Fathers (Latin, *pater*) of the church.

SYNOPTIC Taking a general view of the whole; specifically, used to describe the first three gospels, which are structured similarly and have much content in common, and are thus able to be viewed in parallel.

THEOLOGIAN One who practices the craft of interpreting divine revelation and the divine–human relationship.

TRINITY The doctrine that God consists in three "Persons": Father, Son, and Holy Spirit.

WISDOM The tradition within biblical literature that contains practical advice and insights about the nature of the world.

Roman Power and Religion
Divine Destinies in Conflict

At the time of Jesus' death, c. 30 C.E., the Roman Empire was less than a century old. From its origins in the eighth century B.C.E., the Roman state had been a republic, and as such was ruled by representatives of the people. A revolution that began with civil war in the 40s B.C.E. led to the founding of the empire in 27 B.C.E. with Octavian (who took the name Augustus) as the sole ruler. From that time on, political power tended to be concentrated in a single individual: the emperor. Two characteristics of the Roman state are important for understanding the beginnings of the Christian tradition. One is the desire of Rome to dominate the inhabited world, and the other is the type of power assumed by the emperor.

Both of these factors helped to shape Christianity, forcing it to adapt to a hostile cultural environment. Just as the Roman occupation of Palestine in the first century B.C.E. shaped a Jewish worldview, so the dominance of the Roman Empire throughout the Mediterranean molded the Christian view. But instead of seeing the Roman presence as a temporary punishment that would be overcome by a divine act of redemption, as most Jews did, the early Christians tended to see the world of politics and history itself as a hostile realm, one from which only death would bring deliverance. Thus an environment of intolerance and persecution took on theological significance, being seen not as an unfortunate human situation but as a divinely dominated realm of oppression.

Nothing convinced the early Christian communities of this more forcefully than Roman claims of the divinity of their emperors. The notion that the rulers of this oppressive worldly realm could be "deified" after death intensified the opposition between the Christian and the official Roman worldview and accentuated the otherworldly character of the Christian one.

Christians in the Shadow of the Empire

Rome's desire to dominate the inhabited world had first shown itself in the fourth century B.C.E.; and over the next few hundred years its armies conquered lands all around the Mediterranean and beyond. By the beginning of the first century C.E., Roman power stretched from Spain to India and from North Africa to the British Isles.

The motives behind these conquests varied. A desire to absorb Greek culture led to the conquest of the Peloponnesus (the Greek peninsula at the southern tip of the Balkans), for example, and the need for defense against the Helvetians (ancestors of today's Swiss) prompted Caesar's conquest of Gaul. Control of the Near East was important for economic reasons. It facilitated trade with points east—the Parthian kingdom in modern-day Syria and Iran, and the "silk road" which extended from the Middle East to China.

Economic power has always tended to belong to the state that controls waterways, and the eastern edge of the Mediterranean was a vital component of Rome's economic strategy. Thus, a high priority for the Roman government was to make Palestine—a strategic bridge between the three continents of Asia, Africa, and Europe—safe for commerce. In 6 C.E. Palestine became Judaea, a province of the empire (the name means "Jewish area," derived from Judah, the name for the ancient southern Jewish kingdom—as distinct from the northern kingdom of Israel). Judaea remained relatively independent culturally, but politically it fell under the rule of a Roman governor. It was the last component of the Roman conquest of the eastern Mediterranean.

The emperor did not see himself only as a political ruler. To the Roman mind, he was the agent of cosmic forces that governed the world's history and worked to ensure Roman supremacy over other peoples. These forces, usually referred to under the general term *fortuna* (fortune), were, in effect, the ultimate sovereign; the emperor was their human instrument, charged with fulfilling a supra-human destiny. Most importantly, the concept that the emperor was divine—an idea that became established as early as the reign of Augustus—had profound religious and political implications. It implied that obedience to the emperor entailed recognition of his divine status; and conversely, denial of that status indicated that one did not think that Rome's ascendancy was divinely determined—and no loyal Roman would want to state that. Thus the empire became both a political system and a religion, with laws in force that made denial of the gods' rule, and of the emperor's role as their instrument, a crime.

This fusion of the political and the religious did not bode well for the survival of Christianity, much less for its expansion throughout the Roman world, for it directly contradicted Christianity's central beliefs. Christians believed that their own founder, Jesus, was the true incarnation and agent of divine forces—far different forces from those in which the Romans believed. Furthermore, Christianity shared with Judaism a strict rejection of the idea that there could be more than one god. The monotheism of Judaism and Christianity—their insistence that there is only one God—was absolutely incompatible with the pagan POLYTHEISM (the belief in a number of gods, each associated with a particular set of attributes and responsibilities) that the Romans practiced. For a Jew or a Christian to grant legitimacy to the ancient Roman divinities or to acknowledge the emperor as a divine figure would be breaking the First Commandment of the Decalogue in the most flagrant way. On one occasion Jesus is reported to have said, "Give to Caesar the things that are Caesar's, and to God the things that are God's"; but at this time the cult of the Roman emperor was not yet fully established. The command to divide obligations into religious and political categories would become harder and harder as time went on, for the Roman emperors' sense of their own divine calling would intensify as the empire matured.

In the Face of Persecutions

Even though Jesus and his followers urged obedience to the empire, it was not easy to be a Roman and a Christian too. The Roman government used the full force of the law to keep all practitioners of foreign cults, Jews and Christians among them, within the Roman fold. The method of intimidation was as follows. If a person was suspected of not believing in the absolute divine power of the Roman emperor, he or she was given a chance to prove loyalty by sacrificing an animal to the Roman gods. Since any act of worship of a god other than the divine Creator would be a violation of the First Commandment, Christians were reluctant to capitulate even when faced with the threat of becoming human sacrifices at the public executions if they failed to comply. It was often possible to pay someone to make a sacrifice in the name of the accused Christian, and thereby to keep one's Roman and Christian obligations in balance. But some churches did not approve of this artifice, and came down hard on those congregants who participated in it. By the third century C.E., the compromisers were increasingly ostracized, and became known as "lapsed Christians." Of those who stood firm in their faith, some suffered torture and death. In fact, however, these probably

Condemned Men Being Thrown to Wild Animals, El Djem, Tunisia, 3rd century. Mosaic. Archaeological Museum, El Djem, Tunisia.

In art and writings, the courage of condemned men and martyrs was constantly accentuated. Being mauled by beasts was good evidence of Christian fortitude.

The Passion of Saint Maxima

The passion of the holy virgin Maxima is described, a woman who suffered under Emperor Maximian and the proconsul Anulinus for three days in the month of August.

In those days Maximian and Gallienus the emperors sent letters through the entire province that the Christians should sacrifice on the Cephalitan estate. Anulinus the proconsul entered precisely at the evening hour. Rising at the sixth hour of the night, he called a certain decurion to bring in Modaticius and Archadius the magistrates. When they had come, they were ordered by the proconsul to bring in all the Christians. They immediately sent members of their staff to arraign the Christians. And about the third hour of the day when the proconsul had taken his seat on the tribunal, all the Christians on this estate gathered together. And with all of them standing there, Anulinus the proconsul said: "Are you Christians or pagans?"

They all said, "We are Christians."

Anulinus the proconsul said: "Maximian and Gallienus, the godfearing and august emperors, deigned to deliver letters to me that all Christians should come and sacrifice; however, any who would refuse and would not obey their commands should be punished with various torments and tortures." Then they all feared greatly for themselves and their spouses, and even the young men and women were afraid. Among them were even presbyters and deacons with all ranks of the clergy. Throwing themselves on the ground they all worshipped the cursed idols.

However, there were there two beautiful consecrated virgins, Maxima and Donatilla. Campitana began to shout saying: "We all came to adore the gods and here are these two virgins who have not obeyed the command of the emperors and will not sacrifice."

Anulinus the proconsul said, "Tell me their names."

Campitana said: "They are called Maxima and Donatilla."

Anulinus the proconsul ordered a member of the proconsular staff to bring them out. When they had been led out and were standing there, they said: "Look, here we are. What question do you propose to ask us?"

Anulinus said: "Who authorized you to defy the god-fearing and august emperors?"

Maxima responded: "I am authorized by the Christian faith which I practice."

Anulinus the proconsul said: "How old are you?"

Maxima responded: "So am I the daughter of a magus, the way you are a magus?"

Anulinus the proconsul said: "How would you know whether I am a magus?"

Maxima responded: "Because the Holy Spirit is in us but an evil spirit manifests itself in you."

Anulinus the proconsul said: "By the living God, I adjure you to tell me how old you are."

Maxima responded, "Haven't I told you that you are a magus?"

Anulinus said, "Reveal to me how old you are if you know."

Maxima responded: "May your limbs be broken. I am fourteen years old."

Anulinus the proconsul said, "Today you will finish off [those fourteen years] if you have not sacrificed to the gods."

Maxima responded, "You sacrifice to them. You are like them."

Anulinus said, "Your verdict is about to be pronounced."

Maxima responded, "Greatly do I desire and wish it."

> Anulinus said, "Then prepare yourself for the verdict."
>
> Maxima responded, "It is better for me to receive a verdict from you than to defy the one and true God."
>
> Anulinus said: "How is it that you despair? Will you sacrifice or not?"
>
> Maxima responded: "I stand firm in my God; and I will not worship other gods."
>
> Anulinus said, "I will be patient with you until you make up your mind."
>
> Maxima responded: "I have made up my mind, and the Lord is fortifying me against you: thus you will grow weak but I will grow strong."
>
> (From *Donatist Martyr Stories: The Church in Conflict in Roman North Africa*, trans. Maureen A. Tilley. Liverpool: Liverpool University Press, 1996.)

numbered far fewer than the thousands traditionally supposed to have died, for concerted persecutions were really quite rare and brief in duration.

The persecutions did not succeed in slowing the growth of the church. By the third century Christians in Rome numbered more than 50,000 (out of a population of about 1 million). They met for worship mainly in each others' homes—not in the catacombs, as is popularly supposed, although funeral services, including celebration of the Eucharist, as well as funeral banquets were held in these burial chambers. Catacombs had previously been used by the Romans for burials; under the empire, pagan Romans began to practice cremation, while early Christians, like Jews, continued the practice of burying their dead, using the existing catacombs and creating new ones as required. Some of the catacombs contain chapels dedicated to various saints and are decorated with frescoes, which include some of the earliest Christian art. On occasion, during periods of persecution, the catacombs served as hiding places. One reason for this was the growth of "secret societies," cells of initiates who practiced their rites privately. Being hidden from view, they escaped the authorities; and the safety they provided

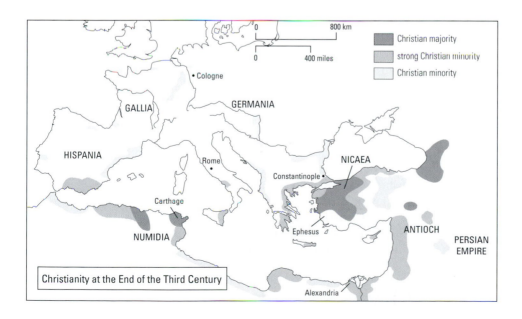

Christianity at the End of the Third Century

The Martyrdom of Zacchaeus and Alpheus

The first great church historian, Eusebius saw martyrdom as a form of divine blessing; his graphic descriptions of the sufferings of Christians were meant to inspire similar levels of dedication. Note the way in which he depicts Alpheus' fortitude as "godliness."

And Alpheus, a lovable man, endured similar sufferings. He was sprung of an illustrious family in the city of Eleutheropolis, and in the church of Caesarea he was honoured with the position of reader and exorcist. Now before he became a confessor he was a preacher and teacher of the word of God. And he used great boldness towards all men, which thing was the worthy cause of his being brought to his confession for the truth. And because he saw that at that time laxity and great fear had fallen upon all men, and many were swept along, as it were, before the torrent of many waters and were led to the foul worship of idols, he considered how he might oppose the torrent of evil by his fortitude. And he, of his own will, threw himself into the midst of the crowd of the torturers, and with words of warning reproached those who from their fear were drawn into error, and turned them from the worship of idols, and brought to their remembrance the words that were spoken by our Saviour about confession. And when Alpheus, valiant warrior that he was, acted thus with boldness, the soldiers arrested him, and forthwith brought him before the judge. Now he was like a man full of the Spirit of God: what expressions he freely used with the utterance of a freeman, and with what words of godliness he made answer, this is not the occasion to tell. Because of this he was sent to prison. And some days later they brought him again before the judge, and with grievous lashings they pitilessly tore his whole body, while the fortitude of his mind stood erect against the judge, and by his speech he resisted all error. And they tortured him on his sides with grievous scrapings. But at length, when he had wearied the judge, as well as those who ministered to the judge's will, he was committed to prison with his fellow-combatant, and there he was stretched a night and a day on that instrument of torture, the stocks.

(From *The Ecclesiastical History and the Martyrs of Palestine*, vol. 1, *Eusebius of Caesarea*, trans. Hugh Jackson Lawlor and John E.L. Oulton. London: Richard Clay & Sons Ltd., 1927.)

made them quite popular over time. (Unfortunately they were so secret that we have little solid evidence about them.)

Although the early Christians worshiped in private, it seems as that they did not do so normally out of fear of being discovered. These were simply the only places available to them; the Roman government would scarcely have allowed them to build churches, even if they had possessed the administrative structure capable of doing so.

When the authorities did launch persecutions of Christians, the effect was the opposite of the one expected: far from losing adherents, the church actually gained more. In believing that they had received eternal life in a realm beyond the present one, the early Christians saw martyrdom as an opportunity to exchange their life of worldly troubles for one of eternal blessedness. (See "The Passion of Saint Maxima" and "The Martyrdom of Zacchaeus and Alpheus.") Thus the horrible punishment imposed by the Romans was received as a boon, and the Romans appeared as agents of God's plan. Thus both Christians and Romans, ironically, saw the persecutions as the fulfillment of a divine plan.

Moreover, the martyrs' own behavior in the face of persecution served as a powerful advertisement for Christianity—more powerful than preaching. Executions were hugely popular public spectacles, attracting large crowds of onlookers. The Romans encouraged this morbid interest, expecting that it would drive Christians from their church and deter others from joining it. But the calmness, even willingness, with which the early Christians met death apparently struck many in the crowds profoundly. The Christians' attitude toward death evinced a degree of commitment that proved to be one of the church's strongest attractions. Of course, no one willingly chose to be persecuted, or joined the church in order to suffer martyrdom. But the ways in which the martyrs died revealed something that perhaps no written text or oral argument could convey. The deaths of the martyrs persuaded others that the church really was a path to a blessed eternal existence, and that the present life was so inferior in comparison that one could leave it without sorrow. The persecutions, therefore, provided powerful "advertising" for the merits of Christianity.

As a result, persecutions drew in more believers than they killed off—something that was not lost on the Roman authorities. News of these persecutions, recorded in martyrologies which were as avidly read as the Gospels themselves, spread throughout the empire; and traveling preachers and priests continued to draw followers. They did so even at times when to profess the Christian faith was a sure path to a martyr's death. Some especially violent waves of persecution are associated with the emperors Decius (c. 201–251; r. 249–51) and Diocletian (245/248–313/316; r. 284–305), both of whom felt that adherence to the older Roman religion was crucial for preserving the empire. Both of them, however, underestimated three things: first, the decline in authentic worship of the ancient Roman divinities, a custom that by the third century was seen more as folklore and mythology than as religion; second, the hold that Christian beliefs had on a wide spectrum of people, including members of the leading Roman families; and third, the political necessity of allowing colonized peoples, including Christians, to preserve their indigenous traditions. Without some tolerance of regional cultures, even recently "imported" ones such as Christianity, any hope of loyalty to an empire is a lost cause.

The Reign of Constantine

The situation of the church changed with the reign of the emperor Constantine (c. 280–337 C.E.; r. 312–337 C.E.). One of the truly pivotal figures in the history of Christianity, Constantine rescued Christianity from possible obscurity—yet in the process changed its nature forever. Constantine's wife was a Christian, and it is understood that she influenced him greatly. Although he may never have converted to Christianity himself—historians are unsure on this point—Constantine declared Christianity a legally recognized religion of the Roman Empire in 324 C.E. How did this come about? In 312 C.E. Constantine, a Roman general who had been proclaimed emperor by his troops in 306, was battling rivals for control of the Roman Empire. According to legend, the night before one battle Constantine dreamed that an angel foretold victory if he had the Greek monogram of Christ on his soldiers' shields. (See "The Prayer of Constantine"

The Prayer of Constantine

Constantine had left the liberation of Rome from the tyrant Maxentius to generals such as Severus and Galerius. When they failed, he fell to prayer and looked to God for a sign.

Accordingly be besought his father's god in prayer, beseeching and imploring him to tell him who he was and to stretch out his right hand to help him in his present difficulties. And while he was thus praying with fervent entreaty, a most incredible sign appeared to him from heaven, the account of which it might have been hard to believe had it been related by any other person. But since the victorious emperor himself long afterwards declared it to the writer of this history, when he was honoured with his acquaintance and society, and confirmed his statement by an oath, who could hesitate to accredit the relation, especially since the testimony of aftertime has established its truth? He said that about noon, when the day was already beginning to decline, he saw with his own eyes the trophy of a cross of light in the heavens, above the sun, and an inscription, CONQUER BY THIS attached to it. At this sight he himself was struck with amazement, and his whole army also, which followed him on an expedition, and witnessed the miracle.

He said, moreover, that he doubted within himself what the import of this portent could be. And while he continued to ponder and reason on its meaning, night overtook him; then in his sleep the Christ of God appeared to him with the sign which he had seen in the heavens, and commanded him to make a likeness of that sign which he had seen in the heavens, and to use it as a safeguard in all engagements with his enemies.

(From Eusebius, *Vita Constantine* [*A Life of Constantine*], in J. Stevenson, ed., *A New Eusebius*. Cambridge: Cambridge University Press, 1987.)

Constantine the Great (detail), Palazzo dei Conservatori, Rome, 325–326. Marble.

Constantine was a heroic figure in every respect, including his own self-regard. Monumental sculpture such as this appeared everywhere throughout his empire.

and "Constantine Enters Rome.") Constantine followed this advice and won the battle, and then the empire. Upon consolidating his power in 313 C.E., Constantine signed the Edict of Milan, officially putting an end to the persecution of Christians.

By the end of the third century it had become clear to most observers of the empire that there were too many Christians in all sectors of society—rich and poor, urban and rural—to make it worthwhile to attempt to control the spread of the religion. The change in the church's legal status brought about by Constantine now enabled the scattered Christian communities to organize under central administrative offices. By making Christianity a recognized religion of the empire, Constantine, in effect, made the church a part of the administrative system of the Roman state (see Chapter 5). No greater reversal of fortune could be imagined than the overnight transformation of the church from a persecuted minority to an officially recognized religion. Among Christians, the prospect of becoming one with their longtime enemies caused a fair amount of agonized reflection; but in the end it was possible to see the liberation of the church as an act of divine benevolence.

Constantine Enters Rome

According to Eusebius, Emperor Constantine's reign was the fulfillment of Rome's destiny and biblical prophecy, and his military successes were the result of divine assistance. Here is a description of his triumphant entry into Rome as ruler of a Christian empire.

Constantine, the superior of the Emperors in rank and dignity, was the first to take pity on those subjected to tyranny at Rome; and, calling in prayer upon God who is in heaven, and His Word, even Jesus Christ the Saviour of all, as his ally, he advanced in full force, seeking to secure for the Romans their ancestral liberty. Maxentius, to be sure, put his trust rather in devices of magic than in the goodwill of his subjects, and in truth did not dare to advance even beyond the city's gates, but with an innumerable multitude of heavy-armed soldiers and countless bodies of legionaries secured every place and district and city that had been reduced to slavery by him in the environs of Rome and in all Italy. The Emperor, closely relying on the help that comes from God, attacked the first, second and third of the tyrant's armies, and capturing them all with ease advanced over a large part of Italy, actually coming very near to Rome itself. Then, that he might not be compelled because of the tyrant to fight against Romans, God Himself as if with chains dragged the tyrant far away from the gates. … Maxentius and the armed soldiers and guards around him went down into the depths like a stone, when he turned his back before the God-sent power that was with Constantine, and was crossing the river that lay in his path, which he himself had bridged right well by joining of boats, and so formed into an engine of destruction against himself.

Thus verily, through the breaking of the bridge over the river, the passage across collapsed, and down went the boats all at once, men and all, into the deep; and first of all he himself, that most wicked of men, and then also the shield-bearers around him, as the divine oracles foretell, *sank as lead in the mighty waters* (Psalms, 8: 15, 16).

These things, and such as are akin and similar to them, Constantine by his very deeds sang to God the Ruler of all and Author of the victory; then he entered Rome with hymns of triumph, and all the senators and other persons of great note, together with women and quite young children and all the Roman people, received him in a body with beaming countenances to their very heart as a ransomer, saviour and benefactor, with praises and insatiable joy.

(From *The Ecclesiastical History and the Martyrs of Palestine*, vol. 1, *Eusebius of Caesarea*, trans. Hugh Jackson Lawlor and John E.L. Oulton. London: Richard Clay & Sons Ltd., 1927.)

The Councils and Christology

Twelve years after granting recognition to Christianity, Constantine gave further assistance to the church by convening a council at which disputes about doctrine could be resolved. Various members of the church at the beginning of the fourth century had differences of opinion about CHRISTOLOGY, the issue of whether Jesus Christ really was divine, or human, or both. In particular, there was a tendency, known as ARIANISM after its first advocate, Arius (c. 256–336), to view Christ as a supernatural being, created by God but not coeternal with him. In other words, Arianism held that the second Person of the Trinity, the "Son," was created by the first Person, the "Father." Being created meant that he exists within the boundaries of time, not eternally or outside them, and is thus subject to the same forces of change and decay that all of nature shares. The adoption of such a doctrine would probably have nullified three fundamental tenets of the

BIOGRAPHICAL PROFILE

Julian the Apostate (332–363; Roman emperor 361–363)

With the exception of Judas Iscariot, probably no other figure in Christian history has been more reviled as a traitor to the faith than the Roman Emperor Julian, who acquired the label "the Apostate" because of his rejection of the Christianity of his youth. Julian was the nephew of Constantine the Great, the first Christian emperor, and was raised as a Christian; however, he was unimpressed by the behavior of his Christian family. Constantine had ordered the murder of several members of his family, and when the emperor died, his son, Emperor Constantius (Julian's cousin) had Julian's father, elder brother, uncle, and six of his cousins murdered also. Julian believed he was spared only because of his youth (he was six years old). Witnessing such bloodshed at the hands of at least nominally Christian rulers and relatives did not endear Julian to the faith of the royal family.

As a boy, however, he was baptized as a Christian and educated in the faith. In fact, during philosophical studies at Athens he got to know St. Basil, the great Cappadocian theologian. He also developed an interest in the Hellenistic religions of ancient Greece, and subsequently rejected his Christian faith in favor of them.

Julian's political career began when Emperor Constantius made him governor of Gaul, the Roman province that included much of present-day France. Julian proved to be a very capable ruler, so much so that Constantius feared he might seek the throne. These fears were not unfounded: when the emperor sought to muster Roman troops from Gaul in 360 to aid him in his war against Persia, they refused to follow him and instead proclaimed Julian as their emperor. Before civil war could break out

over this issue, Constantius died and Julian duly became emperor by right of succession.

As emperor, Julian saw himself as an instrument of the pagan deities, and he attempted to use his political power to restore pagan religion to the prominence it had enjoyed before being eclipsed by upstart Christianity. To accomplish his goal, he supported the pagan priesthood and their sacrificial rituals. He even became a pagan "pope," declaring himself to be its high priest.

Julian refused to persecute Christians, wisely sensing that creating martyrs would only spur the growth of the religion he so detested. He did, however, attempt to stop the spread of Christianity by following the example of Celsus. In *Against the Galileans*, he criticized and ridiculed the biblical stories and Christian doctrines. He also claimed that the Christian God was one worshiped only by uncivilized barbarians. Additionally, to demonstrate once and for all the falseness of Christianity, Julian planned to rebuild the Jewish Temple in Jerusalem. At that time, Christians were convinced, on the basis of various prophecies in the Hebrew Bible, that the Temple would remain destroyed forever. Fortunately for Christianity, Julian was then killed in a battle with the Sassanid Persians. His aim to restore paganism to a position of preeminence had been aborted before it matured.

The reign of Julian reveals the fragile nature of early Christianity, even in the fourth century. Were it not for the fortuitous blow of a Persian spear, Julian, in many respects an effective and wise ruler, may well have stamped out Christianity and dramatically altered the course of Western history.

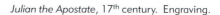

Julian the Apostate, 17th century. Engraving.

Christian belief system that had evolved by the early fourth century: the Trinity, the Incarnation, and the Atonement.

The Trinity is the concept that God is three "persons" in one: Father, Son, and Holy Spirit. The doctrine of the INCARNATION is the belief that God took human form in the person of Jesus, that Jesus is God in the flesh, or "incarnate." Atonement refers to the crucifixion, viewed as the act by which God and humanity, alienated since the sin of Adam and Eve (who, in eating the fruit of the Tree of Knowledge of Good and Evil, incurred God's anger), were reconciled.

The Nicene Creed

It is possible that Constantine was aware of the danger posed by Arianism; certainly he wanted a peaceful and harmonious church in his empire. To this end, he invited bishops and theologians from all over the world to a doctrinal council, to be held in 325 in Nicaea, near present-day Istanbul. Altogether 318 distinguished individuals attended, a remarkable showing. For months the assembled churchmen discussed and debated Christology, finally rejecting Arianism and formulating their position in a CREED. A creed, from the Latin *credo* ("I believe"), is a statement of the essentials of the faith, phrased in a succinct form. Known as the NICENE CREED, after the council at which it was written, this statement affirms the trinitarian character of the Deity and the doctrine of Christ, binding all believers to the idea that Christ was both fully human and fully divine. He was not, therefore, a creature to whom supernatural powers were granted (as in Arianism), nor a god who only seemed human (as in DOCETISM, from the Greek *dokesis*, "appearance"), but completely (if mysteriously) *both*.

Important as this development was for the history of Christian thought, it also reflected the new power of the church. The council not only formulated the creed but condemned all those who taught or believed otherwise. It did this by declaring them anathema (literally, in Greek, "handed over" to their damnation). It is obvious that an authoritative declaration of anything implies the denial of any statement disagreeing with it. But explicit condemnation to Hell is the harshest form of discipline, in a Christian context, against contrary views, and it is significant that the council, in condemning the Arians by anathematizing them, in effect imposed a divine punishment. By declaring the Arians damned, rather than merely stating that they held different opinions or were mistaken in their understanding of Christology, the church set the highest possible value on orthodoxy. A person either believed exactly as the church did in certain matters, such as the person and achievement of Christ, or was destined to eternal damnation.

Although we have been speaking of the church as an association of people—as of course, it was—it is only with the "Constantinian shift"—as the legalization of Christianity under Constantine is sometimes called—that we begin to see it taking the form it would have for the next millennium and a half. The structure of the hierarchy, with power concentrated at the highest levels, is a legacy of the imperially summoned council at Nicaea. And the function of the church as both the formulator of orthodox doctrine and the condemner of HERESY (opinion contrary to the orthodox doctrine), a function that has consumed so much of the church's energy even to the present day, has its origin in an emperor's desire that his reign be a peaceful one.

Jean Fouquet, *Untitled*, c. 1450. Oil on wood panel.

Mary is shown being crowned Queen of Heaven by Jesus, while God the Father and God the Holy Ghost look on approvingly.

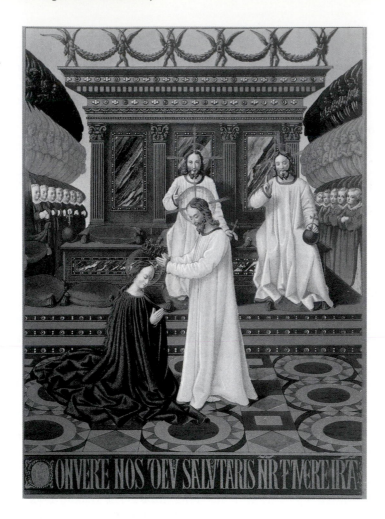

Roman Empire, Greek Church

Thus far we have spoken of the Roman Empire as if it remained unchanged during the first three centuries of Christian history. In some senses, to be sure, there was continuity: throughout this period Rome remained an empire controlling a vast terrain. In other ways, however, the empire changed as much during the reign of Constantine as did the church itself.

Byzantium

During the third century C.E. the western and eastern halves of the empire had been drifting apart. Geography made it difficult for the empire to be governed from a central capital, and this problem was exacerbated by cultural differences between the Latin-speaking West and the Greek-speaking East. For administrative reasons, at the end of the third century, the empire was divided into two parts, with a western ruler in Rome and an eastern ruler in the Greek-speaking part (known as Byzantium), each with a lieutenant, making a tetrarchy, or "rule of four." Thus, there were, in effect, two governments, though only one center of allegiance, Rome. Constantine, eager to have power once again concentrated in a single ruler, himself, defeated his co-rulers, abolished the shared arrangement, and moved the seat of government to the city of Byzantium (present-day Istanbul), which he named Constantinople after himself and which, in the year 330, became the "New Rome."

Relocating the seat of government in the East was strategically important for the defense and eastward expansion of the empire, but it was also symbolically important in its signaling of the beginning of a new empire. The "old" Rome remained an administrative center for Italy, Gaul, and other European possessions, as well as a site associated with a remarkable history. The founding of Constantine's new capital facilitated the abandonment of the ancient paganism of Rome. In 380, under one of Constantine's successors, Theodosius I (347–395; r. 379–395), Christianity became the empire's official religion. In fulfillment of Constantine's vision, the empire became a blend of the old Latin civilization— minus its pagan trappings—and the Christian Greek religious culture.

In the Byzantine world, "Roman" did not mean the Latin-speaking republicanism of the first centuries B.C.E. and C.E., the age of Cicero and Virgil. It meant Greek-speaking Christian imperialism and trust in an emperor who, like Constantine, never lived in Rome or even spoke Latin, but who was seen as the agent of divine forces governing human history. Since the belief that God protected and preserved the church on earth was naturally more acceptable to most Christians than the somewhat convoluted notion that God wished them to embrace martyrdom, and so proclaim the superiority of the next world, the church had little difficulty believing that the new Christian emperors were divinely ordained. Thus, in modified form, the divine role of the emperor— though not his divine status, as in the pagan empire—was acknowledged.

Byzantine culture, the civilization that began during the reign of Constantine, would last until the invasion by Muslims and the collapse of Constantinople as a Christian city in 1453. For half a millennium, from 300 to 800, while the Latin culture of the West was losing ground to invaders from the north and east, the Byzantine Empire flourished. Its scholars preserved the Greek literary and philosophical tradition, perfecting rhetoric—essentially the art of making fine speeches—and reconciling ancient philosophical thought with Christian dogmas. Greek monks and scholars, in their copying and interpreting of ancient classical texts, kept this tradition intact for a thousand years, preserving the writings of Homer, Plato, Demosthenes, and others until the rise of Renaissance humanism in the West and the invention of the printing press in the fifteenth century.

To the Byzantine mind, Greek civilization was a continuous tradition, reaching back to Homer and Hesiod in the eighth century B.C.E. and forming a uniform, if dazzlingly complex, worldview. A crucial element of Greek philosophy was the enterprise of trying to identify the one true reality, an absolute being, in comparison with which everything else is a puny imitation. This endeavor may have begun with the pre-Socratic philosophers and Plato (c. 428–347/348 B.C.E.), but was completed only with the revealed truth of the New Testament. In Greek Christian theology, Jesus Christ was described as the incarnation of Truth, and thus no part of culture or human activity was alien to his work. It is also possible, in more mundane terms, to see the Greek Christians as motivated by pride in their own heritage and determined to keep their written tradition intact. Whatever the explanation, Byzantine learning is largely responsible for handing on to the West the foundations of European thought and culture.

As is often the case, language was more effective at creating boundaries than in forging political links, for the Greek Christendom of the "new Rome" became more and more distinct from the Latin Christendom of the disintegrating old Rome. The Greek Church showed powerful leadership in its office of PATRIARCH, as the supreme head of the church was called; and leaders of the Greek Church made up the majority at the seven councils that were called between the First Council of Nicaea and the Second Council of Nicaea in 787 C.E.

The Latin Church, like the political landscape surrounding it, struggled in the vacuum left by the founding of Constantinople. The West would not see another great secular ruler until Charles the Great (Charlemagne) in the year 800. But the Latin Church would begin to see strong leadership in the 450s with the advent not only of popes, but of papal theory, doctrines concerning the extent and nature of the pope's power, which we will encounter in chapters 5 and 11.

Key Terms

ARIANISM A 4th-century heresy denying that Christ was fully divine and coexisted with the Father before time.

CHRISTOLOGY The doctrine of Christ; thought and writing about the nature and work of the second Person of the Trinity.

CREED A statement of belief, often recited by a congregation as an affirmation of the commonly held faith.

DOCETISM A 2nd-century heresy stating that Jesus only appeared to have suffered and died.

HERESY A doctrine counter to the teachings of the universal church.

INCARNATION God taking human form in the person of Jesus.

NICENE CREED The creed formulated at the Council of Nicaea in 325; it affirms the Trinity and censures Arianism.

PATRIARCH The title for a leader of episcopal rank, mainly in the Eastern Church.

POLYTHEISM A religious system in which many deities coexist.

Worship in the
Early Church
A Case Study in Adaptation

The early church was not a body of ideas or texts; it was made up of persons who met together to worship. This obvious fact tends to be ignored by those who identify the history of Christianity with the development of doctrines or institutions. Before there were written doctrines, there were beliefs and the faithful who held them. And before there were standardized forms of church organization, there were practices that brought the believers together. Yet reconstructing the practices that mark the beginning of the church is no easy task, for customs undergo substantial change, before any formulas or instructions are written down.

Archaeology and social history have revealed a number of details about the activities of the early church. These details amplify and corroborate clues left in the letters of Paul (see Chapter 2), which are among the earliest texts we have in the Christian tradition. It appears that the first Christians met in each others' houses, where they celebrated communion. Their meetings included men and women from many walks of life, and both free persons and slaves were part of the community. Such egalitarianism was radical for its time, but was in keeping with the teachings of Jesus and the lives of the apostles, as recorded in the Acts of the Apostles.

The Jewish Origins of Christian Worship

Whatever the scattered Christian churches had in common was drawn from their Jewish origins. Because Christianity took its principal concepts from Judaism, and defined itself as the culmination of that tradition's history, the pattern of rituals in the early church was also derived from Jewish models. Both the weekly cycle, with Sabbath observance and gathering of the community for instruction and blessings, and the annual cycle, with its celebrations of God's unique redemptive deeds, are adaptations of Jewish worship. Jesus himself was an observant Jew, and his own prayers, as recorded in the Gospels, echo the prayers common among Jews at that time. To take an obvious example, the so-called Lord's Prayer (found at Matthew 6:9–13) contains obvious echoes of the Jewish KADDISH, a prayer in various forms that declares the glory and sovereignty of God. And the blessings over the bread and wine at the Last Supper are similar to the blessings Jews pronounce over bread and wine to this day.

Disagreements over Jewish Law

The role of Jewish observance in Christian life presented a complicated problem to the early Christians. As we have seen in Chapter 1, the beginnings of Christianity were marked by efforts to distinguish the new religion from the rest of Judaism, while still remaining grounded in the ancient Jewish tradition. The same need to balance originality and continuity is seen in the church's LITURGY, the pattern and form of communal worship. From the beginning, disagreement over whether Christians were bound to Jewish law or freed from it—that is, whether they were still within Judaism or outside of it—stimulated efforts to define just what the new faith entailed. Differing viewpoints formed among the apostles themselves about the authority of Jewish law. The relation of old and new was a crucial one for Christian worship, because so much of Jewish ritual had been built around the concept of redemption—not only the historical redemption of the Jews from bondage in Egypt but also the anticipated redemption by a Messiah from present and future oppression. In bringing about this deliverance, observance of the law was crucial.

The Christian community also espoused the concept of redemption by a Messiah but understood it in a new way. In their eyes it had now been achieved, by Jesus Christ. This brought the observance of the law into question, for if the law had been observed in order to bring about the messianic redemption, was it still necessary? The apostle Peter and his followers held that Christ had ushered in a final stage of history, one demanding rigorous observance: "The end of all things is upon us, so you must lead an ordered and sober life, given to prayer" (I Peter 4:7). Similarly, James, who in his letter (James 1:1) addresses the "twelve tribes" of the Diaspora (i.e. the whole Jewish people, descended from the twelve sons of the patriarch Jacob, including Christians) preaches a more faithful and moral life, insisting that faith, to be real, must issue forth in deeds. James' example was the patriarch Abraham, whose obedience to God would have extended even to sacrificing his son, Isaac, as recounted in Genesis 22 (James 2:20–23).

In contrast to these prophetic and possibly legalistic views of Christian duty, some early believers held that Christ's work had the effect of nullifying the law and establishing a new motive for conduct. St. Paul, possibly the most influential New Testament theologian, described the relation between the old and new law in terms of a contrast between Adam and Christ. Adam, for Paul, represented the "old man," the state of humanity in sin and alienation from God, who has been replaced by Christ or the "new man." This means that the relationship between humanity and God was profoundly altered by Christ, so that strict obedience to the law was no longer a means to righteousness, but an opportunity for the sin of pride, which would make one unrighteous indeed. For example, Paul saw circumcision, the ritualized removal of an infant male's foreskin, as a symbol of obedience to the old covenant. Paul claims (against the argument of James cited above) that Abraham was accounted righteous on account of his faith, not his deeds; for in the event, God spared his son, commending Abraham for his trust. Moreover, Abraham was himself uncircumcised when God declared him righteous. (See "On Abraham and Circumcision.")

On Abraham and Circumcision

For Paul, circumcision is symbolic of Jewish ritual observance, which he wants to distinguish from genuine righteousness. Thus Abraham, the progenitor of the Jewish people, is described as righteous because of his faith rather than by his act of self-circumcision.

Consider: We say, "Abraham's faith was counted as righteousness"; in what circumstances was it so counted? Was he circumcised at the time, or not? He was not yet circumcised, but uncircumcised. Consequently, he is the father of all who have faith when uncircumcised, so that righteousness is "counted" to them; and at the same time he is the father of such of the circumcised as do not rely upon their circumcision alone, but also walk in the footprints of the faith which our father Abraham had while still uncircumcised.

(Romans 4:9–12, *The New English Bible: New Testament*. Oxford: Oxford University Press, 1961.)

While Jewish law posed many problems for the early Christians, other aspects of the Jewish tradition were easily absorbed and perpetuated. These included reading from the Scriptures and the chanting of psalms. The latter custom survives today in the medieval plainsong, or Gregorian chant, that is still heard in some Christian churches. The singing of hymns was another early custom, mentioned in the Gospels (for example, in Matthew 26:30). Prayer, of course, was as crucial to the new religion as it was to the old.

The Character of Christian Ritual

The primary purpose of worship, of course, is communication with the deity—through praise, thanksgiving, supplication, and meditation. But worship has other, secondary purposes. People also gather in religious settings to commemorate an event or person with special meaning for their lives, to affirm that their identity has been shaped by that person or event, and to share their experience with others who either have had the same experience or are seeking something similar to it. In addition to this "biographical" function, ritual gives structure to people's lives, often in ways that they find aesthetically, as well as emotionally, satisfying. The stages of life, and the seasons of the year, tend to be marked by ritual of some sort, and the most important of these events are celebrated by the solemn rites found in religion. The task of solemnifying the stages and states of one's life helps to celebrate one's identity as a member of a group. The two functions are interrelated, since a person's private life is partly shaped by associations with groups. As Christianity grew from its Jewish roots, it gave its adherents ample opportunities to commemorate their common historical origins and the stages of their own lives.

Liturgy and Sacrament

To understand Christian ritual, we must first consider two terms: Liturgy and SACRAMENT. "Liturgy," which is derived from a Greek word meaning, literally, "public work" or service to the community, encompasses the various forms of communal worship within the church. The forms of liturgy range from the simple to the complex, and from the everyday to events that occur once in an individual's lifetime. Although the specific formulas varied from place to place, there was apparently early agreement on the basic liturgical year—that is, the sequence of ceremonies that needed to be held every year at fixed times. The most important of these was EASTER, along with the preceding Holy Week, in which Christians commemorated the death and resurrection of Jesus. The Easter event was the Christian counterpart to the Jewish Passover—a unique redemptive event, a central reference point (if not the historical start) for the tradition that followed. Commemoration of Jesus' days of fasting in the desert (Luke 4:1–13), known to us as Lent (from the Anglo-Saxon word for springtime), and the forty-nine-day period between Easter and Pentecost (see Chapter 2: the bestowal of the Holy Spirit on the apostles and thus the "birthday" of the church), became the beginnings of cycles of observance. Each of these seasons was characterized by a "mood," so to speak, of its own: fasting and penitence for Lent, jubilation during the weeks after Easter, and, later, a spirit of expectancy during Advent, the weeks preceding CHRISTMAS, the midwinter celebration of Jesus' birth. In many pagan cultures, too, springtime and winter have celebrations, with the new life of nature being the focus in the spring festival, and the emergence from winter's darkness. Historians have often described the Christian festivals as adaptations of pagan rites. But as we shall see below, Christian celebrations drew their principal meaning from ancient biblical religion, and thus cannot be exclusively associated with pagan seasonal festivals.

Unlike liturgy, which is common to most religions, sacraments are unique to Christianity. These rites have special significance; and although the evolution of Christians' beliefs about their significance is hazy in some cases, it seems that from the outset these practices were thought to bring the participant closer to the divine, into contact with God in some way not possible with other rites. BAPTISM, for example, is an adaptation of the Jewish MIKVAH, a ritual bath that purifies a person for worship, symbolically for standing before God. (Jesus' baptism by John in the river Jordan was just such a rite.) The Christian continuation of this rite, grounded in Jesus' mikvah experience, symbolically purifies one for the presence of God in the church. Similarly, the Eucharist, or Lord's Supper, is a commemoration of an event at the end of Jesus' work: but it too is an adaptation of a Jewish rite, the Passover dinner or SEDER, which celebrates the liberation of the Jews from Egypt in the late thirteenth century B.C.E. (Similarly, the Eucharist is a meal that celebrates the "liberation" of the believer from bondage to "flesh" and law.) These acts, it was later thought, bestowed a supernatural quality upon their participants, called "grace." In other words, they represented a blending of divine and human elements in experience. But the original rationale for these two sacraments is much simpler than that: both rites were associated with Jesus (one as recipient, one as celebrant), and both were acts that he commanded his disciples to continue performing. And in repeating these acts, the participants moved that much closer to Jesus.

In order to understand better the concepts of liturgy and sacrament we will look more closely at baptism and the Eucharist. Both of these sacraments originate in the life and teachings of Jesus, and both served as sources and shapers of meaning in the lives of Christians as the early church grew.

Forming Christian Identity: Baptism

There was no ambiguity in the way the earliest followers of Christ, the apostles, formed a group: they were called directly by Jesus to follow him and help him in his work. Charismatic leaders have no trouble recruiting followers, but keeping a community growing after its founder's demise has been one of the challenges religious groups regularly face, even today. The promise of immortality, evidenced by Jesus' resurrection, gave the early church no shortage of interested members. The difficulty was making sure they believed the right things, for without consensus in matters of faith, calling oneself a Christian could have meant anything and everything. Unlike Judaism, in which one's identity could be evidenced by certain tangible indications (e.g. circumcision), membership in the Christian community was by faith, and could be proved only by making a statement of faith and being baptized. Thus Christians recited such a statement to affirm their own beliefs but also to identify themselves to each other. What they were reciting was the beginning of the Christian creed. As a passage that the believer was expected to recite perfectly, a creed needed to be long enough to express what was particularly Christian, but not so long that it could not be remembered correctly. The length of the Pledge of Allegiance to the U.S. flag is ideal for a creed. The Apostles' Creed and the Nicene Creed (see Chapter 3) are short enough to be remembered, but long enough to encapsulate the essentials of the faith. Later creeds were extremely long, but these were probably not recited.

A sarcophagus relief of a baptism, 3rd century. Terme Museum, Rome.

Baptism often had echoes of Jesus' baptism in the Jordan. The rite on this sarcophagus is depicted as death to the old life and birth to a new one.

Later, as more formal means developed to grant membership in the church, a creed was recited within the liturgy as a common declaration of faith. Like the Eucharist that followed its recitation, the creed bound the believers together by reminding them of their beliefs about crucial past and future events.

Membership in the church was made official with the ritual of baptism. This rite, which, as previously noted, Jesus himself received from John the Baptist before he began his ministry, involved immersion in water, combined with a declaration of the faith. Like the Jewish mikvah (a ritual bath), baptism symbolizes purification and conversion: it represents both cleansing from original sin and entry into the new covenant.

A baptismal font for total immersion, Sbeitla, Tunisia, 4th century.

There are steps on two sides down which the candidate would have descended into the holy water. Visible also are the bases of pillars which would have supported a canopy or dome.

With the passage of time, Christianity evolved from a voluntary to a natural religion. That is, it became one into which a person was born, rather than one that he or she joined voluntarily by conversion as an adult. With this transformation baptism began to be administered soon after birth, taking the place of the Jewish rite of circumcision, the practice that initiates a male, eight days after birth, into the Jewish covenant. In place of that procedure, an infant was symbolically purified through baptism on the eighth day after birth; also, of course, it was performed for girls as well as boys.

In becoming, like Judaism, a natural religion, Christianity faced a question already familiar to Jews: How could a believer born into a religion achieve a greater degree of perfection within his or her faith? This was a question that Judaism had answered with its various sects (see Chapter 1), which had entailed heightened levels of devotion and responsibility. The early church found its answer in MONASTICISM—the withdrawing from society in order to pursue an ordered life of contemplation—a phenomenon that we will encounter in Chapter 7.

Commemorating the Passion: The Eucharist

The central feature of Christian worship, virtually the seed from which its liturgical tradition grew, was the Eucharist, a reenactment of the Last Supper. This sacrament served as a form of fellowship, just like communal meals of many similar sects, and was a commemoration of Jesus' Passion, the crucible from which the church emerged. By re-creating the event at which Jesus prepared to leave the world and entrusted his friends with his work, the followers not only reminded themselves of their founding event, but in a sense brought Jesus back among themselves. In their reenactment, the participants "became" the apostles at the Last Supper. The feeling of oneness and purpose that they shared gave them the sense that Christ was still among them. Eventually the celebrant, or priest, would himself become a substitute Christ figure—although that would not happen for a few centuries. (See "Baptism and the Eucharist.")

The ritual meal was more than just a commemoration; it involved a consecration of the bread and wine, which gave them added significance. According to the records left by the apostles, at the Last Supper Jesus pointed to the bread and said, "This is my body," then pointed to the wine and said, "This is my blood." Few can be certain as to what he meant by these words, if he did in fact say them at all. But at an early date it became a widely held belief that his words were meant literally, and that he was in a real sense present in the bread and wine. Thus, when the faithful were gathered, and the words of consecration—the repetition of Jesus' two statements—were spoken, the bread and wine would be transformed into flesh and blood, so that the participants could consume him. This made the eucharistic meal a powerful form of oneness with Christ, quite unlike anything in Judaism.

As we have seen, the Eucharist was closely associated with the Jewish Passover meal, or seder; indeed, the original Last Supper may have been this very feast, shared by Jesus and the apostles. Traditionally, the seder is held in private homes rather than in a house of worship, to remind the participants that at the time of their redemption the Jewish people did not yet have a temple and were in a state of migration. Similarly, the Eucharist was at first held in private homes, as the church was itself in a form of "exodus," unable to build houses of worship in which to celebrate. The Eucharist combines expectation with fulfillment by recalling both Christ's death and his resurrection, and it is instituted as an enduring memorial. It is highly significant that at the Last Supper Jesus calls the wine the symbol of a covenant (Matthew 26:28, Mark 14:24). "Blood of the covenant" is a pregnant phrase, not, as some suggest, because ancient contracts were sealed with blood (though that is true), but because it recalls the blood of the sacrificial lamb that served to identify the homes of the Israelites and therefore safeguard them when God killed most of the firstborn males in Egypt—passing over the houses so marked (Exodus 12:1–14). By partaking of Jesus' sacrificial blood, his followers would be counted among those redeemed by the new convenant, while all the rest would suffer. The authors of the Gospels may have seen the capture of Jerusalem and the destruction of the Second Temple as a new form of divine punishment, this one inflicted on the Jews—a parallel to the killing of the Egyptians.

Whereas Passover is an annual celebration, the Eucharist was, from early Christian times, part of the weekly cycle of worship. What does this difference mean? For one thing, it suggests that Jesus' followers wished to remind themselves as often and directly as possible of their founder's last day among them. But to keep the weekly repetition of the Eucharist from diminishing in significance, the church consecrated the week before the commemoration of the resurrection—that is, Easter. Thus every Sabbath would serve as a reminder of the Last Supper and the crucifixion, while also looking forward to the annual celebration of the redemptive miracle of his rising from death.

The relation of Sabbath and Easter in Christianity to Sabbath and Passover in Judaism shows how the church adapted the structure of Jewish life. Another indication of how Christianity both affirmed its Jewish roots and yet distinguished itself from Judaism is the shift in sabbath observance from the seventh day of the

Baptism and the Eucharist

The two sacraments at the foundation of Christianity were adaptations of Jewish practices rather than new creations. Here we see familiarity with baptism and the blessing of bread and wine, but not with the Holy Spirit or Jesus' presence in the meal.

When Apollos was at Corinth, Paul traveled through the inland regions till he came to Ephesus. There he found a number of converts, to whom he said, "Did you receive the Holy Spirit when you became believers?" "No," they replied, "we have not even heard that there is a Holy Spirit." He said, "Then what baptism were you given?" "John's baptism," they answered. Paul then said, "The baptism that John gave was baptism in token of repentance, and he told the people to put their trust in one who was to come after him, that is, in Jesus." On hearing this they were baptized into the name of the Lord Jesus; and when Paul had laid his hands on them, the Holy Spirit came upon them and they spoke in tongues of ecstasy and prophesied. Altogether they were about a dozen men.
(Acts 19:1–7, *The New English Bible: New Testament*. Oxford: Oxford University Press, 1961.)

During supper Jesus took bread, and having said the blessing he broke it and gave it to the disciples with the words: "Take this and eat: this is my body." Then he took a cup, and having offered thanks to God he gave it to them with the words: "Drink from it, all of you. For this is my blood, the blood of the covenant, shed for many for the forgiveness of sins. I tell you, never again shall I drink from the fruit of the vine until that day when I drink it new with you in the kingdom of my Father."
(Matthew 26:26–29, *The New English Bible: New Testament*. Oxford: Oxford University Press, 1961.)

week, Saturday, to the first day, Sunday. The early church was aware of the commandment, in the Decalogue, that the Jews must preserve a sabbath day—a day of rest and holiness, a time very different from the rest of the week—and they honored this command. But whereas the Jewish tradition celebrates the creation of the world and the revelation of the law in its sabbath, the church celebrated the redemption of humanity by Jesus. Thus the day on which the resurrection was thought to have occurred, Sunday, became the "Lord's Day," and this became the Christian sabbath.

Belief in Practice

The ritual life of a religious community requires constant explanation and adaptation, and nowhere is this more true than in the case of Christianity, which culturally had to "translate" its Jewish practices to make them meaningful to a non-Jewish world. To this end, leaders within the Christian community prepared explanations of its various rites; some of these took the form of commentaries on the biblical passages in which they were rooted, while others were treatises on the rites themselves. The beliefs that gave meaning to this evolving system of practices were formalized in DOGMA (literally, "opinion" from Greek *dokein*, "to seem"). Gospel accounts, canonical or otherwise, were increasingly supplemented by more recent writings applying Jesus' teachings and actions to new communities; and letters such as we find in the New Testament became models for a tradition of letters from one community to another, or from a bishop to his community, about the proper practice of the Christian life. Here we have the beginning of theology: reflection on the meaning and value of the biblical narrative and the ritual practices that the Bible gave rise to. The development of this tradition will be explored in later chapters.

Key Terms

BAPTISM Symbolic cleansing with water, representing the washing away of an old identity and the assumption of a new one; one of the sacraments.

CHRISTMAS The celebration of Jesus' birth.

DOGMA A belief handed down from one generation to another; literally, an opinion.

EASTER The celebration of Jesus' resurrection.

KADDISH A Jewish prayer sanctifying the name of God.

LITURGY Any religious rite following a set pattern and performed by a community.

MIKVAH A Jewish ritual bath, symbolizing the cleansing necessary for presenting oneself before God.

MONASTICISM A way of life in which people strive for perfection by separating from society and passing their days in prayer and study.

SACRAMENT A ritualized point of contact with God, instituted by Christ and maintained by church tradition.

SEDER The Jewish ritual meal at Passover.

Virgin and Child with Saints and Angels, St. Catherine Monastery, Mt. Sinai, Egypt, 6th century. Encaustic on wood.

PART TWO

The Christian Religion in Late Antiquity

Free of the shadows of imperial persecution, scattered Christian communities began to organize around a diocesan structure in which bishops presided over regional parishes, representing them in councils. While regional churches balanced local customs with universal mandates, Christians who previously would have willingly submitted to torture and death sought other ways to demonstrate total dedication to the Christian ideal. Monasticism became a central institution of the medieval church; monks submitted to a daily pattern of prayer and work, and to an abbot as an earthly father. The monastery became a spiritual preparation for the heavenly world, and a practical training ground for bishops (including some popes) and missionaries.

Christianity became a successor of sorts to the fallen Roman Empire, a standard-bearer of culture and a source of stability in a rapidly changing world of migrations and tribal conflicts. Employing the Latin of the Western Empire (and the Greek of the Eastern), the Christian Church became an international agent of public administration. With a literate clergy, roots in Rome, and a developing system of canon law, the church now served secular as well as religious needs, growing in importance among peoples who otherwise may have resisted its overtures. Although the period 500–800 appears to many secular historians as the sunset of paganism, to historians of the church it represents the dawn of a coherent, international phenomenon that would in time bear the title "Christendom."

The elements guaranteeing the expansion of a centralized church on one level ensured the preservation of vernacular cultures on another. Pagan customs were preserved in a tradition while religious life began to lend obedience to Roman Christianity, or at least to its missionary representatives. The mixture of particular and universal elements in early medieval culture gave rise to two categories of experience: the secular, for that which changes over time, and the sacred, for that which is presumably unchangeable. These terms were not explicit at the time, nor were their boundaries clear.

401	Innocent I affirms his claim as bishop of Rome to lead the church.
413–26	Augustine of Hippo writes his *City of God*.
418	Pelagius is condemned for rejecting predestination and original sin.
419–426	John Cassian's *Institutes* present a model for monastic life.
431	The Council of Ephesus condemns the Nestorian heresy.
432	St. Patrick sets off to convert the Irish.
438	The Codex Theodosianus lists 68 imperial edicts against heresy.
440–461	Pope Leo the Great consolidates the authority of the Roman see.
451	The Council of Chalcedon condemns the monophysite and Nestorian heresies.
476	The last Roman Emperor in the west, Romulus Augustus, is deposed.
484	Schism between the bishop of Rome and the patriarch of Constantinople.
496	Clovis, King of the Franks, is converted to Christianity.

523	Boethius writes his *Consolations of Philosophy* in prison.
527	Dionysius Exiguus establishes a system of counting years from Christ's birth (A.D., B.C.)
529	St. Benedict founds a monastery at Monte Cassino, beginning of the Benedictine Order.
537	Church of Hagia Sophia consecrated in Constantinople, the greatest religious building in Christendom.
c. 540	Roman historian Cassiodorus promotes a mix of classical and sacred learning.
563	Irish monk St. Columba founds a monastery on Iona, Scotland.
c. 583	St. Colombanus sets out from Ireland to convert the heathens in Burgundy.
590–604	Pope Gregory I systematizes church dogma and ritual, including music (Gregorian chant).
597	Augustine of Canterbury is sent by Pope Gregory I to bring Roman Christianity to England.

601	Augustine becomes first bishop of Canterbury.
c. 635	St. Aidan, a monk from Iona, establishes a monastery on Lindisfarne, Northumbria.
638	Muslim armies capture the city of Jerusalem.
664	At the Synod of Whitby, King Oswy of Northumbria accepts the authority of Rome.
c. 699	Work begins on the Lindisfarne Gospels, illuminated manuscripts.

718	St. Boniface embarks on a mission to spread Christianity to Germany.
726	The Byzantine emperor condemns religious images, an iconoclasm resisted in the West.
731	The Venerable Bede completes his *History of the English Church and People*.
754	Pope Stephen II anoints the Frankish King Pepin the Short.
756	First of the "papal states" created with the grant of Ravenna, Italy, to "St. Peter."
771	Charlemagne becomes king of the Franks.
772–85	Charlemagne subdues the Saxons and forcibly converts them to Christianity.
782	Alcuin of York is summoned by Charlemagne to Aachen to head the palace school.
787	In the Byzantine Empire, the Council of Nicaea rules against iconoclasm.
c. 799	*The Book of Kells*, an illuminated manuscript, is produced by Irish monks.

The Emergence of Hierarchy

Papal Beginnings

From the fourth through the ninth century, as the western Roman Empire gradually disintegrated and most of Europe lapsed into political and economic fragmentation, the Christian Church began to emerge as the one institution capable of nurturing a new, viable civilization.

While this new civilization was informed, to a great extent, by Christian beliefs and practices, it was supported and propagated by the church hierarchy: the administrative structure that had begun to develop, slowly, in the years immediately following Jesus' death. Although it was clear during Jesus' life that he was the leader, and the apostles and disciples the followers, his death brought an end to this rudimentary structure, and it was a long time before a new sense of organization emerged. There was an obvious religious reason for this: Who could take the place of the one who had changed the relationship between humanity and God? The sight of Jesus' empty tomb and his subsequent appearances among them created in his followers an acute sense of his unique divinity which they knew they did not possess. Claims to leadership within the Christian community might have been seen as an assertion of supernatural power, and therefore suspect. This was one reason why the early church lacked a strong sense of hierarchical order. So long as the community of believers felt they were being divinely guided, they were reluctant to establish human offices that might interfere with that guidance.

Another reason, of course, was found in the climate of persecution and heresy that surrounded the Christians in the first centuries of their history. Thus, it was simply not possible to create a visible priesthood with unchallenged lines of authority when the threat of punishment by the government loomed over all believers. Although the New Testament spoke of "gifts" of leadership in the church, it was dangerous to assert possession of them. For example, a second-century sect known as the Montanists claimed prophetic inspiration, only to be condemned as heretical by the year 200. For practical as well as pious reasons, therefore, the church remained fragmented.

A Priesthood in Embryo

It was inevitable that as the church grew in membership, some form of organization would emerge. There were already indications in the New Testament that the matter was being addressed, as is evident in St. Paul's description of various "spiritual gifts" in I Corinthians 12:1–11. But these were not specific roles; and it was not until the third century that an ordained ministry became a prominent part of the church's organization. DEACONS and DEACONESSES, who took care of the sick and the poor, are attested to in the New Testament. Women performed other tasks as well, but their roles in time were taken by men.

From the beginning certain members of the church were designated as worthy to perform the Eucharist. Since the act of repeating Jesus' words that transformed bread and wine into something sacred was to take up his role, performing this rite was thought to call for persons with special gifts. When the eucharistic rite began to be understood as a sacrifice, the person performing it became identified with the priests who performed sacrifices in the Jerusalem Temple. Within a short while, the Greek Church had an office of *hiereus*, or priest, and the Latin-speaking Christian community applied the equivalent term *sacerdos*, which was commonly used in pagan religions, to this role within their church.

Bishops and Councils

Within the first century it became obvious that some kind of leader, above the rank of priest, was required to ensure uniformity among individual churches and continuity within them. Originally, this office bore either of two titles, both taken from Greek: *presbyteros* ("elder"—a term borrowed from Judaism) or *episkopos* ("overseer"); but in time the latter prevailed. In Latin, this was slightly modified to *episcopus*, and eventually, through the Old English *bisceop*, it became "BISHOP," the term denoting one who went about in service to the community. A bishop might be assisted by one or more deacons (a rank below that of priest); who assisted him in liturgical and administrative duties.

From about the year 100, the Bishop of Rome held a position of special prestige among the bishops, even though, as a district, Rome was not the most important episcopal see, being later than others. However, the city's association with Peter, to whom Jesus entrusted his "flock," and with Paul, who died in that city, gave the Bishop of Rome a privileged place. This superiority was symbolized in the case of a dispute over doctrine among Alexandrian Christians which they could not resolve. Alexandria, in Egypt, was a major city; its bishop was the first to be called *papa* ("father"); before the fourth century it rivaled Rome in prestige. In their perplexity, there was only one bishop to whom the Alexandrian Christians could turn. By appealing to Rome, as they did, and accepting that bishop's decision, the Alexandrian churches tacitly acknowledged—as did other provincial churches—its central authority. Thus they helped to create a hierarchy among bishops that would continue through the history of the church.

Still, the church as a whole did not expand in an organized fashion, and to see Rome as a hub from which the rest of the church expanded farther and farther would be inaccurate. The church grew on a course of its own, small communities growing and subdividing, as a cell does. So far as life at the parish level was concerned, the local bishop—whose area of jurisdiction was called a DIOCESE (from a Greek word for an administrative division) held all appropriate power, for the bishop was thought to be divinely appointed. This belief, known as the doctrine of APOSTOLIC SUCCESSION (and still held by the Roman Catholic, Anglican, and some other churches), asserts that the first bishops were, in effect, the apostles and that all subsequent bishops—who must be consecrated by another bishop—can thus trace their authority back to Jesus' original consecration of his apostles (John 20:21–23).

Concentrating church authority at the local level in the person of the bishop remained the customary form of rule until the fourth century. At a higher level the church employed a kind of representative government: the COUNCIL. At these meetings, attended by bishops, the principal aim was to ensure uniformity of practice and consistency in teaching. Ever since the council held at Jerusalem around 49 C.E. (see Acts 15), councils had proved a moderately effective means for standardizing religious life, although persecutions under the empire prevented highly visible meetings of all the church's leaders. At the Council of Nicaea in 325 (see Chapter 3), the 318 bishops who assembled found their collective strength to be greater than their individual powers because together they could define doctrine and condemn positions contrary to their teachings. In matters of belief, therefore, they could establish ORTHODOX doctrines and condemn as HERETICAL those that diverged from orthodoxy. Without unanimity preserved in documents (such as the Nicene Creed), individual bishops were not able to set and enforce standards of belief.

In the Greek-speaking world, which was such a dominant milieu during the first three centuries of Christianity, a decentralized church grew in a particular pattern. The community at Antioch, in Asia Minor, expanded westward and established churches, under Antiochean supervision, in Edessa and elsewhere in present-day Syria. Alexandria, in turn, became the base for an expansion to some

Gentile and Giovanni Bellini, *St. Mark Preaching in Alexandria,* 16th century. Oil on panel. Pinacoteca di Brera, Milan.

Connections to the Apostles brought prestige to churches throughout the Mediterranean. Their legends were embellished and episodes in their lives were lavishly depicted.

of the southernmost points of the Roman world; while the city of Ephesus, in present-day Turkey, anchored expansion to the east and north of Asia Minor. Each of these episcopal sites became a METROPOLIS (literally a "mother city") to these other communities.

With the establishment of Constantinople (known as Byzantium before Constantine named it after himself) as an imperial capital, the bishop of that city began to play a new role in the church. Although as a bishopric Constantinople was newer than the apostolic communities of Antioch, Alexandria, and Ephesus, its role as administrative hub of the eastern empire—it was known as the New Rome—gave the city's bishop a measure of superiority over the other "metropolitan" bishops. This was not jurisdictional authority per se, as the regional bishops still exercised sovereignty. But the bishop, or Patriarch, of Constantinople gave the Greek Church a geographical center.

Beginnings of the Papacy

In seeking the beginnings of what would be known as the Roman Catholic Church, we need to look at the secular history of Rome, the capital of the empire. As the administrative hub of a far-flung Mediterranean empire, the city was very much the center of the inhabited world, and certainly the fertile soil for much of high Roman culture. (Roman authors made much of the difference between Romans and provincials, and talented writers or artists from the provinces knew they had to settle in Rome and find acceptance there in order to achieve any kind of fame.) And just as the mayor of a major city, or the president of a highly regarded urbanly situated company or university would nowadays have more prestige than someone farther down in the rankings, so the Bishop of Rome had prestige by virtue of geography alone.

As time went on, and Rome lost its secular importance, its bishop still inspired reverence by virtue of his link with Peter and Paul. Not only had Peter been its first bishop, both he and Paul had, according to tradition, been martyred in that city (sometime during the persecutions by Nero, c. 62–64). It was this association, above all, that perpetuated the ascendancy of Rome over other dioceses. For it was Peter, as told in Matthew's Gospel, whom Jesus called the "rock" (a pun on Peter's name) upon which he would build his church (Matthew 16:18) and to whom he entrusted his "flock" of believers (John 21:15–17). Passages such as these led Pope Leo I (c. 400–461; r. 440–461), also known as Leo the Great, to argue that each Bishop of Rome, by virtue of being a successor to Peter, had inherited the power and mandate given by Jesus to Peter. This made the Roman bishop the PRIMATE, or leader, among bishops, just as it made Peter the prince among the apostles. This was not well received in the East, which saw Constantinople as the center of both church and empire, but it helped to organize bishops in the Latin world.

Gregory I and the First Missionaries

Nevertheless, it was not until the end of the sixth century that the Bishop of Rome began to exert a central administrative authority—as opposed to a spiritual authority—over other churches. In 590 Gregory I (c. 540–604; r. 590–604), later also known as Gregory the Great, became Bishop of Rome, and it was during his rule that the relation of Rome to other dioceses began to change markedly. Gregory had all the right qualifications for a distinctive role in the medieval church: aristocratic birth, training in the legal profession, a successful career in civil administration. At the peak of his civil career he gave up the secular life and entered a monastery (one he had built on family property). (See "Gregory the Great.") In time he became abbot, and his abilities came to the attention of the leaders of the church in Rome. Within a short time he was named bishop of the city; and to make his work more efficient he divided his district into seven regions—the origin of the system of parishes within a diocese.

Gregory the Great, 10th century. Ivory book cover. Kunsthistorisches Museum, Vienna.

Gregory is observed scrupulously writing down the word of God as transmitted by the dove perched upon his shoulder.

It was during Gregory's reign as Bishop of Rome that the papacy began to undertake missionary work. The beginnings of this expansion are obscure, but certain traces can be discerned from the written record. According to legend, one day Gregory saw a shipment of slaves from England waiting to be sold. Admiring their fair hair, the pope asked a companion who these beautiful creatures were. "Angli" (the Latin for Angles) was the answer—to which Gregory is said to have replied, "not *angli* but *angeli*." Then and there he decided to bring these "angels" into the church; and soon he dispatched forty monks from his own monastery to the distant island, thought to be as remote and primitive as any place on earth. This band of monks, led by one later known as St. Augustine of Canterbury (d. c. 609), arrived in England in 597.

The Roman monks expected to find a wild and ferocious people—an expectation that was at least partially confirmed. At this time Britain was an unstable mixture of peoples: some Christian (the descendants of those original inhabitants who had converted during the Roman occupation of the first four centuries) and some pagan (the Angles, Saxons, and other Germanic tribes who had invaded the islands more recently). These various groups were in political disarray and engaged in intermittent conflict. In bringing order, as well as papal Christianity, to the inhabitants, Augustine and his fellow monks faced numerous challenges and questions. These questions (which we shall examine more closely in Chapter 8) tended to be about the degree and form of adaptation to local customs that were permitted without giving up the distinctive elements of Catholic Christianity. Although he presumably had the power to make authoritative decisions, Augustine turned to Gregory for answers. In appealing to the Roman bishop in this way, Augustine was indicating, both symbolically and actually, that the church he represented was Roman.

This deference was rewarded toward the end of his work, when he received from Gregory the PALLIUM. Originally, in ancient Rome, a garment identifying, a

Gregory the Great

Pope Gregory I was considered the indispensable patron of Roman Christianity in England, and contemporary accounts depict him as a larger-than-life figure. Here a British monk tries to capture Gregory's religious, and particularly monastic, spirit.

Gregory was Roman by nationality, his father being Gordianus and his mother Sylvia; so he was noble in the eyes of the law but nobler still in heart in the sight of God because of his religious life. He lived for a long time in a monastery where, as he himself declares, all transitory affairs were of little importance to his mind. He rose above passing events and accustomed himself to think about nothing but heavenly themes.

We can clearly appreciate from his words, even though only partially and imperfectly, how he reached this state of mind. In the first place these writings bear witness to the fact that he was an honourable representative of the apostolic see in the place which he explicitly states was Constantinople. In these passages he speaks straightforwardly, not indeed boastingly but with his habitual humility, about this matter: "For a long time," he says, "I put far from me the grace of godly living: and even after I had been inspired with heavenly longings, I thought it better to wear the secular habit. For though the way of attaining what I sought in my desire for heavenly things was revealed to me, yet inveterate habits bound me so that I could not change my outer way of life." Then he adds that, because his heart compelled him to serve this present world, his cares were thereby greatly increased. So, eagerly fleeing from all these things, he sought the haven of a monastery and escaped naked from the shipwreck of this life. Thereupon, still making use of this charming yet humble simile, he hastened to add that, just as when a storm arises it drags a carelessly moored ship even from the lee of a sheltering shore, "so," he says, "I suddenly found myself, though wearing the dress of an ecclesiastical order, tossed in the waves of secular cares and losing the peace of the monastery because, when I had it, I did not hang on to it as firmly as I should have done." After this he says he was called upon, being faced with the duty of obedience, to undertake the ministry of the sacred altar. "And after this," he adds, "unwilling and reluctant though I was, since the ministry of the altar was in itself a heavy load, the weight of pastoral care was added to my burden. And now I endure it with the greater difficulty because I feel myself unequal to it and I have no self-confidence to encourage or refresh me. So," he said, "a little time after I had undertaken the ministry of the altar, it was decided without my knowledge that I should receive the burden of a sacred office. Many of the brethren from my monastery, compelled by brotherly love, followed me. I saw that this had happened by divine dispensation, so that, through their unremitting example, I could bind myself, as it were by an anchor cable, to the calm shores of prayer; while being tossed about by the ceaseless tide of secular business, I fled to their fellowship as to the refuge of a safe port from the currents and waves of earthly affairs. And though this office of mine had dragged me from the monastery and, with the distraction of business, had cut me off as with a knife from my former life of quiet, yet by my serious conferences and readings with them, I was daily stirred to a desire for devotion."

(From *The Earliest Life of Gregory the Great*, by an anonymous monk of Whitby, trans. Bertram Colgrave. Lawrence, KS: University of Kansas Press, 1968.)

philosopher, the pallium was at this time a band worn around the neck by a bishop as a symbol of his power and his affiliation with Rome, for it could be granted only by the pope. Thus, granting the pallium represented a declaration of papal approval; and bearing it meant that a bishop was a sanctioned member of the Roman-led hierarchy.

There is irony in this development, of course. For submission to a distant bishop to be considered a sign of power for the local one seems self-contradictory, especially if we see autonomy and sovereignty as essential elements for episcopal authority. But it is all too easy to think that such elements are inherent in a position of leadership and to ignore the different cultural assumptions surrounding the position of the time. In short, it may be anachronistic to think that power and autonomy are necessarily connected in religious rulership. In the early Middle Ages, when civilization and religious orthodoxy were the commodities in greatest demand, "Romanness" carried the highest prestige. The populations in the wilderness craved connections to Roman civilization, a system of laws and culture that promised stability and refinement. In religious practice, too, Rome set the standard. It became axiomatic in these centuries that "Christianitas," the church, meant "Romanitas," or recognizing Rome as the reference point. Thus the expansion of the church and the preservation of uniformity were linked.

Another apparent paradox emerges from this process: the expansion of the church is in proportion to the authority of its center. Simply put, Rome became the hub of an extended series of missionary activities, which brought Christianity to northern and eastern Europe. These territories had relatively recently been settled by migrating tribes, such as the Franks, Goths, and Huns, and unlike Britain, they had never come within the colonial reach of the Roman Empire. Yet the promise of Roman culture, its law and literacy, offered a stability sorely needed by the northern peoples; and there can be little question that the missionaries who brought the Christian religion to these regions were aware of this need. Thus as the faith spread, so spread the rule of the papacy, the Roman institution that had assumed the empire's responsibility for preserving order and culture. The stronger the "hub," the farther the "spokes" could extend into untamed regions.

The Second Wave of Missionaries

The story of the religious "Romanization" of continental Europe is told by the successors of Gregory I's missionaries to England. Within a decade some of the original forty monks built monasteries of their own at Wearmouth, Jarrow, Ripon, and elsewhere. Here they re-created the life of prayer and study they had known in Rome and attracted new members from the local population. (Other houses, such as the Celtic monastery at Iona, came under Roman influence in later centuries.) These newer monks implicitly made a threefold commitment: to their religion, to the monastic life, and to Roman authority over their religion and monastic life. This was a new and more exacting level of commitment than simply becoming a Christian, or even, in a Christian country, becoming a monk. In Italy, the authority of Rule and abbot insulated the original Benedictine houses from papal control. (See Chapter 7.) In England, the commitment to monastic life represented a more comprehensive change from life within secular society, as well as a more direct responsibility to Rome. The level of dedication shown by these English monks was demonstrated in a way that may seem the very opposite of monasticism: they left the relative security of their monasteries to spread the Gospel abroad.

Just as monks had traveled to the English shores as missionaries, the monasteries they founded in the north of England began to send out missionaries of their own. These dedicated men traveled to the Continent, establishing monasteries throughout present-day Germany and in the process creating centers for learning and piety. Among these visionaries Boniface (675–754/5) may be considered a typical example, though his story (see also Chapter 8) is better known than that of others. Originally named Wynfrith, Boniface was trained in the monastic arts of study and preaching, and was the first Englishman to write a Latin grammar. In 718 he left his monastery and embarked on a missionary career that would result in the creation of an episcopal see, or bishopric, at Mainz, and the establishment of monasteries throughout Germany, of which the illustrious house at Fulda (founded in 744) was the most distinguished. From this monastery there emerged, in turn, more missionaries and more founders of religious houses, first in Germany and then, in time, through regions to the north and east. In all of these establishments, if the records are to be trusted, obedience to Rome was instituted as a necessary part of authentic Christianity.

Alas, Boniface came to an unfortunate end. This extraordinary man, who had established Roman Christianity in Germany, had built the monasteries at Fulda, Fritzlar, Kitzingen, and Ochsenfurt, and had founded the bishoprics of Mainz, Passau, Salzburg, and Regensburg (among others), died in the Frisian town of Dokkum at the hands of a pagan mob. Boniface's body was taken from Dokkum to Mainz and thence to Fulda, where he was buried. He quickly became regarded as one of the great martyrs of northern Europe. Although his death lacked the heroic aura exemplified by the first Christian martyrs, it was, in its own way, a form of

Who's Who

Spreading the Word

St. Columba (c. 521–597) A missionary figure of Irish origin, he came to England on a pilgrimage. He went on to found a monastery on the Hebridean island of Iona, where he was abbot.

St. Augustine of Canterbury (d. c. 609) The leader of a band of Roman monks sent to Britain by Gregory, Bishop of Rome, to convert the English to Christianity. An influential missionary, he became the first Archbishop of Canterbury.

St. Cuthbert (c. 636–687) A major cult figure, he was a monk who went on to found a monastery at Ripon and became a hermit on the island of Farne, off Northumberland, where many came to seek his

wisdom. He was made Bishop of Lindisfarne in 685.

St. Boniface (originally Wynfrith) (675–754/5) Born in Wessex, this monk became a renowned preacher and missionary, responsible for many converts—especially among the German peoples. He organized several important church Councils and was made Bishop of Mainz c. 746.

St. Willibald (c. 700–786) One of Boniface's helpers and an Englishman, he traveled to Rome, the eastern Mediterranean, and Germany. Responsible for much work in the German Church, he was appointed Bishop of Eichstätt.

suffering for his faith. In the sixteenth century Boniface was widely called the "Apostle of Germany," though the terrain that he evangelized was far broader than the Germanic lands.

Carolingian Culture and Christianity

The long reach of Rome can be seen most clearly, perhaps, in the phenomenon of the Carolingian monarchy's rise to power and the beginnings of the Holy Roman Empire. This institution has long been considered the "First Europe"—a term that may mystify us at first. We can certainly trace the rise to imperial power of Charles the Great, or Charlemagne (748–814; r. as emperor 800–814). It is harder to understand what his regime, and that of his successors, represented culturally. If "Europe" is an essentially modern name, a term current only since the Enlightenment, what can it mean to call the world of the ninth century "European"?

A Christian and a Roman Empire

The Carolingian Empire was the first in the West since the fall of Rome, and the first to be both Christian and Roman—that is, recognizing the central authority of the pope. It was a pope, Stephen II (also, confusingly, known as Stephen III), who in 754 offered military help to the Carolingian king Pepin III (714?–768; r. c. 751–768), a ruler whose power had come in part from having been consecrated king of the Franks (who occupied an area reaching from northern France to western Germany) by Boniface. Anointed a second time by Stephen, who called him a "Roman patrician," Pepin divided his territory between his sons Charles (who would become Charles the Great) and Carloman. After the death of his father in 768, and following a long series of military campaigns, Charles reached the peak of his power in 800, with his coronation as "emperor of the Romans" by Pope Leo III. The "empire"—later called the Holy Roman Empire—was more a papal creation than a restoration of the ancient Roman Empire, which the pope was not in a position to hand on anyway. While it might at the moment have seemed the final step in papal obedience to the Carolingian royal house, in time Leo's gift proved to have strings attached. For if the pope had the authority to grant imperial power (and Charles indisputably did receive the crown from Leo), then presumably the papacy was able also to revoke this power. Thus, instead of being an absolute sovereign, Charles and his successors were seen by the papacy as subordinates, in charge of the material wellbeing of their subjects while the church took care of their souls.

Whatever the potential conflicts of this arrangement between church and state (to be explored more fully in Chapter 9), Charles's empire fostered a decidedly Christian culture and (for the first time on a large scale) a highly educated one. In the East the intellectual tradition had never seriously declined, but the Latin West was in the depths of a dark age in which literacy, law, and piety had sunk to very low levels. If any part of the medieval period deserves the condescending label "Dark Ages," the pre-Carolingian era would be the strongest candidate.

Bede, 12th century. Manuscript illumination. British Library, London.

One of the great scholars of the early Middle Ages, Bede's intellectual interests were wide-ranging, although he rarely left his isolated monastery.

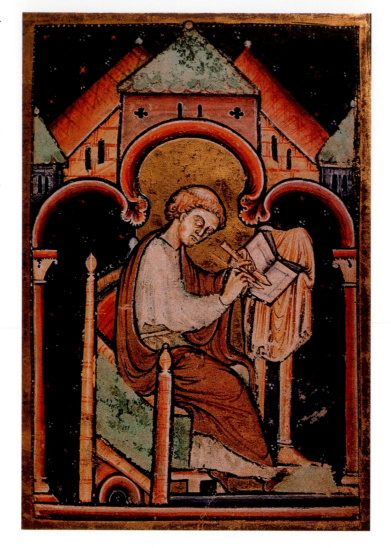

Even before the creation of the Carolingian Empire, however, there had been signs of a rebirth of European culture. With the establishment of monasteries as centers of learning (see Chapter 7) and of bishoprics as centers of religious and social administration, order on a broad scale began to return. The monasteries also played a vital role in political history in the eighth century. A notable example of this influence can be seen in the classic record of this period of history, the *Ecclesiastical History of England* by the Venerable Bede (673–735; "venerable" is a title, like "saint").

Bede, a monk at Wearmouth and nearby Jarrow and one of the most wide-ranging intellects of the period, was never a missionary; in fact he never left his part of England. Yet his *History* tells a story of monasticism and Roman rule as the creators of order and harmony out of a religiously and politically disorganized group of peoples. Bede's *History* is the source of much of our knowledge of

Augustine and his monks, and without it we would be in the dark about most of the seventh century in Britain. (See "Bede's *Life of Cuthbert*.") The care he takes in describing crucial episodes in the history of the church, such as a dispute about calculating the correct date for Easter, offers reassuring evidence that he was scrupulous with his sources. Nevertheless, it sometimes seems a little bit too easy to see the progress of harmony and Roman authority going hand in hand. If this is Bede's thesis, he states it very strongly—indeed suspiciously so. On closer reading we begin to see that Bede may be trying to persuade his readers that Christianity and obedience to Rome bring harmony and stability in the secular sphere. Thus Bede's *History* may be part of a missionary effort, and not merely a record of the facts.

This story of the spread of papal authority sounds too good to have been entirely true, and scholars have questioned it seriously. The historical record, they point out, came from the hands of writers such as Bede, who were sympathetic to the papacy, but few documents survive to confirm that the local populations were really as enthusiastic to embrace Roman rule as the officially

---

Bede's *Life of Cuthbert*

British holy persons were credited with miraculous abilities, such as controlling the behavior of wild animals. Bede is a typical chronicler of these extraordinary events. Here we observe the monk Cuthbert reproaching birds for interfering with the grain crops of the monastery.

At first he took bread from his visitors and water from his own well; then he thought it would be better to follow the example of the fathers and live by his own hands. He asked for implements to work the land with and wheat to sow, but though he planted in spring there was nothing ready by mid-summer.

"It's either the nature of the ground," he said to the brethren, "or the will of God, but the wheat certainly is not growing. So bring barley and we shall see whether that will produce anything. If God does not see fit to give increase, then rather than live off others I shall return to the monastery."

The barley was brought long past the proper time for planting, when there was no hope of it growing, but it soon sprang up and brought forth a very good crop. When it began to ripen the birds came down and set about devouring it. (This tale was told by the pious servant of God himself, for it was his custom, being by nature friendly and cheerful, to strengthen the belief of his colleagues by recounting some of the blessings with which his own faith had been rewarded.)

"Why are you eating crops you yourselves did not grow?" he asked the birds. "Perhaps you have greater need of them than I. If God has given you permission, then do as He bade you: if not, be off with you, stop damaging other people's property."

They flew off at his first word and did no further damage. These two miracles of the venerable servant of God are reminiscent of the doings of two of the fathers. In bringing water out of the rock he reminds one of a similar miracle performed by St. Benedict—only he brought it forth more abundantly because there were more people in need—and in driving away the birds he was following the example of St. Antony who by words alone restrained wild asses from trampling his little garden.

(From Bede's *Life of Cuthbert*, trans. J.F. Webb, in D.H. Farmer, ed., *The Age of Bede*. New York: Penguin Books, 1965.)

pro-Roman narrative suggests. This is quite true, and skepticism may be justified if one sees the authors of the historical record as one-sided. But the more complete picture is very difficult, if not impossible, to fill out. If the material is available at all, it must be collected, sorted, deciphered, and tested for accuracy against other documents—which may or may not be available. The work needs to be done, but it will be only after a long period of investigation that we will know with any assurance whether the narrative associated with Bede is an accurate description of the events of his time.

Key Terms

APOSTOLIC SUCCESSION The historical link from one of the Twelve, transmitted by Christian leaders down the generations to the present day; for churches, having been founded by or possessing a relic of an apostle.

BISHOP An overseer of a group of churches, with authority over clergy of individual parishes.

COUNCIL An assembly, usually principally of bishops but including other clergy, for defining doctrine and disciplining those dangerous to the church.

DEACON A member of the clergy charged with assisting priests and bishops, especially in charitable and material matters.

DEACONESS A woman charged with the care of certain members of a parish—usually the sick and the poor.

DIOCESE A bishop's jurisdiction, comprising a number of individual churches, or parishes.

HERETICAL Adhering to teachings in conflict with those of the universal church; schismatic.

METROPOLIS The "mother city" in Eastern Orthodoxy, whose bishops have primacy over other bishops in their regions.

ORTHODOX Faithful to the teachings of the church; also used as the name of the Eastern Church.

PALLIUM A band of fabric worn by the bishop of Rome and other bishops consecrated by him.

PRIMATE The bishop of the "first" see in a national church; the chief bishop of a given people or state.

CHAPTER 6

The Flourishing of Liturgy
Devotion Through Ritual and Imagery

The question of whether, in any given religion, practice grows out of doctrine or vice versa is a moot one. The earliest Christian practices were, as noted in Chapter 4, adaptations of Jewish rites; and Judaism is commonly, if simplistically, considered a tradition of practices rather than of doctrines. On the other hand, the fact that the Jewish practices were adopted implies the existence of new beliefs governing their transformation. We have also seen in Chapter 4 that doctrine often emerged as a commentary on Christian rites as they began to be practiced in the first century outside the Jewish world. As time went on, however, new rites appeared; some of them were adaptations of the original rituals, others were new rites that emerged within the Christian community. Certainly, both practice and doctrine were and are complex and evolving organisms, shifting and growing with the Christian community itself.

In the first millennium or so of Christianity, practice, especially ritual, was the dominant element of the tradition. In an environment of low literacy and high levels of superstition, where Christianity often supplanted animistic practices and agrarian fertility religions, practice inevitably prevailed over doctrine. Ideas of life-granting sacraments, contact with the holy through everyday objects, and recited formulas able to evoke divine responses formed the religious life of medieval Christians; explanatory discourse was largely redundant. (This attitude would change in the early modern period, as we shall see.) Thus when we look at religious life as practiced in the centuries before the invention of printing, we are looking at Christianity as lived by the laity.

The Objects and Monuments of Early Liturgy

As with so much else in the origins of Christianity, the liturgy of the apostolic community was rooted in Judaism, particularly the synagogue service. As we saw in Chapter 4, the transition from diaspora Jewish worship to early Christian forms was simplified by the reliance of Jesus' followers on the Torah and Writings to shape their understanding of their own founder's redemptive work, and the

Abel and Melchizedek, San Vitale church, Ravenna, 6th century. Mosaic.

Abel (left) offers the sacrifice of a lamb, foreshadowing Jesus, the Lamb of God. The priest and king Melchizedek (right) offers up bread, the body of Christ, while on the altar stands a chalice of wine, the blood of Christ. The hand of God can be seen initiating the act of transformation.

Eucharist as a commemoration of redemption: few experiences would have driven home more clearly the idea that Christianity was a combination of the very old and the very new. And perhaps because the origins of Christian worship were adaptations of traditional practices, the ability to adapt ensured successful transitions to Greek and Roman cultural settings.

From the start, liturgy was more than the recitation of texts and the sharing of a symbolic meal. The idea that God had taken human form in Jesus, and thus became tangible, was understood as a repeal, of sorts, of the Second Commandment, and depictions of Jesus began to proliferate in churches throughout the Mediterranean. (There were no attempts to depict the First Person of the Trinity: in that sense the original Commandment still stood.) These images, *eikones* in Greek (and thence "icons" in English), were more than pictures: they were considered miniature manifestations of divinity (almost, but not quite, miniature incarnations) and thus had a holiness that other images, and certainly other types of object, did not possess. In the Greek philosophical world, especially anywhere Platonism was present, a metaphysics that held that tangible objects "participated" in a superior immaterial realm made rational the belief that Jesus, and images of him, participated in a divine reality. Thus directing one's devotion to an icon of Christ was viewed as one and the same as worshiping the incarnation, Christ, himself.

In time, not just the Christ figure but the whole cast of saints became the objects of such veneration. When Jesus, as a source of divine power, charged his apostles with carrying on his work, they possessed some of the same divine energy that he had; thus images of the apostles would participate in the divine essence to some extent. In more straightforward terms, if icons of Jesus held some of his power, and the apostles held some of Jesus' divine quality, the icons of the apostles had their own divine energy. The power of the apostles, and later of other saints, gave rise to LITANIES, sequences of petitions to all of these figures in the hope of intervention with God. If Christ was God, and not simply a mediator between humans and God, then another rank of mediators was called for: this was the function that the apostles served. And since each of the twelve had connections with various parts of the world, it was not hard to connect even a remote community with one of them.

During the period of persecutions, the ranks of the holy expanded markedly: all who had died in obedience to their faith — by resistance to Roman pressures to renounce it — were embodiments of total commitment to the Christian ideal and thus in a demonstrable way "holy." The Latin term for "holy," *sanctus*, put these martyrs on something of a par with the apostles; and the martyrs too would figure in litanies as intercessors or petitioners on behalf of the faithful. Just as the stories of martyrs spread throughout the Christian network of churches, so did frequently exaggerated tales of the martyrs' holy lives. These narratives left iconographic records, not just textual ones. St. Agatha, for example, a virgin martyr whose torture included having her breasts cut off, was depicted holding a tray with two loaves of bread, since the loaves resembled her amputated breasts. (She thereafter became the patron saint of bakers, even though bread-baking did not form a part of her earthly life.)

The Roman persecutions thus proved to be a rich resource for Christian devotion, and if believers mourned the victims of the empire's actions, they redeemed

Hagia Sophia, Constantinople (Istanbul), 532–537.

This monument of Byzantine architecture reflects the power of the Eastern Empire. It served as a church for 900 years and since the 1450s has been a mosque.

their suffering by investing each of the martyrs with special powers. If there was a protective function in the saints' relationship with God, the Roman Christians understood well what this meant. In pagan Roman religion, families had protective divinities, often called *lares* or "household gods," who watched over the members of each generation and ensured the continued prosperity and fame of lesser families—as well as of the major dynasties. Altars to these divinities were a part of the Roman home, and devotions to the ancestral deities were a common feature of pagan life in the early empire. The ever-increasing risk among distinguished Roman families that relatives would become martyrs to the new religion helped domesticate the *lares* in Christian families.

Thus the Christian liturgy quickly absorbed elements foreign to its Jewish roots. The apostles and martyrs became points of contact with divinity, traces of a world inhabited by the incarnate God. Reminders of the Jewish and Near Eastern origins of this worship were found in the retention of phrases in Hebrew and (in the Latin-speaking world) Greek, as well as in the custom of churches facing east, toward Jerusalem. And of course the biblical readings of the LECTIONARY (the arrangement of texts to be read on given days of the year) would have seemed foreign to most pagan hearers. Over time, however, the themes of the Hebrew Bible became part of the Roman worldview, with their Christian culmination as the natural conclusion to the long-awaited redemption.

Art and Architecture

Images of biblical scenes, mosaics in ceilings and walls, and reliefs of stone and metal began to fill Christian churches; and together with icons they became prominent elements of church décor. Intended as illustrations and reminders for a populace that had heard the stories recited but who might not have read them themselves, images of patriarchs and apostles served a pedagogical purpose by giving human form to names and events that were chronologically distant and culturally still somewhat alien.

Architecturally, though, continuity with ancient Roman religion was the norm. A number of prominent pagan temples were converted to Christian use—mainly by the addition of mosaics and reliefs—and new Christian churches were built along similar lines. Colonnades, or rows of columns within the nave, together with rounded arches and flat or coffered ceilings, all echoed the design of pagan temples and reinforced a sense that this religion was quite at home in the Roman cultural world, and was not an ill-fitting importation from the colonized Orient. Certain features could not be dispensed with: altars, for example, signifying the notion that the Mass is a sacrifice offered to God; and baptismal fonts, usually at the entrance of a church to symbolize the believer's entry into the Christian community. (Holy water, also at the entrance to churches, allowed members to reaffirm their baptism by dipping their fingers in it and blessing themselves.)

With the rise of imperial power in Constantinople, the "Roman" elements of church decoration gave way to a more distinctly Byzantine sense of design. Eastern churches saw a richer use of mosaics and a rise of non-biblical iconography: contemporary figures, royal and otherwise, became immortalized in historical mosaics. Emperors and their relatives began appearing as faces in apostolic or patriarchal scenes. And images associated with liturgy, such as baptism, consecration of the eucharistic host, and processions of priests, became visual reinforcements of the services themselves, reminders to the participants that they were part of a divine tradition originating with creation and continuing in their own day.

The sheer scale of Byzantine church architecture helped underscore the grand sweep of divine sovereignty. Additions, in the form of chapels and ambulatories, radiated from central sanctuaries; churches often became the largest buildings in their cities. This is certainly true of the Cathedral of Divine Wisdom, known in Greek as *Hagia Sophia*, built in Constantinople by the Emperor Justinian in 532–37. Designed by Asian architects, this cathedral had an area of almost 49,000 square feet (well over an acre) with a 101-foot wide dome that rose 179 feet into the air. The cathedral underscored the greatness of the empire as well as divine sovereignty (the emperor himself being an agent of the divine will).

At the other end of the architectural spectrum, catacombs served a special function in early Christian piety. Belief that physical death was only the transition to eternal life, and that bodies would rise from the dead at the end of time, demanded that bodies be preserved; hence vast labyrinths of underground burials became the final resting place of the Christian dead, usually buried with their identification and age at death. Images from their lives often accompanied these inscriptions, as did images of doves (representing the Holy Spirit, which would restore them to life) and representations of the final resurrection.

While their bodies awaited resurrection, the souls of the dead were active in heaven; and before long the cult of the saints became a widespread feature of Christian worship. Those who had died as martyrs were said to enjoy glory in heaven, and those who lived pious lives and died in the service of the church were also in a blessed state. Their proximity to Christ, like that of the apostles and martyrs, meant that they might be able to intercede with God on behalf of those still in the world. Thus these souls became helpers of the living, supposedly persuading God to show his mercy toward them, to heal them, and extending to him any number of other petitions. In this role they took up the function left by the Roman household deities, the *lares*, and served as patrons for individuals and families. In time there would be patron saints of certain professions (for example, St. Agatha for bell-makers and bread-making).

The Virgin Mary

Crowded as the cast of saintly characters became, the central role of Jesus and his intimate circle was never diminished. In fact, during the first six centuries, as the person and work of Jesus Christ became broadly and more clearly understood, his divine and human parentage became a subject of special devotion. Specifically, the role of Mary in the redemptive work of Christ emerged from the relative shadows of the New Testament and apostolic writings, where her significance is just hinted at (when mentioned at all), to a prominence that gave her a status almost equaling that of her son. The declaration of the Council of Ephesus (431) that Mary was *theotokos*, or the bearer of God, was an important step in the creation of her cult status, even though some theologians had seen her as such for two centuries already. By 600 believers held that she had been physically assumed into heaven, and her ascent, known as the Assumption, became a part of Christian worship; it did not become a defined dogma of the Roman Church, however, until 1950.

John Chrysostom's *On Virginity*

Virginity allowed lay persons to achieve a holier state than their more carnal neighbors and relations, and exhortations to sexual purity abound in Patristic literature. Here St. John Chrysostom (see p. 105), one of the great preachers and theologians within the Greek tradition, elevates virginity above married life.

You say that her clothes are shabby, but virginity resides not in clothing nor in one's complexion but in the body and soul. Is it not strange that we have different standards? We will not judge the philosopher by his hair or his staff or his tunic, but by his way of life, his character and soul; the soldier too we will not approve for his mantle or belt but for his strength and manliness; yet the virgin, who represents a state so admirable and superior to all others, we will simply and offhandedly assume practices her virtue because of the squalor of her hair, her dejected look and grey cloak. We do not strip her soul bare and scrutinize closely its inner state.

But he who has drawn up the rules for this contest does not permit this. He orders that those who have entered not be judged by their clothing but by the convictions of their souls. "Athletes," Paul says, "deny themselves all sorts of things," all that troubles the health of the soul; and "if one takes part in an athletic contest, he cannot receive the winner's crown unless he has kept the rules." What, then, are the laws of this contest? Hear again his words, or rather Christ himself, who has established the contest: "The virgin is concerned with things of the Lord, in pursuit of holiness in body and spirit;" and again, "Let marriage be honored and the marriage bed be kept undefiled." But even as on a ship, if you remove the rowers, you disable the ship, and as in war, if you cause the soldiers to revolt, you bind up and surrender the general to the enemy, so too in this case, if you banish marriage from the position of honor, you betray the glory of virginity and place it in extreme danger.

Is virginity a good? Yes, I fully agree. But is it better than marriage? I agree with this, too. If you wish, I will illustrate the difference like this: virginity is as much superior to marriage as heaven is to earth, as the angels are to men, and, to use far stronger language, it is more superior still. For the angels, if they do not marry and are not given in marriage, are not a mixture of flesh and blood. They do not pass time on earth and endure trouble from the passions. They require neither food nor drink. Sweet song cannot appease them, nor can a radiant face win them over, nor any other such thing. Their natures of necessity remain transparent and brilliant, with no passion troubling them, like the heavens at high noon clear and undisturbed by any cloud.

("We Must Judge Virginity On The Basis of One's Soul, Not One's Clothing," in John Chrysostom, *On Virginity* and *Against Remarriage*, trans. Sally Rieger Shore. New York: Edwin Mellen Press, 1983.)

Devotion to Mary did not diminish in the Middle Ages; if anything, it expanded, in part because she was seen as more than a saint. If the saints were intercessors with God for the benefit of the living, then the mother of the incarnate God was the intercessor *par excellence*, for Jesus surely listened attentively to his mother. The Annunciation (Luke 1:28–38) became the subject of art and devotion alike, the word "graced," in the Latin *gratia plena*, or "full of grace," signaling a uniqueness among humans. The angel's greeting at Luke 1:28 became the basis for the most widespread Marian devotion, the rosary. The "Ave Maria," a prayer affirming

Limbourg Brothers, *Annunciation*, from *Les Très Riches Heures du Duc de Berry*, 1413–1416. Manuscript illumination. Musée Condé, Chantilly, France.

Illuminated manuscripts juxtaposed text and images in inventive ways, so that pictures sometimes told a story even more powerfully than words.

Mary's blessedness and appealing to her on behalf of the faithful, was recited repetitively; 150 of them were seen as a popular substitute for the Psalms for illiterate Christians. The rosary was a pattern of one Lord's Prayer, ten Ave Marias, and one "Gloria Patri" (a doxological formula affirming the Trinity), with the reciter keeping count by holding a sequence of beads. Said to have been given by the Virgin Mary herself to St. Dominic, the thirteenth-century founder of the Dominican Order, the rosary was a form of devotion embraced by believers, both lay and religious, everywhere. Considering the ratio of ten Ave Marias to one Lord's Prayer, Mary came close to eclipsing Christ in the devotions of the unwary believer.

Churches dedicated to Mary, variously called "Notre Dame," "The Church of Our Lady," the "Marienkirche," and the like, sprung up throughout Europe in an extended wave of medieval church building. Between the eleventh and thirteenth centuries, as church architecture in the West shed the Romanesque style of rounded arches and flat ceilings in favor of the Gothic style of vaults, spires, and windows reaching toward heaven, Mary became a focal point of popular devotion, with stained-glass windows depicting various stages of her life (especially the Annunciation and Assumption), and sculpture representing her sufferings during the Passion. The theme of the *pietà*—Mary holding her crucified son after he was lowered from the cross—became a prominent one in Christian sculpture. In the iconography of the Passion itself, identifying with Mary as she saw her son die was thought to be an ideal devotional posture.

The Music of Early Liturgy

The music of the Christian liturgy has a long history, though our knowledge of much of it is fragmentary from lack of evidence. We do know that liturgy in the Latin West was chanted, with some parts chanted in the same manner at all times, while others were chanted in different ways according to the day or the service. Each chant had its own mode, or pattern, usually an ascending series of notes that returned to the original one. Early liturgy had eight of these modes, and their use ranged from the very basic to the very ornate, the latter being the result of a creative blending of them. Certain parts of the liturgy, such as psalms, were recited by the choir, often led by a cantor, rather than by the priest. Thus they had different settings, sometimes quite complex ones, especially in responsorial psalms, which often employed one mode for the cantor and another for the choir.

The part of the chanted liturgy most familiar to modern churchgoers is the "Alleluia," a verse of praise before communion. Often it is sung in three parts, beginning with a threefold "Alleluia," each one longer than the one before; then there is a phrase affirming some aspect of God's greatness; finally another threefold "Alleluia." Intonation that tends to rise in the middle, as if heavenward, and then returns, is a common feature of this chant.

Hymns are an ancient part of the liturgy. They originated in the Eastern Church, probably in Syria. The words of some early hymns were attacks against heretics and pagans, and some of the early hymnodists were themselves condemned as heretics. But the popularity of the melodies of many hymns ensured their survival in popular memory, despite numerous attempts to restrict and even eliminate them. One fourth-century council, at Laodicea (361), even banned the singing of hymns altogether—with little effect. Hymnody spread throughout the West due to such Fathers as St. Hilary of Poitiers (c. 310–366), who may have encountered the genre during his own travels in Syria. Hilary was followed by the great St. Ambrose (c. 340–397), whose musical innovations included the use of rhythmic stress, a reflection of shifts in the pronunciation of Latin at the time. Ambrose, like Hilary and their Eastern counterparts, used hymns as polemics against heresy; praise of God became the dominant theme only in later centuries. But the "Ambrosian" pattern became a standard one throughout the Middle Ages.

Innovative Solutions

Not all of the Christian Church's liturgy was an adaptation of Jewish ritual. As we have indicated, the "metamorphoses" of ancient Jewish rites may have held deep meaning for the first generations of Christians, but those meanings would have been lost on Christians from other cultures; and the survival of the church depended on attracting these and extending beyond the bounds of any single culture. But how could the monotheism of Christian devotion appeal to adherents of Roman religion, with its cast of deities and ancestral divinities in each family? The archaic pantheon of Roman gods had largely passed into the realm of folklore by the time Christianity began its spread throughout the empire. Some emperors tried by official means to restore ancient Roman worship, generally unsuccessfully. Household deities were more difficult to dispose of, for it was reassuring to have the spirits, or "shades," of one's ancestors present as examples and protectors: even before its long decline, Roman culture honored the dead as models from a heroic past.

The church managed to incorporate this veneration into its own devotional life by instituting a realm between the human and the divine, in which the spirits of the dead watched over the living and intervened with God on their behalf. These are, of course, the saints, and the Latin Church made much of them. (They are less prominent in the Eastern Church, possibly because the Greeks did not have so strong a devotion to their ancestors as the Romans had.) Martyrs, who had proved their devotion to God by dying for the faith, were thought to be especially powerful agents; and soon they became the objects of prayer and devotion, not merely venerable examples of piety. That is, their spirits were viewed as still active, exercising a residual energy of sorts for the good of those who asked for their help. In view of the fact that the Christians saw the next life as the "true" one—the present one being merely a preparatory stage—the creation of a spiritual realm was perfectly consistent. What is surprising is that this spiritual realm is as much the product of accommodation to paganism as it is a logical development from Christian theological principles.

Perhaps nothing illustrates the partly Jewish and partly pagan character of the Christian liturgical cycle more effectively than the feasts of Easter and Christmas. Easter is unambiguously the Christian passover, and even shares that name in certain languages. (For example, in French it is *pâques*, from the Hebrew *pascha*, from which comes the English term "paschal lamb.") So it is no surprise that a number of churches thought that it should be celebrated on a date as close as possible to the Jewish holiday. In England in the seventh century, a number of dates were considered, with the matter finally settled by the Synod of Whitby. One of the obvious marks of unity in the church is clearly the sense of synchronicity in worship.

Christmas, on the other hand, seems to have been linked to astronomical phenomena—in particular to the winter solstice on December 21. Across many regions in antiquity this marks the turning of a season, the end of a period of growing darkness and the beginning of lighter days; thus it serves well as a celebration of new beginnings. Since Christians felt that a new age had dawned with the birth of Jesus, it was natural to locate his date of birth around the solstice. By placing the date slightly later, on the 25th, they avoided making the connection completely obvious. Once this date was set, it was possible to fix the beginning of the year at March 25, nine months before Christmas. (It was assumed that his delivery was not premature.) Thus the coming of spring and the passover/Easter season mark the beginning of the yearly cycle, while the period of greatest darkness is another occasion to celebrate a new beginning. Contradictory as it may seem, the world-renouncing worldview of the ancient church was relieved by these

Epiphany, 15th century. Oil on panel. Palazzo Pitti, Florence.

Episodes from the life of Jesus shaped the Christian year. Some, such as the homage of the three kings, underscored the submission of secular to holy powers.

luminous bright spots. For every dark winter there is spring directly ahead; and for every Lent and Good Friday there is a period of new life and spiritual energy.

The Liturgical Year

These dates in the calendar are some of the reference points in the liturgical year, the boundaries of its seasons. The period leading up to Christmas is ADVENT, a season of expectation, symbolized by light. (Christians often put lights in their windows during Advent.) The symbolism has a tantalizing double meaning. Since it is a period of natural darkness, the lighting of lights serves as a way of staving off the darkness, refusing to give in to the mysterious nocturnal unknown in the belief that the light of more sun is right around the corner. But the lights also represent hospitality, openness to strangers, a willingness to accept a new member in the community, such as the infant Jesus. The following Christmas season is a time that includes the feast of the circumcision (eight days after Christmas) and the Epiphany, celebrating the arrival of the three kings from the East.

As winter progresses, the period leading up to Easter is known as LENT, a word derived from the Germanic root for springtime. This season recalls Jesus' forty days in the desert (and behind that, Moses' forty days on Sinai [Exodus 24:18]), and is marked by a regime of fasting and penitential prayer. Just as Jesus' time in the desert was a time of trial and preparation, so the individual believer is expected to endure pains and self-searching in preparation for the Easter event. In monasteries, it was not uncommon for the asceticism and the intensity of devotion to heighten over the course of Lent. The period after Easter, known as the Easter season, is very different in tone: it is jubilant, for it commemorates the resurrection and the period when Jesus stayed with his followers before the ascension to heaven.

The rest of the year is known as ORDINARY TIME, a misleading term if it suggests that the Christian year was led like any ancient pagan's year. The term actually means the "ordered" time, the sequence of weeks outside the special seasons. Throughout the year the Christian community lived as a redeemed people, remembering the deeds that shaped their identity and looking forward to the fulfillment of divine promises. During the special seasons these events were not just remembered; they were in some degree reenacted, so that the Christian Church continually experienced its shaping moments, as well as remembering them.

Key Terms

ADVENT The period of expectation before Christmas.

LECTIONARY A book with the fixed readings for services during the Christian year.

LENT The time of spiritual preparation before Easter, usually marked by self-denial in commemoration of Christ's 40 days in the desert.

LITANY A recitation calling on a series of saints for intercession.

ORDINARY TIME In the calendar of the Latin Church, the weeks outside of special seasons.

The Monastic Microcosm
The Benedictine Norm and Reform

The legalization of Christianity under Constantine (see Chapter 3) created an unforeseen and somewhat ironic problem. Martyrdom was no longer a risk for Christians. While the danger of a gruesome death may seem a strange thing to miss, the fact was that Christians had developed a view of the world that gave religious meaning to being a victim of persecution. Christians had seen martyrdom as a way of participating symbolically in the crucifixion of Jesus and thus achieving union with him. Although not all could have this experience (martyrdoms were in fact rare occurrences), the danger of being regarded as an enemy of the Roman Empire was enough to guarantee that membership in the church entailed a serious—even dangerous—commitment.

In Chapter 4 we noted the evolution of Christianity, early in its history, from a voluntary community into a natural one, to which one belongs by virtue of one's birth. So long as Christians were occasionally persecuted, however, the church remained to some exent a voluntary religion, for even those born into Christian families and raised in the faith remained in it through deliberate choice.

Once the danger of martyrdom had passed and Christians became truly a natural community, they lost some of the emotional energy that had fired them in earlier days—even if many possessed the same degree of devotion. In other words, since they had seen martyrdom in a positive light, and had given powerful religious meaning to it, the lifting of criminal status left a void in their Christian experience. A form of life was needed that could reflect, as martyrdom had done, the totality of the believer's commitment and offer a means of oneness with God. Monasticism filled this gap.

The creation of monasticism formed a voluntary community within the natural one and gave Christians an opportunity to live a committed and intentional life within the church, and thus to show a dedication similar to that of Jesus' earliest followers. It entailed withdrawal from the world, and thus was a form of world-denial. It offered a life of prayer, and thereby a means of intimacy with God. And it presented to the wider world, both Christian and non-Christian, an example of religious dedication that they might be inspired to emulate to some degree.

Beginnings of the Christian Monastic Tradition

Monasticism, a part of religious practice in both the West and Asia, is older than Christianity. It was practiced within Hinduism and Buddhism, and the Essenes and John the Baptist represented Jewish forms of it. Within a generation after Jesus' death, some pious Christian men withdrew from society to live in prayer and contemplation in the desert. Such dedication was thought to indicate special spiritual gifts and privileged access to God. Thus the DESERT FATHERS, as they were called, acquired a status in the eyes of Christian followers, who often sought their wisdom and prayers. The lessons preserved by these followers, known as APOPHTHEGMATA, or "sayings," constituted a wisdom tradition rivaling—in bulk if not in influence—the sayings attributed to Jesus. Those who wished to lead lives of perfect dedication, or at least to bring more perfection into their worldly lives, followed these precepts faithfully.

Eremitic and Cenobitic Monasticism

The solitary monastic life is easy to describe but almost impossible to imagine. The aridity of the landscape in which the Desert Fathers lived served as a form of sensory deprivation. Isolation from human society removed cultural distractions, and the barrenness of the terrain precluded the pleasures offered by nature itself. Like exiles from Eden, these solitaries lived lives of penance and prayer, subsisting on rudimentary nutrients and spending all their time seeking oneness with God. Although hardly an organized body like a philosophical "school," these monks were unified by the same goal and pursued similar paths to reach it: they chose an unworldly life to reach an otherworldly destination, heaven. Some were probably widowers, who had withdrawn from the pain and loss of living in the earthly world. The movement could have begun with St. Anthony of Egypt (c. 250–355), who enclosed himself in a tomb for twenty years and set an example for later desert monks. It also included such characters as Simeon Stylites (c. 390–459), the first of a number of pole-sitters, who spent many years on a platform high above the world (in order to be closer to heaven).

The monastic life attracted women as well as men, and some ancient estimates put their number at double the population of male solitaries. Their routine was as rigorous as that of their male counterparts, though their demographic composition may have been different: scholars suspect they comprised a high proportion of impoverished and abandoned women, nearly all of them older and drawn from the upper classes; many, no doubt, were widows who wished to end their days in the embrace of the church.

This form of life, called EREMITIC after *eremos*, the Greek word for "desert," would have been ideal for the purpose of intense spirituality were it not for geographic and demographic factors. Withdrawal from civilized life is possible only where there are vast expanses, such as the deserts of North Africa, that can provide the space necessary for the solitary life. But the northern coast of the Mediterranean—Italy, southern France, Spain, and Greece—presented a very different landscape, one of fertile land. And the solitary life of prayer is obviously possible only when there are few people around, which also was not the case in

Gherardo Starnina, *La Tebaide*, 14th century. Oil on panel. Uffizi, Florence.

From the vantage point of the Renaissance, Starnina has created an imaginary scene depicting Egyptian desert hermits from an earlier age.

Greece and Italy, both densely populated. Add to these obstacles the fact that a growing number of Christians sought the life of prayer and study, and the need for a better alternative to eremitic monasticism becomes clear. Some new form of religious life was required.

The life of prayer and study did not necessarily depend on eremitic solitude; other circumstances might be able to support it. What emerged in the West, through processes still disputed by historians, was a communal form of monasticism, known as CENOBITIC, from the Greek for "common life," *koinos bios*. In cenobitic monasticism the discipline of orderliness performed a function similar to that performed by the rigors of life in the desert. Just as the Desert Fathers had renounced worldly temptations by subjecting themselves to life in the Egyptian sands, so the Western monks could practice restraint within the daily routine of the monastery. Times were set for rising, eating, numerous prayers throughout the day, study, and labor. In its original conception, cenobitic monasticism was a rigorous and pious life, a replacement for martyrdom as a voluntary form of Christian witness and an adaptation of the eremitic model in promoting and inspiring piety.

Cenobitic monasticism originated in a monastery in Egypt founded by Pachomius (292–346), an Egyptian monk who had converted to Christianity from a pagan background. As in eremitic monasticism, the goal of communal life was the search for perfection through ASCETICISM, a life of self-denial. Since the presence of other people presented new temptations and distractions, the cenobitic life was strictly regulated, with fixed times for prayer, set duties for all members of the community, and rigid limits set upon the monks' interaction.

The phenomenon spread rapidly throughout the eastern Mediterranean, with substantial houses being founded in Asia Minor and the Peloponnesus. These were centers of learning, as well as piety, and many Greek texts, both pagan and Christian, survive thanks to the efforts of monastic scribes of the fourth and fifth centuries. Among the founders of cenobitic monasticism in the Eastern church are Basil the Great (c. 330–379), Bishop of Caesarea and author of a "RULE," or set of regulations, that was used throughout Asia Minor, and John Cassian (360–435). The latter began his monastic life in a community, spent ten years in the desert, then returned to the inhabited world to be ordained deacon by the great theologian St. John Chrysostom (c. 347–407). Later, as a priest, he established the monastery of St. Victor in Marseilles.

St. John Chrysostom, 17th century. Engraving.

Named "Golden mouth" on account of his eloquence, Chrysostom was one of the few fathers to be almost as influential in the Latin West as in the East.

Basil learned about the solitary monastic life from some of the centers in which it flourished, and he saw certain dangers in this life: the sin of pride probably chief among them. As a remedy against this spiritual pitfall he advocated a kind of communal life that would become the dominant form of monasticism in the West. Basil's writings on the monastic life, condensed in two forms (the *Longer Rules* and the *Shorter Rules*) give us a clear picture of early Greek (more accurately "Cappadocian" from the city, in modern Turkey, where his monastery flourished) religious life. To avoid the sin of pride, a hazard of over-zealous asceticism, the life was only moderately austere. And to prevent preoccupation with physical survival at the expense of prayer, the monks were provided with the food and spiritual means to adequately sustain them.

Like Basil, John Cassian was an influential writer, whose *Institutes* (419–26) and *Conferences* (or *Collationes*, 426–28) would be among the charter documents of Western monasticism. (See "John Cassian's *Institutes*.") In the first four books of the *Institutes*, Cassian provides a monastic operating manual, with instructions for the times for various duties and liturgies. But he goes on in Books 8–12 to offer serious psychological guidance, counseling his readers of the dangers of gluttony, anger, and other sins, and offering useful techniques for averting them. Cassian's work was overshadowed somewhat, but never completely replaced, by later giants of the monastic tradition.

John Cassian's *Institutes*

The beginnings of monasticism were organizationally and conceptually complex, and one of the masterminds of the Western tradition, John Cassian, combines elements from the Egyptian Desert Fathers and the Hebrew Bible in his manual for monastic organization, the Institutes.

1. The history of the Old Testament relates that the most wise Solomon—after he had received from God "exceedingly great wisdom and prudence and a breadth of heart like the countless sands of the sea," such that by the Lord's testimony it is said that no one was like him in times past and that no one like him would ever arise in the future—wished to build that magnificent temple for the Lord and that he requested the help of the king of Tyre, a foreigner. When Hiram, the son of a widow, had been sent to him, he undertook whatever splendid thing the divine wisdom suggested to him with respect to the Lord's temple and the sacred vessels, and thanks to his assistance and oversight he brought it to completion.

2. If, therefore, the princedom that was loftier than all the kingdoms of the earth, and the noble and excellent scion of the Israelite race, and the divinely inspired wisdom that surpassed the skills and institutes of all the people of the East and all the Egyptians by no means disdained the advice of a poor foreigner, rightly also do you, most blessed Pope Castor, instructed by these examples, deign to summon me in my utter want and poverty to collaborate in your great work. You are setting out to construct a true and spiritual temple for God not out of unfeeling stones but out of a community of holy men, one that is not temporal and corruptible but eternal and impregnable; and you also desire to consecrate very precious vessels to the Lord, not forged out of the dumb metal of gold or silver and afterwards captured by the Babylonian king and set apart for the pleasure of his concubines and princes but out of holy souls that shine in the fullness of innocence, righteousness, and chastity and that bear within themselves the indwelling Christ the king.

3. Since your wish is to establish in your own province, which lacks such things, the institutes of the Eastern and especially of the Egyptian cenobia, inasmuch as you yourself are accomplished in every virtue and in knowledge and are so laden with all spiritual riches that not only your speech but your very life is a sufficient and abundant example to those who seek perfection, you request and demand that I too, rude and wanting in word and knowledge, contribute something from my poor intelligence to the accomplishment of your desire and lay out in order, however inexpertly, the institutes of the monasteries that we have seen observed throughout Egypt and Palestine, such as they were handed down to us there by our fathers. In this you are not looking for a pleasing style, with which you yourself are particularly gifted; rather, you are concerned that the simple life of holy men be explained in simple language to the brothers in your new monastery.

(From John Cassian, Preface to *The Institutes*, trans. Boniface Ramsey. New York: Newman Press, 2000.)

The Benedictine Rule

The greatest of these monastic figures was surely St. Benedict of Nursia (c. 480–c. 547), from northern Italy, who withdrew to the eremitic life in a cave after his exposure to the decadent culture of Rome. On leaving the cave after a few years, he established a residence for himself and a few other monks at Monte Cassino in southern Italy; this became the center of Benedictine monasticism until its destruction in World War II. As leader of the community, Benedict composed the *Rule* that remains the operating manual for monasteries throughout the world. (See "St. Benedict's Rule for Monks.") This document is a patchwork of precepts taken from the Greek monastic tradition, with observations and instructions from Benedict himself. The biographical record does not tell us whether Benedict hoped that his compilation would become a standard for so much of the Western monastic tradition; it does not even reveal whether Benedict thought of establishing an order, as well as his own monastery. But in fact adherence to the Rule, like the traditional monastic vows of poverty, chastity, and obedience, has been a necessary element of the monastic tradition, as has obedience to the abbot who

---

St. Benedict's Rule for Monks

The founder of the Benedictine tradition appeals to piety in introducing his Rule, but never ignores the practical needs of an establishment made up of many men from a wide range of backgrounds; his detailed instructions give us a snapshot of domestic monastic life.

PROLOGUE

Hearken, my son, to the precepts of the master and incline the ear of thy heart; freely accept and faithfully fulfil the instructions of a loving father, that by the labour of obedience thou mayest return to him from whom thou hast strayed by the sloth of disobedience. To thee are my words now addressed, whosoever thou mayest be that renouncing thine own will to fight for the true King, Christ, dost take up the strong and glorious weapons of obedience.

And first of all, whatever good work thou undertakest, ask him with most instant prayer to perfect it, so that he who has deigned to count us among his sons may never be provoked by our evil conduct. For we must always so serve him with the gifts which he has given us, that he may never as an angry father disinherit his children, nor yet as a dread lord be driven by our sins to cast into everlasting punishment the wicked servants who would not follow him to glory.

CHAPTER 22

HOW THE MONKS ARE TO SLEEP

Let them sleep each one in a separate bed. Let their beds be assigned to them in accordance with the date of their conversion, subject to the abbot's dispositions. If it be possible, let them all sleep in one place; but if their numbers do not allow of this, let them sleep by tens or twenties, with seniors to supervise them. There shall be a light burning in the dormitory throughout the night. Let them sleep clothed and girt with girdles or cords, *but not with their belts*, so that they may not have their knives at their sides while they are sleeping, and be cut by them in their sleep. Being clothed they will thus always be ready, and rising at the signal without any delay may hasten to forestall one another to the Work of God; yet this with all gravity and self-restraint. The younger brethren shall not have their beds by themselves, but shall be mixed with the seniors. When they rise for the Work of God, let them gently encourage one another, on account of the excuses to which the sleepy are addicted.

(From *The Rule of St. Benedict*, trans. Abbot Justin McCann. London: Broadway Press, 1952.)

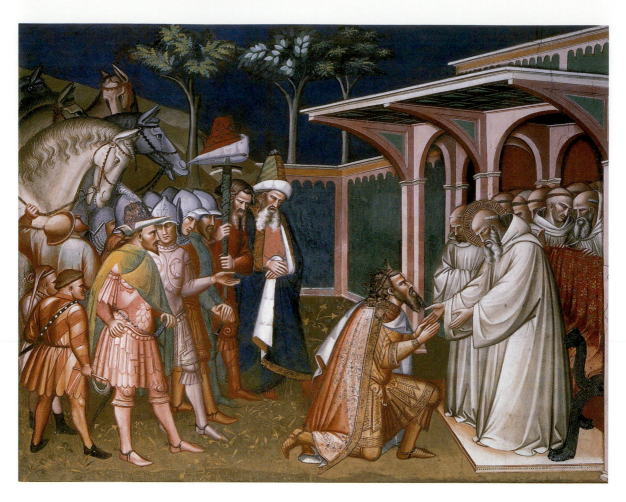

Spinello Aretino, *The Saint Prophesies to Totila, King of the Goths* (detail from the *Life of Saint Benedict*), sacristy of San Miniato al Monte, Florence, 1387. Fresco.

Illustrations of St. Benedict proliferated in the Middle Ages. The power of his words is here underscored by the genuflecting submission of a king.

governs it. And the dominance of the Order of St. Benedict (O.S.B.) has endured into our own time.

On first impression, the *Rule* does not look like a very spiritual document. It specifies the number of hours for outdoor labor, kitchen duties, and the like—as well as the required liturgies. However, this degree of detail was meant to restrain the inclinations that, if left unchecked, would have interfered with the spiritual life. The effect was to make the whole life one of self-denial and service to God, not just one in which devotion occupied a large part of a life interspersed with "worldly" elements.

Along with a highly ordered way of life regulated by the Rule, the second influential part of cenobitic monasticism that helped it to thrive in the West owed to the leadership of the abbot. The community of monks was bound to obedience to a master, who was both a governor of the monastery's activities and a model of the spiritual life. The term "abbot" derives from the Hebrew for "father," and the abbot was fatherly in two senses. He was a father figure in the monastery, someone who would guide the monks with paternal goodwill. He was also understood as the representative of God the Father, and hence an embodiment of divine benevolence and power. By submitting to the authority of the abbot (a submission analagous to submission to the pope outside the monastery), a monk believed that he was yielding his own will to the will of God.

Monastic Life

Life in a Benedictine monastery was rigidly structured. The Rule governed virtually every aspect of life, and the abbot applied and enforced the Rule. It was a life of labor and prayer (*orare et laborare*, "pray and work," became a motto of the order), with labor never being for its own sake, but for the sake of the individual's spiritual life. The plan of worship set the schedule for the monastic day, with all other activities arranged around it. A cycle of liturgies, beginning early in the morning and ending at the end of the day, gave devotion an importance it could not possibly have in the secular world and served as a way of keeping discipline in the monks' everyday life. There is little chance of becoming over-involved in an activity when a chapel service is only a few hours away.

Preserving the Classical Tradition

Paradoxically, the emphasis on piety allowed monasticism to play a vital role in transmitting the literature inherited from pagan antiquity. The necessity for reading Scriptures and their commentators, and reflecting on points of commonality and difference between pagan and Christian cultures, made literacy a requirement of monastic life long after it had ceased to be expected in the outside world. Not just literacy but scholarship was necessary for the monastic system for

---

Who's Who

The Birth of Christian Monasticism

St. Anthony of Egypt (c. 250–355) The first of the "Desert Fathers"—pious figures who lived extraordinarily poor, isolated lives in very harsh or barren places—he spent much of his life in the desert, and twenty years encased in a tomb, emerging briefly to organize a community of hermits.

St. Pachomius (292–346) A convert to Christianity from paganism, this Egyptian soldier-turned-monk founded the first cenobitic Christian monastery. (Cenobitic monks live devoutly in a community, rather than as hermits.)

St. Basil, or Basil "the Great" (c. 330–379) *See "Fathers of the Early Church," Who's Who, p. 48*

John Cassian (360–435) A founder of cenobitic monasticism in the Eastern Church, he spent periods both in a monastic community at Bethlehem and in

the desert. He served as a priest and a deacon, established the monastery of St. Victor, Marseilles, and wrote an influential set of rules for monks.

St. Simeon Stylites (c. 390–459) Another "Desert Father," he was a monk before living as a hermit in northern Syria. He then became the first Stylite—a hermit who lived on a small platform atop a pillar as high as 60 feet—to be as close as possible to heaven, surviving on food donated by followers.

St. Benedict of Nursia (c. 480–547) A major figure of monasticism and founder of the Benedictine order. He became the leader of a community east of Rome, establishing several monasteries there, and then moved to Monte Cassino, where he founded the main monastery of the Benedictine Order and wrote a famous set of rules for monastic life.

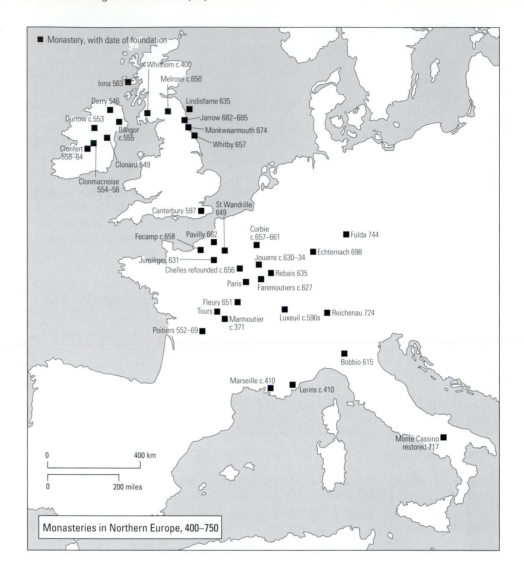

■ Monastery, with date of foundation

Whithorn c.400
Iona 563
Melrose c.650
Derry 546
Lindisfarne 635
Durrow c.553
Jarrow 682–685
Bangor c.555
Monkwearmouth 674
Clonfert 558–64
Whitby 657
Clonard 549
Clonmacnoise 554–58
Canterbury 597
St Wandrille 649
Fecamp c.658
Pavilly 662
Corbie c.657–661
Fulda 744
Echternach 698
Jumièges 631
Jouarre c.630–34
Chelles refounded c.656
Rebais 635
Paris
Faremoutiers c.627
Fleury 651
Tours
Luxeuil c.590s
Reichenau 724
Marmoutier c.371
Poitiers 552–69
Bobbio 615
Marseille c.410
Lerins c.410
Monte Cassino restored 717

0   400 km
0   200 miles

Monasteries in Northern Europe, 400–750

in the absence of secular institutions of learning, the monks themselves were obliged to preserve, copy, and correct these texts, as well as interpret them. The resources for such work were found in the classical tradition itself, not the Christian one, since the rules of rhetoric and grammar, not to mention history and geography, had been perfected in the Greek and Roman traditions before Judaism or Christianity made any impression on the classical world. In fact, many Christian theologians saw the history of civilization as divided into clear periods, with classical culture serving as the "preparation" for Christianity.

If, as we saw in Chapters 1 and 4, the early Christians took pains to establish a balance between innovation and continuity with Judaism, so the Latin monastic tradition made an effort to clarify the relationship between what was uniquely Christian and what was an inheritance from the traditional Roman culture. As in the earlier process, Latin Christianity tried to keep as much as it could of the earlier culture, adapting where necessary (turning Roman household deities into saints, for example; see Chapter 6) but preserving wherever possible. The intended result was an impression of continuity between classical and Christian civilizations.

The monks' awareness of, and emphasis on, this continuity ensured that the classical tradition would be preserved. Monasteries became hives of scholarly activity, with their members producing commentaries, reference works, and guides to the workings and history of a civilization that, by the early sixth century, existed mainly in texts. The monastic enterprise has proved as valuable for later ages as it was at the time of its inception, for most classical literature would be completely lost if not for the copies made and preserved by monks. In some cases, the original classical texts of many compilations and compendia have been lost; thus monastic abridgments or accounts are the only sources of information we have about a vast but now vanished library of ancient works.

Obedience to Rome

During this period of transition from classical to Christian civilization, the intellectual program of the monks also helped ensure the spread of Christianity. The monks were literate and organized; moreover, they represented, in their scholarship, a civilization that offered all the political and legal infrastructure, not to mention stability and cultural prestige, that the recently nomadic peoples of northern Europe needed if they were to build their own civilization. Monks were generally given a warm welcome by the leaders of these tribes, for Christian culture offered the best of two worlds: a religion for the people and, for the leaders, a connection to ancient Rome and its institutions.

The early success of monasticism gave rise to an influential missionary movement by the Benedictines, beginning in the 590s with Pope Gregory I's mission to England (see Chapter 4) and lasting for half a millennium. Remaining within the monastic enclosure—part of the essence of the Benedictine life—was not something a devoted and talented monk could expect. Instead, monks were frequently sent from their home monasteries to establish houses elsewhere, or to convert the "heathen" in the hinterlands. Interestingly, it was the very rigidity of monastic organization that may account for the success of this movement. With little opportunity to adapt to regional circumstances, the government of abbot and Rule could exercise an authority that remained relatively unchallenged, bestowed by the Roman hierarchy and so ultimately, through the papacy, by Christ himself. As the missionary movement grew, so did obedience to Rome, because no matter where the monks came from, it was to Rome that they were bound, and obedience to Rome was integral to the Christianity they brought with them on their travels.

Evidence of the strength of this concept, and of the monastic ideal generally, is the fact that archaeological remains, as well as written records, reveal a striking uniformity among Benedictine monastic houses. Not only was the daily life set by the Rule preserved, but even the physical layout of monastic buildings remained remarkably consistent, throughout most of Europe. It consisted of a chapel, or church, flanked by a CLOISTER, a covered walkway surrounding a courtyard, and, adjoining these, the other buildings: refectory, kitchen, scriptoria (in which manuscripts were copied), cells, and all the other rooms and outbuildings required for a communal life. Perhaps this uniformity is understandable when we consider the way that monasticism spread, by initiative from parent Benedictine houses; but it is a useful reminder of the trans-cultural power of Christianity and its links to Rome.

The Monastery and the Outside World

The monastic world was an idealized form of the larger society and, as an ideal, necessarily contrasted markedly with it. This may be seen most obviously in the centrality of worship in the typical monk's life. Whereas the secular person might normally fit his or her devotions into a life dominated by worldly tasks, in the monastery the worldly activities took second place to the spiritual life. Life in a monastery was thus a mirror image of life in the "world."

In other ways also, the monastery offered a contrast to the world outside. The culture of a monastery was shaped by love of God and charity for one's neighbor, instead of the instincts and personal ambitions that would have dominated life in an untamed medieval society (or indeed in our own). In monasteries, individuals were guided not by self-interest, but by surrender to the authority of the Rule and the abbot. In secular society, constitutional order was neither so uniform nor so powerful in the last centuries of the first millennium, and rulers with few restraints on their power were more often feared than venerated. For much of the medieval European world at the time, the presence of any social order—and certainly to the extent displayed by monasticism—offered a striking contrast to the prevailing circumstances.

We may see the monastery as a microcosm of medieval society, but if so it was an inverted one. It was a microcosm to the extent that it was complete and self-sufficient, its members representing the world outside. But it was inverted in that it held to values that contrasted with those of the world outside: values such as prayer, study, and the priority of the spiritual life over the physical. Because the secular world of that time recognized the value of the spiritual life, despite its own limits in achieving it, worldly society supported monasteries in the hopes that the monks' prayers would benefit them. In turn, within the monasteries the needs of the outside world for spiritual help provided the occasion for the monks' spiritual "labor." They genuinely felt that through their prayers they were performing a valuable service for the outside world, and that withdrawal from the world was necessary for this work. And the world seems to have agreed with this, for secular support of monastic institutions was generous and widespread, a phenomenon that still echoes in certain forms of religious philanthropy to this day.

In the medieval mind, the world depended on the monks' activity. The salvation of humanity would have been in far more doubt without the prayers of monks and nuns to intercede for secular society—prone as it was to give priority to physical matters at the expense of the spiritual. Thus, in the Middle Ages, monastic life was considered by many to be the most important of callings.

The Psalms played a substantial role in the liturgical life of the early monasteries, for a fairly obvious reason. They are, of course, rich expressions of piety and the center of worship for both clergy and laity. But more significantly, the Psalms are affirmations of faith in a benevolent deity even amid evidence of destruction and persecution. (Many were composed around the time of the Babylonian Exile in the sixth century B.C.E.) In a world that seemed to course from one disaster to another—marked by the collapse of the Roman Empire, the migrations of numerous nomadic peoples, numerous wars and social turmoil, and the threat from the rise of Islam in the seventh century—the Psalms never lost their relevance.

Reform Movements

Preserving the monastic ideal over time was not easy. As new monasteries developed their own patterns of activity, and as monasticism grew in popularity, deviations from the Benedictine norm also increased. What may have seemed suited for Monte Cassino in the sixth century might not be the best way, so it was thought, for northern France in the ninth century. Establishing and supporting monasteries became a pious pastime for landowning families, and often there were strings attached to such patronage. In many cases, monastic life seemed to offer itself as a convenient livelihood for second and third sons, the ones who might challenge the authority of the firstborn son and natural heir to the family's land and titles; or for daughters who either chose not to marry or were not married off by their parents.

However much the monastery gained from the favor of rich families, the quality of monastic life itself did not benefit from being used in this way. Wealth and monastic life were a paradoxical combination, yet many monasteries had become rich as a result of the reciprocal relationship between monks and laity. And as to patronage, was that not also a deviation from the ideal of self-sufficiency? To those who saw the monastic ideal in this way, something had gone seriously wrong with the institution itself.

The Abbey of Cluny

The increase in monastic wealth prompted a number of REFORM movements, efforts to return to the Benedictine ideal in terms of organization and an austere way of life. The earliest and most influential of these reform movements began at the abbey of CLUNY, in Burgundy, in eastern France. Founded in 910, this monastery represented a serious attempt to return to the spiritual foundations of Western monasticism. At Cluny liturgical devotions acquired new prominence, as the Mass, the eucharistic service, was celebrated daily, and monks had more time for pious pursuits, because much of the menial work in the fields and kitchen was turned over to LAY BROTHERS.

The need for reform along these lines was strong enough to spread beyond Cluny's boundaries. Under the abbot Odo (927–942), Cluny became a model for reform in neighboring houses, and under the remarkable abbot Odilo (994–1049), it became the center of a monastic reform movement, the "mother house" to a network of "daughter houses" bound to it by loyalty and organizational obedience; what the abbot of Cluny decreed became law in the daughter houses as well. With Cluniac reform, the Benedictine movement may be said to have reached a critical point, for the sovereignty of the abbot came under scrutiny and the recently won autonomy of each house was threatened. These measures may have been necessary for the sake of reform, but they nevertheless mark a turning point in the development of monasticism.

For centuries after the founding of Cluny, reform would be the driving force within Western monasticism. Some movements, such as the Gorz Reform in Germany which began in the 970s, were conscious efforts to return to the Benedictine ideal. This German movement differed from its Cluniac counterpart in its submission to local bishops and intensification of ascetic practices. Other movements were reformist in name only, such as the Cistercian Order, an original phenomenon of the early 1100s which we will have a chance to observe closely in Chapter 14. For now, it is sufficient to understand the origins and development of the Benedictine system, and to recognize the impact that this tradition had on the development of medieval Christendom.

Women's Monastic Houses

Although we tend to think of the monastic world as a masculine one, women's religious communities existed from the early Middle Ages. Noble Roman women like Melanie the Elder and Paula in the late fourth century were instrumental in establishing monasteries for both men and women. Paula's Roman monastery, established on an inherited estate, became a place where visiting bishops stayed, among them St. Jerome, theologian and translator of the Bible. Jerome translated the Psalms into Latin for the women of Paula's monastery; and many of his exhortations to virginity and the religious life may have been inspired by the examples of both that he witnessed while visiting Paula and her daughter Eustochium. During these decades, women such as Olympias (361–408) were creating an ordered religious life for women in Constantinople. Noble and wealthy, Olympias was able to attract the interest and support of an important Greek theologian, St. John Chrysostom, then bishop of Constantinople. At its peak her monastic house was home to 250 women.

Women's houses spread throughout Europe, in pace with men's. Some establishments were near men's monasteries, so that priests could minister to the women; some were attached to men's monasteries, with women abbesses presiding over both the men and the women, to make sure that the priests did not neglect the women under their care.

Female monasticism took a number of forms during the early Middle Ages, but none like Fontevrault in the northwest of France in the early twelfth century. Founded under the auspices of Robert d'Arbrissel (1060–1116), Fontevrault was intended to create a house where women could live in community with men. It was a "double" monastery, women and men alike under the governance of an abbess, with the male authorities yielding to her power more and more. Fontevrault represents the high point of women's power in the tradition of Christian monasticism.

The Premonstratensian Order was made up of hermits, male and female, living in the French woodlands of Prémontré (*Premonstratensis* in Latin). This was an order in which women made up the majority, though they lived under the authority of an abbot. Cistercian women, similarly, lived in the shadow of their male superiors; but their growth within the order is astonishing, with houses for

Cistercian women appearing in locales that had no male communities of that order.

The Mendicant orders had women also. Most famous among these are the Poor Clares (or "Poor Ladies"), the "second order" or female branch of the Franciscans, founded when Clare of Assisi (1194–1253) joined Francis in his work shortly after the Friars Minor were founded. This branch was privileged with papal protection even before the male branch. A similar but less prominent pattern followed within the Dominican order.

Key Terms

APOPHTHEGMATA Collections of sayings by the Desert Fathers, taken down and disseminated by their followers.

ASCETICISM Any form of self-discipline practiced for a spiritual end; often a life of strict self-denial.

CENOBITIC Of the communal monastic life (from the Greek *koinos bios*, common life).

CLOISTER The inner colonnade of a monastery; the term is often used for the religious life generally.

CLUNY A monastery established in the early 10th century; it became the center of a network of houses seeking a return to the Benedictine ideal.

DESERT FATHERS Monks who lived in isolation in the desert; the earliest Christian hermits.

EREMITIC Of the solitary monastic life (from the Greek *eremos*, desert).

LAY BROTHER or SISTER A member of a monastic community who helps in the work of the house and shares in its religious life, taking vows of celibacy and obedience, but is exempt from the study required of monks or nuns.

REFORM A movement aimed at correcting the corruptions of a monastic establishment and restoring the life to its original form.

RULE The governing document of a monastery, setting times and tasks for the community.

The Expansion of the Church

First Missionary Movements and the Crusades

A missionary element, the impulse to spread the teachings and draw new members into the church, has been present in Christianity since the first Easter. Although Jesus' own ministry was confined to Palestine and to his own Jewish community, according to the Gospels he clearly intended his message for all persons, and his disciples believed that through his crucifixion and resurrection he had atoned for ORIGINAL SIN, the common condition of all humans. In the view of the early Christian theologians, the disobedience of Adam and Eve, as related in Genesis, had caused humanity's fall from grace—or simply the Fall, as it is commonly called—but Jesus' sacrifice on the cross had reversed this condition. His death and resurrection were seen as the mirror image of Adam's fall, and something that, like original sin, affected all of humanity. Thus it is not surprising to find the resurrected Jesus in the Gospels (see Matthew 28:19) instructing his followers to spread the news of his work through all of the inhabited world.

The Roman regime in the Mediterranean made the work of spreading this message as difficult in practical terms as it seemed necessary in religious ones. The siege of Jerusalem at the end of the first century C.E. (see Chapter 1) scattered the Jews and Jesus' followers, leading both Jews (perhaps for the first time in their history) and Christians to encourage conversion among the gentiles: such converts were called PROSELYTES, or, in Latin, *proselyti* (from a Greek word meaning "foreigner"), a term the Jews seemed to have used before the Christians did. But imperial decrees against Christianity, with their constant threat of persecution, kept these efforts from acquiring much public visibility.

We can see how essential missionary work was to the early church when we recognize that the word "apostle" literally means one who has been "sent" on a given mission (as opposed to a disciple, a student of a particular master). The term "mission" is derived from the Latin *mittere*, "to send"; and without much of a stretch we can translate the Greek-derived word "apostle" with the Latin-derived one "missionary." Thus the first teachings of the apostles were in their own way missionary work, almost by definition. Even Paul, at Galatians 1:16, sees mission as his most important work. And the late-first-century Greek text

Didache, also known as *The Teachings of the Twelve Apostles,* is an attempt to illustrate the difference between the false path of paganism and the authentic way of life, namely Christianity.

Apologetics

Among the foremost areas where Christians sought followers was the Greek-speaking world; thus they needed to "speak" Greek intellectually as well as linguistically. They needed, that is, to describe their faith in a way that would appeal to the Greek mentality—a mentality unfamiliar with such Jewish concepts as monotheism, covenant, and divine law; one that, instead, was nurtured by paganism but that otherwise tended to be rationalistic. They needed to present an ascetic and otherworldly ideal to a mentality that took pleasure in this world and was somewhat skeptical toward ideas of an afterlife. And they needed to reshape the Christian perspective so that it looked more like a philosophical school than a sect from an alien culture.

Among the active Greek philosophical schools of the first few centuries C.E. it was Platonism that had the closest affinities to Christianity. Although Plato (c. 427–347/348 B.C.E.) lived long before the Christian era, his otherworldly idealistic philosophy blended well with some central Christian claims. For Plato, the material world is just a copy of a "real" world that exists in a separate realm of ideas. Each individual table, for example, is but an example, necessarily incomplete and flawed, of an unchangeable and perfect "tablehood" in the realm of ideas. Thus, while we can touch any number of material tables, "tablehood" itself can only be contemplated. The philosopher lives a life of contemplation of these ideas, alone in knowing that they are the only things that are truly real.

In later developments within the Platonic tradition, the opposition between the real world (as Platonists saw it) of ideas and the false world of matter was diminished by a concept of progress in which these worlds would eventually be united. NEOPLATONISM, the term for this newer school, held that something called "The One" was the end to which everything within the changing world was moving. This conception of time reconciled the present with the future, the "real" and the "false," the relative and the absolute. By casting Christian ESCHATOLOGY —that is, the Christian idea of the end of the world—in these Neoplatonic terms, the early APOLOGISTS—philosophical defenders of the Christian worldview— were able to present the Christian message of a transcendent reality as superior to a frail and changing world of falsehood.

The apologists' best friend was not Plato, but the author of the Fourth Gospel. At the very beginning of the Gospel of John, Christ is depicted as the embodiment of the Logos, a Greek term for speech, reason, rationality, and the divine intellect itself. Taking this passage (John 1:1–5) as their premise, the apologists argued that Christ was the incarnation of what the Greek philosophers understood as the ruling mind that governs the universe—not the human manifestation of the Hebrew YHWH. By accentuating the common features between the Christian and Platonic traditions, the apologists were able to argue that Christianity was the true and complete shape of the Platonic worldview. A large literature, mostly in Greek, emerged in the first four centuries, exhorting pagans to consider the persuasiveness of Christianity.

The Latin Christian tradition, too, though less rich in apologetic writings, had some noteworthy defenders of the new faith against pagan opposition. Tertullian, one of the earliest Latin Fathers (see Chapter 2), composed a work called *On Prescription against Heretics* which argues in forceful and clear Latin for the superiority of the Christian over the "Greek" worldview prevalent in Roman culture at the time. In one of the best-known rhetorical questions of Western thought, Tertullian asked, "What does Athens have to do with Jerusalem, the [Platonic] Academy with the church, heretics with Christians?" The answer was "Nothing"; for, as Tertullian put it, "There is nothing else that one ought to believe" besides Christianity. Philosophy, Tertullian says in his *Apology*, does not drive out demons. Clearly the Latin tradition diverges radically from the Greek, but this mirrors the contrast between the pragmatic Roman temperament and the speculative Greek one. Among the less philosophically inclined, such a foursquare stance might surely have its appeal.

The First Western Missions

When we speak of Christian missionary work we are more likely to think of individual agents bringing the faith to supposedly godless peoples, rather than of the kind of rhetorical appeals described above, although the principle is the same. The more active type of missionary work began to get under way (as we noted in Chapter 5) in the early 600s. It deserves serious attention, for without it the church might never have extended beyond the Greco-Roman milieu of its first five centuries.

We should remember, of course, that that milieu was hardly a very limited one. Instead, it extended well beyond the cultural borders that we identify with the "Greek" and "Roman" worlds. To the east it encompassed areas only then being populated with peoples later called Slavs and Magyars; to the west it included the Iberian peninsula, distinctive enough that Latin writers from Seneca (c. 55 B.C.E.–C.E. 40) to Isidore (d. 636) made a point of identifying themselves as Spanish in origin. But both of those provinces were dwarfed by the region to the south: North Africa. From present-day Morocco to Egypt, the Mediterranean shore of the continent was a strategic element in the security of the Roman state (in the three centuries before the Caesars) and the growth of the Roman Church (in the first three centuries of the Christian era). Yet in the final analysis, North Africa seems to have been more fertile soil for Christianity than for Roman paganism.

It was here, for example, that the martyr Perpetua (see Chapter 3) was consigned to her death; here too was a church that was Roman in language (when much of the rest of the church was still Greek-speaking) and organized enough to have a sizable number of bishops (100 by some accounts) under the authority of Carthage alone. This church expanded during a time of severe persecutions: the 250s tested the church harshly, and even under the leadership of St. Cyprian (d. 258, himself a martyr), who tended not to take a lenient stand toward those who had "lapsed" in order to save their lives, the church continued to grow.

There was also a native form of Christianity, and conflict between it and the Roman form proved a precursor to a number of other episodes during these centuries. The Donatists, for example, were a band of Christians who held to a theology that claimed that the sacraments were valid only when administered by a priest with pure hands—i.e. one not in a state of sin. This was a vital consideration in the era of the persecutions, when tolerance of the "lapsed" might have been taken as a sinful tendency—not to mention trying to save one's own life amid Roman campaigns against Christians. The Donatists thus became a purity sect *par excellence* in the early church; and in time their beliefs would run head-on with the thought of Augustine, who may at that point have had a more realistic sense of the inevitability of human sinfulness. Donatism was a local form of Christianity that never completely gave way to Augustine's Catholicism; and we shall see that native forms of Christianity became a "second paganism" that missionaries had to combat.

To get an idea of the enormous challenge faced by the early missionaries it is important to have some grasp of the political flux prevailing in Europe during the last years of the Western Empire and the first few centuries after its fall. In the lands ruled from Rome, civilization was in decline, weakened by the shift of power to Constantinople and by incursions from barbarian tribes from the north and east. The rest of Europe was a hodge-podge of peoples in the uneasy transition from a nomadic to a sedentary way of life. In the north, the Goths moved south and east in the years 150–400, breaking up, in the process, into Ostrogoths and Visigoths ("eastern" and "western" Goths). Central Burgundians moved from present-day Poland to what is now east central France in the early fifth century, about the same time that Lombards and Vandals moved south: the former from present-day Germany to southeastern Europe, the latter from the region around the modern Polish-Czech border to northern Italy. During this century also, Angles and Saxons were moving from Germany into eastern and southern Britain. These are but a few of the migrations taking place in Europe at this time. Consider the jostling of cultures, most of them distinct and in mutual opposition, and the things any people needs in order to settle into a new territory, and you have a sense of the social turmoil of the fifth and sixth centuries.

Missionaries in Britain

The missionary movement, like much else in the Latin tradition, owes its origins mainly to Pope Gregory I (r. 590–604), a Roman patrician who gave up high office in secular society to withdraw to the seclusion of monastic life, only to rise to the top of the hierarchy in the Latin Church. Gregory, as we are told by Bede in his *Ecclesiastical History of the English People* (731), sent a delegation of monks from his monastery, led by Augustine (St. Augustine of Canterbury), to bring Christianity to the English (see Chapter 5). The mission to England was the beginning of a process that would extend into the eighth century, for the success of the first Roman missionaries led their followers to continue this work throughout the northern lands.

Arriving as agents of the pope in 597, Augustine and his companions found themselves among peoples practicing polytheistic religions that had arrived with the earliest settlements, together with indigenous traditions and the remnants of a Christianity that had come over with Roman soldiers in the first and second centuries. This native form of the faith, known as Celtic Christianity, was a blend of Roman belief and Celtic pratices: relics of the paganism of the Scots, Welsh, and Irish who inhabited the islands before the Angles and Saxons. The most

*St. Augustine of
Canterbury,
c. 607. Engraving.*

*The founder
of Roman
Christianity in
England is here
shown wearing the
pallium, a symbol
of his link with the
bishop of Rome.*

noteworthy feature of Celtic Christianity may be the monastic impulse, which found holiness in withdrawal from society and a rigorous asceticism.

This clash of several religious cultures was unusually complex, involving, between the two Christian communities, variations among such things as marriage restrictions, the celibacy of clergy, and the limits of bishops' jurisdictions. To persuade the native Christians that obedience to the papacy was the only valid form of Christian practice, and to convince the pagans that this imported tradition, Christianity, was superior to their own religious traditions, would have been daunting for any missionary. As Bede's narrative relates it, the Benedictine missionaries presented their questions to Gregory, whose answers always seemed to work. Thus the Bishop of Rome ruled, from a great distance, the Christian Church in the British Isles.

A number of symbolic events in Bede's narrative (which is our main source for this episode of church history) are intended to reinforce in the reader's mind the notion that this is the "Romanizing," and not merely the Christianizing, of these peoples. Augustine's receipt from Gregory of the pallium is one such instance. This bestowal, in 601, was accompanied by Augustine's appointment as the first Archbishop of Canterbury, a Roman town in southeastern England where Augustine had previously baptized the Jutish king Ethelbert of Kent. Augustine's successors would have authority over the church in England down to the present day.

Bede's description of the Synod of Whitby, in 663–64, illustrates the degree to which conformity to Roman practice served as a unifying force among peoples. This meeting was called by King Oswy of Northumbria, another Christian ruler, to settle a dispute concerning the day on which Easter was celebrated. At this time, Easter might be celebrated on three different dates: the 14th day of the Jewish month of Nisan, the date on which Jews celebrate Passover, regardless of the day of the week; the first Sunday after the 14th of Nisan; or the date followed by the Roman Church, which adhered to the Julian calendar, devised by Julius Caesar in 46 B.C.E. King Oswy, raised in the Celtic tradition which observed the 14th of Nisan as Easter, recognized that unifying the Christian community on this most holy day was imperative. There were two defenders of the Celtic dating: Colman, Abbot of Lindisfarne, and Hilda, Abbess of Whitby, and two advocates of the

The Martyrdom of St. Boniface, the church of St. Salvatoris, Fulda, 10th century. Manuscript illumination.

The suffering and death of those who helped spread Christianity throughout Europe gave a sacred power to the sites with which they were associated.

Roman dating: Wilfrid, Abbot of Ripon, and Agilbert, Bishop of the West Saxons. The debate is an illuminating look at early cultural conflict, and one is struck by the persuasiveness of Colman's argument for preserving the tradition of the ancestors. But Wilfrid argued that St. Peter, who supposedly held the keys to the kingdom of heaven, was always correct. The Roman practice prevailed—the first step in the unification of the English Church.

Missionaries on the Continent

The Benedictine monks who were sent to England from Rome quickly set about establishing monasteries. Some of the great religious houses of Britain—Jarrow and Wearmouth, for example—should be seen as products of the missionary strain in Western religion. From these centers the Benedictines sent monks to the Continent, where they built yet more monasteries. One of these monks, named Wynfrith (see also Chapter 5), was an English Christian who exemplified the "traditional" disciplines of monasticism: prayer, study, seclusion from the world. Nothing in this cloistered life, except the submission to authority essential to monasticism, could have prepared him for the role that won him his place in Christian history.

St. Boniface to Bishop Pehthelm

The principal missionary to the Germanic peoples, Boniface was adept at gaining the favor of other church leaders. The spread of "Roman obedience," loyalty to the papacy, would not have been possible without their support. Here he encourages and instructs a fellow bishop.

To his reverend brother and beloved fellow bishop, Pehthelm, Boniface, humble servant of the servants of God, sends sincere greetings of love in Christ.

We turn to the fatherly kindness of Your Holiness with earnest supplication, because we feel ourselves in serious peril, and beg you to aid us with your prayers acceptable to God. This German ocean is dangerous for sailors and we pray that we may reach the haven of eternal peace without stain or injury to our soul, and that while we are striving to offer the light of Gospel truth to the blind and ignorant who are unwilling to gaze upon it, we may not be wrapped in the darkness of our own sins, neither "run or have run in vain," but, upheld by your intercessions, may we go forward unspotted and enlightened into the splendor of eternity.

We are sending you some little gifts: a garment decorated with white spots and a coarse towel to dry the feet of the servants of God. Deign to accept them, we beg you, as a reminder of us.

There is one matter about which we desire your opinion and your advice. The priests throughout Gaul and Frankland maintain that for them a man who takes to wife a widow, to whose child he has acted as godfather, is guilty of a very serious crime. As to the nature of this sin, if it is a sin, I was entirely ignorant, nor have I ever seen it mentioned by the fathers, in the ancient canons, nor in the decrees of popes, nor by the Apostles in their catalogue of sins. If you have found anywhere a discussion of this subject in ecclesiastical writings kindly inform us and let us know also your own opinion.

I desire, for Christ's sake, that Your Welfare may advance in all holy virtues, with health and long life.

(From Austin P. Evans, ed., *Letters of St. Boniface*, trans. Ephraim Emerton. New York: Columbia University Press, 1940.)

The Life of St. Boniface

Hagiography, the genre of saints' lives, emphasizes those qualities that make the subject unusual and unique, and often this will include precocious displays of piety and learning. In this early life of Boniface, we witness the saintliness manifested very early in his clerical career.

The first section of our narrative is now completed, though in outline. Next we shall briefly make known the virtuousness to which the saint trained himself in the beginning of his studious life: in order that after we have laid the foundation of the fabric of our work, the loftiness of the structure may little by little be raised higher to the summit.

For after he waxed in age and in admirable strength of knowledge, and the seven years of infancy glided away, and the glory of boyhood came, by the inspiration of heavenly grace he was enriched with great and unutterable dignity of mind, as is shown by the examples given later in this work; and, living according to the model afforded by the earlier saints, and in obedience to the ordinances of the venerable fathers, he was manifested and adorned by the purity of many virtues. Moreover he was so kindled by divine genius, and so applied himself especially to the exercise of reading, that in all the moments and hours and revolving years that were added to his life, the helps and the divinely augmented gifts of the Protector on high were also increased within him. And the more he progressed in the school of the priesthood, the more, as trusty men who were his intimate associates have borne certain witness, did his daily studies, in continual meditation day and night upon literary training, incite him to the increase of eternal blessedness, and protect him marvellously against the inimical persecutions of diabolical suggestion, which among men are wont often to cover the tender flower of youth as it were with a kind of fog of cloudy darkness; so that also, because of his ceaseless care and long solicitude and his perpetual examination of the sacred laws, and by the help of the Lord God, the seductive passions of youth within him, and the assaults with which fleshly lusts at first assailed him, for the most part subsided. And more and more his studies carried him forward to the general instruction of the people, which, after the passage of no great interval of time, he began, enlarged, and perfected, in accordance with the episcopal ordinance of ecclesiastical prescription. For he despised the perishable adornments of this world, and in his childhood, under the moderate government of Father Wulfhard, kept the pattern of the monastic life well and duly for many years; until, when sportive boyhood was over and manly youth began, the more glowing desire of his spirit fired him to go, with the consent and advice of his trusty fellow servants and of the father of the monastery, to neighboring monasteries also, whither he was summoned by the want of teachers of reading.

(From *Life of St. Boniface Willibald*, trans. George W. Robinson. Cambridge, MA: Harvard University Press, 1916.)

Taking the Latin-derived name Boniface, meaning "doer of good deeds," Wynfrith first left England in 718 to do missionary work among the Frisians, in present-day Holland, but without success. A few years later, he returned to the Continent, to work among other Germanic tribes. (See "St. Boniface to Bishop Pehthelm" and "The Life of St. Boniface.") With his learning and eloquence he drew converts among the Bavarians, Swabians, Franks, and Saxons, who had formed settlements between the Elbe and Rhine rivers. Boniface was instrumental in establishing the first bishopric among the German peoples, creating an episcopal see at Mainz, south of Frankfurt. With helpers such as his fellow Englishman Willibald (c. 700–786), who was sent north from an Italian monastery by Pope Gregory III (731–741) to aid the mission, Boniface built communities both German in their local leaders and Roman in their obedience. To use an image from Willibald's writings, these missionaries sowed Christian "seeds" in the Teutonic soil, yielding "plants" that combined both Roman essence and regional context in ideal synthesis. Like the first Gregory, these former monks became highly visible leaders in their secular environments: Boniface as first Bishop of Mainz, where he was succeeded by another countryman, Lull, and Willibald as first Bishop (consecrated by Boniface) of Eichstätt, in southern Germany.

Besides establishing and occupying bishoprics, these missionaries built monasteries, which continued a vibrant tradition of study and piety and, like their English prototypes, would supply bishops and priests for generations to come. Willibald is credited with founding a double monastery (mixed-sex), one with houses for men and women alongside each other; Willibald's brother Winebald served as its first abbot until his death in 761, and their sister, Walburga, as his successor in the abbot's role until her own death (c. 779). This monastery, at Heidenheim, a village in Bavaria, became the model for a number of other double-monastic foundations, and gave women religious a much more solid place in institutional life than they had before. In later centuries (see Chapter 14) German nuns and abbesses would create a rich spiritual and mystical tradition.

Surviving by Adapting

The story thus far indicates that Christianity survived into the Middle Ages in conflict on two frontiers, which have usually borne the labels "classical" and "barbarian." At the beginning of our historical period, Christianity was hardly a self-contained community, much less a civilization in its own right. By the tenth century Christianity was the core of a civilization that offered much-needed stability. The church thus saw itself transformed from being the most "outside" of outsider groups to being the "inside" group that could facilitate the transitions of newer tribes from migratory existence to settled statehood. Considering the unsettled state of Christianity during its own first centuries, this emergence is truly remarkable.

The quality that above all accounts for Christianity's ability to become the core of medieval civilization is its adaptability, a trait honed during the era of persecutions. Operating as an underground movement, with no central organization, the early Christian communities had learned quickly to adapt to circumstances, preserving their faith in the shadow of an intolerant regime (see Chapter 3). Then, with the legalization of Christianity in the fourth century, the communities had organized themselves along secular Roman lines, with regional representative government by bishops and a well-stocked hierarchy (see Chapter 5) to keep the institution orderly. The seeds of the later equation of "Romanitas" with "Christianitas," or "Romanness" with Christianity, were sown during this period.

The missionaries who brought Christianity to northern Europe brought with them far more: literacy, knowledge of the international language Latin, familiarity through their monastic studies with the classical tradition, and a knowledge of law, both Roman and ecclesiastical. All of these were essential components of a stable society. All were absent among the migratory tribes. Thus Christianity—and the more "Roman" the better—must have seemed to these people the key to their transformation.

The church showed its adaptability in various ways. Some of the adaptation allowed certain indigenous practices to continue, modified into Christian form. The blessing of agricultural things—soil, animals, harvests—seems to have originated as pagan fertility rites, and the tying in of Christian holidays, such as Christmas (see Chapter 6), with pagan festivals is another example of this adaptability. The clergy also demonstrated a readiness to take on political duties where necessary. Bishops often represented authority in secular as well as religious matters, and clergy were looked up to as judges in disputes when local law proved unable to solve problems. In social as well as religious ways, the Romanization of Europe was the work of the missionary arm of the Latin Church.

Eastern Missions

Byzantine Christianity is occasionally called a non-missionary religion, since it lacks the forceful missionary tendencies of the modern Western Church. During the early Middle Ages, however, the Eastern Orthodox Church was for a time just as active in missionary work as was its Latin counterpart. In the ninth century it was the Eastern Church that undertook the conversion of the Slavic peoples in the North. As in the West, it was the head of the church—in this case the Patriarch of Constantinople—who took the initiative, and it was monks who went out among the peoples to be converted. Photius (810–895) was the patriarch, and St. Cyril (c. 827–869) and St. Methodius (c. 815–885), two brothers, were the monk-missionaries. However, their missions differed in some ways from those of their Western predecessors. First, not all their missionary attempts were successful: their first mission was with a people (the Kazars) who rejected their efforts and converted to Judaism. Second, some of their missions were launched in reply to calls for their services.

The first Orthodox mission to the Moravians (in the present-day Czech Republic) was in response to a request from the ruler, Rostislav, for preachers in Slavonic—a language that these two missionaries knew well. In preparation for their mission, they translated the Bible into Slavonic—more exactly into the Macedonian dialect they had learned, which became known as Old Church Slavonic; this remains the official liturgical language of Orthodoxy in Russia and elsewhere. In the process, Cyril and Methodius adapted the Greek alphabet into something better suited to the sounds of Slavonic: still in use, it is known as the Cyrillic alphabet, after Cyril.

The work of translating the Bible and disseminating doctrine in the language of the people was a stroke of genius, for it very literally "vernacularized" Christianity. Now conveyed in the language that the people could understand, the new religion no longer seemed a foreign cultural graft. Unfortunately, the brothers' mission to the Moravians failed, because German missionaries were promoting the Roman form at the same time, and did so forcefully enough to weaken the Eastern mission drastically. (On Methodius's death, the German missionaries persecuted and expelled his followers.) Nevertheless, they moved on to Bulgaria, Russia, and Serbia, and after initial struggles managed to establish a thriving Christian community. Bulgaria first, then Serbia and Russia, adopted Orthodoxy as their national faith.

The Royal House of Kiev

The Russian episode has a history of its own, beginning with Photius but far from auspiciously, as there was considerable resistance to Christianity in the royal house of Kiev (predecessor of the Russian state) at the end of the ninth century. This changed when the Russian princess Olga of Kiev (d. 969) received baptism in 957. Her grandson Vladimir I (c. 956; r. 980–1015) not only was baptized but married into the family of the Byzantine rulers; both he and Olga were declared saints, or CANONIZED, by the Eastern Orthodox Church. Under Vladimir, Russia became officially Orthodox; and a Christian renaissance similar to that of the Carolingians in the West (see Chapter 9) got under way. Icons, relics, and sacred artifacts of all kinds were crafted and imported. Monasteries were established. Church courts held power even in secular matters. Vladimir's sons and successors, Boris and Gleb, continued the work. Their capital at Kiev became the center of a culture that blended Slavic and Byzantine elements, both artistically exuberant. In the city's hundreds of churches, liturgy, vestments, and icons reflected a sense that the Holy is approachable in this world and that human abilities can craft and shape it appropriately. Like Byzantium itself, Orthodox Kiev was a remarkable civilization.

Over the next two centuries, the Kievan state split into a number of smaller principalities. Most of these fell to Mongol invaders during the thirteenth century, and Kiev itself was sacked by the Mongols in 1240. Thus came to a halt this splendid Orthodox Christian culture, two centuries before the fall of Byzantium itself. But Christianity itself had gained a foothold in Russia, and its culture would flourish once again in later centuries.

The Crusades

In their intertwining of religious and secular concerns, the Crusades are a typically medieval phenomenon. In conception, nothing could be closer to the heart of medieval Christianity than a desire to restore the Holy Land to the church. As we have seen, the church came into being in a geographical landscape that, according to tradition, had been promised by God to the Jews but was occupied and then conquered by Roman powers. The idea of recovering Jerusalem from foreign occupation dates from that time. The city's occupation by non-Christian peoples was a disruption of the idea that God is in complete control of human events. Symbolically, Jerusalem had been recognized as the capital of religious culture since the second century when Tertullian contrasted it with Athens, the symbolic capital of pagan culture. Pilgrimage to the Holy Land was an ancient practice, suggesting that the Christian during this life is only at home in Jerusalem, specifically at the tomb where Jesus was laid after his crucifixion.

The rise of Islam in the seventh century and beyond brought a new power onto the scene, one that reinvested the land with equally religious significance. Islam is self-consciously a continuation of Judaism and Christianity, and thus sees itself also as the heir to the Promised Land. Politically and culturally, Islam became a Mediterranean superpower while religiously it appeared to stand in denial of core Christian teachings.

The Crusades themselves owed their origin to the Gregorian Reform of the early eleventh century. Gregory VII himself wanted to come to the aid of the Eastern Church (recently separated from Rome) and liberate the Holy Land from Muslim occupation. It was his hope that cooperation in that campaign would reunite the Eastern and Western Churches; but neither his expedition nor the desired reunification would come to fruition.

Gregory's idea was a compelling one, though, and crusading enterprises got underway in earnest in 1095. At the synod of Clermont, Pope Urban II (r. 1088–1099) appealed to the knights and nobles to undertake an expedition, promising spiritual benefits (absolution from sins) and declaring the liberation of the Holy Land to be the will of God. The First Crusade began in 1096 under the leadership of various French, Norman, and Flemish nobles; a French bishop served as papal representative. The crusaders advanced through Europe in three formations, converging on Constantinople before moving south in unison toward Jerusalem, which they reached and stormed in July 1099. In the process, the armies

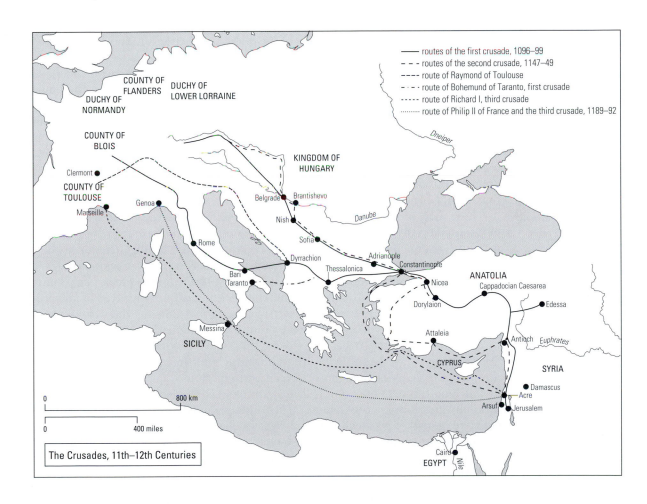

The Crusades, 11th–12th Centuries

celebrated the religious imagery of warfare: the church was an army, with Christ as its head, and the cross as its banner. In various forms this language had been part of Christian lore since the time of the early Fathers.

With the conquest of Jerusalem (after five weeks of battle), a new state was created. The Kingdom of Jerusalem was founded by Godfrey of Bouillion and sustained after his death in 1100 by his brother Baldwin, who ruled until 1118. Jerusalem's organization and leadership were more a clone of a European feudal kingdom than a throwback to an ancient or indigenous civilization; this situation lasted less than a century, ending in 1187 as a result of disputes about succession and administration.

Other Crusades followed. The Second Crusade of 1147–49 was remarkable not only for the secular figures involved (German and French kings, whose efforts were impeded by Sicilian and Byzantine rulers), but also for the role that Bernard of Clairvaux (see Chapter 14) played in initiating it. In preaching the duty to take up the Cross and embark on a campaign to recover the holy sites of Christianity, Bernard gave a pious dimension to an activity that had been largely military and secular. The notion that the church had a destiny in this world, and that it could be realized by the exercise of military might, comes into full focus during these decades. Preaching about Crusades would be the church hierarchy's counterpart to the secular nobility's idea of embarking on them.

Prominent as the Crusades were in the popular imagination, they represented different ideas for different persons. For example, as the leader of the Third Crusade (1189–92), Emperor Frederick Barbarossa saw himself as the head and unifying force of a campaign embracing the entire West. Dying before he could reach his destination, he was succeeded by his son, Frederick of Swabia; but he too died along the way. Acre, in present-day northern Israel, was finally conquered in 1191 by armies led by two kings, Richard III (the "Lionhearted") of England and Philip August II of France. Richard achieved a truce with the Islamic populace after occupying a large part of the Mediterranean coastline. From 1191 onward, pilgrimages to Jerusalem became the desired goal for large numbers of European Christians.

There were incentives for Crusades at every level. From the original promise of penitential credit there developed an elaborate program of crusaders' privileges, which in time included not only spiritual benefits but also legal and material ones. Spiritual benefits comprised credit in heaven for the good deed of embarking on a Crusade: the crusader would be rewarded in the afterlife for his piety. Legal benefits included immunity from prosecution for certain deeds committed by the crusader; and material rewards consisted of benefits such as the release of a crusader's heirs from debts incurred by him if he was killed on a Crusade. These were offers too good to be ignored by many. We should recognize that the Crusades may have been the church's initiative, but they were undertaken for a number of reasons—some more mercenary than pious.

The long-term effect of the Crusades was to force Christianity and Islam into a mutually antagonistic relationship. The influence of Islamic science and scholarship had been flowing steadily to the West since the ninth century, and the shape of Scholastic theology in the West would have been very different without the impact of Islamic philosophy. But by regarding Islam as the enemy of Christianity, and failing in their strategy to eradicate it, Christian crusaders served to ignite generations, and subsequently centuries, of Western hostility to it. This has proved to be the durable, and tragic, legacy of the Crusades.

Key Terms

APOLOGIST A defender of Christian teachings, usually with philosophical arguments.

CANONIZE To declare somebody a saint or grant special authority to a book or set of books.

ESCHATOLOGY That part of theology concerned with judgment and the afterlife.

NEOPLATONISM A late-antique philosophy holding that the present material world of dividedness is on a path toward union with the One.

ORIGINAL SIN The doctrine that humanity was compromised in the Fall of Adam and Eve, and unable to restore itself without divine help.

PROSELYTE A convert, often one prompted by missionary efforts.

SYNOD OF WHITBY A council that met in 664 and symbolically unified the English Church by fixing the date for Easter observance.

Giotto di Bondone, *Last Judgment*, Arena Chapel, Padua, c. 1305.
Fresco, approx. 33 ft × 27 ft (10 × 8.3 m).

PART THREE

Medieval Western Christian Culture

With the coronation of Charlemagne in 800 and the beginning of the Holy Roman Empire, Christendom completed the process of establishing a successor to the first Roman Empire, never completely Christianized despite Constantine's initiatives in the early fourth century. Charlemagne's dynasty witnessed a considerable expansion of learning and piety in both monasteries and schools, while the courts of bishops, with their jurists and theological counselors, became centers of social and religious discipline.

Divisions within Christendom prevented it being a fully unified civilization. Nevertheless, a common foundation supported a system of churches, schools, and political alliances far more extensive than that of any previous empire.

Although far from being a world empire, the Holy Roman Empire became a notable rival to the Byzantine Empire in the East, centered at Constantinople. Less aggressively expansionistic than its Western counterpart, the Byzantine Empire nevertheless oversaw the spread of Orthodoxy among Slavic peoples.

This period of Christian history was marked not only by expansion but also by intensification. Monasteries became centers of mystical writings. Cistercian and other "schools" actively reconceptualized the Christian life. In cities, some schools developed into universities, drawing students from all over Europe and sending them out into the world to practice law, medicine, the arts, and theology. Parts of the classical tradition that had been lost for a millennium were rediscovered and provided material for study and new scholarship.

In the early 1200s a new class of religious individual arose. The mendicant friar was a homeless, penniless wanderer whose peregrinations and preaching reinvigorated Christian communities bored with parish clergy or discouraged by stories of lazy (or corrupt) monks. Innovators and in some cases intellectuals, these friars included Thomas Aquinas, Bonaventure, and William of Ockham. Their work helped shape intellectual life from 1200 to 1500. Much of what we call "medieval" has its origins in such religious orders.

800		
	800	Pope Leo III crowns Charlemagne as Holy Roman Emperor.
	c. 819	Hrabanus Maurus, abbot of Fulda, composes influential treatise on priestly duties.
	862	Sts. Cyril and Methodius embark on a mission to convert peoples of eastern Europe.
	909	The abbey of Cluny is founded; origin of the Cluniac Order of monks.
1000	988	Vladimir, Prince of Kiev, converts to Orthodox Christianity.
	1054	Papal legates excommunicate Constantinople's Patriarch; final breach between Orthodox and Latin Churches.
	1075	Pope Gregory VII asserts the pope's right to depose monarchs and bishops.
	1077	Emperor Henry IV goes to Canossa in symbolic acceptance of papal authority.
	1078	St. Anselm proposes the ontological argument for God in his *Proslogion*.
	1088	The founding of the University of Bologna, first university in Europe.
	1095	Ivo of Chartres compiles *Tripartite Collection*, a comprehensive body of canon law.
1100	1095	Pope Urban II proclaims the First Crusade to liberate Jerusalem from Muslim rule.
	1123	Pope Calixtus II holds the First Lateran Council.
	1126	St. Bernard, abbot of the Cistercian monastery of Clairvaux, writes *On loving God*.
1200	c. 1140	Gratian's *Decretum* codifies canon law.
	1209–71	Followers of the Albigensian heresy are repressed with great ferocity.
	1210	Pope Innocent III grants St. Francis of Assisi permission to create a mendicant order.
	1215	St. Clare forms the mendicant order known as the Poor Clares.
	1215	The Fourth Lateran Council defines the seven sacraments.
	1216	The Dominican Order is recognized by Pope Honorius III.
	1224	St. Francis receives the stigmata.
	1232	Pope Gregory IX grants a constitution to the Dominican Second Order of nuns.
	1249	The founding of the University of Oxford.
1300	1265	Thomas Aquinas begins his *Summa Theologiae*.
	1308	Death of John Duns Scotus, influential Scottish Scholastic philosopher.
	1309	The papacy moves from Rome to Avignon.
	1327	Death of German mystic Johannes Eckhart.
	1328	The views of English theologian William of Ockham are denounced by Pope John XXII.
	1349	The Black Death sweeps throughout Europe.
	1373	English mystic Julian of Norwich experiences a series of visions.
	1378	The church is torn by the Great Schism; rival popes claim power in Avignon and Rome.
1400	1382	Teachings of English religious reformer John Wycliffe are condemned by the church.
	1416	The Bohemian religious reformer John Huss is burned at the stake.
	1417	The Council of Constance ends the Great Schism.
	c. 1436	*The Book of Margery Kempe*, an account of the life of an English mystic, is written.
	1453	Constantinople falls to the Ottoman Turks.
	c. 1455	Gutenberg's *Bible* is published, the first printed book in Europe.

Carolingian Culture and Religion
A Medieval Renaissance

The events that brought Christianity to the tribes of northern Europe did more than establish religious practices and beliefs. They also ensured obedience to the papacy in Rome, as might be expected from monks continuing the work begun by the pope's envoy Augustine of Canterbury. They brought literacy and the Latin language, essential connections to the previous great civilization that had flourished in Europe. And they brought conceptions of culture, both political and intellectual, that would develop, during the ninth century, into the structure of a new civilization, the first one in the West since the fall of Rome. The political institution that began in the ninth century would continue, in some form, for a thousand years.

Not so long lasting, but of equal importance to the story told in these pages, were the cultural and religious aspects of this political milestone, which together formed the beginning of medieval civilization.

Carolingian Ascendancy

The political institution that would become the Holy Roman Empire had somewhat shaky beginnings. It began with the ascendancy of a usurper's dynasty, the Carolingians, and their recognition by the papacy. In these early years, the late 700s, there were alliances created for the sake of expediency and military advantage, efforts to consolidate power in the West as a defense against control by the Greek-speaking East, and the unprecedented bestowal by the pope of the imperial authority of the Caesars long after their empire had collapsed.

The story, briefly, is as follows. In 751 the Carolingian prince Pepin III had become (with the church's blessing) king of the Franks (see Chapter 5). Pepin's son Charlemagne (Charles the Great), who became king in 768, aided by Charlemagne's younger brother Carloman (751–771), embarked on a program of conquest and annexation so thorough that they were able to forge a realm extending from modern-day France to Bohemia (in the present-day Czech Republic),

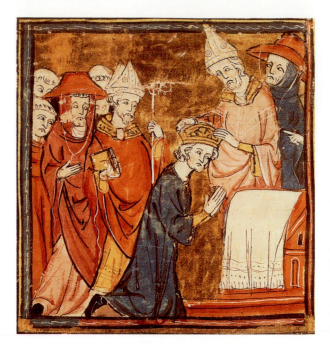

The Coronation of Emperor Charlemagne by Pope Leo III in St. Peter's, Rome, in 800, 14th century. Vellum. Bibliothèque Nationale, Castres, France.

A turning point in Western Christendom, the coronation of Charlemagne set the stage for centuries of dispute about the relation of secular to sacred institutions.

including alliances with the Anglo-Saxons in the north and Spain and Italy in the south. Considering the numbers of peoples involved and the amount of provincial administration required, their program must be considered one of the most ambitious expansion efforts in history. One of the crucial components of the strategy was the cooperation of the papacy, for without the support of the church these new rulers would have been unable to forge alliances (which in many cases were naked annexations) with their new member states.

The church, for its part, stood to gain from a partnership with the powerful new monarchy. Not only did stronger and centralized rule promise to facilitate missionary movements into the unchristianized territories, but the political and military power of the Carolingian house offered crucial support for a papacy vulnerable to the powers in the East. The Roman Church was still technically a subordinate branch of the Eastern Church in Constantinople, under the supervision of an "exarch" (roughly equivalent to a bishop) in the imperial city of Ravenna, near Italy's Adriatic coast. By the eighth century, however, the Roman Church had reached a point at which it could not be considered truly a branch of another church. An alliance with a powerful Western monarchy would ensure Rome's independence from the Greek world; and the military aid of Charlemagne's forces would protect Rome from the attacks from east and north that constantly threatened the papal realm.

A Pope Kneels Before a King

The assorted needs and priorities of the two ambitious institutions came together, symbolically and actually, in Rome on Christmas Day, 800. On that occasion, Charlemagne was met by the relatively new pontiff, Leo III (c. 750–816; r. 795–816), and declared "king of the Franks and patrician of the Romans," while the people acclaimed him as their emperor. The pope, who had just that week escaped being deposed, and who had been the victim of a botched assassination attempt less than a year earlier, set a crown on Charlemagne's head and knelt in obedience to the ruler he had just crowned—the only time in history a pope would kneel before a king. At that moment a new civilization, one that would dominate the West culturally for centuries and continue politically for a millennium, was born.

As later events and controversies would prove, however, all sorts of things were wrong with this apparently authoritative coronation. Charlemagne was already king of the Franks, however illegitimate the beginnings of his family's dynasty. The term "patrician of the Romans" was too vague to convey even much prestige, let alone power. The papacy had never had the power to crown kings, and Leo III was in a very powerless position. If this was a transfer of rule, it lacked the clarity that ensures the success of such transfers. According to one "official" account of the ceremony, by Charlemagne's biographer Einhard, Charlemagne is said to have remarked that had he known what was going to happen that day, he would never have entered the church. But other evidence indicates that he had, in fact, known, and well in advance. The comment may indicate mainly remorse over sharing power with anyone else; this was the king who called himself a new David, after the biblical king, saw himself as chief of the "chosen people," and referred to his capital at Aachen (in present-day Germany) as the "New Rome."

The "Carolingian Renaissance"

Charlemagne built more than an empire: he guided the creation of a civilization, doing more in this role, perhaps, than any individual in Western history. Thus when we use the term "Carolingian," we mean more than we do when, for example,

Four Evangelists, from a Carolingian Gospel book, Palace Chapel school, Aachen, Germany, early 9th century.

The culture supported by the Carolingian Dynasty took several forms, of which the most remarkable was the making and decorating of books.

referring to something of the late nineteenth century as "Victorian," after the monarch at the time. Something that is called Carolingian is likely to owe its origin to Charlemagne's own work and conception of culture. However, the revival of learning that we call the "Carolingian renaissance" actually began in the generation before Charlemagne's reign (indeed, scholars have distinguished a "first" and "second" Carolingian renaissance with a subtlety that we can ignore).

Empires, by definition, imply a degree of uniformity at some level of administration: all the inhabitants must in some sense understand themselves as subjects of a single ruler. In a similar vein, religion can become standardized throughout an empire, with all subjects belonging to a single church and recognizing that the worldly as well as the spiritual elements of their lives are directed by God. Thus, even before the coronation of 800, the Carolingian dynasty had made attempts to standardize, and Romanize, religious life in the lands under their rule. With powerful bishops installed in influential cities such as Mainz, Trier, and Cologne, loyalty to Rome and guidance from Rome became noticeable during the 760s in the reign of Charles's father, Pepin III. Worship was conducted according to Roman liturgical books, while Benedictine monastic houses multiplied, and spread ever eastward, for a century or more. Whether the creation of such a system was the inevitable conclusion to the process begun by Gregory I in the 590s (see Chapter 5), the Carolingian bishops certainly capitalized on the momentum that had built up over the preceding century by reinforcing Roman practice in their dioceses.

Education was another major component of this new cultural world—the factor that, above all, justifies the term "Carolingian renaissance." Charlemagne's predecessors had given new emphasis to the building of schools associated with cathedrals and parish churches, but efforts in the mid-700s were rare and difficult. Charlemagne wanted to make sure that all his clergy, from bishops down to deacons, were trained well enough to guide the people in prayer and belief. In a "General Admonition" of 789 a new law of the land prescribed that reading,

Who's Who

Shapers of Medieval Christianity

Alcuin (c. 732–804) An English priest who joined Charlemagne's court and became Abbot of St. Martin in Tours, France. A notable teacher, he contributed greatly to church culture and is a major figure in the Carolingian Renaissance.

Charlemagne (Charles I, or Charles "the Great") (c. 742–814) The first emperor of what became known as the Holy Roman Empire—much of Christian western Europe. Responsible for a flourishing of Christian learning, reform, and church building, his reign became known as the Carolingian Renaissance.

Johannes Scotus Eriugena (John the Scot) (c. 810–877) Despite his name, this outstanding Latin and Greek scholar and philosopher was actually an Irishman. Head of the palace school at Laon, his controversial work dealt with God's all-encompassing role in the world.

Peter Abelard (1079–1142/3) A major French theological and philosophical figure famed for a doomed love affair with Héloïse. His copious writings include *Sic et Non*, intended to open up debate about the nature of authority. He became Abbot of St. Gildas in 1127.

writing, singing, arithmetic, grammar, and stenography (important to the church for recording the speeches of religious leaders) should be taught to boys by every monastery and bishopric. (There had been measures along these lines for a couple of centuries already, but now they were standardized and given the force of law.) In support of his program, Charlemagne appointed the English priest Alcuin (c. 732–804) as master of his own new school, and Alcuin brought with him the already mature British tradition of monastic scholarship.

Bishops throughout the empire took up the challenge posed by Charlemagne, establishing cathedral schools, "public" schools (meaning that they would be under secular control), and schools for the liberal arts and sacred studies. In all of these institutions, at least some of the Latin classics were included in the curriculum, and commentaries were prepared for the sake of explaining these texts. Thanks to these studies, the general quality of Latin improved, so that more of the ancient tradition could be read, and texts written in the ninth century could be read more easily later on. (As with any language, bad Latin is harder to understand than correct Latin.) And given the variety of languages spoken throughout Charlemagne's empire, teaching exact Latin was a way to create and preserve some uniformity—even if only among the educated few.

At the Carolingian court of Aachen (also called, in French, Aix-la-Chapelle) an intellectual elite dominated. In addition to Alcuin, a number of theologians and learned men in a variety of other disciplines (geography and music, for example), created something resembling a modern think tank, aimed at bringing Roman thought and religious practice into general use in the territories. In patronage of the intelligentsia, however, Charlemagne was surpassed by his grandson Charles II, the Bald (823–877; r. as emperor 875–877) who commissioned scientific and historical works that became standard texts. This Charles was also a patron of monasteries, one of them being that of St. Denis near Paris, named after France's patron saint, who was, according to legend, Bishop of Paris sometime in the third century and was martyred for his faith. Another legend associates him with one Dionysius the Areopagite, who was converted by St. Paul (Acts 17:34). This is pure fabrication.

However, by this time there were some texts circulating in Greek, attributed to this early convert, which dealt with some of the most subtle theological issues: the hierarchies of heaven and earth, the way God can be known, the terms for God and what they actually express. The texts date from c. 500, and we still have no clue to the identity of the author; but in the mid-800s they were assumed to have been the work of Dionysius/St. Denis. Accordingly, Charles the Bald commissioned one of the sharpest thinkers of his age, Johannes Scotus Eriugena (c. 810–877), to translate these works from Greek into Latin, and in so doing he inaugurated a Latin mystical tradition. For these texts are our source of such concepts as the *via negativa* and *via positiva* toward knowing God, the hierarchy of the heavens being mirrored by the structure of rulership on earth, and knowledge of God being unlike the knowledge of any created thing (see Chapter 14). Thus some of the most powerful ideas in mysticism were introduced to the West by an emperor who mistook the identity of the first bishop of Paris and believed a false attribution of some Greek texts.

Early Medieval Spirituality

It is important to remember, while examining the intellectual aspects of Carolingian Christianity, as seen among its rulers and the church hierarchy, that these developments were inextricably linked to, and supported by, deeply cherished religious beliefs—unchallenged, as such beliefs are today, by sophisticated scientific discoveries. The Carolingian world was one in which the spiritual permeated all aspects of life, and in order to understand it we must look at this aspect of religion.

However much we talk about doctrines and the history of Christianity, and imagine that we actually know what our subject is because it is a tangible tradition like other aspects of culture, as students of religion we need to be reminded that the core of our subject is profoundly intangible: the belief in God held by people living, for the most part, in a world very different from our own. Because the piety of ordinary people has left a very meager written record, we cannot study medieval religiosity in the same way we can trace the history of the papacy, for example. In the absence of such direct sources, we must make a choice: either avoid this aspect of religious history altogether and confine our study to those aspects for which we do have remains, or attempt to understand religious sentiment from texts available to us. Imperfect as it is, we will pursue the second choice.

Interest in spirituality has been on the rise in recent decades, as churches continue to seek ways of earning the loyalty of their existing members and attracting new ones. And since many of these people had been at least partially alienated from organized religion by its supposed emphasis on the rules and regulations of church membership, spirituality has been marketed as an alternative to the rigid structures of institutional Christianity—even by the churches themselves. The first thing to recognize is that this understanding of spirituality is peculiar to our time. In the Middle Ages, spirituality did not develop as a counterculture within the organized church or advertise itself as something separate from the dominant focus of the tradition. Spirituality was part and parcel of the life of the medieval church. This means—fortunately for us as historians—that the body of material available to us is much more extensive than we might imagine. Indeed, instead of having too little material to study, we might actually have too much. Amid a potential embarrassment of riches, the essential task is to limit the topic, so that we may discuss it concretely and identify texts pertinent to the subject.

Let us identify spirituality as that aspect of religious life that expresses the attitudes and aspirations of the human spirit in its relation to God. Even though all of Christianity has to do with humanity's relation to God, individual sentiment does not find its expression in aspects like church organization, ritual, or doctrine. The spiritual "voice" is distinct from these aspects but not contradictory.

Lay Spirituality

Like Molière's comic character Monsieur Jourdain, who was surprised to discover that he had been speaking prose all his life, students of religion may be astonished to realize just how much of their subject is concerned with spirituality—the line between religion and spirituality being a hazy one. Very little from the documentary record has been left by the medieval laity. The majority of people may have been thoughtful and articulate in religious matters, but most were illiterate; and few, if any, of those who could write composed personal testimonies to their piety.

Evidence of spiritual life among the people of medieval Europe has tended to come from two sources: liturgical texts left by the literate elite, and the material culture of everyday life. Neither category is completely adequate for this historical purpose. The literate populace was dominated by clergy and the upper levels of secular society, both unconcerned with recording the sentiments of the peasantry, while the material artifacts of everyday existence tell us more about the practicalities of daily life than about attitudes toward divine realities. Yet even these incomplete bodies of evidence show us a form of popular piety that combines Christian and pagan elements into an eclectic religious system, one mirroring, perhaps, the sometimes awkward coexistence of "Roman" and indigenous strains in medieval culture generally. Among the Roman elements were the sacraments of baptism and the Eucharist, both of them ways of making tangible contact with divine power. Local or pagan practices that were absorbed into Christian life in various places included the blessings of crops and animals (this was a farming culture, after all), celebrations of the solstices (relics of astronomical religion), and the incorporation of local patron deities into the pantheon of saints—spirits who protected their devotees and interceded with God on their behalf.

The regional variations that occurred at the level of popular practice had one thing in common: they tended to make religious power appear to be something tangible, and holiness something accessible to the senses. Genuine benefits were available through contact with the energy supposedly present in sacred artifacts such as relics (see Chapter 6) and rites. As early as the fourth century, supposed fragments of the cross were being identified and venerated and the bones of martyrs began circulating shortly afterwards. The intimacy with God that was felt in these forms no doubt made individuals more devout and led them to see more divine activity in their own lives than if they had felt that God became accessible to experience

A Tassilo chalice, c. 770. Copper, gilded. Donated by Duke Tassilo and his wife Liutpirc. Kremsmuenster, Germany.

The uniqueness of Eucharistic devotion, central to religious experience in the Middle Ages, was symbolized by elaborately crafted chalices.

only once, with the Incarnation. Such a view would have restricted God's presence to Jesus' contemporaries and left medieval European society with an image of an exclusively transcendent God: that is, one beyond human experience. The tangible (supposed) manifestations of divine power in medieval culture helped to balance the distance of the transcendent God with the closeness of sacred matter. (The Orthodox tradition, with its icons and highly sensuous devotional life, never lost a sense of the immediacy of the sacred: icons, for example, were themselves considered manifestations of their subjects' qualities; see Chapter 6.)

In the West, the sensory character of popular religiosity is most clearly perceived in the art that adorned medieval churches. Sculpture and stained-glass windows were two art forms—one old, one new—put into the service of piety. It was generally felt by a number of religious figures (including Pope Gregory I) that these visual depictions were "bibles" for the illiterate. For the artists who produced the works, aesthetic criteria were of only peripheral importance. Nor did an artist aim simply to exercise skill and imagination. Instead, the main purpose of creativity was to arouse, guide, and instruct the piety of the viewer; aesthetic works were visual aids, so to speak, in a program of spiritual education—as well as a means of glorifying God. (The Decalogue's prohibition of graven images was not thought to apply here, possibly because the artists were reproducing stories already in scriptural revelation, not trying to shape an image of the intangible God of the Hebrew Scriptures.) The viewer could concentrate on the image and gain a new understanding of a divine quality or truth: the anguish of the Virgin Mary in an image of the crucifixion, for example, or the power of faith to gain eternal life in a depiction of Jesus summoning Lazarus from the tomb.

Such "understanding" was real, but it was not the same as understanding facts and concepts. Rather, it was an AFFECTIVE awareness of God, something that occurred within the emotions. If you could look at a religious image and come to a greater emotional sense of God—greater love, awe, gratitude—then you were achieving a new level of spirituality. It is not surprising that most of this experience was visual; but the other senses, too, were engaged. The sound of bells and the chanting of priests and choir were elements of lay spiritual life, as was the smell of incense and candles and the tactile contact with oils and holy water. All of these facets of religious practice are aspects of popular spirituality.

Material Culture

As intangible as beliefs ultimately are, they are nevertheless expressed in forms; and the forms in which piety is expressed reveal much about the culture. In the ninth century and later there was a revival of attention to books; indeed, if we may speak of a Carolingian renaissance, it was one in which the book became an art form. In the schools, a new manuscript style had been developed in some of the monasteries. This hand, called Caroline or CAROLINGIAN MINUSCULE, brought greater accuracy to the texts being copied and allowed for easier reading than the hodge-podge of manuscript styles that had existed before. (To ensure uniformity in the text of the Latin Bible—the Vulgate—Charles the Great had Alcuin prepare a new "official" edition. The greater accuracy surely ensured that more classical texts survived in readable form than would otherwise have been the case; and the comparatively greater ease of reading may have aided the spread of literacy and learning throughout the empire. Most of the typefaces still in general use throughout the world are variants on the ninth-century letterforms. (Ironically, Charles himself never mastered even basic writing—though he could read, unlike most of his contemporaries.)

Alongside the beautiful Carolingian hand the pages of sacred books often bore magnificent illustrations; and the books were enclosed in elaborate bindings. The Bible had become an object of study as never before—in the West, at least—and an object of religious veneration in its own right. Hence the preservation and copying of Bibles became a favored avenue for creativity, and in this era we find some of the most beautiful ILLUMINATED MANUSCRIPTS: texts in which the words are accompanied by colorful and detailed graphic renderings of the events being narrated. Just as impressive as the pages were the bindings crafted for many of these tomes: intricately tooled covers of precious metals, inlaid with jewels. In a way similar to that of the sacred icons of the Eastern church, these books became points of contact with divine power.

The quality of the silverwork and goldsmithing in these books is matched by the craft and artistry found in other sacred Carolingian artifacts. Chalices, patens (plates used for communion wafers), crucifixes, and other ritual items from this period show an impressive level of culture, one we would hardly associate with the barbarian tribes of the North—although that is how the Franks had been seen only a few centuries before. (They might have been more literate and cultivated than their historical stereotype suggests.) If the artifacts of this culture tell us anything, it is that the rise of the Carolingians to imperial status was evidently joined by a sense that great political power must be linked to a great cultural tradition. And the Carolingian achievement proved to be almost as remarkable in the arts as it was in the political shaping of western Christendom.

Key Terms

AFFECTIVE Taking place in the emotions, as opposed to the intellect; as a form of spirituality, one that sees the heart as the locus of piety.

CAROLINGIAN MINUSCULE A style of writing that facilitated the copying and reading of texts, one of the aesthetic innovations of the 9th-century renewal of classical culture.

ILLUMINATED MANUSCRIPT A highly decorated handwritten book, in which the images interpret and help tell the story contained in the verbal text.

Scholasticism
From Anselm to Aquinas

The term "scholastic" nowadays is taken to mean a number of different things: academic, pedantic, overly rational, obsolete. But in the Middle Ages, when the term came into use, it referred simply to what was done in school (*scholae*)— first the cathedral schools, and eventually the universities. What pupils did in these schools was study, of course; but what they studied was focused, and how they studied it was just as precisely defined. This chapter will look at the developments in thought from the early "schools" to "Scholasticism" as a form of religious thought.

The sample of Scholastic thought with which people are most likely to be familiar from their introductions to philosophy or theology is usually drawn from St. Thomas Aquinas (1224/1225–1274), but in several respects Aquinas is quite atypical of Scholastic thought (he actually came to epitomize Scholasticism only in the late nineteenth century). He was one thinker in a movement far more diverse and controversial than most people suppose. In fact, a case might be made for the plural "scholasticisms" as the more accurate label for medieval philosophy; but we can remain content with the singular form so long as we keep in mind that it designates a variety of theologies, not a unified program. Any unity that Scholasticism does possess comes from its common purpose: to understand God by means of reason. But this criterion could apply just as well to other, quite separate episodes in theological history which have nothing to do with the Scholastic movement (for example, the Greek apologetics discussed in Chapter 8).

Beginnings of Scholasticism

In its original conception, the Scholastic enterprise is easy to describe. Scholasticism derived its name from the schools in which men trained for the priesthood. Largely a legacy of Carolingian culture, these schools were attached to cathedrals in various European cities, and beginning in the twelfth century some developed into the first universities. The schools thus took a new place alongside monasteries as centers of theological study. By all accounts, Scholasticism arose from attempts by scholars in these schools to explain passages of the Bible. As an EXEGETICAL project (that is, one devoted to the critical interpretation of texts), Scholastic thought can claim continuity with Patristic schools of theology, and the connection should not be underestimated. In the course of their work interpreting scriptural passages, scholars—or "schoolmen," as they were called—inevitably would come across discrepancies that needed resolving. How, for example, can the affirmations of God's unity be reconciled to the doctrine of the Trinity, held as orthodox by all councils after Nicaea (see Chapter 3)? Or, if Jesus knew that he was the Messiah and that the atonement could be achieved only with his death, why did he ask (Mark 14:36) for the "cup" of suffering to pass him by? Also, if God knew that Adam and Eve would fall from grace and that all humanity would, as a result, need to be redeemed, why did He give humanity free will in the first place? These and other questions, some subtle, some obtuse (at least they seem so from a modern vantage point), posed very real problems to medieval interpreters. Also, it should be remembered that the thinkers entertaining these problems did not have the scholarly means to resolve questions by appealing to different sources or manuscripts of various texts. For them, all Scripture was a unified revelation, and discrepancies could be resolved only by the use of reason.

One of the first schoolmen to grapple with these problems was Alcuin, theological counselor to Charles the Great (see Chapter 9). Another was John the Scot, also known as Johannes Scotus Eriugena (c. 810–877). John is noteworthy for asserting that true philosophy and true religion are one and the same: a view that many modern thinkers have accepted, even though it had been rejected in earlier centuries. Eriugena is only now beginning to come into his own as a theologian, and it is likely that coming generations will be more appreciative of his work than twentieth-century scholars generally have been.

St. Anselm

As a theological tradition, Scholasticism began in earnest with the work of St. Anselm (1033–1109), an Italian-born priest, later Archbishop of Canterbury, and one of the most creative medieval philosophers. Anselm set the terms for much of Scholastic thought by exploring the extent to which reason, unaided by scriptural revelation, could arrive at a knowledge of God. It was obvious to Anselm that human reason was capable of knowing many things without the aid of revelation. No one needs biblical corroboration of a mathematical formula, for example. On the other hand, there seem to be things that reason is incapable of discovering for itself, and for which revelation is needed. From the outset, the early church had assumed that God chose to reveal in the Bible those things that humanity needed to know for its salvation but was unable to know rationally. For Anselm, reason and revelation were viewed as complementary. Revelation started where reason ended. Humanity needed both reason and revelation, each working in its own sphere, in order to know all that was necessary to know for salvation. (We should not forget that these were issues on which eternal life and death were thought to depend; academic games they certainly were not.)

St. Anselm's *Why God Became Man*

An early master of Scholastic thought, St. Anselm offers a philosophical explanation of the Incarnation and Atonement. As he explains in this excerpt from the preface, he wrote it as a defense of Christianity rather than as a philosophical exercise.

Because of some people who, without my knowledge, began copying out the first parts of this work before it was finished and fully researched, I have been compelled to complete the work that follows, to the best of my ability, in greater haste than would have been opportune from my point of view. For, if I had been allowed to edit it in tranquillity and for the appropriate length of time, I would have included further additional material which I have left unmentioned. It has been amid great heartache—what the source of this has been, and the reason for it, God knows—that I began this work in England in response to a request, and have completed it, while on a journey, in the province of Capua. I have named it, in consideration of its subject-matter, *Why God Became Man* …, and have divided it into two books. The first book contains the objections of unbelievers who reject the Christian faith because they think it militates against reason, and the answers given by the faithful. And eventually it proves, by unavoidable logical steps, that, supposing Christ were left out of the case, as if there had never existed anything to do with him, it is impossible that, without him, any member of the human race could be saved. In the second book, similarly, the supposition is made that nothing were known about Christ, and it is demonstrated with no less clear logic and truth: that human nature was instituted with the specific aim that at some stage the whole human being should enjoy blessed immortality, "whole" meaning "with both body and soul"; that it was inevitable that the outcome concerning mankind which was the reason behind man's creation should become a reality, but that this could only happen through the agency of a Man-God; and that it is from necessity that all the things which we believe about Christ have come to pass.

It is my earnest request that all who wish to copy this book should place before its opening this little preface, along with the chapter-headings of the whole work. My intention is that anyone into whose hands it comes may discern, as it were, from its facial appearance, whether there is anything, within the whole body of the work, which he may find worthy of respect.

(From St. Anselm, "Why God Became Man," in Brian Davies and G.R. Evans, eds., *Anselm of Canterbury: The Major Works*. Oxford: Oxford University Press, 1998.)

Anselm challenged this epistemological division of labor by holding that if the mind is an endowment given by God, then it should serve the purpose of knowing God: the same purpose that is served by biblical revelation. Beginning from this hypothesis, Anselm sought to determine whether certain statements found in revelation could be derived from reason alone. Thus, in his treatise *Cur Deus Homo* (*Why God Became Man*; 1097–99), Anselm tried to prove, without recourse to revelation, why the atonement was necessary and why Christ needed to possess both a divine and a human nature for the atonement to be possible. (See "St. Anselm's *Why God Became Man*.") In Anselm's rendering, humanity incurred with the Fall a debt which it needed to repay, but could not. God, on the other hand, was able to pay the price, but did not need to. In assuming human form in the person of Jesus Christ, God took on humanity's accountability for original sin and paid the price of restoring humankind to grace. Therefore, in Anselm's view, the divine atonement for sin needed to take the form that it did.

Anselm takes his place in the history of philosophy owing to the ONTOLOGICAL argument for the existence of God—that is, one that argues for the necessary existence of God on the basis of the definition of God. This argument, developed in his *Proslogion* (1078), has drawn perhaps more critical attention than any other position in Western philosophy between the eras of St. Augustine and Descartes. The position itself is a relatively simple one. Anselm holds that of all the beings one can imagine, there must be one so great that it is impossible to think of one greater. Such a being, in Anselm's view, possesses all attributes, one of which must be existence. Thus God exists not only as a concept—an idea of something than which there can be nothing greater—but also as a being, since a perfect being that did not exist would not be so great that one could not imagine a greater one. (In other words, one could always imagine a greater one, i.e. a supreme being that does exist.) The point is that a being that exists has one more attribute than one that does not exist, all other things being equal. The issue at conflict is whether existence is a predicate: that is, something that can be affirmed or denied about the subject of a logical argument—in this case, a being. Put more specifically: can one add "is" alongside other qualities of a thing?

Many philosophers now hold that existence is not a predicate, so that God's being is not entailed by the definition of God as the being that is so great that one cannot imagine a greater. Other thinkers continue to hold Anselm's view that God necessarily exists. Wherever one stands, the Anselmian formula raised questions that remain important to this day.

Authorities Must be Weighed, not Counted

Over the following century, the twelfth, Scholasticism would develop in method to become an efficient way of solving theological problems. The heart of the Scholastic discussion is the *quaestio*, or "question," which is ordinarily based on a discrepancy in two or more texts. The author will pose the question in the form of a supposition, provide all the evidence in support of that supposition, then introduce a source that overturns all the other evidence. He will then spend the rest of the *quaestio* explaining why the evidence that had been cited in support of the initial statement must be seen as false, inaccurate, or misread. (The result is a clearer and more certain understanding of the body of faith.)

Such a procedure demands great attention to authorities, and it is in the weighing of evidence that Scholastic thinkers made genuine contributions. The awareness that sources could be in apparent contradiction, together with confidence that no discrepancy is irresolvable, led to concerted efforts to establish criteria for discriminating between weak and strong authorities. In principle, a single valid source is sufficient to overturn a dozen spurious ones; and this is a far cry from earlier tendencies to pile up scriptural PROOFTEXTS as evidence in support of a given position. "Authorities must be weighed, not counted" (*auctoritates ponderantur, non numerantur*) is a watchword of Scholastic method, one usually observed faithfully. Where Scholastic thinkers frequently disagree is in their reading of their predecessors; and in their disagreements they helped establish the critical stance toward sources that has shaped modern academic method.

Peter Lombard and the Search for Structure

As Scholastic thought developed, it became increasingly comprehensive in scope. It was felt that a method that is valid for resolving specific disputes about the meaning of revelation should in principle be applicable to the whole body of Christian teaching. As time went on, the number of questions grew, and ways of structuring these questions were needed. Without a fixed order, the teachings of theologians would be no more than series of observations: no more unified or structured, necessarily, than a large collection of short essays. The need for organizing this unwieldy material was evident, and it was met by a particular book that offered a comprehensive set of categories.

Peter Lombard's *Sentences*

A standard text of Scholastic theology, the Sentences *of Peter Lombard offered an anthology of earlier views and attempts to reconcile differences among them. Lombard here answers the question of whether Christ was Mary's natural or adopted son.*

If it is asked whether Christ is an adopted son, as man, or in some other way, we reply that Christ is not an adopted son in any way, but only a natural Son. For he is a Son by nature, not by the grace of adoption.

He is not called Son by nature as he is called God by nature; for he is not Son from that by which he is God, since he is Son by the property of nativity, while he is God by the nature of divinity. However the term nature, or Son of nature, is used because he is a Son naturally, having the same nature as he who begot.

Moreover he is not an adopted son, because he did not first exist and then become adopted as son, as we are spoken of as adopted sons in that when we were born we were "sons of wrath" but have been made "sons of God" through grace. There never was a time when Christ was not a son and therefore he is not an adopted son.

But against this one can argue thus: If Christ is the son of man, that is of a virgin, it is either by grace or by nature, or by both. If this is so by nature, then it is either by divine nature or by human nature; but not by divine nature, therefore either by human nature or else he is not by nature the son of man. If it is not by nature, then by grace alone; and indeed, if by human nature, not thereby less through grace. If, therefore, he is the son of the virgin by grace, he seems to be an adopted son, so that the same man is a natural Son of the Father and an adopted son of the virgin.

To this it can be said that Christ is the son of the virgin by nature, or naturally and by grace. He is not, however, the adopted son of the virgin, since it is not through adoption, but through union, that he is called the son of the virgin. For he is called son of the virgin in that in the virgin he received a man into the unity of a person; and this was by grace, not by nature.

Thus Augustine in *On John* says: "That the Only-begotten is equal to the Father is not from grace but from nature. However that a man was assumed into the unity of person of the only-begotten, is from grace, not from nature." Christ, therefore, is the adopted son neither of God nor of man, but the Son of God naturally and the son of man naturally and by grace.

(From Peter Lombard, *The Four Books of Sentences*, in Eugene R. Fairweather, ed. and trans., *A Scholastic Miscellany: Anselm to Ockham*. New York: Macmillan, 1970.)

The book was the *Sentences* by Peter Lombard (c. 1100–1160), and it served a number of purposes. (See "Peter Lombard's *Sentences*"). For all his influence over the course of medieval theology, Peter Lombard himself was not an original formulator. Instead, he was a compiler, and the *Sentences* served as a sourcebook for theologians for nearly five hundred years. As its title suggests, Lombard's work is a collection of sayings from the church fathers on every theme in the theological universe. Such compilations have always been useful, and never more so than during the Middle Ages, when even the most learned minds of a given age lacked genuine familiarity with the classic texts. By means of the *Sentences* a theologian could find out what any of a dozen or more of the most authoritative thinkers of the church had said on a topic. Then as now, a compendium could give the least erudite the appearance of great learning, and the more obscure the citation, the more likely it was that the person using it had never read the work from which it came.

But Lombard's *Sentences* had a more durable effect than providing classic sources for untrained theologians. The order of the work provided a structure, and often an impetus, for the researches of others. Commentaries on the *Sentences*

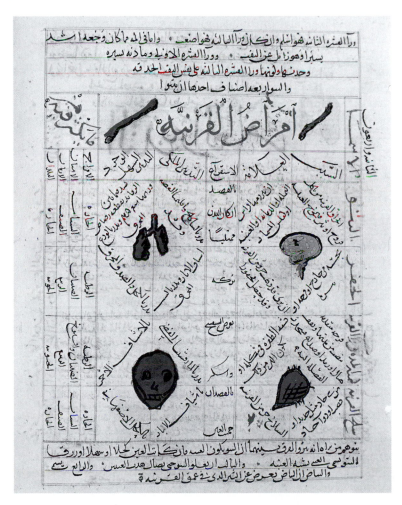

Avicenna (Ibn Sina), from *Canon of Medicine*, 14th century. Vellum. National Museum, Damascus.

Arabic science and philosophy were transmitters of the classical intellectual heritage. Philosophers such as Avicenna helped build the foundation of Christian Scholasticism.

became a genre in itself, embodying each commentator's efforts to reconcile differences, prioritize authorities, and create a coherent system of doctrine from the daunting patchwork of quotations. The writing of a *Sentences* commentary would become for centuries the test of a theologian's intellectual dexterity. Such works, which can run to several times the length of the *Sentences*, should best be seen as technical projects, as they have little stylistic or rhetorical appeal. Logical cogency and organizational clarity were the marks of a good *Sentences* commentary, which was invariably based on the belief that all the valid sources in the tradition could in fact be reconciled, and that the system of Christian theology could be intellectually mastered. Different as it was in style from Anselm's works, this genre continued the early Scholastic enterprise of seeking certainty in matters of belief, or of using understanding to corroborate faith.

During the twelfth century the path of European philosophy takes a number of turns. In the newly founded universities, such as those of Paris, Oxford, and Cambridge (all dating from the early-mid 1200s), Scholasticism formed part of the curriculum; meanwhile a monastic strain of this discipline flourished in the religious houses, especially in the Cistercian order.

Around the same time, extra-Christian influences began to appear in the shape of the philosophies of the Islamic thinkers Avicenna (Ibn Sina) (980–1037) and Averroes Ibn Rushd (1126–1198), and the Jewish theologian Maimonides (1135–1204). All three, and a number of their students, had encountered Greek thought and had struggled with the relation of philosophical reason to divine revelation. In many cases the questions they raised became important issues for Christian theologians, and a number of Scholastic arguments were adaptations of, or responses to, the work of these non-Christian thinkers.

Thirteenth-Century Scholasticism

The Scholastic tradition reached a high point in the middle of the thirteenth century, the era of Albertus Magnus (c. 1200–1280), Thomas Aquinas (1225–1274), and Bonaventure (1217–1274), among others. Theologians such as William of Auvergne (1180–after 1236) and Robert Grosseteste (c. 1170–1253) preceded them, and many followed them; but the mid-thirteenth century was a golden age for Scholastic thought. Two external factors contributed to the ascendancy of this tradition. The first of these was the establishment of universities throughout Europe, and the importance given to their theological faculties. The second was the formation of the mendicant orders (see Chapter 12), the Dominicans and Franciscans, whose friars occupied many of the theological faculties. As we shall see, rivalries between these two orders stimulated prolific and creative work among them.

The Influence of Aristotle

A third factor must be mentioned here, and that is the discovery and assimilation of classical thought, especially the works of Aristotle (384–322 B.C.E.). The Greek philosopher represented human rationality at its finest; his comprehensive system, which encompassed the natural sciences as well as ethics and political theory, provided a structure for the curriculum of the medieval university. Aristotle's emphasis on method and on METAPHYSICS, which deals with the fundamental nature of reality, stimulated Christian reflection on these concepts. For Aristotle, things that exist do so as the result of four causes: material (what something is made of), formal (what shape it is supposed to have), instrumental (what makes it), and final (what its ultimate purpose is).

Medieval Christian philosophy saw validity in this division of causes, but modified it by asserting God as the ultimate, or final, cause of all things—in short, their ultimate purpose. This means that whereas for Aristotle the final cause of a person is fulfillment of his or her individuality, for the Scholastics a person's ultimate end is God and union with God.

Aristotle posed a threat to the Scholastics, not because he was a pagan Greek but because his thought differed from that of Plato. Christian thought had absorbed some form of Platonic idealism, by way of the theology of Augustine (see

Universities in the Middle Ages

▲ University, with date of foundation
( ) date uncertain

Uppsala 1477
Aberdeen 1495
St Andrews 1411
Glasgow 1451
Copenhagen 1475
Rostock 1419   Griefswald 1456
Frankfurt-on-Oder 1496
Cambridge 1209–25
Oxford 1249
Cologne 1388
Leipzig 1409
Erfurt 1379
Louvain 1425
Mainz 1476
Prague 1347
Trier 1454
Wurzburg 1402
Cracow 1364
Caen 1432
Heidelberg 1385
Ingolstadt 1459
Vienna 1366
Orléans c.1236   Paris c. 1170
Tubingen 1476
Angers c.1250
Freiburg 1457
Piacenza 1248
Verona (1339)
Dole 1422
Parma 1412
Vicenza 1204
Poitiers 1431
Basle 1459
Treviso 1318
Grenoble 1339
Pavia 1361
Venice 1470
Bordeaux
Turin 1404
Padua 1222
Cahors 1332
Avignon 1303
Ferrara 1391
Toulouse 1229
Montpellier
Reggio 1188
Bologna (1369)
Genoa (1471)
Florence 1349
Salamanca 1218–19
Valladolid 1300
Perpignan 1360
Arezzo 1215
Coimbra 1308
Lerida 1300
Gerona (1446)
Pisa 1343
Rome
Alcale 1499
Barcelona 1450
Siena 1246
Naples 1224
Lisbon 1290
Salerno
Valencia 1500
Palma 1483
Seville (1254–60)
Catania 1444

0   400 km

0   200 miles

Chapter 2). It was evident from any reading of Augustine, or indeed of Anselm, that this world was the "shadow" realm and that the immaterial and eternal one was the "real" one. Such a metaphysics, known as IDEALISM for its claim that the world of abstractions (*idea* in Greek) is the real one, seems incompatible with Aristotelian thought, and it is worth remembering that Aristotle's system is in large measure a critique of his teacher Plato. Aristotle's thought, known as HYLOMORPHISM for its focus on matter (*hyle* in Greek) and form (*morphe*), recognizes the reality of the material world, but organizes and authenticates objects within it by specific terms, known as "categories." They include—to use Aristotle himself as an example—quality (philosopher), quantity (say, 5 feet 5 inches, 175 pounds), relation (student of Plato, teacher of Alexander the Great), location (Athens), time (morning), state (standing), and the like. There are ten categories, and everything in experience can be analyzed according to them.

Although Aristotle's categories are themselves abstractions, which contain sense objects (for example, Socrates and Aristotle both fall into the "philosopher" category), his system includes no ultimate realities or immaterial forms—only the tangible realm (except for a concept of deity as the ultimate "knower" of the material realm). Such a view would seem at odds with the otherworldliness of Christian Platonism—if we can use that term for Augustine's philosophy. The "Doctor of Grace," Augustine, and the "Master of Those who Know," Aristotle (as medieval scholars described these giants), could not remain mutually exclusive. The most urgent task for thirteenth-century philosophers was therefore to reconcile these two modes of interpreting experience.

Thomas Aquinas

For a resolution we can turn to St. Thomas Aquinas, an Italian Dominican friar and the most prominent Scholastic to wrestle with this problem. Others, such as the English Franciscan Roger Bacon (1214–1292) were better known in their own day, but their work has been eclipsed by that of Aquinas. Like Aristotle, he recognizes a difference between what is, which he calls ACTUALITY, and what is capable of developing from what is, which he calls POTENTIALITY. However, Aquinas attributes reality to potentialities, and in so doing subordinates the "what is" to the "what can be." Beyond this, however, he sees the plurality of things in the "is" world itself as being subordinate to a unity of all things in the "can be" world of potentiality. And this unity is God, the sole source of all matter and its ultimate end. The world, in brief, is like a giant jigsaw puzzle, each piece of which has its meaning only in reference to the whole. Now God may cosmically be putting all the "unfree" pieces—inanimate objects—back together; but humans, being free, have to will to be restored to the divine One, and moreover need a model to which to conform. The model, according to Aquinas, is Christ, and the means of achieving restoration is provided by the church.

This understanding of the relationship between God and the world, known as EXITUS-REDITUS (meaning "emanation and return"), comes closest to reconciling pagan thought (identifying the One was a dominant problem for Greek philosophers) and unifying it with Christian belief in God as the origin and end of all matter. Thus the "oneness" that was the absolute in classical Greek philosophy

BIOGRAPHICAL PROFILE

Thomas Aquinas (1225–1274)

Thomas Aquinas was born into a noble Italian family, probably in 1225, and spent his early years in the Benedictine monastery at Monte Cassino, where he learned the curriculum of the seven liberal arts. At fourteen he entered the University of Naples, where he was taught by Dominican friars who made a strong impression on him. Joining the Dominicans in 1244, Aquinas traveled to Paris and became a student of Albertus Magnus, whom he subsequently followed to Cologne when the Dominicans established the Order there. Albertus Magnus also introduced Aquinas to the works of Aristotle, many of whose writings were at that time being translated into Latin. The Greek philosopher would prove to be a major influence on Aquinas's thought.

Returning to Paris in 1252, Aquinas received a bachelor's and a master's degree in theology from the university, and then became one of their Dominican professors of theology. He continued studying Aristotle (and his leading Arabic commentators) and began writing a prodigious body of theological work. He also traveled around Italy from one Dominican house to another, including a term as Master of the Dominican Order in Rome. In 1268 he moved to Paris for the second time. In these final years of his life he wrote the *Summa contra Gentiles* (1259–64), and most of the *Summa Theologiae* (1266–73; it remained unfinished at his death), and a series of commentaries on Aristotle's works. He did this amid growing suspicion of Aristotelian thought, at least those parts interpreted by the Western followers of the Islamic philosopher Averroes. (A condemnation by the church in 1270 put Averroes and Aristotle under scrutiny; 219 statements by Aquinas himself would be condemned in 1277, after his death.) Undeterred, Aquinas continued his work on the *Summa Theologiae*, returned to Italy to manage the Dominican Order at Naples, and was on his way to a Council at Lyon when he died, in a Cistercian monastery, on March 7, 1274.

Aquinas's work is a comprehensive synthesis of the Christian (and neo-Platonist) theology of Augustine and the philosophy of Aristotle. Aquinas sees God as the "One" beyond the sensible world, from which everything within it emanated and toward which it is destined to return. Christ, for Aquinas, indicates the path back to that reintegration; therefore, the Catholic Church, as the extension of Christ, is the means by which God draws everything that is separate and finite back to its absolute source. Within this broad canvas are contained all individual lives, and Aquinas is concerned that the big picture coheres with the small. Thus no individual may do anything that diminishes the larger whole: commit murder, assassination, or suicide, for example. According to Aquinas, God has implanted in rational persons an innate sense of right and wrong, which guides actions even in the absence of "positive law," explicit commands issued by authorities. This view of a divine moral governance of all human society, known as Natural Law, would dominate Western religious thought into the twentieth century. Pluralistic constructions of culture and post-modern skepticism about all things divine and absolute have cast a shadow over this philosophy in recent decades.

Six centuries passed after Aquinas's death before his philosophy acquired its status as a model for thought in the Roman Catholic tradition. In the Encyclical *Aeterni Patris* of August 1879, Pope Leo XIII waxed poetical about the "Angelic Doctor," asserting that "Reason can scarcely rise higher, while faith could scarcely expect more or stronger aids from reason than those which she has already obtained through Thomas."

Giovanni Battista Bertucci the Elder, *St. Thomas Aquinas*, 1512–1516. Tempera on panel. Robert Lee Memorial Collection. Gift of Sarah C. Blaffer. Museum of Fine Arts, Houston, Texas.

was reconciled with the dynamic worldview of later Neoplatonism. The Thomistic view also very handily explained the role of Jesus Christ in this cosmological process, and identified the crucial role of the church as an agent in this process. The Greeks, according to Aquinas, understood the structure of the process, and both Plato and Aristotle made essential contributions to understanding it, but they fell short of grasping the complete truth because they lacked Christian revelation.

With his philosophical acumen and formidable industry (he produced more than 1,000 words every day of his adult life and could dictate to several scribes at once), Aquinas was responsible for producing many other doctrines, as well as a host of other religious works, including some hymns. He is the most prolific author in the Christian tradition. Unlike Peter Lombard and most of his other predecessors, Aquinas was a truly original thinker, one who sought to synthesize the Neoplatonism of St. Augustine with the newly discovered Aristotelianism taught in the schools. Since both Aristotle and Plato were pagan thinkers, Aquinas's work was a three-way synthesis, careful to preserve Aristotelian hylomorphism and Platonic idealism within a Christian framework, in which both the Greeks' reason and Christian revelation coincided—just as Anselm said they would, before the rediscovery of Aristotle would make such a synthesis much harder to achieve.

In the Thomistic view, humanity was compromised in the Fall, but not destroyed; thus grace was not a necessary and total replacement for a fatally flawed human nature, but an aid (a necessary one, to be sure) toward achieving salvation. Similarly, natural human goodness was such that God might regard the works of the baptized Christian with some, but not complete, favor; grace was the necessary supplementary quality that made one just, or righteous, before God. Thus revelation was an auxiliary to reason, and grace was an additional endowment—a *donum superadditum*—to nature or the natural faculties by which humanity operated. From these principles, as from others, Aquinas' thought

Who's Who

Christian Philosophers

Robert Grosseteste (c. 1170–1253) A theology lecturer at Oxford University, England, he became the first lector (reader) of a Franciscan community at Oxford and later Bishop of Lincoln. He was an important writer of theological, scientific, and philosophical works, and an outstanding Greek scholar.

William of Auvergne (1180–after 1236) A theologian and philosopher, Bishop of Paris, and influential at Louis IX's court, he supported a controversial group of orders known as the Mendicants, who operated outside the recognized clerical system. He adopted many of Aristotle's principles.

Roger Bacon (1214–1292) An English theologian and a scholar in many disciplines from languages to natural sciences. He entered the Franciscan Order and went on to write a major work on the state of Western education, known as the "Opus Maius."

St. Thomas Aquinas (1224/5–1274) A hugely influential Italian philosopher and theologian, and a major figure in the Dominican Order. His enormous output includes *Summa Theologiae*, which deals with man's relationship to God and Christ.

acquired a reputation for optimism and regularity that would come under attack in the fourteenth century and afterward.

So in the end, Aquinas and his fellow Scholastics would say, there *are* things we can understand, and we can understand them with the aid of those pagan thinkers who understood them best. And there are also things that we must simply believe, but these beliefs are not incompatible with understanding. On the contrary, they illuminate the understanding, providing insights and explanations that give certainty and completeness to our awareness of the world. Reason and revelation, understanding and belief, are, in Scholastic thought, mutually necessary and complementary.

In the end, Scholasticism cannot be regarded as a movement, for there were too many disputes about substantial points for that; nor can it be considered a method, since there were a number of methods at work within the broad span of Scholastic thought. Our safest way of characterizing Scholasticism is to identify it as the forms of systematic theology carried on in medieval schools and universities. In its academic setting, these forms of thought reflect one crucial assumption: confidence in the ability of reason to grasp divine truths as revealed in Scripture. Scholasticism sought to minimize the gap between reason and faith and to make knowledge of God something real and possible for rational persons. Over the course of developing this project, Scholastic thinkers expanded the scope of their inquiry to include the ways in which we know things, all human experience, and indeed the whole history of the created world. It may seem that this was an impossibly ambitious project, almost sacrilegious in its presumption. But at this time, the Middle Ages, the claims of reason were an affirmation of faith in the divine source of reason and of revelation, and in the order and power of God's providential activity. Scholasticism is thus just as much a religious phenomenon as it is a philosophical movement.

Key Terms

ACTUALITY What an entity is at any given point, regardless of its origin or destiny.

EXEGETICAL Based on interpretation of the biblical text; a theology closely bound to scriptural revelation.

EXITUS-REDITUS A cosmological structure in which the material world emanated from, and will return to, a single absolute unity.

HYLOMORPHISM A metaphysical doctrine in which entities are understood according to both matter and form.

IDEALISM A branch of metaphysics which holds that immaterial entities are the only real ones.

METAPHYSICS A branch of philosophy concerned with existence and the nature of reality.

ONTOLOGICAL Concerning arguments for the existence of God based on the nature and essence of things.

POTENTIALITY What any given entity is ultimately capable of being.

PROOFTEXT A biblical passage used in support of a given argument.

CHAPTER 11

The Church and the Law
The Investiture Controversy

In the preceding chapters we have seen the church developing its doctrines and practices, including various forms of worship and new ways of living a dedicated religious life. As the church progressed from being a loose collection of semi-autonomous communities in the first century to being a cohesive institution, it inevitably became increasingly concerned with law: both the secular laws of the world in which it existed, and the laws it formulated to govern itself.

The secular laws of the pagan Roman Empire were basically antagonistic to the church, which survived on the wrong side of the law for more than three centuries. From the reign of Constantine onward, the church enjoyed favored status under imperial law; and then, after the collapse of Roman government in western Europe, the Latin Church—now a reasonably well-structured organization—found itself the only ruling institution left standing. Thus it became, almost by default, a governing agent in society. With the revival of secular government and the continuing development of a strong papacy, the stage was set for frequent conflict between the spiritual and the temporal realms.

Internally, the church began to formulate a complex system of laws to govern itself. This lengthy process, involving numerous councils and the writings of countless theologians and jurists, led to the full flowering, in the eleventh and twelfth centuries, of the legal system known as CANON LAW, after one of the terms for an ecclesiastical ruling. It would be inaccurate to see this law merely as a substitute, created from necessity, for secular law, for it is grounded in theological principles and developed not only as a way of regulating moral behavior but as a way of integrating the public moral life with the exercise of piety. Canon law, especially when studied historically, will always seem remote and perhaps esoteric, the work of papal councilors and Scholastic specialists; but in fact its subject is the life of a Christian society, and it thus impinges on the lives of the medieval laity.

From its earliest times, the church has had the power to govern the lives of believers—as indeed most religions do, to a greater or lesser extent. The idea behind canon law may lie in the rabbinical authority exercised in the Judaism of

Jesus' time. In the New Testament, certain "assignments" that Jesus gives his apostles contain a sense that their power possesses a special, even unique, quality: think for example, of the power to cast out demons (Acts 5:16) and the power to bind and loose (Matthew 16:19). And in Paul's epistles we have instructions given to various communities, which presuppose Paul's power to guide, if not to rule, these churches. We have also seen how, in later centuries, the papacy came to dominate Christianity in the West.

Theoretical Foundations of Canon Law

Like any large organization, the Christian Church needed to be governed by a consistent set of rules, maintained and reinforced by recognized authorities. Some guidance was available in the New Testament books; some in other early writings; and some from the laws of the Roman Empire. Church law was therefore an eclectic blend of precepts, intended to ensure uniformity in organization and discipline from parish to parish. From early on it had two goals: providing pastoral guidance for the laity and establishing disciplinary procedures for the clergy.

The concept of law in the early church is as complex as the collections of laws themselves. Predictably, it has more in common with Roman legal thought than with the Jewish idea of revealed law and rabbinical authority (see Chapter 1). In the Latin world, a sense of right and wrong was instinctive in persons, so that certain behavior was natural in all: for example, honoring parents, obeying authority, or avoiding harm. There was no need to legislate such behavior, for it fell under what was known as the natural law. Natural law, being part of every person's constitution, is universal, not something that changes from culture to culture. On the other hand, each culture has certain practices and priorities that it wants to reinforce, and thus issues written law, also known as positive law, to make them explicit. Canon law is the positive law of Christian people, maintained, developed, and enforced by the clerical hierarchy.

Together with the expansion of papal powers, councils of bishops played a significant role in the evolution of canon law. The decrees of these assemblies, beginning with Nicaea in 325 (see Chapter 3), became the law of the church in both east and west; collections of papal decrees and conciliar documents represented the rulings in effect throughout Christendom. Councils, after all, represented the consensus of belief among the church hierarchy; they addressed difficult or urgent matters; and they were considered to be the embodiment of the Holy Spirit's guidance of the church. Councils, in short, were the points at which the church was most unified and thus most powerful.

In addition to these general, or ECUMENICAL (from the Greek *oikumené*, "the inhabited world") councils, regional councils were frequently held. Here, churchmen from a given territory met and issued decisions on matters of local concern. These rulings were binding for those bishops' jurisdictions, but not beyond. In Gaul, for example, more than fifty such councils were held between 500 and 700. And of course local bishops, as the ecclesiastical rulers of their dioceses, could issue their own decrees. All of these became the codified law—the statutes literally on the books—of the church, a record preserved and interpreted by clergy.

As we might expect, however, given the laborious way in which books were produced and copied in a manuscript culture, these collections of authoritative documents varied from region to region, and even from volume to volume. Manuscripts of these compilations survive today, providing valuable evidence of differences in practice and piety. Over time, some of these compilations took precedence over others, becoming standard sources on particular issues. All the while, a number of spurious decrees—documents falsely attributed to certain authors or councils—began entering these collections. In an age in which it was difficult to discern authentic from false, the conflicts among codes created widespread confusion and disagreement. It is not surprising, then, to see canon law becoming one of the more active, and intellectually demanding, pursuits of the Middle Ages.

The Annals of Fulda

The monastery at Fulda was a bastion of Roman Christianity and a center of Carolingian culture; its monks became chroniclers of their empire's history. Here we see a military expedition being planned, coupled with a disciplinary case concerning a heretical priest.

Lothar and Louis had a meeting in the castle of Koblenz in February. It was rumoured that Lothar's party was mainly concerned to see that Louis should put aside his friendship with Charles and ally himself with Lothar as their brotherhood demanded. Louis, however, remembering the treaty which he had long ago made with Charles and confirmed by an oath in God's name, cleverly avoided their skilled persuasion, and returned to his own kingdom. Around the middle of August he sent an expedition under his son Louis against the Bohemians, who were planning rebellion, and crushed them, forcing them to send ambassadors to sue for peace and to give hostages. Around October 1 he held a general assembly at Mainz, where he received, heard and dismissed ambassadors from his brothers and from the Northmen and Slavs. He also reconciled the men of [Arch]bishop Hrabanus [of Mainz], who had been publicly proved to have conspired against their lord, to him. He sent his own ambassadors to his brother Lothar in Thionville, where he was holding an assembly, to intercede for Gislebert, who had returned to his allegiance that same year.

   A certain priest called Gottschalk, who held wicked opinions about divine predestination, namely that the good were predestined by God to life and the evil to eternal death, was condemned at an episcopal synod, reasonably as it seemed to many. He was sent to Hincmar, his own bishop, at Rheims, but first took an oath that he would never return to the kingdom of Louis.

(From *The Annals of Fulda*, trans. Timothy Reuter. Manchester: Manchester University Press, 1992.)

The earliest efforts to systematize the various codes and regulations came around 600 in the work of Isidore of Seville (c. 560–636), an organizer and transmitter of an extraordinary range of knowledge, best known for an encyclopedic work in twenty volumes titled *Etymologies*. In addition to preserving the contents of ancient documents (some of which have since been lost) concerning the governance of the church, Isidore's compendium contained fragments from Roman law, the system that had developed over the centuries as Rome evolved from a monarchy (under Etruscan rule) to a republic and then to an empire. As the

Scenes from the Life of St. Isidore, 15th century. Vellum. Musée Condé, Chantilly, France.

Isidore's compilations and treatises served as sources and models for scholars in the Renaissance.

Catholic Church began, both actively and passively, to assume the functions of the defunct empire, the legal system that pagan Rome had left behind became a valuable inheritance for the Roman Church. The transition was aided by the fact that Roman law had received its final systematized form under the rule, and according to the commands, of Christian emperors, heirs of Constantine who wished to combine the pagan civilization with Christian beliefs. Theodosius I (347–395), who became co-emperor in the East in 379 and was converted to Christianity the following year, had seen the Roman Empire as the model on which Christian orthodoxy could be patterned. He matched his actions to his theory, issuing a series of edicts which imposed increasingly tight restraints on religious belief and practice; in 391 Christianity became the official religion of the empire, with a corresponding prohibition of all other beliefs. The restrictions culminated in the *Codex Theodosianus* of 438, a compilation of sixty-eight imperial edicts against heresy. All of this became material for the compilations and codifications of Isidore and his successors.

Hence, the initial task of creating canon law was largely one of adapting it from imperial sources; and this meant that much of the original "Roman" material remained in place as church law. With so much of the basic material already on hand, it was possible to prepare comprehensive treatises fairly early. The ninth century was a time of rich production in lawmaking, as we might expect with the rise of the Carolingian dynasty (see Chapter 9). One of the leading figures during this period was Hrabanus Maurus (780–856) the Abbot of Fulda and later Archbishop of Mainz, who, around 819, composed a treatise, in both a long and a short version, on priests' duties; it remained influential for centuries.

The Holy Roman Empire and the Church

In the Edict of Milan (313) Constantine gave lawmaking powers to the church, setting it higher in status than the secular state. In the Latin world, theologians such as St. Augustine (see Chapter 2) asserted the superiority of the heavenly "city of God" over the "human city," the state or earthly civilization, and supported this division with substantial philosophical arguments. On the basis of these arguments and the importance of Rome in the culture of late antiquity, the papacy accumulated more and more power over the Latin Church, aided by the claims to authority made by Pope Leo I (see Chapter 5). Thus when Pope Gelasius I (r. 492–496), in one of his many writings on the authority of the papacy, defined the secular and sacred realms as independent sovereign powers, he was consolidating opinions already current rather than stating a new doctrine. The novelty lay in identifying the Bishop of Rome as the "monarch" with sacred power, a ruler with influence equal to the secular emperor.

The promising partnership between Charlemagne's empire and the papacy (see Chapter 9) was short-lived. The Carolingian Empire gradually disintegrated after Charlemagne's death in 814, but it was reconstituted a century and a half later by Otto I (r. 962–973), the first of a series of Saxon rulers of that name, who was crowned emperor in 962. The name "Holy Roman Empire" was not applied to these domains (which, at their greatest extent, included most of central Europe, the Low Countries, eastern France, and northern Italy) until the middle of the thirteenth century.

Always an unwieldy political entity, the empire continually struggled to retain or regain control over its constituent states, while at the same time engaging in a long-running power struggle with the papacy. Establishing the boundaries of imperial and papal authority within the empire kept jurists on both sides constantly employed; and each disruption of the equilibrium brought a new wave of juristic writing. Within the empire, the church developed with the patronage of the local overlords, but nevertheless it remained bound to obey Rome. To which of these two, the local secular rulers or the Roman episcopacy, did control of the church actually fall? Those who saw the local rulers as sovereigns over the churches in their territories were reminded by the pope of western Christianity's ties to Rome as the anchor and reference point for all religious matters. Those who claimed that Rome alone should exercise sovereignty over churches could not explain away the fact that it was the local rulers who built, cared for, and in many cases sustained the churches—functions that Rome, for the most part, had never been expected to fill. This conflict of jurisdictions was one of the earliest problems that ecclesiastical jurists had to face. Despite their efforts, this issue continued to create problems throughout the medieval period—and beyond. (Nor, of course, was the church-versus-state problem confined to the empire; in one form or another it caused friction in other countries and would do so for centuries to come.)

Proprietary versus Imperial Churches

An attempt was made to solve this problem by defining different forms of church. In one category was the *Eigenkirche*, or "proprietary church," an institution of the FEUDAL SYSTEM. The *Eigenkirche* was the "family parish" of a landowning sovereign: a church built by the family and maintained physically by that family, which served the feudal lord, his household, and his subjects. Quite obviously, the family's investment in the local church under such an arrangement was assumed by them to grant them control over other churchly matters as well. In particular, they reasoned that they should have a say in the appointment of its clergy—whose salary, after all, they paid.

In a different category was the *Reichskirche*, or "imperial church," an institution that, as the name indicates, was answerable to the emperor. A number of parishes and monasteries had been founded by the secular powers. Their bishops and abbots saw themselves as answerable to those powers, and especially to the emperor, as the supreme secular authority, rather than directly to the pope. Because the empire had itself been founded by the pope, this did not represent a conflict of loyalty. Instead it revealed an ordering of powers that gave the empire a high degree of control over church affairs

The early decades of the Carolingian Empire had seen a number of such churches instituted by imperial authority. The eastward expansion of the empire under the Carolingians was accompanied by a parallel expansion of the Latin Church, which made converts among the Carolingians' new subjects. In the following century, Emperor Otto I ("the Great"; r. 962–973) founded a number of new bishoprics in eastern lands, including those at Brandenburg (948), Magdeburg (968), and Prague (973). These bishoprics served as bases for missions among the Slavic peoples, but they were all ruled from the archbishop's see at Mainz.

The different natures and loyalties of these churches came into sharpest conflict whenever the time was ripe to appoint new clergy. The secular patrons of the proprietary *Eigenkirche* parishes insisted that their custody of a church included a say in the selection of its clergy, despite their own personal subordination, as laity, to the church. The bishops who presided over the imperial *Reichskirche* parishes, recognizing that their service was ultimately sacred rather than secular, held that the theoretical superiority of the clergy over the laity superseded the rights of secular patrons and dictated that the hierarchy alone had sole power to appoint—and dismiss—local clergy. Such a deadlock could not easily be resolved; indeed, it would lead to the INVESTITURE CONTROVERSY of the eleventh century.

The Investiture Controversy

A turning point in the history of the empire and the church alike, the investiture controversy demonstrated the extent to which events in one affected the course of the other. The second half of the eleventh century saw upheavals in the politics of ecclesiastical appointments, beginning, as they often do, with minor incidents, and ending with redefinitions of jurisdictions.

The minor incident that set off the controversy was the appointment, in 1075, by Emperor Henry IV (1050–1106; r. 1056 [with regent until 1070]–1106) of a German archbishop to the bishopric of Milan, a move that would give the German cleric control over (and income from) a diocese he might never have visited. Such an appointment might have caused little stir if the reigning pope at the time had not been Gregory VII (c. 1020–1085; r. 1073–1085). Gregory was a monk (he may have spent some time at Cluny; see Chapter 7) and had been part of a reform-oriented papal hierarchy since the late 1040s. In March 1075 Gregory set out certain assertions about the sanctity and supremacy of the papacy, among them the right to depose princes, both "temporal" and "spiritual," that is, secular princes and bishops alike. The reason for such assertions of power was to curb corruption within the church, a state that Gregory attributed directly to the practice of LAY INVESTITURE, or the appointment by laity (the feudal nobility) of clergy (including bishops). There had been a number of abuses in this area, particularly NEPOTISM, the appointment of relatives, and SIMONY, the sale of church offices. By reclaiming the papacy's right to appoint bishops, Gregory hoped to end these practices, or keep them within church circles; and by asserting the right to depose princes, he wanted to show that the secular realm had no sovereignty in church matters. The system of patronage and the *Eigenkirche* seemed to have been brought to an end.

Letter from Gregory VII to the Bishop of Metz, 1081

The struggle with Henry IV was going against Gregory at this time. His deposition of Henry had provoked sympathy for the emperor, and at councils at Mainz and Brixen, called by Henry, the pope was declared deposed. This letter to Bishop Hermann is the fullest expression of the pope's point of view.

Bishop Gregory, servant of the servants of God, to his beloved brother in Christ, Hermann bishop of Metz, greeting and apostolic benediction. …

Thy request, indeed, to be aided, as it were, by our writings and fortified against the madness of those who babble forth with impious tongue that the authority of the holy and apostolic see had no authority to excommunicate Henry—a man who despises the Christian law; a destroyer of the churches and of the empire; a patron and companion of heretics—or to absolve anyone from the oath of fealty to him, seems to us to be hardly necessary when so many and such absolutely decisive warrants are to be found in the pages of Holy Scripture. Nor do we believe, indeed, that those who (heaping up for themselves damnation) impudently detract from the truth and contradict it have added these assertions to the audacity of their defense so much from ignorance as from a certain madness.

For, to cite a few passages from among many, who does not know the words of our Lord and Saviour Jesus Christ who says, in the gospel: "Thou art Peter and upon this rock will I build my church, and the gates of hell shall not prevail against it; and I will give unto thee the keys of the kingdom of Heaven; and whatsoever thou shalt bind upon earth shall be bound also in Heaven, and whatsoever thou shalt loose upon earth shall be loosed also in Heaven"? Are kings excepted here? Or are they not included among the sheep which the Son of God committed to St. Peter? Who, I ask, in view of this universal concession of the power of binding and loosing, can think that he is withdrawn from the authority of St. Peter, unless, perhaps, that unhappy man who is unwilling to bear the yoke of the Lord and subjects himself to the burden of the devil, refusing to be among the number of Christ's sheep? It will help him little to his wretched liberty that he shake from his proud neck the divinely granted power of Peter. For the more anyone, through pride, refuses to bear it, the more heavily shall it press upon him unto damnation at the judgment.

(Gregory VII's Letter to the Bishop of Metz, in Henry Bettenson, ed., *Documents of the Christian Tradition*. New York and London: Oxford University Press, 1947.)

However, Henry IV had just as strong a will as Gregory did; moreover, since lay investiture had been practiced since Carolingian times, he had centuries of precedent on his side. Unwilling to yield to Gregory, Henry accused the pope of abusing church officials; of usurping the emperor's legitimate duties; and of passing judgment over the emperor, who was as divinely anointed (in Henry's view) as Gregory thought himself to be. In a 1076 letter to Gregory, Henry, with the German bishops on his side, declared the pope deposed and demanded that he descend from his throne, so as to allow it to be occupied by a pope who could restore purity and humility to the holy office.

Gregory was the wrong pope to treat in such a manner, and he countered immediately—by deposing Henry, releasing all Christians (the pope's "subjects," in a spiritual sense at least) from obedience to him, and forbidding anyone (including bishops) to serve him as king. Most seriously (from the point of view of a believing Christian), he excommunicated Henry. This meant that Henry would die without the benefit of the sacraments and that his subjects would no longer be under the sovereignty of a Christian ruler. The papal claim to be able to depose an emperor was only a year old, and it rested on shaky historical grounds; the other rights, apart from excommunication, seemed to have been made up on the spot, or so it appears in hindsight. At the time it was enough to intimidate Henry, who capitulated in January 1077 by appearing at Gregory's estate at Canossa, in northern Italy, dressed like a penitent sinner and standing barefoot in the snow. Gregory was suitably appeased, granted Henry absolution (thus returning him to the church), and declared him restored to power.

However, the drama was just starting, for as soon as Henry returned from Canossa he was plunged into war with his "successor," Rudolf Duke of Swabia, who had been made king after Henry's deposition by the pope. As civil war raged north of the Alps, the pope tried to mediate, finally in 1080 calling an assembly to resolve the dispute and decide on a ruler. Henry, however, tried to prevent the conference from taking place, and was once again deposed and excommunicated. As the deposition was valid, Rudolf had no challenger in Henry and thus became the rightful emperor. Henry went down swinging, calling an assembly of his "own" bishops to depose Gregory as pope and appoint his successor, the "antipope" (a rival to the legitimate pope), Clement III (r. 1080). This action had its effect, for thirteen cardinals and a number of other supporters withdrew their allegiance from Gregory. (See "Letter from Gregory VII to the Bishop of Metz, 1081.") Henry continued his campaign against Gregory with military force, taking control of Rome in March 1084 and installing Clement as the true Pope (1084–1100). Gregory, who had troops on his side as well, was forced into exile in Salerno; he died a year later, professing his love for justice and hatred of iniquity. He was later canonized.

The King Begs the Abbot and Implores Mathilde, from the *Vita Mathilde des Donizo,* 1114. Manuscript illumination.

Henry IV, as guest in 1077 of the margravine Mathilde of Tuszien and under the guidance of the local abbot, gains readmittance to the church of Pope Gregory VII.

The conflict between empire and papacy had repercussions for decades, with treatises appearing in support of each side, and clergy being forced into difficult choices of loyalty and obligation. In 1100–1107 a new investiture controversy broke out in England; and Emperor Henry's successor, Henry V (1081–1125; r. 1106–1125), was excommunicated by a French synod in 1111. Controversy over episcopal appointments within the Holy Roman Empire came to an end only with the Concordat of Worms in 1122.

Compilations and Systems of Canon Law

In the end it was canon law that clarified the boundaries of sacred and secular and identified the jurisdiction of each power. The Gregorian Reform, the movement begun with Gregory VII, required, above all, clarification and codification. As early as 1076 the papacy began to compile laws and privileges relating to the clergy, some of which were invoked in the pope's dealings with Henry. By 1085 a *Collection of Four Books* was available to serve as the legal manual for the papal CURIA (governing body) and its satellite offices. And at a time when secular governments had little but customary law (law established through practice) to guide them, the efforts of church jurists to determine the duties of the state seemed wonderfully helpful. The disadvantage of this arrangement, of course, was that the secular state had little to contribute to the process. As a result, the state was not the governing agency in society, but part of the governed body: this was hardly the ideal situation for secular rulers.

Canon law reached a new level of importance in the wake of the Gregorian Reform. Pope Urban II (1042–1099; r. 1088–1099) was an unwearying compiler of his predecessors' writings, second only to Ivo (or Yves) of Chartres (c. 1040–1116), a bishop and canon jurist, whose *Tripartite Collection* (c. 1095) became the most comprehensive corpus of canon law; this was a collection of precepts divided into three parts and destined to be influential in the later development of the Christian tradition. The first of the three parts contains more than six hundred and fifty papal documents, beginning with St. Clement (r. c. 92–c.101), the third successor of St. Peter, and ending with Urban II, then still ruling. It also contained almost eight hundred conciliar documents from Greek, African, and other councils, as well as extensive passages from the Greek fathers, then largely unknown because of linguistic barriers. The second part of Ivo's great work is known as the *Decretum*, a massive collection of fragments of legal rulings and discussion, divided into seventeen books. The third part, the *Panormia*, is divided into eight books and serves as a practical manual for clergy. Though unwieldy and difficult to use, Ivo's collection of documents and fragments was nevertheless the most complete effort yet to collect everything bearing on church authority.

The most enduring effort to systematize a millennium's worth of law was the work of a theologian and canon jurist named Gratian (d. c. 1160), whose *Harmony of Discordant Canons* (c. 1140) aimed to resolve the discrepancies in all the surviving legal documents and thus to arrive at unambiguous law. A work of impressive precision, the *Decretum Gratiani* (as it came to be called) begins its discussion of an issue with a "dictum," or explanation of the differences between the texts pertinent to a problem; it proceeds with citations of *auctoritates*, or passages in support of his own reading of the pertinent law; discusses the limits of applicability; and relates each topic with others in the collection. The student of Gratian's work is exposed, in a rather dizzying kaleidoscope of citations, to Roman law, the Bible, the church fathers, and official rulings by popes and councils throughout the ages. Indeed, the peripheral erudition it contained may have given the *Decretum* an appeal quite apart from its utility as a tool for understanding canon law. Although it never received official papal recognition as an authoritative code of law, it was taught and commented upon throughout the university world, and its influence may even be detected in the method of scholastic theology.

The Eastern Orthodox Church

In terms of cultural richness and cohesiveness, the Eastern tradition offers an instructive counterpart to the Latin West. A longstanding philosophical tradition in the West supported the New Testament doctrine of Christ as the *logos*, or word, of God; and the prevalence of philosophical schools and religious sects in the West offered settings in which Christian communities could emerge, thrive, and spread the word. The word spread eastwards. So did the Greek version of the Bible, both in the Septuagint (the Greek translation of the Hebrew Bible) and the New Testament, and it gave the early church a more "domestic" character than a Latin tradition that was linguistically as well as culturally alien. Thus even though the biblical narrative appeared to be another people's story, it was accessible in the Greeks' own idiom; and the Christian belief that the new covenant included gentiles as well as Jews was understood as an official welcome to the Greeks.

Eastern Christianity came into its own in the fourth century (as we saw in Chapter 3). During the reign of Constantine and owing to the Council of Nicaea (in 325), Christianity had become the dominant culture in the Greek-speaking world. Its capital, Byzantium, was renamed Constantinople (literally "Constantine's city") and became, actually and symbolically, the seat of a new government. It was called the "second Rome," the Christian successor to the ancient (and still pagan) Italian city; and like the first Rome in its golden age, Constantinople would become the center of a wide-ranging cultural world. The principal difference between it and first-century Rome was that Byzantine culture would be Christian rather than pagan.

A variety of factors account for the religious and cultural renaissance that emerged in Byzantium. First, the Byzantine world was more unified than the West, not having undergone centuries of expansion and colonization. Thus its adaptation to Christian culture was much more uniform compared with what had occurred in the Latin world. Second, a more introspective and intellectual culture dominated in the Greek world, which both allowed theologians to construct a profound system of beliefs and primed the general population to understand and take them seriously. Contemporary accounts describe the agitation of ordinary persons over the wording of certain parts of the Creed: one could hardly buy food or go to the barber without discussing theology. Although surely exaggerated, the reports of such an engagement with religious ideas bear within them some kernel of truth.

Due to its strong secular government, the Orthodox Church was able to focus more on theological matters than civic and organizational ones. The church was ruled by bishops and the deliberative body was the council. From the Council of Nicaea onward, assemblies of religious leaders dictated the teachings and proclamations of the Orthodox Church. Some of them were quite controversial. For example, in the eighth century the Iconoclastic Controversy (see Chapter 11) consumed the attention of theologians and created a schism between Western and Eastern Churches. In 787 the Seventh Ecumenical Council met again at Nicaea and declared that icons were to be revered with the devotion that was owed to crucifixes and the Gospel itself. (However, in Orthodox theology icons were not themselves worshiped; instead they were revered or venerated, in much the same way as Western saints were.) Some theologians within the Eastern Church, and many in the West, considered that such visual representations of the Divine constituted "idolatry" rather than authentic Christian piety, and they attacked the practice. But the support of secular rulers, particularly the Empresses Irene and Theodora, ensured that by 843 the veneration of icons would remain a permanent and distinctive practice within the Orthodox Church.

In an unstable world in which only the intangible forces of divinity promised any security, and in an environment in which social confusion threated peaceful existence even at the family level, the law of the church offered order and stability. The uniform governing of society by a church hierarchy that claimed sovereignty over spiritual and material realms alike probably gave much needed coherence to an otherwise disorganized world. The church became the successor to the collapsed Roman Empire, and in turn helped establish a medieval monarchy that was a self-consciously Christian restoration of that empire. The resulting sense of God being in control of human history led persons to vocations either within the church hierarchy or in lives of prayer and withdrawal from the world. Let us now turn to some of these forms of religious life.

Key Terms

CANON LAW The system of laws and procedures used by the church in the West.

CURIA Literally, the "court," and particularly the hierarchy closest to the papacy.

ECUMENICAL Literally, universal; specifically, concerning the shared beliefs of Christians throughout the inhabited world.

FEUDAL SYSTEM A medieval social and economic structure that granted power to a small number of landowners and subjugated a large population of peasants.

INVESTITURE CONTROVERSY A crisis over the ability of secular nobles, as opposed to the papacy, to appoint clergy—especially bishops—in their territories.

LAY INVESTITURE The appointment ("investiture") of bishops by the secular nobility, considered by the papacy a usurpation of papal jurisdiction.

NEPOTISM The placement, usually by secular nobility, of relatives in positions of power within the church.

SIMONY The purchase and sale of church appointments.

The Mendicant Orders and Lay Movements
New Forms of Religious Life

By the beginning of the thirteenth century, western and central Europe had undergone a great transformation from an almost entirely agrarian society, in which most people lived at a subsistence level, to a thriving civilization, with numerous towns and cities, splendid cathedrals and growing universities, guilds of craftsmen and merchants, and a busy international trade. Inevitably, all these developments impinged upon the church and upon the Christian life of both laity and clergy. Perhaps the most noteworthy outcome of the transformation of Europe, within a specifically Christian context, was the rise of the mendicant religious orders: the Franciscans and the Dominicans, followed in later years by others such as the Carmelites.

These orders resembled the monastic communities (notably the Benedictines and Cistercians) in several respects: their choice of the spiritual over the worldly life, and their vows of poverty, chastity, and obedience. They differed from the monastic orders primarily in that they did most of their work out in the secular world and were quite literally dependent for their livelihood on donations from the laity—hence the name "mendicant" (from the Latin *mendicare,* "to beg"). The mendicants did not have property of their own, like the laity, nor did their orders have endowments of land that allowed for the fairly comfortable lives of monks in old and well-established houses. Because they were not attached to monastic foundations, but lived among the people in fairly well-populated areas, the mendicants did not run the risk of accumulating property, either individually or collectively.

Nor were the mendicants priests, in the same sense as the members of the SECULAR CLERGY, such as parish priests. They were called "friar" (from the Latin *frater,* "brother"), rather than "father": peers rather than superiors. The hierarchical organization that held the secular world as subordinate posed no problem for them, as it allowed—indeed forced—them to live humbly among their secular neighbors. Thus this form of religious life started out as a type distinct from both monasticism and the secular clergy.

The names for the orders themselves continue to reflect a complexity behind a seemingly simple appearance. Franciscans are the order founded by St. Francis of

Giotto di Bondone, *St. Francis Preaching to the Birds*, 1296–1297. San Francesco Upper Church, Assisi. Fresco.

Nature for Francis was an abundant source of knowledge about divine goodness; he stood out among his contemporaries for his reverence for all life.

Assisi (c. 1181–1226), the son of a prosperous Italian merchant, who gave up all he had to help the poor; Dominicans are named after St. Dominic, or Domingo de Guzmán (c. 1172–1221), a Spanish scholar and priest, who sold all he had, even his books, to aid the poor. The formal name for the Franciscans is the Order of Friars Minor (the abbreviation "O.F.M." appears after their individual names), meaning literally the "little brothers" who are bound by service to others and obedience to the pope and the head of the order. And the Dominicans are known formally as the Order of Preachers (or "O.P."), and are thus explicitly dedicated to pastoral care mainly through preaching.

Although poverty and preaching have always been elements of the religious life, they took on special importance in the thirteenth century in the context of the aforementioned changes in political and economic life. The previous century had seen a shift in the population away from the countryside and toward towns and cities, which in turn became influential trading centers with laws and privileges of their own. An essential element in this complex process was the "reinvention" of money, or the replacement of a barter economy with a monetary one. An agrarian economy can operate on a barter system; the farmer who grows wheat can do business in kind with the one who raises cattle, provided they can agree on an appropriate exchange. In a town, merchants conduct business with traders from farther away, and in quantities that make barter impractical. Thus money—silver and gold—becomes the medium for exchange. Coin is not only more portable than any commodity that it may represent; it is also more durable, as it does not rot, smell, get eaten by pests, or burn. As a result, it becomes easy—in theory at least—to accumulate more than one needs. The reinvention of money (it had been used in antiquity, mostly in the trading cities) brought with it a materialism that had not been seen since the time of the Roman Empire.

The new urban environment in which many Christians lived also presented spiritual challenges. A denser population brought closer proximity to the liturgy and sacraments, since the local church would be within easy walking distance. But people engaged in commerce, or even a craft, would be tempted to practice a particular craft beyond a necessary level, in order to make more money. So, paradoxically, while townspeople lived closer physically to the spiritual realm, they were increasingly seduced by the material one. The more demanding and exciting the physical world became, the less directed

people's energies were to the eternal. A special kind of missionary movement was needed to keep the heavenly and earthly in their earlier relationship, with the earthly serving the heavenly. The mendicants—each order in its own way—took on this difficult task.

In their poverty, the Franciscans served as living antitheses to the greedy merchants who apparently cared only about accumulating as much money as possible. The Dominicans supplemented that lesson with structured sermons on the nature of creation and the world to come, demonstrating the transitoriness of this life and the value of the next. Each of these orders assumed to some degree the functions of the other. The Franciscans also preached and taught; the Dominicans were also dedicated to a life of poverty. Hence the "missionary" work of the mendicants had two dimensions: one practical, exemplified mainly by the Franciscans, and one intellectual, exemplified mainly by the Dominicans.

St. Francis and St. Dominic

Some of the differences between the two orders go back to Francis and Dominic themselves. It is not far-fetched to see each order as the continuing embodiment of the virtues peculiar to its founder, and the perpetuation of their names in the informal names of the orders somewhat reflects this personal element. But the legacy of these two saints goes far deeper; they are seen, even today, as special instruments of divine work in the world.

We see one ideal in the life of St. Francis, who was raised in the comfortable surroundings of the merchant class we have just described. His life was a carefree one until he experienced warfare and illness. The turning point in his life, however, came one day when he was praying in the church of St. Damian, near Assisi, and is said to have heard Christ asking him to repair his "falling house." Thinking that Jesus was referring to that particular church building, Francis sold some of his father's textiles for its restoration. Alienated from his father for this well-intentioned theft, Francis left home. He embraced "Lady Poverty" as his "bride" and lived as her "husband." (He was never ordained as a priest.) He called the birds and other animals his brothers and sisters. In 1210 Pope Innocent III (1160–1216; r. 1198–1216) granted him and eleven companions (note the parallel with the Twelve Apostles) permission to be wandering lowly preachers. Their message was one of penance and hope in salvation. Like the apostolic community of the first century C.E., these friars initially functioned without an organization or headquarters, and subsisted instead only in some living quarters attached to local churches. A rule, like that of the Benedictines, but stressing humility and poverty, was already in its second version by 1221, and soon the order became so numerous that it needed to be organized into "provinces."

The culmination of Francis's spiritual life, for himself and certainly for his followers, was his STIGMATIZATION in 1224. According to legend, in the course of his prayers one day, five wounds appeared on his body: on his hands, feet, and abdomen. These wounds, known as STIGMATA, were seen as matching the wounds Christ endured during the crucifixion, and served as a sign that Francis had himself achieved oneness with God. (See "The Epiphany of St. Francis.") These were not innocuous marks. On the contrary, they apparently caused genuine suffering, and thus allowed Francis to experience the pains of martyrdom; more-over, these wounds remained with him for the last two years of his life. Emulating Christ's submission to his own death, Francis calmly awaited the arrival of "Sister Death," who visited him in 1226. That Francis was viewed as uniquely

---

The Epiphany of St. Francis

All hagiographies are about saints, but few are also by them. Francis of Assisi and his Order were fortunate in having his life composed by St. Bonaventure, a major theologian and himself a Superior of the Franciscans. Here we observe Francis' conversion to a life of poverty.

God afflicted his body with a prolonged illness in order to prepare his soul for the anointing of the Holy Spirit. After his strength was restored, when he had dressed as usual in his fine clothes, he met a certain knight who was of noble birth, but poor and badly clothed. Moved to compassion for his poverty, Francis took off his own garments and clothed the man on the spot. At one and the same time he ful-filled the two-fold duty of covering over the embarrassment of a noble knight and relieving the poverty of a poor man.

The following night, when he had fallen asleep, God in his goodness showed him a large and splendid palace full of military weapons emblazoned with the insignia of Christ's cross. Thus God vividly indicated that the compassion he had exhibited toward the poor knight for love of the supreme King would be repaid with an incomparable reward. And so when Francis asked to whom these belonged, he received an answer from heaven that all these things were for him and his knights. When he awoke in the morning, he judged the strange vision to be an indication that he would have great prosperity; for he had no experience in interpreting divine mysteries nor did he know how to pass through visible images to grasp the invisible truth beyond. Therefore, still ignorant of God's plan, he decided to join a certain count in Apulia, hoping in his service to obtain the glory of knighthood, as his vision seemed to foretell. ...

From that time on he clothed himself with a spirit of poverty, a sense of humil-ity and a feeling of intimate devotion. Formerly he used to be horrified not only by close dealing with lepers but by their very sight, even from a distance; but now he rendered humble service to the lepers with human concern and devoted kindness in order that he might completely despise himself, because of Christ crucified, who according to the text of the prophet was despised *as a leper* (Isa. 53: 3). He visited their houses frequently, generously distributed alms to them and with great compassion kissed their hands and their mouths.

To beggars he wished to give not only his possessions but his very self. At times he took off his clothes, at times unstitched them, at times ripped them in pieces, in order to give them to beggars, when he had nothing else at hand. He came to the assistance of poor priests, reverently and devoutly, especially in adorning the altar. In this way he became a participator in the divine worship, while supplying the needs of its celebrants. During this period of time he made a pilgrimage to the shrine of St. Peter, where he saw a large number of the poor before the entrance of the church. Led partly by the sweetness of his devotion, partly by the love of poverty, he gave his own clothes to one of the neediest among them. Then he dressed in the poor man's rags and spent that day in the midst of the poor with an unaccustomed joy of spirit. This he did in order to spurn worldly glory and, by ascending in stages, to arrive at the perfection of the Gospel.

(From St. Bonaventure, *The Life of St. Francis*, trans. Ewert Cousins. New York: Paulist Press, 1978.)

gifted with divine favor is indicated by the fact that he was canonized only two years later.

The story of St. Dominic's life includes no dramatic conversion episode, but like that of Francis's life, it recounts the emergence, in one man, of a strong sense of purpose in a changing world. As a young man, ordained as a cathedral canon (a member of its regular staff), he accompanied his bishop on a trip to France to investigate a sect of heretics, the Albigensians. Living simply and in poverty, Dominic and Diego, his bishop, entered into serious and searching dialogue with the Albigensians, investigating and debating points of doctrine with a thoroughness that other church officials did not display. The Albigensians proved stubborn adversaries; a few years later in 1207, they murdered the papal legate, or emissary, Pierre de Castelnau. Shortly afterward, Innocent III ordered a military campaign against the sect. Only after five years of bloodshed were the Albigensians subdued. During this time, however, Dominic had recruited a few followers; and with their help he made peaceful conquests among the Albigensians, converting many of them with reasoned argument. Clearly, Dominic's methods were more effective than papal militarism.

By now, Dominic had conceived the plan of forming an order of preachers and teachers, and in 1216 this plan received papal approval. The few dozen new Dominicans were dispersed toward the larger cities, especially those with universities—Paris, Bologna, and Oxford among them. There they studied, taught (and thus attracted students who could join them in their work), and preached to the townspeople.

Mindful of the circumstances that had brought their order into being, the Dominicans became guardians of orthodoxy and correspondingly vigilant opponents of heresy—not only in the universities but also through the Inquisition. This institution, which had been established in the late twelfth century, was the

---

The Canticle of Exhortation to St. Clare

The Franciscan tradition was notable from its very beginnings for giving a place to women. Francis charged his follower, Clare of Assisi, with a special religious mission, setting out his precepts in poetic form.

Listen, little poor ones called by the Lord,
   who have come together from many parts and provinces:
Live always in truth,
   that you may die in obedience.
Do not look at the life outside,
   for that of the Spirit is better.
I beg you through great love,
   to use with discretion
   the alms which the Lord gives you.
Those who are weighed down by sickness
   and the others who are wearied because of them,
   all of you: bear it in peace.
For you will sell this fatigue at a very high price
   and each one [of you] will be crowned queen
   in heaven with the Virgin Mary.

(From *Francis and Clare: The Complete Works*, trans. Regis J. Armstrong and Ignatius C. Brady. New York: Paulist Press, 1982.)

The Master of Santa Chiara, *St. Clare with Scenes from her Life*, 14th century. Tempera on panel.

Episodes from the life of Clare of Assisi provided instructive models for her followers.

means by which the church investigated and punished heresy. The prominent roles played by many Dominicans in the Inquisition—including the notorious Tomás de Torquemada (1420–1498), Grand Inquisitor of the later Spanish Inquisition—should not eclipse the positive contributions of such eminent members of the order as Thomas Aquinas (1225–1274), patron saint of students; his teacher Albertus Magnus (c. 1200–1280), the "Universal Teacher"; the mystics Johannes (Meister) Eckhart (c. 1260–1327), Johannes Tauler (c. 1300–1361), Heinrich Suso (c. 1295–1366); and Dominic himself.

The early mendicants' engagement with the world and rejection of the cloistered life also included a significant role for women. Whereas the laws of monasticism insisted on the separation of men and women into separate establishments, within mendicant life cooperation between men and women was approved, even encouraged. Among Francis's early followers was a young noblewoman of Assisi, who left her home and became the leader of a number of women religious. Despite efforts by parents and siblings to bring her back into the family, St. Clare (1194–1253) prevailed (she later even brought her mother and two sisters into the mendicant life), becoming the head of a community at St. Damian's Church, the same one Jesus had supposedly asked Francis to restore. Known first as Poor Ladies, and later as Poor Clares after their founder, these women received permission in 1215 to live entirely on the charity of others and, like their brother Franciscans, to own nothing either individually or as a group. Their life was a strenuous one, but the order spread widely throughout Europe despite the austerities of its regimen. (See "The Canticle of Exhortation to St. Clare.")

Dominic, too, recognized the value of women, and one of his order's first achievments, in 1206, was to establish a convent of nuns—converts from heresy—in Prouille, France. Dominic felt that women could help the work of the friars through a life of prayer and penance. His Second Order, as the female branch was called, lived according to a document known as the Rule of St. Augustine (research has shown that this was not written by Augustine himself). In 1232 it received a constitution, or governing plan, from Pope Gregory IX (1148–1241; r. 1227–1241). Unlike their male counterparts, these women religious lived strictly cloistered lives, isolated from the world. The aid they provided their brothers and the world was the immaterial kind: they prayed, and in so doing, it was thought, helped bring divine favor and protection to humanity. Only in the modern period, and especially in the United States, has the Dominican Second Order taken a more active role in the world.

Franciscan versus Dominican Theology

Because so much of the mendicants' work, especially that of the Dominicans, involved preaching, the two orders inevitably developed their own theological systems. In the churches they built in towns, and in the universities, their ideas achieved wide currency among the laity in general as well as the educated few. In outlining the distinguishing characteristics of these two systems, there is a danger of oversimplification; however, certain generalizations are possible.

Franciscan theology tends to define the sacred as IMMANENT: that is, as existing within the natural realm. Such theology sees the world as the abode of God, and humanity as able to achieve oneness with God. The role of Christ is less that of an atoning victim and more that of a model for humanity's own struggle toward perfection.

The rivalry between the two schools was surely real. There are too many records of Dominican-led Inquisition trials against Franciscans to allow doubt about their mutual opposition. In some other respects, however, the extent of the opposition may have been exaggerated. In the late nineteenth century certain Austrian and German scholars coined the term *Wegestreit* ("conflict of ways," or of *viae*) to describe the charged atmosphere at late-medieval German universities. What may have been true at Heidelberg and Cologne, upon which some of these studies focused, may not have been true at many, if not most, other centers of learning at the time. But research in the field is continuing, and we cannot yet answer the question about how general the conflict of old and new *viae* really was.

Thomas Aquinas and John Duns Scotus

The pre-eminent figure in Dominican theology is, of course, St. Thomas Aquinas, whose work was introduced in Chapter 10. His influence as one of the leading Scholastics has extended down the centuries into our own time, although the view of Scholasticism that places Thomas Aquinas at the center of that tradition is a modern one, decisively shaped by the papal declaration of 1879 which made him the authorized "doctor," or teacher, of theology in the Catholic Church. For half a century a philosophical view known as Neo-Thomism dominated Christian thought, with outstanding intellectual efforts applying the Dominican worldview of the thirteenth century to the realities of the twentieth. Although this viewpoint still has its adherents, in the second half of the twentieth century it appeared that no single philosophical system could meet the demands for certainty in an age of rapid cultural change. In short, Thomas's world was deemed too different from the modern West for his thought to be relevant to it. In the wake of Neo-Thomism there arose new investigations (many of them stimulated by serious theological concerns) into some of the thinkers whose work had been eclipsed by Thomas's since 1879. These other medieval scholastic thinkers have not yet fully entered the mainstream, but interest in their work is growing.

Although all attempts to encapsulate the work of thinkers as complex as Thomas Aquinas are to some extent distortions, we can try to capture its essentials in brief terms. For Thomas, the created order is arrayed in a hierarchy of levels of being, all emanating from God as a creative source and all ultimately destined to return to God. Original sin, for Thomas, is the continued deviation from God as the source and goal of all being, and redemption is the path back to that ideal oneness. Thus Jesus Christ is, for Thomas, the guide for humanity's return to God. In this sense the Franciscan and Dominican theologies share a common doctrine of Christ.

Thomas's theological system, mostly shared by other Dominicans, is known as REALISM. This is possibly a confusing term, since it fails to specify what it considers real. Modern readers who equate "real" with "tangible" need to recognize that within Thomism ideas and abstractions have a reality of their own: they are, in fact, the reality, and individual things in the material world are copies. This system is usually contrasted with NOMINALISM, the school of thought that actually dominated late-medieval theology. Here, too, the label is an imprecise one, since it suggests that it deems something "nominal" but does not indicate what that something is. Some scholars have suggested that "terminism" is more accurate; but it would be even less correct if it were taken to mean that only terms are real.

Equally provocative is the theology of the Franciscan order, as exemplified by the work of John Duns Scotus (c. 1265–1308), known as the "subtle doctor" because of the difficulty of his thought. Duns Scotus's work is grounded in metaphysical principles, definitions of "being" and "reality." For Duns Scotus (the "Scotus" simply denotes his Scottish origin), the greatest certainty lies in stating that an individual thing exists. Thus the most real things are individual entities.

Medieval Religious Life

St. Dominic de Guzmán (c. 1172–1221) A Spanish priest who founded the Dominican Order in Toulouse, France, and sent missionaries out far and wide. He also established the makings of an order for Dominican nuns.

St. Francis of Assisi (c. 1181–1226) From a wealthy Italian merchant family, he experienced what he believed was a personal call from the Lord during Mass and gave up all he possessed to help the needy. He founded the Franciscan Order.

St. Clare (1194–1253) From a noble family in St. Francis's native Assisi, Italy, Clare left home to follow Francis and became a leader of religious women. She ultimately became head of a community at St. Damian's Church.

Albert the Great (c. 1200–1280) Called the "Universal Teacher," this Dominican philosopher-theologian held teaching posts at various Dominican and academic establishments in Europe. He was a great influence on other philosophers—especially St. Thomas Aquinas, a former pupil.

St. Bonaventure (Giovanni di Fidanza) (1217–1274) A theologian and Minister General of the Franciscan Order, he was appointed Cardinal Bishop of Albano. His "Life" of St. Francis was validated as the official biography of the saint in 1263.

Common features that they share or the concepts that might categorize them are what Duns Scotus calls "passions," what we would call "perceptions." All of these beings are the product of the divine will, which Duns Scotus describes as the creative energy of the material world. Theologically, this means that the world is the way it is because God willed it so, no more and no less. Because of the importance of the divine will in this system, it is known as VOLUNTARISM. God could have willed in an infinite number of other ways, but the divine will is beyond our understanding. Thus God's justice, and the system of redemption through the sacraments of the church, are products of an inscrutable will, to be accepted but not necessarily to be understood.

The contrast of Duns Scotus's voluntarism with Thomas's very ordered way of seeing the world is obvious. Both are ways of interpreting experience, and attempts to see the world as the work of an omnipotent and benevolent deity. But whereas Thomas sees God as an active intellect, bringing all things into intelligible order, Duns Scotus's God is more an impulse, bringing the world's contents into being, without any perceptible order other than their created state. It is easy to see why the Franciscan system dominated in the decades after the outbreak of the Black Death in 1349. The notion that God is not accountable to human standards of order is easier for voluntarist theology to maintain; and this theological position held more explanatory power in an age when whole populations were decimated by an apparently capricious, misunderstood disease.

Beghards, Beguines, and the Devotio Moderna

The urbanization of European society brought about a number of other changes in the patterns of Christian life. Indeed, there was so much desire for variety in inventing new forms of religious ritual that the mendicant orders, innovative and reformist by nature, acquired extraordinary importance in these years. Additionally, the boundaries between religious and lay forms of Christian life began to shift in the thirteenth and fourteenth centuries, and what had appeared fixed in 1200 seemed, by 1400, bewilderingly fluid.

One new phenomenon in this trend was the group known as the Beguines, communities of women who lived a semi-religious life, but without taking the vows of poverty, chastity, and obedience integral to monasticism. This movement originated in the Low Countries, where it mostly flourished, around the beginning of the thirteenth century; the origin of the name is uncertain. The Beguines dedicated themselves to good works, such as teaching and caring for the sick and the poor—not unlike many present-day orders of nuns in this respect. Their life also resembled that of the mendicant orders of their own time: it was a combination of the discipline of the religious life and involvement in the secular world. The houses in which they lived, called *béguinages*, served not only as their residences but also as schools and places of refuge for the urban poor. Each community had its own rule; there was no "mother house," as there is for monastic orders. A Beguine was free to own property and to leave the community and marry if she chose.

The male counterparts of the Beguines were the Beghards. Unlike the Beguines, who came from all social classes, the Beghards were mainly of humble origin.

They worked as craftsmen to support themselves, though some established schools and "hospitals" (in the medieval sense of lodgings for pilgrims), and cared for the poor in the towns in which they were located.

In time, the Beghards (and to a lesser extent the Beguines) became suspected by the church of having heretical tendencies, and many of these communities were suppressed during the religious conflicts of the sixteenth century; others closed down for a variety of reasons (although a few *béguinages* survive in

---

Thomas à Kempis' *Imitation of Christ*

The devotional bestseller of the later Middle Ages, the Imitation of Christ *offered a much needed antidote to the abstruse reasoning of Scholastic thinkers. Here we observe the essence of eucharistic piety expressed in the simple terms of the gift of, and a desire for, holiness.*

Lord I come unto Thee to the end that wealth may come unto me of Thy gift and that I may joy at the holy feast that Thou hast made ready unto me, poor wretch, by the sweet benignity in the which my Saviour is all that I may or ought to desire: for Thou art my health, my redemption, my strength, honour and joy.

Alas my Lord God make thy daily servant joyous. For my Lord Jesu I have raised my soul unto thee and now desire devoutly and reverently to receive thee into my house to the end that I may deserve with Zacchaeus to be blessed of thee and to be accompted among the children of Abraham.

My soul desireth the body, my heart desireth to be united only with thee. Give thyself unto me good Lord and then I am sufficed, for without thee no consolation nor comfort is good; without thee I may not be and without thy visitation I may not live; wherefore it behoveth me oftentimes to come and approach to thy high presence to receive thee for the remedy of my health to the intent I fail not in the way of this mortal life if I am defrauded of thy spiritual nourishing.

Also my right merciful Lord Jesu when thou hast preached unto the people and healed them of divers sickness thou hast said "I will not leave them fasting and without any refection lest peradventure they might fail in their way."

Do with me then, good Lord, in that manner since thou hast left this holy sacrament for the comfort of all faithful people; for thou art the sweet refection of the souls of them that have worthily received and eaten thee and they shall be partners and also inheritors of the eternal joy....

My Lord God I shall more often receive thee, my loving Lord, with a devout thought. O marvellous gentleness of thine unspeakable pity towards us that thou, Lord God, creator and giver of life unto all spirits, hath willed to come to one so poor a soul with thy deity and humanity and hath granted to my poor lean and dry soul to be made fat with thy grace and thy holy unction of thy sweet spirit.

O happy thought and well happy soul that deserveth devoutly to receive his God his Lord and creator and in that receiving to be fulfilled with joy and spiritual gladness.

O what great Lord receivest thou. O what and how great an host entertainest thou into thy lodging, how joyous a fellow takest thou into thy house, how faithful a friend thou admittest unto thee, and how good noble and sweet a spouse embracest thou which ought to be beloved and desired above all things.

O right sweet beloved Lord, the heaven and earth and all the ornaments of them hold silence in the presence of thy face. For what praise, honour and beauty they have it is of thy mercy and largeness and cannot be like unto the honour and beauty of the holy name and of thy wisdom, whereof there is no number neither end.

(From Thomas à Kempis, *Imitation of Christ*. London: J.M. Dent & Sons Ltd., 1937.)

Belgium to this day). At the time of their founding, these communities broke new ground by offering a middle way between leading a formal religious life, secluded from society, and a secular, worldly one. For women, especially, whose options had previously been limited to marriage or the nunnery, this new way of life—in the world but not of it—was most attractive.

After the Beguines and Beghards came other popular movements, such as the Devotio Moderna, or Brethren of the Common Life, another "order" made up of laity seeking a more purposefully religious life. These groups may have seemed subversive to some, but theirs was a subversiveness in the service of the church. The Devotio Moderna was the creation of a visionary Dutch cleric, Gert Groote (1340–1384), and the movement was unusually active in northern European cities in establishing schools and educating the laity generally in matters of piety. Among the many Christians influenced by the Devotio was Thomas à Kempis (c. 1380–1471), who is generally credited with the religious classic *The Imitation of Christ* (c. 1425), a book that offered spiritual guidance to a wide-ranging lay audience. A medieval bestseller, translated from its original Latin into a number of languages even before the invention of printing, the *Imitation* explains the mysteries of the sacramental life, especially the Eucharist, with clarity and without condescension. (See "Thomas à Kempis' *Imitation of Christ*.") It was in the same spirit that Desiderius Erasmus (c. 1466–1536; see chapters 15 and 18), who had also been exposed to the teachings of the Devotio, would write his own spiritual classic, the *Enchiridion Militis Christiani* (*Handbook of the Christian Soldier*) (c. 1500). These are not dense philosophical treatises, and this has led some to think of the Devotio as an anti-intellectual movement. It would be fairer to see it as a reaction against Scholasticism. Whereas the Scholastics spoke, in both their writings and arguments, to a university-trained elite, the members of the Devotio spoke to an uneducated laity, whose desire for a deeper understanding of their faith was just as great as that of monks and mendicants.

Heretical Movements

As the power of Christian institutions increased during the Middle Ages, more and more dissident groups began to appear. Deviant thought had been a part of the Christian tradition since its beginning, and various forms of it, such as Arianism, had been virtually crushed by the early councils. In the eleventh century some of these ancient heresies began to revive, and to be augmented by new ones. For example, the CATHARS—also called the Albigensians, after the French city of Albi, near which they lived—held a dualistic worldview similar to that of the Manichaeans. Founded in the third

Pedro Berruguete, *The Burning of the Books*, or *St. Dominic de Guzmán and the Albigensians*, 15th century. Oil on panel. Prado, Madrid.

Known for its defense of church teaching, the Dominican Order became the most feared scourge of opposition or heterodox groups.

John Wycliffe (c. 1330–1384)

John Wycliffe was an extraordinarily creative philosopher and theologian. He rose through the ranks teaching philosophy at Oxford University without the benefit of belonging to either of the mendicant orders that dominated academic life in England and on the Continent. He was a fellow of Merton College, and later master of Balliol College, in the 1350s and 1360s. He composed treatises on logic (then the preferred method of investigation), optics (then closely connected to epistemology), and metaphysics. Between 1365 and 1372 he wrote *Summa on Being*, which was made up of treatises on various philosophical problems. He became rector of Lutterworth parish, Leicestershire, in 1374.

Nominalism was a medieval philosophical theory according to which general terms (called "universals") have no real existence; for example, redness doesn't exist, only red things (called "particulars"). In an age when nominalism reigned, Wycliffe was by contrast a steadfast realist, insisting that universals, no matter how abstract they seemed, did actually designate "real" things. Realism would be vindicated in the nineteenth century with the revival of interest in Thomas Aquinas; and the reality of universals was one of the critical issues posed by twentieth-century analytical philosophy. As a philosopher, therefore, Wycliffe was considerably ahead of his time.

He also went against the grain in holding that all things happen by necessity, that human freedom is an illusion. All things in nature exist in God, who determines all that happens. The reason for this is that God knows everything that has happened, all that is, and all that will be. Unlike human will, God's will is unchangeable, so that what God knows about the future cannot be changed.

Wycliffe was not just a philosopher, however. Concern for church management led him to argue, in his work *On Civil Dominion*, that possessing religious office presupposes proper use of it, and that being in a state of sin prevents a priest from functioning properly. The worldliness of the clergy and the papal hierarchy at Avignon appeared to Wycliffe to disqualify them for legitimate rule. The laity, especially the nobles, endorsed this argument.

However, the church hierarchy took him to task, issuing orders for his arrest and imprisonment; this was to be carried out by the secular authorities, but they did not carry out their orders.

At a time when Wycliffe's arguments were drawing hostility from the church hierarchy, the papacy returned to Rome and the Great Schism (1378–1417) broke out. Amid disputes about legitimate lines of authority, Wycliffe wrote a treatise on *The Truth of Sacred Scripture*, in which he argued that the Bible alone is sufficient authority for belief. In contrast to a church establishment that asserted that the Bible needed amplification and interpretation, Wycliffe boldly insisted that a lack of clarity in understanding scripture was the result of human error, not the divine intention to make an interpreting agency such as the church necessary. (Wycliffe was anticipating the arguments for "sola scriptura" found in the sixteenth-century Reformers.) He also issued the first English translation of the Bible.

Fearless in his convictions, Wycliffe spent his last years exploring the doctrine of the Eucharist. He drew further criticism from church authorities with his assertions that the elements of bread and wine remain after consecration (conversely, the doctrine of transubstantiation denied that the bread and wine remained as anything but "accidents," or appearances), and that Christ's presence in the Eucharist was figurative rather than literal. Exiled from Oxford for his beliefs and decried as a heretic in 1378, he retired to Lutterworth where he defended the peasantry in a wave of rebellion and attacked the clerical establishment even more boldly than before. His followers were known as "Lollards," forerunners of English Protestantism.

Wycliffe died peacefully in his sleep in 1384 and was buried, but, because in the eyes of the church the earth cannot bear the remains of a heretic, his bones were later ignominiously dug up and burned, and his ashes thrown into the sea.

James Posselwhite (after a print by G. White), *Portrait of John Wycliffe*, 19th century. Engraving. Private Collection.

century C.E., the Manichaeans (whose numbers included St. Augustine before his conversion) believed that good and evil are opposing principles which have become entangled and that salvation is achievable through separating the two. In the rigidity of their asceticism, the Cathars (their name is Greek for "the pure ones") probably were much more severe than their Manichaean predecessors.

In the early thirteenth century, just as the mendicant orders were evolving, a school of followers grew up around Peter Waldo (d. c. 1215), a wealthy merchant of Lyons who gave his property to the poor and taught the simple precepts of the Sermon on the Mount. The Waldensians, as his followers were called (they were also known as the Poor Men of Lyons), were not quite so rigorous as the Cathars, but they practiced community of property and preached in the vernacular (women preached, too).

Toward the end of the fourteenth century, just as the Brethren of the Common Life were coming into being, English followers of John Wycliffe (c. 1329–1384) known as LOLLARDS (so called because they were thought to mumble their prayers) also preached in the vernacular and were instrumental in having the Bible translated into their native language. Of these three medieval heretical movements, the Lollards were perhaps the most radical in their attacks on the church, for they openly condemned many of the most popular practices at the time, such as pilgrimages and veneration of saints. In a number of ways the Waldensians and Lollards were forerunners of the Reformation of the sixteenth century.

Key Terms

IMMANENT Dwelling within, pervading; a belief in God's immanence holds that the divine is present to human experience.

LOLLARD A follower of John Wycliffe; any member of a loosely organized anticlerical sect in late-14th- and 15th-century England.

NOMINALISM A philosophical and theological doctrine holding that individuals, and the terms denoting them, are ultimately real.

REALISM A philosophical and theological doctrine which teaches that only abstractions are ultimately real.

SECULAR CLERGY Priests who do not belong to religious orders.

STIGMATA The wounds on hands, feet, and side that have marked certain holy men, among them Francis of Assisi.

STIGMATIZATION Receiving the wounds that Jesus bore during the Crucifixion.

VOLUNTARISM The theological position that all that exists, including the Incarnation and the church, has come about through the will (Latin, *voluntas*) of God.

Scholasticism and Salvation
The Sacramental System

The fourteenth and fifteenth centuries in Europe saw a continuation of the Scholastics' efforts to construct a comprehensive system that would explain the interaction of matter and spirit in creation. While they labored at this task, they also addressed the crucial matter of individual salvation. For although it was agreed that Christ had died to redeem humanity from original sin, it was still incumbent on individual Christians, with many personal sins on their consciences, to become worthy of the eternal life that God had promised.

After Aquinas

The elevation in 1879 of Thomas Aquinas to sainthood profoundly altered Western Christianity's awareness of the medieval theological tradition. The papal declaration of Leo XIII had the effect of aiming a spotlight on Aquinas and a few of his contemporaries, with the result that this left those out of the spotlight in the dark. Hence, modern students of theology, Protestant as well as Catholic, know a great deal about St. Thomas Aquinas; but they still know very little about the course of Scholasticism after his death in 1274. Histories of the Christian tradition have long contributed to this distortion by identifying the thirteenth century as the true culmination of Scholasticism and the following two centuries as a long period of decline. Moreover, very few of the original texts from this later period ever appeared in modern scholarly editions, much less in accessible translations. The resulting picture was that the period 1300–1500 has been seen as a two-century-long theological "dark age."

Since the 1960s this picture has been changing, and what had been dismissed as a period of deterioration has now been appreciated as one of culmination and harvest. Of great historical importance has been the recognition that theology in the late fifteenth century was a very different creature from that embodied in the two massive "Summas"—the *Summa Theologiae* and the *Summa contra Gentiles*—that Aquinas left in 1274. But many texts remain unedited, most are

CHAPTER 13

178

still in their original Latin, and research into this area remains the preserve of specialists. Still, it is a period of Christian thought too important to ignore.

Nominalism

In Chapter 12 we indicated the basic differences between nominalism and realism. Both ways of thinking are forms of deciding what is real and what is illusory—or, more accurately, what is the truth and what is its shadow. Realists as represented by Thomas Aquinas hold that the realm of ideas, as described by Plato, is the "real" one—even though, like Thomas, they make constructive use of Aristotle's thought also. Although realism continued to be an active school of thought during the later Middle Ages, it was eclipsed by nominalism, in many ways a more difficult mode of construing experience, and certainly a revolutionary program in theological thinking.

"Nominalism" may be a misleading term, since it suggests, falsely, that what is real in another school is only nominal or insignificant to this one. Philosophically (as opposed to theologically) nominalism comes closest to twentieth-century positivism, the rejection of things beyond the material world and a corresponding attention paid to experienced reality. If, after reading Plato's discussion of universal essences and concepts such as "chairness," you doubt the existence of an "idea" of chair but know a chair when you sit on one, you are ready to approach nominalism.

The most difficult aspect of nominalism to grasp is the fact that despite its emphasis on physical reality, it is a theological school, one with a Christian conception of God and a very clear doctrine of the church. Unlike modern positivism, which tends to reject theological claims as incompatible with observed reality, medieval nominalism sees the world of experience as the necessary unfolding of the divine nature, so that there is nothing in experience that does not derive from God; nor is there anything in human action that is not controlled in some sense by the divine will. To an extent one hardly finds in modern philosophy, the Scholastics invoke biblical proofs for their metaphysical programs.

John Duns Scotus and William of Ockham

The Franciscan theologian John Duns Scotus, whose work was introduced in Chapter 12, offers both a positivist metaphysics and a doctrine of God. For Duns Scotus, the only thing that can be said unequivocally of all existing things is that they exist; hence the fundamental concept in his thought is being. (Notice that this is a quality that God shares with tables and chairs: What is God? God *is*, Duns Scotus would say, and God exists in the same sense that this book does.) This being so, it is individuals that participate in being, not universals: we have a lot more certainty that a given number of chairs exist in this room than we have of the existence of an idea of "chairness"; thus individuals take precedence over universals. To give precision to this concept, Scotus applies the term *haecceitas* (Latin for "thisness") to this particular, present form of being. A certain chair may share all sorts of abstractions—woodenness, four-leggedness, brownness, etc. (cf. Aristotle's categories, Chapter 10)—but what it really *is* is this chair, no more and no less.

God enters the picture when we try to account for why and how this world of individuals came into being. For John Duns Scotus, all individuals are the products of the divine will; God brought everything into being. God is, however, bound to the terms of logical possibility: it is impossible for the divine will to create something both round and square, or something that is and is not. There is thus a logical order and predictability (of sorts) to the created realm: we needn't fear the appearance of self-contradictory entities. Duns Scotus's elucidation of the divine will does not stop there, for to him the divine will is bound also to a moral order, since God, who is the source of all good, can create only good. This concept is intended to offer some reassurance in the presence of the evil and the unpredictable, for people are more likely to wonder about the presence of evil in the world than the possibility of something like square circles.

John Duns Scotus,
17th century.
Engraving.

The Scholastic theologian is here depicted seeking inspiration from a painting of the Virgin Mary for his thesis on the Immaculate Conception.

The divine will is linked to moral as well as ontological values, and the human will shares the same boundaries. We can effectively will only what is capable of existing, and we can only will what we consider good. When we consider a given object and seek to understand whether it is a good or bad thing, we ask ourselves whether we would will such a thing to be. (Have you ever wished you could paint your favorite landscape, or play music like the musician you admire most? Thus you see the part the will plays in evaluating goodness.) Thus will takes precedence over intellect in the Scotist program, just as individuals take precedence over universals.

In conceptual subtlety and historical influence, William of Ockham (c. 1280–c. 1348) stands out as the dominant figure of fourteenth-century thought.

Founder of the so-called "new path" (*via moderna*) of Scholastic theology, in contrast to the older way (*via antiqua*) of Aquinas and Duns Scotus, Ockham is best known for a principle that extends and radicalizes the Scotist preference for particulars over universals. The principle, formulated as "Ockham's razor" (for its paring away of the non-essential), is that entities are not to be multiplied beyond what is necessary. In brief, this means that if you have four chairs in a room, you have four distinct entities and not four examples of an abstract fifth entity, the idea of "chairness." Assuming a universal, to Ockham, is creating an unnecessary entity, and thus a violation of the "razor."

Ockham differs from Duns Scotus and other predecessors in identifying the extent of divine freedom. Whereas Duns Scotus had said that God was able to will only the good, and was logically bound to non-contradiction, Ockham attributes absolute freedom to God, so that God is able to will evil and can reverse the course of nature. This is termed the divine *potentia absoluta*, or God's unrestrained power. Other thinkers, including Thomas Aquinas, have also attributed such power to God, but it does not form so prominent a part of their systems.

For God to hold such power is not an entirely comfortable notion. The comfort we take in the order and harmony of the world is quickly overshadowed by fear that God's sovereignty is able to disrupt that stability at any moment. What if God should halt the heat of the sun? What if the order of the seasons becomes a random sequence? What if, in the sphere of human activity, everything declared good becomes bad, or only the wicked are saved? The uncertainty would be terrifying. In response to this, the Ockhamist program makes a critical distinction between the *potentia absoluta* and the *potentia ordinata*, in other words the "ordered" or "ordained" power of God. This category of divine power declares that God has willed to order creation in a certain way—the predictable and orderly way of experience—and will not disrupt that order (even though the right to do so is never relinquished). In this way the two most important and inviolable concepts in the nominalist doctrine of God—stability and sovereignty—coexist in tension.

William of Ockham, c. 1494. Woodcut. University of Leeds, England.

An influential contributor to science and philosophy, Ockham became something of a patron saint to late-medieval academics.

The Operation of Grace

It is difficult to exaggerate the importance of the doctrine of grace in later Scholastic thought. Although grace has always been a central doctrine in Western theology, under nominalism it took on new significance in the life of the church. For if the whole created order is the product of a single divine will, then the means for realizing the divine goal must also be present in this order.

In practical terms, this meant that grace was already available in the world—in the form of the church and its sacramental system. Through the sacraments, the Christian already possessed all that was needed to attain salvation; the key was to make such grace a reality in one's own life. Like an exam in which the answers are concealed within the questions, the world of the nominalists needed no external inspiration, as grace was contained within nature. The key lay in cooperating with this grace.

By cooperating we mean something quite specific. In this theological system, baptism represents grace "operating" upon the individual; it is given freely with no spiritual effort on the part of the baptized person. But once a person has received this "OPERATING GRACE" through baptism, he or she becomes a participant in a program demanding active "cooperation." This program is the set of works and rites that constitutes the life of the church. In participating in these works, the believer exercises COOPERATING GRACE, which, unlike the "operating" form, does demand effort on the Christian's part. To be precise, it is not the believer's own power that cooperates; rather, he or she possesses this cooperating grace as something that is given in baptism. Perhaps the best way to imagine this concept is to think of someone with an ability so unusual that we might describe it as a gift. Such talent requires constant practice and refinement, so that even though we recognize a unique endowment in our talented friend, we see him or her constantly working to perfect this ability. In the Middle Ages grace was considered such a gift.

Merit as Spiritual Credit

There are, of course, differences between the modern view of earthly gifts and the medieval sense of grace. Grace is a spiritual endowment and therefore is measured in a different way from a talent. In the medieval worldview, spiritual accomplishments were marked by MERIT. Merit is spiritual "credit," a substance that a person can accumulate by performing certain good works, both ritual and moral. Just as sins bring demerit—that is, they subtract from one's balance of merit—so good deeds replenish the merit and add to the sum. At death, a person's merit will determine the ultimate fate; with luck and many good deeds, there will be enough merit for salvation, in other words heaven and the BEATIFIC VISION, or direct experience of God, which the redeemed will enjoy in the next world.

How much merit is enough, and how do persons know when they have it? This was a critical issue in medieval religious life, and one that would ignite the Reformation. One of the most notorious statements in late-medieval theology claims that "God will not withhold grace from those who do all they can" to merit it, but also that no one can know with certainty when that level has been attained. Thus a Christian was expected to work out his or her salvation "in fear and trembling" (to use terms from the New Testament), knowing that salvation is possible but never knowing how much merit is sufficient. The result was that people scrupulously sought merit in various works, but their anxiety was subsequently heightened rather than lessened by the impossibility of knowing the divine justice that would evaluate their efforts. The *facere* doctrine (which takes its name from the Latin verb "to do" in the formula "to do all that is within you") may have been intended as a source of comfort, but like the professor who assures students that there is no limit on the number of A's to be awarded (provided their work is almost perfect), this doctrine inspired apprehension rather than appreciation.

The Sacramental System

The doctrine of grace that emerged in Scholastic thought had far-reaching effects on religious life and practice. The idea that God had presented humanity with the freedom and means to attain salvation required that a definite program for achieving that goal be in place and available for all believers. Since salvation could be attained only within the church, the church's task was to guide its members toward heaven. It did so by attributing values of merit to various works—especially, but not solely, the seven sacraments.

Sacraments, Merit, and Indulgences

Sacraments are of course as old as Christianity (see Chapter 4), but their number and importance have changed over the centuries. At the Fourth Lateran Council in 1215 the church settled on the seven sacraments of baptism, confirmation, Eucharist, penance, matrimony, ordination, and extreme unction (last rites). These ceremonies structure and sanctify the Christian life in its two forms, clerical and lay. (Marriage thus offers a form of sanctity for the secular life analogous to that offered by ordination for those entering the clerical state. Only widowers who entered the priesthood would be able to receive all seven sacraments.)

The sacramental life began with the "operating" grace of baptism, at which the Christian, usually an infant, entered the church. At a given age, he or she was confirmed—a word signifying confirmation of the vows made on his or her behalf by the godparents. The newly confirmed Christian would then begin the "cooperating" work of accumulating merit through devotional works. Each sin needed to be atoned for through penance (confession and forgiveness, or absolution); and the obligatory Eucharist needed to be received with a clear conscience, which meant that penance and satisfaction (the works needed to expiate a sin) needed to precede communion. (This is continued today in many churches, in which a communal confession and absolution are part of the Eucharistic service.) Since, in addition, it may be impossible to make a complete confession immediately before death, the final absolution conferred in extreme unction was a valuable supplemental dose of merit. However, since doubt was a sin (and the particular work of the devil, it was believed in the fourteenth and fifteenth centuries, was to induce fear and doubt in believers), having serious questions, even on one's deathbed, about the efficacy of the sacraments and the assurance of salvation was enough to compromise one's chances of salvation.

There were, however, ways to supplement the sacramental program and gain merit outside the ritualized world of liturgy. Going on pilgrimages to see and

Domenico di Michelino, *Dante and His Poem*, 1465. Fresco. Florence Cathedral, Florence.

Holding an open copy of the Commedia, *Dante points to Hell with his right hand. Purgatory with its seven levels looms behind him; at its summit stand Adam and Eve in the garden of Eden. Paradise rises in the form of Florence Cathedral on Dante's left, the brightest of stars shining above it.*

The Triumph of Death, 1503. Fresco. Bibliothèque Nationale, Paris.

This work depicts the catastrophe of the Black Death of 1348. The Grim Reaper stands triumphant over the body of a young woman cut down in her prime.

venerate relics of saints, venerating the saints and observing their special days, and engaging in various other "para-sacramental" activities (even crossing oneself with holy water) were sources of merit—as was almsgiving, the sharing of one's worldly goods with the poor (including the clergy). Each act was a deposit in a kind of spiritual retirement account, meant to ensure blessedness in the next life—if one had led a saintly life. For less saintly individuals, the trick was simply to die with a credit balance.

A "debit" balance, so to speak, did not mean damnation to hell, but did signify something short of heaven. Quite simply, it meant that the believer's sins needed to be removed to a state known as PURGATORY—literally, "place of purgation." Depicted in contemporary images as a fiery place (fire being an effective way to purify things), purgatory served as a kind of spiritual halfway house, where persons' souls would be purified so as to become worthy, posthumously, of heaven. Their sentences could be lightened, however, by the prayers of those they left behind; and there seems to have been much anxiety about whether one's survivors cared enough to pray on one's behalf so as to mitigate the pains of the fiery realm. This belief survives today in the memorial Masses that are offered for the souls of specific departed believers— anyone from a recently deceased family member to the founders of an ancient institution. In every case, the piety that leads to the Mass being said, or any other good work being performed, is a payment of merit for the deceased.

It is not difficult to see that this system can create as much anxiety as the *facere* doctrine. Not only does one have to make sure that there is sufficient merit for oneself; it is also necessary to take care, spiritually, of one's departed loved ones and to make sure that one dies with the ordinary human goodwill that will lead others to pray on one's own behalf—or else the capital to establish endowments to have others do this on a regular basis. In the Middle Ages, one way in which this burden was lightened was by the issuing of INDULGENCES, declarations by the church that one's purgatorial penalty was lessened by a stated amount. Indulgences were granted for pious works such as pilgrimages, but almsgiving was also effective. From here it was but a short step to giving "alms" to the church— in effect, buying indulgences. Thus a person could exercise "cooperating grace" and gain indulgence for a life of misdeeds with a financial transaction; and, of course, the rich were best placed to take advantage of this offer.

The theological concepts behind indulgences go back to early Scholastic distinctions between operating and cooperating grace. The former, as we saw, was seen as the initial work of God on behalf of the Christian: the gracious act of baptism, an initiation into the covenantal relationship between the Christian God and the saved. The latter was the way God drew persons to salvation: the individual, in this early form of the doctrine, still remained largely passive in the process. In later forms of the Christian doctrine of salvation, the "cooperating" component depended far more on the believer's own initiative. Certain types of pious works, especially pilgrimages and acts of veneration toward saints, accrued supernatural merit, as did other devotions, but also gained a rare benefit in the INTERCESSION of the saints. It was thought that saints—and above all, the Virgin Mary—would intervene on behalf of certain faithful persons, so that needs and prayers would elicit the desired responses from God.

Such a belief had its benefits and disadvantages. On the one hand, belief that a particular saint values one's devotion and has one's own interests at heart strengthens the believer's piety and creates, to some degree, a sense of security. The observance of saints' feast days with special devotions, and perhaps celebrations, also added an extra dimension to everyday life. On such days it was thought that the saints might be particularly receptive to the requests of their devotees. Belief in the efficacy of the saints also sent many people on pilgrimages to sites associated with them—either because the saint had lived or died there or because a relic of the saint, such as a body part or an item of clothing, was kept there. Despite the physical hardships of such journeys, they were exhilarating experiences—socially, culturally, and spiritually—for many people who otherwise rarely traveled more than a few miles from home.

On the other hand, these pilgrimages, and even some of the devotions, cost money. So the privileged stood to gain more than the underprivileged who made up the majority of medieval Christians. Moreover, there was a tendency, often encouraged by priests, to feel that none of these activities would ever be enough. The more people did, the more they sensed the extent of their sinfulness—a cycle that intensified anxieties over salvation.

The system of indulgences began to get seriously out of hand when they began to be applied to the souls of the departed in large numbers and for high prices. Members of rich families could protect themselves against purgatory and provide for their deceased parents and other immediate relatives—and for all their ancestors as far back as they might care to go. Since there was great prestige in having an "old" family, based on generations of landowners, there was an almost boundless market for such spiritual insurance. The church benefited greatly

Lucas Cranach the Elder, *The Pope's Selling of Indulgences*, 1521. Woodcut.

Artists sympathetic to the Reformation lampooned the church's trade in spiritual commodities, depicting the hierarchy as greedy and the lay purchasers as gullible victims.

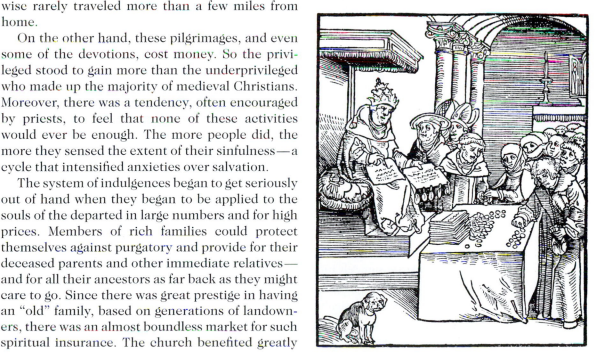

from the system. St. Peter's Basilica, in Rome, was built on the proceeds of indulgence sales, and probably every parish in Europe gained in some way from this commerce.

Inflation on the monetary side of this economy put unbearable pressures on those who could only barter. That is to say, with the rich paying handsome sums for their ancestors' souls, the poor, who had only their good deeds and sacramental works to their credit, became increasingly anxious about their own—and their relatives'—spiritual state. (On the principle of the Fifth Commandment, "Honor thy father and thy mother," devotion to family and concern for its salvation was thought to be one of the marks of the pious Christian.) What was the exchange value between humble prayers and a few Masses by those with nothing else, and stupendous endowments for whole families? Did a person's poverty mean that his or her parents or grandparents were destined to a harder fate in purgatory than those whose children paid their penalties in cash?

The concept of original sin and its effects in each believer's life dominated the late-medieval worldview, especially in the wake of the plague, which most saw as divine punishment for their sins. Penitential rituals took on unprecedented importance in the lives of the faithful. Fear of dying without the benefit of the final sacrament made many people zealous about penance, and in the process they became more submissive to the authority of the church. The penitential rite became a means of pastoral control as never before, allowing clergy to shape the lives of their parishioners. Some of this control offered opportunities for extortion and manipulation.

Thus, the late-medieval system of merit, sacraments, and indulgences tended to be anything but a source of comfort. For many persons, these teachings reflected the capriciousness of divine justice and demonstrated that purely material transactions were favored over earnest gestures of piety. Toward the end of the fifteenth century, a wave of anticlerical sentiment gained momentum; but the system would persist until an alternative arrived in the form of the Reformation.

Key Terms

BEATIFIC VISION The immediate knowledge of God granted to saints in heaven.

COOPERATING GRACE That part of the process of salvation in which the believer becomes an agent, by means of grace, in his or her own salvation.

INDULGENCES A reduction in purgatorial penalties obtained by ritual works or purchase from the church; a certificate representing such reduction.

INTERCESSION Pleading on behalf of someone else; the intervention of departed saints on one's behalf before God.

MERIT Spiritual credit accumulated by good works for the church; a sufficiency was believed to ensure salvation.

OPERATING GRACE That part of the process of salvation in which grace is active and the believer is passive; usually applied to baptism.

PURGATORY A state after death in which baptized Christians are believed to purge themselves of residual sinfulness, and in the process gain salvation.

Spirituality and Mystical Experience
Medieval Mystics

So far, we have discussed the religious life in monasteries and other religious communities mainly as one of active work: in copying manuscripts, developing theological systems, and ministering to the laity in various ways. It should not be forgotten, however, that much of the life of these communities (in some orders virtually all of it) consisted of prayer and meditation. Among those committed to the cloistered life, SPIRITUALITY—a focusing on communication with the divine—was not simply a component of daily life but its very fabric.

Certain extremely gifted persons were able to take spirituality much further, entering a dimension we call MYSTICISM. The word "mystical" is a familiar one, describing something that is strange, remote, elusive, knowable to only a few. All of these terms can be applied to the phenomenon of mysticism, which is the direct experience of an ultimate reality—what Christians call God. This experience, although elusive, is overwhelming, and is seen by those who have undergone it as a divine gift. The Middle Ages produced a number of mystics—most of them, but not all, members of religious orders. In their writings they attempt to describe the pathways to achieving a mystical experience and the nature of the experience itself.

Despite being considered a gift from God, mystical experience requires much preparation. Without an exacting program of discipline, the believer would be in no condition to receive the divine experience. In medieval Europe (and in other cultures, too) desire for God led to a system of ascetic practices, forms of self-discipline (*askesis* is Greek for "discipline" or "exercise") intended to make a person receptive to divine grace.

Mystical Ways Toward God

In some of the earliest texts of Christian mysticism, a distinction is made between two ways to attain knowledge of God, one "positive," one "negative." The VIA POSITIVA was the path toward understanding God that attributed, or "posited" (hence the term), certain qualities to God. Thus one could form an understanding of God as good, for example, by considering such matters as the quality of goodness, its forms in human experience, and the ways in which divine goodness may be felt. This method had the merit of making God more understandable, but that virtue was achieved at the cost of the very quality that makes God different from everything else in human experience—unknowability. Thus we find many authors who describe the positive path, but always with the reservation that at the end one has a picture of God, but not God's self in the most authentic sense.

The VIA NEGATIVA offered a way to attain knowledge of God that was as demanding as it was promising. With this method, the devout person would identify a quality customarily attributed to God, such as goodness, and try to imagine a being so perfect as to be beyond any human conception of goodness. God's goodness could not be imagined; thus to contemplate God one needed to "negate" the traditional attribution (whence the term for this method). The mystic who practiced this method rose beyond rationality to a "cloud of unknowing" where God might be imagined in God's own terms. But that realm, once attained, was impossible to describe. Thus we have no records of what that state of oneness with the unknowable God was or is like.

The most influential early theorist of mystical experience in the Christian Church is known as Dionysius the Areopagite, the name attached to texts titled *The Celestial Hierarchy*, *The Ecclesiastical Hierarchy*, and *On Divine Names*. For centuries these texts were attributed to the Greek convert whom Paul had evangelized, and who thus held a type of apostolic authority; but they actually date from about 500 C.E. For the Pseudo-Dionysius (scholars add the prefix for the sake of accuracy), the positive and rational path is valid and authentic; but the true goal of the soul is to rise through the levels of the "ecclesiastical hierarchy" (the things we associate with external religious life: sacraments), through the "celestial hierarchy" of the angelic realm, to culminate in mystical ECSTASY (literally to be displaced from one's self) and union with the Infinite. In such union there is no longer individuality; the believer ceases to be an entity apart from God. At this level the attributes of God have been replaced by the absence of describable attributes, and selfhood is replaced by loss of individuality. Language and rationality have lost their uses, for the Infinite cannot be conceived, nor can the ecstatic state be described. All the mystic can communicate is that such experience is possible.

Although the mystical state could not be described with exactitude, some medieval mystics did find it possible to indicate what this special oneness with God was like: and thus we find in their writings numerous images, metaphors, and allusions employed in an effort to convey the unique state of unity and the path toward it. Not surprisingly, given that God was described as dwelling in the heavens, the images are spatial in character: ladders and paths appear frequently as attempts to conceptualize the mystical discipline. Some authors also adopted poetic metaphors to convey the mystical relationship with God. Often these were drawn from the Bible and adapted to mystical purposes. The most frequent source of descriptive language was the Song of Songs, otherwise known as the Song of Solomon, a book in the Old Testament. By all appearances, this text is a richly poetic love poem, possibly a marriage song, and in fact it has strong similarities to marriage songs from other parts of the ancient Near East. In the medieval Christian tradition, this understanding of the Song is excluded. Instead, interpreters saw it as an allegory of the love between God and the Christian soul, or between Christ and his church. The union of a man and a woman and the emotional intensity of erotic love are likened to the union of the soul and God—only the human, physical union is considered a puny imitation of the soul's fulfillment.

The method of interpretation that allows one to see such books as the Song of Songs in this religious light is the ALLEGORICAL method of exegesis, pioneered by the Alexandrian Jew Philo (c. 30 B.C.E.–c. 40 C.E.), who wanted to reconcile the Hebrew narrative with the philosophy of Plato, and so gave all the historical details of the Torah a supernatural, Platonic, reference point. The Christian Father responsible for bringing this method to maturity was Origen (c. 185–254), one of the most versatile and prolific thinkers of the Greek tradition. Origen held that Scripture had a "corporeal," or literal, meaning which all could grasp, as well as a "spiritual" or "mystical" one, which only those who were perfect could understand. The heart of divine revelation is contained in the mystical meaning. Hence we may identify an "allegorical preference" in interpreters of the Origenist type: readers who move quickly beyond the corporeal meaning to the remote, mystical one, and there find divine secrets. It is hardly any wonder that the "perfect" among these Western monks would have sought the deepest meanings in books such as the Song of Songs.

Bernard of Clairvaux, St. Bonaventure, Johannes Eckhart

In all likelihood, the most influential figure after the Pseudo-Dionysius in medieval mystical thought is St. Bernard of Clairvaux (1090–1153), the abbot of a Cistercian monastery he had himself founded. In Bernard's thought, true knowledge of God is love of God, for God is love itself. And just as it would be ridiculous for a thoroughly disagreeable person to claim to know what love is, so it makes no sense to claim to know that God is love without actually loving. Love is something that can only be understood by experience. And God's love, as Bernard understands it, is so powerful once one has experienced it, all other loves are thrown into its shadow.

Bernard arranged human affections in an ordered hierarchy. At the basest level, a person loves oneself for one's own sake. Self-love of this sort is empty and fleeting. At the second level, one loves God for one's own sake. God is here little more than a guardian angel or a patron of your own interests. At the next level, a person loves God for God's sake—that is, because God is God and inherently worthy of love—instead of loving God purely because of possible divine benefits. Fourth and finally, one loves oneself for the sake of God. At this stage a person becomes an agent of divine love, sharing in God's nature by helping to extend love throughout the world. For Bernard, union with God is not the contemplative oneness that we might find in Pseudo-Dionysius, where all sense of personal identity is lost. Instead, it is an affective and practical union: affective because the experience takes place in the emotions, not reason; practical because the mystic must share in God's work by loving what God loves: humanity.

Le Rattine (from
a painting
by Raphael),
St. Bonaventure,
15ᵗʰ century.
Engraving.

*Both mystic and
philosopher,
Bonaventure's
works helped
articulate a
distinctively
Franciscan
spiritual path.*

This form of mysticism was suited to the ceno-bitic monastic life (see Chapter 7), rather than to solitary existence or life in the secular world. Bernard called the monastery a "school of charity," and one can see why. Only in a monastery, where personal ambitions are discouraged and economic concerns minimized, can one devote oneself fully to properly ordered love: first, love of God, and second, love of one's neighbor—or charity. So it comes as no surprise that the Cistercian tradition is rich in two types of literature: exegetical works on the Song of Songs, and treatises on love of God and neighbor. Works from this tradition are just coming to light in English translations; some of them had remained in manuscript virtually unknown until recent decades. Cistercians such as John of Ford (c. 1140–1214), William of St. Thierry (c. 1080–1148), and St. Aelred of Rievaulx (c. 1110–1167) are joining Bernard of Clairvaux as renowned figures in the tradition of monastic mysticism. Another remarkable center of writing on mysticism was the Augustinian monastery of St. Victor in Paris: here, in the twelfth century, Hugh, Adam, and Richard of St. Victor applied their remarkably creative imaginations and mystical vision to interpreting Scripture.

One reason why monastic life was the ideal condition for experiencing love of God and practicing love of neighbor lay in its peculiar imperfections. According to accounts from the monasteries themselves, monks were frequently tempted by the sin of pride, thinking themselves actually capable of achieving perfection. Not perfection but humility was the ideal of Cistercian spirituality, which required a continuing awareness of the monks' sinfulness. And there was enough to be humble about—not in the sense that the monks were flagrantly immoral, but certainly in the fact that they could surely be (like the rest of us) truculent, harsh, and generally not very lovable. And the fact that one found it hard to feel complete charity toward one's brothers reinforced one's own sense of limitation and sinfulness.

Yet this is how it was supposed to be, apparently. In Bernard's view, God loves a sinful humanity despite its sinfulness: that is, God loves an *unlovable* humanity, and does so absolutely. To love one's neighbor in the same way is to love unconditionally, oblivious to any unpleasant qualities. Loving your most generous friend, most understanding boss, most caring teacher is easy, and exactly *not* how God loves humanity. Loving the difficult and selfish person is how God is toward *you*—and thus how you must be toward that neighbor whom you'd rather avoid. Hence there is a spiritual need, in the Cistercian view, for these "bad" monks; for without them one cannot experience the union with God of loving a sinful humanity.

Mysticism figured in the lives of many other religious orders, including the mendicants. In the thirteenth century the Franciscan St. Bonaventure

(c. 1217–1274) and, in the next century, Dominican theologians such as Johannes (or Meister) Eckhart (c. 1260–1327) and Johannes Tauler (c. 1300–1361) would attempt to synthesize the rational and affective dimensions of religious understanding, often in the form of highly poetic accounts of creation and the life of Jesus. In Bonaventure's writing, it is the life of St. Francis, the perfect Christian who has achieved the blessed union with Christ, that is depicted. Bonaventure's *The Itinerary of the Mind to God* shows Francis as an angelic being inhabiting heaven and enjoying the mysteries of the divine order by fully understanding it. In this work the Scholastic and the mystical elements are so closely intertwined that it is useless to speculate whether it is a Scholastic work with a mystical component, or a mystical work cast in Scholastic terms. In either case, it offers a useful lesson by proving that mysticism and Scholasticism are not mutually exclusive, and that some medieval thinkers did not reject one in turning to the other. Any theologian who wanted to do justice to the range of human awareness of God needed to address, to some extent, both the rational and affective dimensions.

Johannes (Meister) Eckhart was the initiator, almost single-handedly, of a revival of mysticism that lasted until the dawn of the Reformation in the sixteenth century. In a number of works, in both Latin and German (he is one of the great medieval authors in German), Eckhart articulates a cosmology of divine "outpouring," a process of creation in which God overflows like a boiling pot—and which makes everything in the realm of experience a speck or remnant of that divine being. The mystical path then becomes one in which the divinity of all things is clearly recognized; through that recognition, the divine oneness can be restored. Eckhart's mystical style is a complex one, but it has affinities with the exitus-reditus theme of certain Scholastic theologians (see Chapter 12); and it proved as influential as any theological system of his time. Medieval religious culture was one in which the sacred was experienced in a number of ways, ranging from simple acts of coming into contact with, for example, a saint's relic in a shrine, to describing the blessed visions and sensations of a holy Christian like St. Francis. Such a range makes it difficult to speak of spirituality or mysticism as unified traditions. Rather, they should be considered categories of the pious life, just as varied as other realms of religious activity, and with the continuing new attention they are receiving, increasingly fascinating aspects of medieval Christian experience.

Female Medieval Mystics

The study of mystical writings by women has expanded dramatically in recent decades and has become an area attracting some of the most creative scholarship in religious studies. Every year has seen the appearance of texts whose existence in many cases was previously unknown; new monographs and articles appear frequently, forcing scholars to reexamine provisional earlier understandings of these authors. As exciting as this area of research is, any attempt at a comprehensive assessment at this point is at best incomplete. That being the case, it is best to look at a few representative figures from this tradition, keeping in mind that what makes them representative may simply be the accident of their accessibility to modern readers.

Hildegard of Bingen

Hildegard von Bingen, c. 1230. Biblioteca Governativa Statale, Lucca, Italy.

Hildegard used an imaginary architectural motif to convey the divine in the world. Here we see a rendition of that motif.

The German Benedictine abbess Hildegard of Bingen (1098–1179) stands out for a number of reasons. She was one of the first women to write seriously about the religious life, one of the earliest German writers (possibly the first to write theology in that language), and one of the more sensitive poets to write about religious feelings. (See "Hildegard of Bingen's Visions.") She also wrote works on natural science and medicine. Today she is perhaps best known as a composer of hymns and other liturgical pieces; recordings of her work have become deservedly popular.

In her own time Hildegard was widely revered for her prophecies and visions, which she recorded, in Latin, in a three-volume work entitled *Scivias* ("Know the Ways"). Completed c. 1151, *Scivias* contains twenty-six visions, some of them rendered in poetic form and later set to music. They include a great range of images depicting such subjects as the Fall, the church (represented as the ark of the Old Testament flood), and the end of the world. In these writings Hildegard displays a genius for using imagery to express Christian concepts. As an active leader in a church that was expanding its artistic and liturgical canons, she stands near the beginning of a tradition that uses the senses, as well as the emotions, as the means of apprehending the divine.

The prominent displaying of the crucifix, with its graphic representation of the suffering Christ on the cross, was but one way in which understanding of the divine was conveyed through the visual. Stories from the Old and New Testaments and the lives of the saints were also depicted. Toward the end of Hildegard's life, this would begin to be done through the medium of stained glass; but during her lifetime, the great tradition of European religious sculpture was well under way, and churches began to be richly embellished with images of saints and even of Christ and God the Father.

This trend, of course, was a striking divergence from Jewish prohibitions against "graven images," as stated in the Second Commandment. Which brings us to a less attractive aspect of Hildegard: her attitude to Judaism. One of her visions is of a woman of dark color and sinister features, which Hildegard identifies as the "Synagogue." However, we should remember that such prejudice was almost to be expected in the

Hildegard of Bingen's Visions

A true visionary, Hildegard of Bingen was a powerful articulator of popular piety. As a woman outside the circles of authority, she had to present her work as something inspired by God—so that her marginal status ironically gave her even more power.

For five years I had been troubled by true and wonderful visions. For a true vision of the unfailing light had shown me (in my great ignorance) the diversity of various ways of life. In the sixth year (which marked the beginning of the present visions), when I was sixty-five years of age, I saw a vision of such mystery and power that I trembled all over and—because of the frailty of my body—began to sicken. It was only after seven years that I finally finished writing down this vision. And so, in the year of our Lord's incarnation, 1163, when the apostolic throne was still being oppressed by the Roman Emperor, Frederick, a voice came to me from heaven, saying:

> O poor little figure of a woman; you, who are the daughter of many troubles, plagued by a grave multitude of bodily infirmities, yet steeped, nonetheless, in the vastness of God's mysteries—commit to permanent record for the benefit of humankind, what you see with your inner eyes and perceive with the inner ears of your soul so that, through these things, people may come to know their Creator and not recoil from worshipping him with the reverence due to him. And so, write these things, not according to your heart but according to my witness—for I am Life without beginning or end. These things were not devised by you, nor were they previously considered by anyone else; but they were pre-ordained by me before the beginning of the world. For just as I had foreknowledge of man before he was made, so too I foresaw all that he would need.

And so I, a poor and feeble little figure of a woman, set my hands to the task of writing—though I was worn down by so many illnesses, and trembling. All this was witnessed by that man [Volmar] whom (as I explained in my earlier visions) I had sought and found in secret, as well as by that girl [Richardis] whom I mentioned in the same context.

While I was doing this, I looked up at the true and living light to see what I ought to write. For everything which I had written since the beginning of my visions (or which I came to understand afterwards) I saw with the inner eyes of my spirit and heard with my inner ears, in heavenly mysteries, fully awake in body and mind—and not in dreams, nor in ecstasy, as I explained in my previous visions. Nor (as truth is my witness) did I produce anything from the faculty of the human sense, but only set down those things which I perceived in heavenly mysteries.

And again I heard a voice from heaven instructing me thus; and it said: "Write in this way, just as I tell you."

(From Hildegard of Bingen, "The Book of Divine Works," in Fiona Bowie and Oliver Davies, eds., *Hildegard of Bingen: Mystical Writings*, trans. Robert Carver. New York: Crossroads, 1990.)

exclusively Christian milieu in which Hildegard lived. The negative side of intense devotion to the founder of Christianity was apt to be intense hostility to the people who had failed to acknowledge him as their Messiah. Hildegard was unfortunately typical of her time in this respect.

Julian of Norwich, Margery Kempe, St. Birgitta of Sweden, Hadewijch of Brabant, Catherine of Genoa

Among mystical writings in vernacular languages, some are attributed to women who may or may not have been directly responsible for them. This does not mean that these mystics are falsely credited as authors; it means, rather, that authorship was a more fluid concept then than it is now. The mystic Julian of Norwich

Julian of Norwich's *Revelations*

Julian of Norwich was an anchoress, enclosed in a cell within the walls of a church, and a visionary, whose record of visitations by Jesus Christ gave comfort to her and her contemporaries. Here she receives a vision of divine love for the world.

These revelations were shown to a simple and uneducated creature on the eighth of May 1373. Some time earlier she had asked three gifts from God: (i) to understand his passion; (ii) to suffer physically while still a young woman of thirty; and (iii) to have as God's gift three wounds....

It was at this time that our Lord showed me spiritually how intimately he loves us. I saw that he is everything that we know to be good and helpful. In his love he clothes us, enfolds and embraces us; that tender love completely surrounds us, never to leave us. As I saw it he is everything that is good.

And he showed me more, a little thing, the size of a hazelnut, on the palm of my hand, round like a ball. I looked at it thoughtfully and wondered, "What is this?" And the answer came; "It is all that is made." I marvelled that it continued to exist and did not suddenly disintegrate; it was so small. And again my mind supplied the answer, "It exists, both now and for ever, because God loves it." In short, everything owes its existence to the love of God.

In this "little thing" I saw three truths. The first is that God made it; the second is that God loves it; and the third is that God sustains it. But what he is who is in truth Maker, Keeper, and Lover I cannot tell, for until I am essentially united with him I can never have full rest or real happiness; in other words, until I am so joined to him that there is absolutely nothing between my God and me. We have got to realize the littleness of creation and to see it for the nothing that it is before we can love and possess God who is uncreated. This is the reason why we have no ease of heart or soul, for we are seeking our rest in trivial things which cannot satisfy, and not seeking to know God, almighty, all-wise, all-good. He is true rest. It is his will that we should know him, and his pleasure that we should rest in him. Nothing less will satisfy us. No soul can rest until it is detached from all creation.

When it is deliberately so detached for love of him who is all, then only can it experience spiritual rest.

God showed me too the pleasure it gives him when a simple soul comes to him, openly, sincerely and genuinely. It seems to me as I ponder this revelation that when the Holy Spirit touches the soul it longs for God rather like this; "God, of your goodness give me yourself, for you are sufficient for me. I cannot properly ask anything less, to be worthy of you. If I were to ask less, I should always be in want. In you alone do I have all."

Such words are dear indeed to the soul, and very close to the will and goodness of God.

(From Julian of Norwich, *Revelations of Divine Love*, trans. Clifton Wolters. Baltimore, MD: Penguin Books, 1966.)

The Book of Margery Kempe

Margery Kempe was a laywoman free to travel in the world, but she did so with frequent episodes of fits, weeping, and shouting that were thought to be evidence of contact with God. Here we observe her in one of her encounters with God.

As this creature was in the church of the Holy Apostles at Rome on St Lateran's Day, the Father of Heaven said to her, "Daughter, I am well pleased with you, inasmuch as you believe in all the sacraments of Holy church and in all faith involved in that, and especially because you believe in the manhood of my son, and because of the great compassion that you have for his bitter Passion."

The Father also said to this creature, "Daughter, I will have you wedded to my Godhead, because I shall show you my secrets and my counsels, for you shall live with me without end."

Then this creature kept silence in her soul and did not answer to this, because she was very much afraid of the Godhead; and she had no knowledge of the conversation of the Godhead, for all her love and affection were fixed on the manhood of Christ, and of that she did have knowledge and would not be parted from that for anything.... Therefore it was not surprising if she was still and did not answer the Father of Heaven, when he told her that she should be wedded to his Godhead. Then the Second Person, Christ Jesus, whose manhood she loved so much, said to her, "What do you say to my Father, Margery, daughter, about these words that he speaks to you? Are you well pleased that it should be so?"

And then she would not answer the Second Person, but wept amazingly much, desiring to have himself still, and in no way to be parted from him. Then the Second Person in Trinity answered his Father for her, and said, "Father, excuse her, for she is still only young and has not completely learned how she should answer."

And then the Father took her by the hand [spiritually] in her soul, before the Son and the Holy Ghost, and the Mother of Jesus, and all the twelve apostles, and St Katherine and St Margaret and many other saints and holy virgins, with a great multitude of angels, saying to her soul, "I take you, Margery, for my wedded wife, for fairer, for fouler, for richer, for poorer, provided that you are humble and meek in doing what I command you to do. For, daughter, there was never a child so kind to its mother as I shall be to you, both in joy and sorrow, to help you and comfort you. And that I pledge to you. ...!"

Our Lord also gave her another token which lasted about sixteen years, and increased ever more and more, and that was a flame of fire of love—marvellously hot and delectable and very comforting, never diminishing but ever increasing....

When she first felt the fire of love burning in her breast she was afraid of it, and then our Lord answered in her mind and said, "Daughter, don't be afraid, because this heat is the heat of the Holy Ghost, which will burn away all your sins, for the fire of love quenches all sins. And you shall understand by this token that the Holy Ghost is in you, and you know very well that wherever the Holy Ghost is, there is the Father, and where the Father is, there is the Son, and so you have fully in your soul all of the Holy Trinity.

(From *The Book of Margery Kempe*, trans. B.A. Windeatt. New York: Penguin Books, 1985.)

(c. 1342–1416 or later) claimed to "know no letter"—that is, not to know how to read or write—and her *Sixteen Revelations of Divine Love* (date unknown) ends with a statement by the priest who claims to have recorded these revelations. (See "Julian of Norwich's *Revelations*.") Some scholars believe that Julian was not only literate but actually quite learned in theology, while others take her dis-

St. Catherine of Genoa Carrying the Cross, 15th century. Fresco. St. Catherine's church, Genoa.

Solidarity with the suffering was symbolized in many ways during the decades of plague. Imitating the way of the Cross connected one's own pains with those of Jesus in his final hours.

claimer at face value. Each scenario yields its own set of questions. If she was literate, why the pretense of "knowing no letter"? Could she have sensed that her revelations were so astonishing that the ruse of naiveté was necessary to keep her from suspicion of heresy? Or, if she was indeed illiterate and communicated her insights to a confessor-friend, how much of the text is his rather than hers? Might the scribe himself have added his own controversial teachings to the text, his subordinate role shielding his own thought from suspicion? We will probably never know the answers to such questions, but we must consider them if we are to make sense of these texts.

Within the vernacular mystical tradition stands Margery Kempe, an English laywoman (c. 1373–1438/1439) who, according to her contemporaries, possessed unusual spiritual gifts. Margery had a habit of being seized by emotional fits at significant moments, often during church services, and would weep and shriek inconsolably. Although the tendency was highly distracting to those around her, many thought she was blessed by divine impulses, and so were unable to cast her aside completely. Her narrative was preserved in a work called *The Book of Margery Kempe*—not a work of her own authorship (she was illiterate), but rather an account of her travels and travails. (See "*The Book of Margery Kempe*.") A considerable cult developed around her in England, but she was never a candidate for sainthood.

The religious life was a respected one which attracted many of the elite: men and women from property-owning and noble backgrounds. Within the church such persons could extend their influence or continue to serve their families' interests—though only a cynic would deny that piety ran deep in most of those who entered the religious life. Nevertheless, in a culture that saw leadership as a genetically inherited power, it made sense to ensure that both church and the civil realm would be ruled by naturally powerful persons.

St. Birgitta of Sweden (1303–1372/1373) is a case in point. The daughter of a prosperous father, and the wife of an equally prominent husband, Birgitta herself raised a large family of children who would go on to lead distinguished lives themselves; one daughter, Katherine, even became a saint like her mother. On becoming a widow in her early forties, Birgitta turned her back on secular concerns and decided to devote her life to God and the church. In particular, she is said to have received a command from Jesus in about 1349 to go to Rome and stay there until the papacy returned to the city. At that time, the papacy had been located in Avignon for four decades, and few imagined its return to Rome at any time; so, when she received this message, Birgitta faced possible exile for life. Undaunted, she left for Rome, where she did in fact spend the rest of her life, dying in 1372/1373. In 1367 the papacy was restored to Rome, but only briefly; it returned to Avignon three years later.

Birgitta wrote a number of provocative mystical works—*The Word of the Angel* (1354) is possibly her best—but also was a familiar figure in the Catholic Church, becoming a correspondent and associate of popes and cardinals. Possibly because of her mystical gifts, seen as divinely inspired, her exhortations to the hierarchy were taken seriously, and when, in 1378, the papacy returned to Rome permanently, Birgitta's earlier intervention was given part of the credit. Given the unlikelihood in 1349 of such an event ever taking place, to have helped, possibly, to bring it about must indeed have seemed miraculous.

Some of the mystics found their inspiration not in religious experience but in the mundane sensations of secular life. The Dutch mystic Hadewijch of Brabant (thirteenth century) drew on the tradition of courtly love, so that the language with which she describes her love for God echoes the poetry of erotic love. The poems of Hadewijch also draw on the poetry of the seasons; many celebrate the arrival of spring or the new year, which in the medieval calendar came on March 25, the feast of the Annunciation. Just as the earthly is used as a symbol for the

Who's Who

Medieval Women Mystics

St. Hildegard of Bingen (1098–1179) A German Benedictine abbess and writer. She was one of the first people to write in German and also one of the first women to produce serious works about leading a religious life.

Hadewijch of Brabant (13th century) A Dutch mystic whose writings draw heavily on medieval ideas about courtly love.

Julian of Norwich (c. 1342–c. 1416) An English mystic who claimed to be illiterate (supposedly a priest transcribed her "revelations"). Others have discredited this and believe that she was both literate and learned.

St. Catherine of Siena (1347–1380) An Italian Dominican who believed she had been called by Christ to carry out his work. She became involved in high-level church matters.

Margery Kempe (c. 1373–1438/9) An ordinary Englishwoman who became something of a cult figure. She was given to having dramatic "fits," which many believed were proof of divine spiritual knowledge and power.

St. Catherine of Genoa (Caterina Fieschi) (1447–1510) Having had a series of powerful "spiritual" experiences, Catherine devoted her life to caring for the sick, notably as Director of the Pammatone Hospital at Genoa.

The Fire of Love

An English mystic whose writings include some gems of medieval vernacular religious writing, Richard Rolle describes the relation between God and humans as one of intense and constant love. Such affective piety offered comfort in an anxious age.

The love of God takes up to itself with marvelous rejoicing the soul of the man whom it perfectly penetrates and sets it truly ablaze by the fire of the Holy Spirit, and does not permit it to stray for a moment from the memory of so great a love. It ties the spirit of the lover so that it does not fly away toward vain things and continually tends in to the Beloved.

We are able, certainly, if we are true lovers of our Lord Jesus Christ, to meditate on Him while we go on, and to hold on to the song of His love while we sit in the assembly, and we shall be able to keep the memory of Him at the table, even in the very tastes of food and drink. But we ought to praise God for every little morsel of food or every small cup of drink, and among the intervals of the acceptance of nourishment and of small morsels, we ought to resound these praises with honeyed sweetness and spiritual cry and desire. We ought to pant toward Him in the midst of feasts.

And if we should be engaged in manual labor, what prevents us from raising our heart to heavenly things and from retaining the thought of eternal love without ceasing? And thus at every time of our life we should be burning with fervor, not torpid; nor will anything remove our heart from this love, except for sleep.

Oh, how great the joy and gladness that flows into the lover! Oh, what blessed and truly desirable sweetness fills his soul! For love is life, lasting without an end, where it is fixed and made solid in Christ, when neither prosperities nor adversities will be strong enough to change that love following its loving affection rooted in heavenly things, as the wisest men have recorded. Then, without a doubt, it turns night into day, shadows into light, annoyance into melody, punishment into pleasure, and labor into the sweetest rest.

For this love is not imaginary or simulated, but true and perfected, directed inseparably toward Christ, resounding melody to the Beloved with harmony. And if you have loved in that manner (as I have shown), you will stand glorious with the best and the most honorable in the kingdom of God for that life-giving vision Itself.

(From Richard Rolle, *The Fire of Love and the Mending of Life*, trans. M.L. del Mastro [CHK]. Garden City, NY: Image Books, 1981.)

heavenly in love poetry, so with these seasonal pieces the cycles of the physical world are used to describe the relation of the world and God.

One of the variables in the study of medieval religious writing is the degree to which a work reflects the time in which it was created. Every work is to some extent the product of its context; but how much of that context is discernible in the work is a question of interpretation. Some of the most animated debates in the study of Western religious thought are about whether certain works are understandable "only" in the light of their context or can be fully comprehensible without reference to external factors. In the case of mysticism in the late Middle Ages, however, it is clear that the existence of the plague must be taken into account. The Black Death cast a shadow over religious life and practice from its first outbreak in 1347 until the end of the fifteenth century, and in some places even later. Although few texts mention the plague directly, the existence of divine wrath that the plague suggested inspired a number of responses.

One mystic whose work reflects the influence of the plague is Catherine of Genoa (1447–1510), a woman who devoted her life to the care of the sick. Both in her work as director of the Pammatone Hospital in Genoa and in the writings recorded by her spiritual advisor, Catherine exemplifies a theology that stresses oneness with God through both pain and love. Oneness in pain is achieved by voluntary acceptance of suffering, a form of asceticism. Unlike other ascetic paths, sickness is not something one can will; to the medieval mind, all diseases were thought to come from God. What one can will is the attitude one takes toward disease. One can see the onset of disease as something bad and an occasion for resenting God, or one can embrace illness as an expression of God's will. In the latter choice, in Catherine's view, the believer expresses true piety, for he or she is grateful for every expression of God's will, even those that put the natural self at risk.

The time in which Catherine lived was, as we have noted in the last two chapters, one marked by fear—of the plague and of the fires of purgatory. However, European civilization was also undergoing great intellectual development at this time. In Italy the cultural transformation known as the Renaissance was well under way. And in northern Europe, a new spirit of self-confidence was about to tackle the fears that ordinary people suffered and to shake the foundations of the church until it split asunder.

Key Terms

ALLEGORICAL Symbolical; this method of interpreting scripture sees the literal sense as symbolic of a deeper and hidden meaning.

ECSTASY Being transported outside of oneself into a state of union with God.

MYSTICISM Immediate experience of God, often in the form of a sensation of oneness with the divine.

SPIRITUALITY Personal piety, usually expressed through prayer, song, or devotional writing.

VIA NEGATIVA A form of theological writing that tries to understand God by removing (or "negating") conventional terms and attributes; it emphasizes the unknowability of God.

VIA POSITIVA A form of theological writing that describes God by applying (or "positing") terms and attributes; it holds that God is, to some degree, knowable.

Lucas Cranach the Elder, *Family Altar* (center of three panels), 1509. Oil on wood.
Städelsches Kunstinstitut, Frankfurt.

PART FOUR

From Medieval to Modern, from One Church, Many

Changes within and outside the Catholic Church laid the foundations for the gradual collapse of medieval Christendom, an entity that had never been as unified as it appeared. The plague from the late 1340s unleashed new anxieties about divine goodness and the possibility of salvation. The fall of Constantinople in 1453 brought an end to the Byzantine Empire, a minor consolation for a papacy already weakened by schism. Gutenberg's invention of printing with movable type allowed the Christian liturgy to be standardized, facilitated the promulgation of ecclesiastical laws, and gave broad circulation to works of classical and Christian literature.

The rise of humanism permitted critical studies of the Bible and the works of the church fathers. New insights into ancient texts provided alternate interpretations of core doctrines, some of them critical of the Roman Church hierarchy. The sixteenth-century Protestant Reformation that ensued was a complex mix of political, cultural, and religious elements. For a laity anxious about salvation, new religious programs offered a path minimizing the importance of seemingly arbitrary "works." For secular monarchs seeking independence from the Holy Roman Empire, the possibility of sovereign Protestant states promised independence and power. For humanists and theologians, there followed decades of debate and dispute, much of it held within the newly formed universities.

During this Reformation era the Catholic Church was engaged in both reform and reaction. New religious orders were founded and old ones reorganized, and concerted attention was paid to the state of piety at the parish level. Attacks against the institutions of the Catholic Church were met with polemical tracts and treatises defending its traditional practices.

1500		
	1503	Humanist scholar Erasmus publishes his *Handbook of a Christian Soldier*.
	1506	Pope Julius II begins building a new St. Peter's, financed by the sale of indulgences.
	1517	Luther nails his 95 theses to Wittenberg church door, starting the Reformation.
	1521	Luther defends his views at the Diet of Worms, but is excommunicated.
	1529	At the Marburg Colloquy, Luther and Zwingli fail to agree on the eucharist.
	1529	Lutheran princes set up the Schmalkald League to defend their faith.
	1534	King Henry VIII is declared supreme head of the English Church.
	1536	John Calvin publishes his influential *Institutes of Christian Religion*.
	1539	Ignatius Loyola's Society of Jesus — the Jesuits — is approved by the pope.
	1541	Calvin establishes religious rule in Geneva.
1550	1545–63	The Council of Trent launches the Catholic Counter-Reformation.
	1553–58	Mary Tudor briefly reestablishes Catholicism in England.
	1555	The Peace of Augsburg allows German princes to choose between Lutheranism and Catholicism.
	1555–59	Pope Paul IV reforms the Catholic Church.
	1559	John Knox introduces Calvinist teaching to Scotland.
	1562–98	Wars of Religion in France between Catholics and Calvinist Huguenots.
	1562	St. Teresa of Ávila founds the Discalced (Barefoot) Carmelites.
1600	1578	St. John of the Cross completes his mystical work *The Dark Night of the Soul*.
	1605	Catholic conspirators in England attempt the Gunpowder Plot.
	1611	The Authorized Version of the Bible is commissioned by King James I of England.
	1618–48	The Thirty Years' War between Catholics and Protestants in Europe.
	1620	The Pilgrim Fathers, English Calvinists, found a settlement in Massachusetts.
	1632	Catholics found the colony of Maryland.
	1636	Puritan preacher Thomas Hooker founds the town of Hartford, Connecticut.
	1639	Roger Williams sets up the first Baptist church in North America, in Rhode Island.
	1638	In Scotland Presbyterians revolt against the imposition of the Church of England.
	1640	Cornelius Jansen's *Augustinus,* the founding text of Jansenism, is published posthumously.
	1642–48	The English Civil War leads to the fall of Catholic-leaning King Charles I.
	1648	George Fox founds the Society of Friends, or Quakers.
1650	1649–60	Puritans dominate England under Cromwell's Commonwealth.
	1653	Pope Innocent X condemns aspects of Jansenism as heretical.
	1656–57	Jansenist Blaise Pascal attacks the Jesuits in *Provincial Letters*.
	1675	Spener's *Pia Desideria* is published, boosting Lutheran Pietism.
	1679	Pope Innocent XI condemns Jesuit "laxism."
	1682	Quaker William Penn founds the city of Philadelphia.
	1684	Massachusetts theologian Increase Mather publishes *Remarkable Providences*.
	1685	Huguenots flee France when Louis XIV revokes the tolerant Edict of Nantes.
	1688–89	England's "Glorious Revolution," deposing Catholic King James II, allows tolerance for "dissenters."

Launching the Reformation

Martin Luther's Revolution

According to a sixteenth-century quip, "Erasmus laid the egg that Luther hatched." The "egg" was the Protestant Reformation, the religious upheaval that split Western Christianity in two, leaving some Europeans within the Roman Catholic Church and others outside it, in new "protestant" (that is, protesting) denominations that owed no allegiance to Rome. Erasmus of Rotterdam (c. 1466–1536; see Chapter 18) was arguably the leading humanist of his age: a scholar, teacher, editor of classical and Patristic texts, author, and theologian. He was also a critic of the Catholic Church (despite being an ordained priest), attacking the foibles of clergy and theologians, as well as a number of supposedly pious practices. But when the crisis came, in 1517, it was not Erasmus who precipitated it, but a relatively obscure priest named Martin Luther (1483–1546), whose revolutionary activities we shall be examining in this chapter.

The Advent of the Printing Press

It could be argued, in fact, that the "egg" was hatched by an invention that had appeared more than sixty years earlier, in the 1450s: the printing press. Generally credited to Johann Gutenberg (c.1400–1468), this invention made possible the rapid dissemination of ideas to an increasingly literate population. The writings of humanists such as Erasmus (who stayed loyal to Rome despite his criticisms), of Luther, and of other reformers circulated throughout Europe with a speed unimaginable only a few decades earlier. Ideas viewed as heretical by the church and heretofore suppressed were now available for all to read.

The printing press made possible the production of books by the hundreds in a fraction of the time taken to produce a single book by hand. The first printed books were lavish and expensive productions, often designed to resemble the most elaborate manuscript volumes; within decades, however, cheaper and more utilitarian books began to appear. As the market for books expanded, so did the range of literature available: local histories, popular romances, and stories that had been preserved orally began to appear alongside the biblical and classical texts that had predominated among the works preserved by the time-consuming and costly craft of manuscript writing.

Religious Books

Even so, religious books still dominated the fledgling industry—understandably since it began in Mainz. Then a semi-autonomous archbishopric within the Holy Roman Empire, Mainz was sometimes called the "Rome of the North"; here, ecclesiastical supervision was at its strongest. (Not even Rome itself was as vigilant, in the second half of the 1500s, in protecting doctrine.) For the church the benefits of printing were obvious: missals (Mass books) and other service books could ensure that liturgy was regularized throughout a diocese; a standardized biblical text gave the clergy an alternative to faulty or incomplete editions of Scripture; and new rulings could be promulgated and distributed very effectively to parish churches.

Publication of the Bible affected the life of the church in numerous ways. Translated into vernacular languages, it could now easily be read by the laity for the first time. New editions of sermons and treatises by the church fathers, brought out by theologians of the day, provided influential insights into the meaning of certain biblical passages for the reading public. Literate members of the laity were not limited to hearing Scripture read aloud and interpreted in sermons by the parish priest. The first cracks in the dominance of the church were made by the appearance of the printed Bible.

Members of the educated laity who knew Latin had access to a far greater range of material. Editions of the works by the early church fathers appeared almost as frequently as new editions of Greek and Roman classics, opening up worlds previously so clouded in obscurity that they must have seemed more legendary than real. For people without Latin there were vernacular psalters and saints' lives, books offering formulas for prayer, and handbooks for leading a pious life.

Whether printing was advantageous or detrimental to the life of the church is a question that can be endlessly debated. Did access to the New Testament and stories of the saints reinforce piety or instill doubt? Did readers feel closer to the church when they could read books of doctrine, or more independent —feeling that they could find out on their own what the faith demanded? Stated differently, was the religion of the past, as recorded in books, different from what the church was teaching, or were they one and the same? It was crucial for the church that they be the same thing. But as it turned out, they were indeed different.

Plague, Death, and Absolution

According to a widely accepted account of the later Middle Ages, between the outbreak of the plague, in the mid-1300s, and the dawn of the Reformation in the early 1500s, death seemed to hang in the air. The disease was a devastating one, the course of its symptoms rapid, and its path random. In the absence of medical explanations, much less any means of prevention, many people saw it as the

A page from the "Gutenberg Bible," c. 1455. Manuscript illumination. British Library, London.

This Latin Bible in missal script was completed around 1455 in Mainz, Germany. The initial "I" (left) begins the prologue of Proverbs and the initial "P" (right) begins chapter 1 of the Parabolae Salomonis.

Albrecht Dürer, *Erasmus of Rotterdam*, 1526. Engraving. Reproduced courtesy of the Trustees of the British Museum, London.

A Christian humanist and prodigious scholar, Erasmus helped publish much of the Greek and Latin Patristic tradition and the Greek New Testament.

punishment of a sinful people by a wrathful deity. The sense of sinfulness was instilled by the biblical narrative of the fall of Adam and Eve. God's wrath seemed self-evident, for only God could bring so much pain and death to so many. Since it was heretical not to view God as just and good, Christians were obliged to view their suffering as proper justice for their sins.

The inevitability of death—and the near-inevitability of spending time in purgatory, with or without the last rites—was possibly the dominant theme of the fifteenth-century church. As we know from the martyrdoms of the first century, death in itself could be seen as something to be embraced. But there are glorious deaths and inglorious ones; and the ordinary man or woman dying with unabsolved sins died, by and large, an inglorious one. A shortage of priests, and the sudden onset of symptoms in the case of the plague, meant that the risk of dying without absolution was real. The sins with which a person died would have to be removed in purgatory. As we noted in Chapter 13, the church held that the pains of purgatory could be diminished by the prayers of the faithful still living. Thus the merit of the surviving relative's pious act was applied to the condition of the dead person.

But since no one had any assurance that they were doing enough for their departed loved ones, a better alternative seemed to be to obtain one or more indulgences. One of these certificates would release the recipient from purgatorial punishments, either partially or, in the case of the plenary indulgence, completely. Since it was beyond dispute that the church had the right to "bind and loose" and thus to determine Christians' salvation, no one doubted that these indulgences worked. But whereas initially they had been granted for good works, such as caring for the sick or going on a pilgrimage, by the early sixteenth century they were for sale—for oneself or one's deceased relatives.

Naturally, the rich benefited spiritually under this sytem and the church benefited in real terms. To allow the wealthy to buy their ancestors' salvation, while the poor had only their prayers to help shorten the time their loved ones spent in purgatory, aroused distrust and hostility in many quarters—including some ecclesiastical ones. Satires and outright attacks against greedy clergy began to appear in profusion: another by-product of the invention of printing. ANTICLERICALISM was at an all-time high, while fears of a harsh afterlife did not diminish. The people were in a difficult position indeed.

The situation came to a head when a Dominican friar named Johann Tetzel (c. 1465–1519) undertook, on the instructions of Albrecht (or Albert), Archbishop of Mainz (1490–1545), a campaign to sell indulgences throughout Germany. With the skill at preaching for which the Dominicans were well known, and with the supposed value of these certificates becoming ever more highly touted, this sales tour (the proceeds of which helped finance construction of the present-day Vatican buildings) aroused skepticism and scorn wherever it went. It was clear that something was wrong with selling happiness in the afterlife for cash.

Martin Luther

Many people felt instinctively that the sale of indulgences violated the fundamental convictions of Christianity. But a biblical scholar developed this idea into a

BIOGRAPHICAL PROFILE

Martin Luther (1483–1546)

Martin Luther, traditionally considered the initiator of the Reformation, was born in Eisleben, Saxony, in 1483, the son of a peasant who achieved financial success in the mining industry. Ambitious for his son, Hans Luther wanted Martin to study law. Legend (much of it of his own making) has it that Martin was saved from death during a storm by St. Ann, and in loyalty to her for her favor he entered the monastic life instead. While a member of the Augustinian Hermits, he came under the tutelage of Johann von Staupitz who encouraged his study of the Bible. Trained in theology at Erfurt, Luther was ordained as a priest and became a professor of scripture and philosophy at the newly established university at Wittenberg in 1507. Driven by what he called a search for a righteous God, he probed scripture for a revelation of divine righteousness, finding his answer finally in Romans 1:17 ("The just shall live by faith"). Defining faith, rather than works, as the essence of Christian righteousness, Luther insisted that trust in the divine promise of salvation was the sole means of salvation. This meant that "works" and their substitutes, such as indulgences, did not count at all toward salvation.

Indulgences were certificates that could be bought for a fee, entitling the purchaser to benefits in the afterlife for good works done in this life. Such an exchange of spiritual benefits for worldly goods irritated Luther, who insisted that total faith in the complete atonement by Christ was the only path toward salvation. By eliminating "works" from the process of salvation, Luther angered the Catholic hierarchy. In the wake of the 1521 Diet of Worms he was excommunicated from the Roman Church. Instead of capitulating, however, he seemed to bask in the condemnation of a church that he would come to regard as diabolical rather than divine.

Luther had opened up a new understanding of the Christian message of revelation, one that did away with the view that the church was the indispensable vessel through which that message had to be channeled for the benefit of believers. His alienation from the Roman Church is thus easily understood.

Theologically, Luther is known for his doctrine of justification by faith. Pastorally, his greatest influence lay in his efforts to make Christian teaching intelligible to the German laity. The vernacular liturgy made the mass and sacraments more accessible to his contemporaries, not just in Saxony but throughout all Germanic and Scandinavian lands. His gift for language, and his own bluntness, gave new life to the old Latin liturgy. Many today, even non-Lutherans, know the words and tunes to hymns that he composed: "A Mighty Fortress Is Our God" is surely the best known. His translations of the Bible into clear and forceful German brought scripture—to the Protestants, the only form of divine revelation—alive for readers and listeners who had for centuries been told that it was too obscure for them to understand by themselves.

Luther's personality was naturally iconoclastic. He not only rejected the Roman system of canon law: he publicly burned copies of it. He defended his work at Heidelberg, Augsburg, and Worms by summoning his knowledge of the Bible and an obstinacy that would not yield to secular or ecclesiastical coercion. He demonstrated his rejection of the vow of celibacy by marrying a former nun. The Luther household in turn became a model for generations of pastors. (His opponents saw his marriage as evidence of his contempt for the vows of the religious life.)

Luther's harshness was coupled with a surprisingly tender piety. He often spoke of his "assaults" (*Anfechtungen*), periods of intense spiritual turmoil; and friends would be surprised to find him at prayer with tears streaming down his cheeks. His final words were "We are beggars: this is true" and they seem to reveal an utter dependence on God.

Lucas Cranach the Elder, *Martin Luther*, 1533. Oil on panel. City of Bristol Museum and Art Gallery, England.

strong conviction that the indulgence trade was contrary to the teaching of the Bible and proceeded to "go public" with it. Martin Luther, an Augustinian monk and professor of biblical theology at the University of Wittenberg, in northeast Saxony, had been wrestling for at least five years with the question of divine right-eousness. What did it mean to call God righteous? After intensive study of the Psalms and the writings of St. Paul, Luther supposedly suddenly perceived that God's righteousness was the power to save freely—without regard to any human ability to earn it. Luther had rediscovered the Augustinian understanding of grace (see Chapter 2) as something completely free. The whole system of merit and penitential works, as well as the indulgences that were based on it, began to appear to be so much fiction.

Luther has long been cast as a man of heroic proportions, and he was indeed one of those individuals who seem able to change the course of history by sheer force of personality. But his fascination for historians lies not in his greatness but in his complexity. Along with his boldness in challenging centuries of church teaching, at a time when doing so often meant excommunication or even death, went a sensitivity to the anxieties of the ordinary Christian. The Luther who con-demned monasticism because it seemed to be a means toward attaining perfec-tion had been a monk who suffered over the penitential rites, anxious about his own sins and his unworthiness of divine forgiveness. The one who scoffed at the superstitions of medieval Catholicism was himself intimidated by natural phe-nomena such as thunderstorms, and fearful of death. The braggadocio of some of his writings is counterbalanced by a personal piety so intense that he was fre-quently brought to tears while praying.

Luther's background helps explain some, but not all, of later history's fascina-tion with him. He was a Saxon of peasant stock, whose father had risen from miner to mine owner and thus had become a member of the bourgeoisie. Like many ambitious fathers, Hans Luther wanted his son to raise the family's place in society even higher, and so he hoped that Martin would follow a career in law. Martin complied, until on one occasion (according to a well-known account) a sudden storm struck such fear into him that he vowed to St. Anne that he would enter a monastery if spared. True to his word, he then entered the order of Augustinian Hermits (an order formed in the thirteenth century from several groups of hermits, hence the no-longer-applicable name). Luther was apparently a conscientious, dedicated monk. But his scruples over the sacrament of penance (see Chapter 13), and his struggles to understand, through the Scriptures, the meaning of divine righteousness troubled him greatly. Eventually he was led to feel that if the righteousness of God is absolute, then no human works can merit it; and if grace is free, the only way to receive it is to accept it freely and gratefully. Language of "cooperation" and the *facere* doctrine seemed to Luther a violation of the work of Christ and even a fraud perpetrated by the church upon its people.

For Luther, the doctrine of purgatory was the test case. The idea of purgatory, and certainly the notion that one could buy one's relatives out of it by means of indulgences, was impious and cynical in his view; and he condemned the buying of these certificates as much as their sale. Popular sentiment was on his side, as various bits of popular doggerel mocked indulgence sellers like Tetzel—though without much impact on the business itself. It took a grand gesture to challenge the entire system. This was Luther's moment.

*The Typographer,
16th century.
Woodcut. Victoria
and Albert
Museum, London.*

*The invention of
printing helped
shape a new
historical
awareness in the
early modern
period, and
allowed rapid
dissemination of
controversial
religious ideas.*

Luther's Theses

Devotion to the souls in purgatory is at its highest on All Souls' Day, and it was on the eve of this holiday in 1517 that Luther made his first public declaration. The popular story that has come down through the ages is of Luther bravely nailing his "ninety-five Theses" to the door of the Wittenberg Castle church. The accuracy of this image has been called into question, but the fact remains that in issuing his Theses he fired the first shot in a conflict that would rapidly embroil the German-speaking territories. In his Theses Luther identified ninety-five issues for dispute, many of which went to the heart of the Catholic church's teachings about sacraments and justification.

In fact, however, Luther may not have intended to cause a public scandal. In the medieval educational world, theses were the topics offered for disputation. They did not need to represent the proposer's own views; they might just have been ideas he wanted to discuss with other scholars. To attract the greatest amount of public interest, he would state his theses in their most controversial form. Thus an academic theologian at a university might have been intrigued by the topics suggested by Luther in his Theses—but would probably have seen them as something like debate resolutions: intellectual exercises, not real demands for reform. Ideas such as those that Luther presented in his Theses had surely been the subject of academic disputation for decades before 1517.

Luther's Theses took on a life of their own thanks to the printing press. The fact that a member of a religious order, and an academic theologian, would question core teachings of the church and expose them to public scrutiny was too much for the German printers and their readers to ignore, and within weeks, news of Luther's Theses had spread through the German lands. Whether intended as such or not, the issue had become a public affair, and thus it needed to be addressed at the highest levels.

The German hierarchy thus became involved in the "Luther affair" from the beginning. Some response was necessary, since the Theses had, in their original form, been accompanied by a letter to Albrecht, the Archbishop of Mainz. Although Albrecht remained coolly aloof, the wrath of the hierarchy of the German Church and Empire, at Heidelberg, Augsburg, Worms and elsewhere, came down upon Martin Luther—putting him repeatedly in the position of a persecuted believer. It was a role that he was determined to exploit. Gradually, the authorities who might have provided a forum for dialogue became transformed into a sixteenth-

Shaping the Reformation

Who's Who

Johann Tetzel (c. 1465–1519) A German Dominican and preacher who supported the sale of religious "indulgences" (reductions in punishment) in return for money for the church's coffers. His enthusiastic promotion of this practice precipitated Luther's nailing of the "Theses."

Erasmus, Desiderius (c. 1466–1536) A major humanist figure and the leading scholar of his day, especially of Greek; he was the first lecturer in Greek at Cambridge University. He wrote the hugely influential *Praise of Folly*, a biting attack on monasticism and corruption in the church.

Martin Luther (1483–1546) The main figure of the German Protestant Reformation. A theological professor at Wittenberg University, he is best known

for nailing ninety-five "Theses" attacking decadent practices in the Roman Church to the door of the church in Wittenberg Castle, 1517.

Martin Bucer (1491–1551) A former Dominican and an important Protestant reformer. Head of a parish in Strasbourg, he later traveled to England to take up a professorship in Divinity at Cambridge University.

Philipp Melanchthon (1497–1560) A leading scholar and reformer, and a Greek professor at Wittenberg University. Melanchthon and Luther were major influences on each other and the former carried the main torch of reform during Luther's exile at Wartburg Castle.

century version of Pilate's court, with Luther the Christ figure punished for his absolute devotion to an idea the "pagans" cannot absorb. At least in hindsight, this was Luther's image in the making.

In his trials before the hierarchy, Luther invoked the memory of Jan Hus (c. 1372–1415), the Czech martyr of a century earlier, whom he saw as the valiant victim of a capricious hierarchy. Called early in 1518 to Heidelberg to answer charges about his challenge, Luther proved an eloquent enough defender of his Theses to draw several members of the Dominican Order to his cause. One such was Martin Bucer (1491–1551), a German friar who would become one of the most influential theologians of the second generation and a shaper of the Reformation in England (see Chapter 16). Meetings at Augsburg with Cardinal Tomasso de Vio Cajetan (1469–1534) and at Leipzig with Johann Eck (1486–1543) soon followed. The notoriety that his Theses had brought him obliged Luther to defend his position with a force and a clarity that might not have emerged if the controversy had not instantly become bitter. Thus the initial success of the Reformation was due largely to the opposition it drew.

Luther's Reformation Principles

In the next chapter we shall pursue the story of the events following Luther's challenge to the church; however, it is important first to take a closer look at his theology. Luther's defense of his ideas was marked by an appeal to biblical authority, a strategy that he felt would force the Catholic Church to recognize that its teachings were unbiblical and thus false doctrine. In Luther's view, the church emphasized human ability and thus encouraged pride in human achievements—which might be anything from almsgiving by a layman to an outstanding treatise by a theologian. The focus, he felt, should be on divine revelation, as found in the Bible. In the face of this powerful and yet paradoxical authority, human reason should accept its own inadequacy. Similarly, for Luther, grace was so total and uncontrollable that human confidence in natural abilities was inevitably humbled. To the extent that the Catholic Church relied on reason and taught the value of works, it diminished, in Luther's view, the work of revelation and grace.

Luther's appeal to the Bible and his insistence on grace over works are represented by two principles: SOLA SCRIPTURA and SOLA GRATIA. The first means that Scripture, rather than reason or the power of the church, is to be the only source of Christian doctrine. The Patristic tradition (see Chapter 2) had value as a body of interpretive literature, he maintained, but no independent authority. The second principle holds that the divine work of grace is the sole source of righteousness before God; no works, no virtues, no gestures or professions of piety can elicit or influence grace. Stated another way, one is made righteous, or justified, by no efforts of one's own, but only by faith in the promise of forgiveness. This is often referred to as the doctrine of JUSTIFICATION BY FAITH, in contrast to the idea that devotional "works" can make one righteous before God.

These two "sola" principles are joined by a number of other doctrines that set Luther's theology in sharp distinction to that of the Roman Church. One of these is the PRIESTHOOD OF ALL BELIEVERS, a potentially misleading term, since it does not mean that all Christians are clergy. (In any case, Luther preferred the term "pastor" to "priest".) What the priesthood of all believers does mean is that all Christians are equal before God, and bear a special responsibility, like priests, to maintain the faith in its pure form. Ancient divisions into clergy and laity, in which the clergy are superior to the laity, are eliminated in Luther: the lowliest worker is as much a "priest" in God's eyes as the loftiest bishop. Clergy still needed to receive special training, like the other professions, but symbols of their separate status were eliminated in Lutheran liturgy. For example, whereas in the Catholic liturgy only the priest partakes of both elements, with the laity receiving only the wafer (see Chapter 6), in the Lutheran the laity, too, receive both bread and wine.

Perhaps the most far-reaching doctrine of Luther's early years is that of the two kingdoms, a direct challenge to the medieval construct of a secular and a sacred arm of God's governance of the world. In Luther's system, human experience takes place in two realms, or kingdoms: a godly one and an earthly one. The godly kingdom is the one in which God is sovereign, acting on the hearts of believers. It is an intangible and spiritual realm, experienced by piety. The earthly kingdom is the material world, with nature, states, human institutions, and the like. We experience it in our outward lives and in social relations.

This doctrine is radical in its implications, for according to it the church, as a material institution, falls into the earthly kingdom—and thus under the jurisdiction of the secular powers. Hence, in Luther's thought, the governance of the churches belongs to the civil government, who must guard the purity of worship in their territories. The role of the church was limited to preaching and sacraments, not the moral control of the people. The Catholic Church, for Luther, was a usurper of secular power, its error a "confusion of realms" insofar as it invoked spiritual authority while exercising worldly power. In powerful essays such as the *Address to the Christian Nobility of the German Nation* (1520) Luther asks the secular government to recognize its rights and duties with regard to religion.

In theory and practice, then, the Reformation was from the start as much a political phenomenon as it was a religious one. Some princes were sympathetic to the reformers, protecting them and imposing their reforms in the churches within their domains; the resident clergy either went along with the reforms or left for other territories. In many cases the theologians and the courts worked closely to ensure an effective and smooth transition. Lutheranism was thus imposed "from above," and is an example of magisterial reform, or reform by the magistracy. Without the support of rulers such as Frederick III (the Wise), Elector of Saxony (1463–1525; r. 1486–1525), and the youthful Philip, Landgrave of Hesse (1504–1567), the movement Luther inaugurated might have remained an academic diversion and a case for ecclesiastical discipline.

The German princes had more than religious motives for imposing reform. The papacy, as a centralized hierarchy, was an alien power demanding obedience and financial support from all subjects, which meant that both rulers and ruled felt themselves under the dominance of the church. Politically, the princes' sovereignty was limited, to some extent, by the Holy Roman Empire, under whose jurisdiction some of them felt more like provincial governors than true princes. Autonomy from these two Roman powers, church and empire, meant greater power at the local level, as well as greater economic strength: revenues would be more likely to remain in the territory. Luther's challenge to the church on

October 31, 1517, not only launched the Protestant Reformation; it also gave a powerful impetus to a political phenomenon that would dominate the following two centuries: the rise of the modern nation-state. It would be some time, however, before either of these two institutions would reach maturity.

Key Terms

ANTICLERICALISM Popular hostility to the clergy, often in the form of satirizing their imagined gluttony and sexual habits.

JUSTIFICATION BY FAITH A Reformation doctrine holding that only belief in Christ's atonement is necessary and sufficient for salvation.

PRIESTHOOD OF ALL BELIEVERS A Lutheran doctrine stating that all Christians are equal before God and share a holy or "priestly" mission.

SOLA GRATIA A doctrine which teaches that the believer is saved solely by divine means— grace (Latin, *gratia*)—and not through any amount of human effort.

SOLA SCRIPTURA A theological principle that seeks to base all doctrine in scriptural revelation; it is associated with 16th-century Protestantism.

CHAPTER 16

Development of the Reformation

The Spread of Protestantism

The Catholic authorities who thought that Luther would, if pressed, recognize the error of his ways soon learned that here was an antagonist who would not depart easily. Luther was armed with an arsenal of scriptural and Patristic texts and no small measure of self-assurance. If he was to be the diminutive David to the Goliath of the Roman Church, so be it. The course of his career as a reformer would take him through controversy after controversy, and he would die in 1546 sure in his conviction that the papacy was the seat of the "antichrist" foretold in John's Epistles (I John 2:18, 22) and that the end of the world was near. That the world has continued for several centuries, and that antagonistic branches of Christendom would seek mutual understanding and even union, would have struck him as preposterous.

Luther was certain that his age marked the end of history, and that the Last Judgment was not far off: a view fairly typical of his age, especially among his fellow Protestants. These thinkers tended to read the signs of the times and gather from them a sense that the world could not get far worse than it was. The devil had taken the place of Christ, the Turks were threatening to overtake Christendom, and the body of true believers (the reformers and their followers) were being viciously persecuted. For a biblically versed theologian like Luther it was clear that history was repeating itself, and that the sufferings of the Jews during the sixth century B.C.E. and of the Christians in the first century C.E. were repeating themselves. In the reformers' manner of Bible reading, the text was not just a record of the past but a depiction of what would happen in the future.

Being aware of such a perspective helps us appreciate the urgency with which the reformers viewed their situation. Because they saw the Last Judgment as imminent, they felt the need both to clarify their own faith and to separate themselves from the damned—most of whom, they assumed, were still active in the Roman Church seeking salvation through their own efforts. But that church would have its say, and then some; and the Reformation would have decades of struggle before it was recognized by the Catholic Church as an independent, if misguided, form of Christianity.

The Diet of Worms

The progress of the Reformation can be marked by a number of turning points, the first of which is certainly the Diet of Worms in 1521. A Diet (from the Latin *dies*, "day") was a session of the imperial government, called by the emperor in order to address various urgent problems. When the emperor, Charles V (1500–1558; r. as emperor 1519–1555) called the Diet that met in the Rhine city of Worms in 1521, issues on the agenda included various urgent political matters as well as the case of Martin Luther. But Luther's stance before the empire was a dramatic showdown and has become a symbol of personal courage.

According to the records, some of which may have been embellished, Luther was shown a stack of his own books and was asked if he wished to retract anything he had said in them. Luther not only refused to retract his criticisms of the church, but reinforced his opposition to those teachings which in his view conflicted with the authority of the Bible. In his most famous words (which unfortunately he may not have said), Luther declared: "Here I stand; I can do nothing else. God help me." In the wake of his defiance of both church and empire, he was declard an outlaw—a decision announced in the 1521 EDICT OF WORMS.

More troubles followed. Luther himself was safe enough, in hiding at Wartburg Castle, near Eisenach, under the protection of the Elector of Saxony. There, he embarked on a translation of the New Testament into German, a theological and stylistic achievement of the highest order. But his religious movement was under threat. While he was away, a number of theologians with more radical tendencies came to the University of Wittenberg and tried to incite a revolutionary fervor among the students and faculty there. This so-called "Wittenberg move-

P.A. Labouchère (engraver Nargeot), *The Diet of Worms*, 1521. Engraving.

Luther defends his opinions at the Diet of Worms before the emperor and a gathering of the church and social hierarchy.

ment," which involved the radical reformers Thomas Müntzer and Thomas Strauss, with Philip Melanchthon (1497–1560) as the defender of moderation, was an early crack in the cohesion of the Reformation movement. Other points of tension were more subtle, as when Ulrich Zwingli (1484–1531) in Zurich began a program of preaching and writing that resembled the Lutherans' theology in many respects but differed in the doctrines of the Eucharist. This would later become a significant point of division between Lutherans and the Reformed tradition.

The radicals who descended on Wittenberg in 1521–22 continued to believe, despite Melanchthon's efforts to persuade them otherwise, that the freedom they saw proclaimed in the Gospels called for social reform also. The leaders of this movement embarked on a program of preaching and expansion throughout the German lands. In 1523 Thomas Müntzer (c. 1490–1525) preached to the same Saxon princes to whom Luther had appealed in his *Address to the Christian Nobility*, but Müntzer's rhetoric was fiery, predicting the immediate arrival of the Last Judgment and urging the princes to join the ranks of the redeemed and abandon the multitude who were doomed to hell: the Catholic Church and the defenders (like Luther) of the old social hierarchy. Meanwhile, in southwest Germany, the preacher Balthasar Hubmaier (1480–1528) advocated a different kind of revolution: withdrawal from society in pacifistic communities in which all goods would be shared. Hubmaier's teaching was one of the beginnings of the ANABAPTIST movement.

The Peasants' War

Not surprisingly, the nobility did not fall in behind Müntzer's and Hubmaier's calls for upheaval in the social order; but these leaders persisted. In 1524–25, with several thousand disgruntled peasants, miners, and other laborers, they began a series of acts of resistance against the authorities. Beginning in 1524 with a peaceful refusal by some peasants to pay taxes, the movement escalated in early 1525 into an armed band professing loyalty to a divine and supposedly apostolic ideal and vowing to overthrow the social order. Wave after wave of rebellious peasants fanned out from southwestern Germany, creating havoc in Franconia to the north, Thuringia to the east, and even farther, to alpine Austria. The conditions under which this part of the population lived were so horrendous that some rebellion was inevitable, and many scholars, especially those of a Marxist bent, have long seen the Peasants' War (as it was called) as a social movement. But the preaching of the instigators of the revolt, and their claims to divine authority and evangelical freedom, or liberation from all secular or "pagan" rule, give this event a place in the history of the Reformation.

Reaction from the Lutherans in Wittenberg was swift and decisive. Luther had been seen, especially by Catholics, as the godfather of the Peasants' War, and he and his colleagues worked hard to distance themselves from the radicals. Association with politically revolutionary forms of Christianity would have been the kiss of death for the Lutherans, since they depended on the favor of the secular nobility and defended the traditional structure of society as part of a divinely instituted order. Changes in the university's theological program included more attention to ethics (Aristotelian social thought re-entered the curriculum at this point, despite Luther's 1520 rejection of Aristotle as an obstacle to Christian doctrine) and a broadening of studies to include the natural sciences. Instead of being extraneous to theology, these studies were meant to reinforce a sense of divine order—cosmic, social, and personal. Thus the expansion of intellectual life in Wittenberg was, to some extent at least, a response to the radicals—and insurance against such tendencies in the future.

Church and State

The reformers' alliances with secular government became increasingly important factors in the spread of Lutheranism—and probably more important than Luther and Melanchthon wished, as they made it possible for secular rulers to assume control of churches without the theologians' counsel. In 1529 the rulers of a group of Protestant territories formed a confederation called the SCHMALKALD LEAGUE, asserting their right to defend themselves against the empire, in whose eyes they were heretics and outlaws; this was an early milestone in the growing association of church and state. According to the principles of Luther and Melanchthon, churches properly came under the governance of the secular authorities. The church was not an independent entity, and the Catholic Church was a usurper, because it claimed divine authority to control what the reformers saw as a secular institution.

The other side in the dispute was also marshaling its forces. The Holy Roman Empire had been charged by the papacy with the duty of protecting the interests of the church, and this was surely an occasion for special action. Early in 1530 the emperor, Charles V, called a Diet to be held in Augsburg to resolve the religious disputes that threatened to tear his empire apart. "Resolve" is perhaps too generous a term, since the Catholic participants arrived already prepared with detailed condemnations of Lutheran teachings. The Protestants, represented by Melanchthon, delivered their declaration of faith, known as the AUGSBURG CONFESSION and still regarded as one of the authoritative definitions of Lutheran belief. Subscribed to by a number of the Protestant nobility, it was a declaration of independence from the Roman Church and the Holy Roman Empire.

The empire did not take this declaration peacefully. In addition to issuing a condemnation of the reformers' teachings as expressed in the Confession, the Diet threatened military action against the Schmalkald League, and for the following year the danger of war was never far off. In this environment of hostility, both Lutheran and Catholic theologians worked on theological positions designed to refute the other church—since from each perspective, the other church was necessarily the false one. Bitter pamphlet exchanges dominated the 1530s, while differences within Protestant ranks became sources of grave concern. If the Protestants could not achieve unity in their thought, how strong a defense could they erect against the Catholics?

Despite agreement on such matters as the authority of Scripture and the nature of the church, Protestants differed in a number of substantial articles, such as the necessity of good works in the life of the justified Christian and the meaning of Jesus' words when he established the practice of the Lord's Supper. These differences would increase and intensify as Protestantism spread to other parts of Europe. Among the Lutherans, the first of these issues came to the forefront in the late 1520s, when a theologian named Johann Agricola (1492–1566), a Wittenberg graduate, asserted that Luther's doctrine of justification eliminated any need for works. (In fact, Luther's principle of justification by faith alone meant that works do not count *before God*, but are still necessary for civil life.) Agricola's position, known as ANTINOMIANISM, amounts to a rejection of all law. The rule of law is replaced by love of neighbor, so that a person is no longer bound even to the Decalogue. Agricola returned to Wittenberg in 1536 and caused such a stir with his ideas that a small pamphlet war ensued (with some of the works coming from Luther himself), and disciplinary measures needed to be taken against Agricola. He ended up as court chaplain to the Elector of Brandenburg in Berlin.

Disputes over the Eucharist

The Eucharist was just as contentious an issue. The reformers' trust in the clarity and authority of the Bible forced them to take literally, if at all possible, such statements as Jesus' claim that the bread and wine at the Last Supper were his body and blood. The Catholic Church had taught this, and, as the Reformers discovered, the church fathers had apparently believed it too. But how could such an amazing idea be taken as true? Did it mean, as the Catholic Church had taught since the Fourth Lateran Council in 1215, that the bread and wine, while still retaining their normal appearance, actually changed their natures into flesh and blood? Perhaps the bread and wine remained, but were augmented with a divine substance, such as when metal is put into a fire: the metal is there, unchanged *as metal*, but now with the additional quality of "hot." Maybe the bread and wine were augmented by these properties of body and blood. Or was Jesus speaking metaphorically on this occasion, as he had, for example, when calling himself a door (John 10:7); thus the words "This is my body" would amount to his saying "This bread represents my body"? That alternative has some merit too, since it suggests that when the faithful are together, the sense of unity at the Last Supper is recaptured, with the master once again present, at least in spirit. These were difficult options.

The first of these three positions is known as TRANSUBSTANTIATION, and it is associated with thirteenth-century Scholasticism and the revival of Aristotle, whose *Metaphysics* presents the distinction between the SUBSTANCE of a thing (what it really is) and its ACCIDENTS (things that can change without affecting its

Ugolino di Prete Ilario, *The Miracle of the Host*, 1357–1364. Fresco.

The effect of the Eucharist's words of consecration became a controversial issue that bitterly divided Reformers.

substance). The reformers were reluctant to bring Greek philosophy—with its link to paganism—into theology to explain the sacraments. So Luther, Scholasticism's most vocal opponent, offered an alternative, known as CONSUBSTANTIATION, in which body and blood coexisted with the bread and wine. The image of an iron in the fire is Luther's, and it means that Christ in some way enters into the elements of the Eucharist at the point of consecration, but they still remain bread and wine. The third view of the Eucharist, known as SACRAMENTARIANISM, holds that Jesus' words "This is my body" must be understood as "This *represents* my body." This approach was the view upheld by the "reformed" (or Calvinist) Protestants, such as Zwingli, but it was attacked by the Lutherans for "removing" Christ from the Eucharist.

All of this disagreement came to a head first in the MARBURG COLLOQUY in 1529 and later in the WITTENBERG CONCORD of 1536. At the Marburg Colloquy, Zwingli and Luther met and debated whether the words "This is my body" are to be taken literally or figuratively. It was here that Luther most forcefully articulated his doctrine of consubstantiation, affirming the real presence of Christ in the Eucharistic elements. Zwingli was unable to agree with this, and rejected a fifteen-point proposal of Luther's, known as the MARBURG ARTICLES, which served as a record of points of agreement and disagreement. Zwingli's objection was that the Bible is a rationally understandable text, and that when there is a passage that reason cannot make sense of (such as "This is my body"), then the passage must be understood figuratively—in this case, by holding that the bread and wine merely represent Christ's body and blood. Luther, in Zwingli's view, was too willing to suspend rationality and endorse paradoxical doctrines. The Colloquy failed to unite the factions, but helped both sides understand their differences.

Calvinism

By the time of the Wittenberg Concord, in 1536, the Reformed Protestants, who were concentrated especially in Switzerland, had a new leader. This was the Frenchman John Calvin (1509–1564). Trained in both law and theology, Calvin was first exposed to Protestant teachings in Paris, where they had won some adherents, especially among intellectuals; and sometime in the late 1520s or early 1530s he became convinced of their truth. But the French authorities dealt severely with the reformers in their midst—some were burned at the stake—and Calvin, fearing for his life, eventually found a refuge in the more congenial atmosphere of Geneva. There, after becoming a pastor in the Reformed Church, he helped to establish a state based on their religious principles. (See Chapter 17.) The influence of Calvin's theology on the Reformed movement resulted in the gradual adoption of the name "CALVINISM" for this branch of Protestant Christianity.

Although neither Zwingli nor Luther was present at the Wittenberg meeting in 1536 (the former had died five years earlier), their respective views on the Eucharist were once again at issue. Of course, in the end no agreement was reached. If any had been, the division of Protestantism into Lutheran and Reformed, or Calvinist, branches would not have occurred. At Wittenberg, theologians such as the ex-Dominican Martin Bucer and Philip Melanchthon signed a declaration affirming that the body and blood of Christ were truly present in the elements of bread and wine. The language used was very much Luther's, as befits an initiative by Wittenberg to bring all the Protestant churches into line on this issue.

Such union was not to happen. Many of the south German cities that appeared to follow Bucer's lead ended up in the Calvinist camp, where Zwingli's sacramentarian position ultimately prevailed. To this day, the Eucharist remains the chief boundary marker between Lutherans and Calvinists—and one of the main obstacles to Christian unity. (See chapters 17, 20.)

For John Calvin and his fellow Geneva theologians, Luther had paved the doctrinal way—up to a point; beyond that point it was Calvin's duty to clear a path. And clear a path he did, especially in his 1536 *Institution of Christian Religion*, which in later editions became known as the *Institutes* and would go down in history for its presentation of the rigidity of Calvin's thought. The *Institutes* is, in fact, not so rigid as its critics assert. Calvin intended his work as a guide to understanding Scripture, not as its replacement. Thus the final authority on any issue of faith was the Bible, and human judgment (like Calvin's or his readers') needed always to be open to correction by revelation. Or, as Calvin put it, the church was not just *reformed* by the word of God (this is what the name of his tradition signifies), but always in the *process of reforming* (*reformata semper reformanda*, as he puts it).

The church that took shape in Geneva under Calvin's leadership was independent of Rome, like the Lutheran Church, but it was also (unlike Luther's church) free of interference by the secular nobility, since Geneva was a free city with an elected governing body, and the church was ruled by a council. With this form of organization Calvinism was able to exercise a substantial level of control over the Genevans' lives. Both moral and religious violations came under the jurisdiction of a "Consistory," which within decades would become known far and wide for its severity and caricatured as a Protestant counterpart to the Catholic Inquisition. In reality, it bore little resemblance to that formidable court, but it was a powerful disciplinary agency nonetheless.

Geneva owes its association with religious intolerance especially to a particular incident: the execution of Michael Servetus (c. 1511– 1553). Servetus was a multi-talented Spanish humanist whose work on the New Testament convinced him that God is not trinitarian: that is, that the doctrine of the Trinity was an unbiblical later invention, reminiscent more of polytheism than of monotheism. This was too much for Christianity, in all its forms, to bear; and Servetus was condemned by the Catholic Church in France, where he was living at the time. Thinking that he might find

John Calvin, 16th century. Engraving.

A theologian of unusual learning and clarity, Calvin introduced a new form of Protestantism to Geneva and thence as far as Scotland and Hungary.

refuge among fellow French exiles like Calvin, he went to Geneva, where he was discovered despite living under a false name; tried for heresy a second time; and burned at the stake. (His ideas survived him and gave rise to Unitarianism, a form of religion that would attract followers in both Europe and America.) Advocates of tolerance attacked Calvin for his part in the execution, while other Protestants, Melanchthon among them, supported Calvin's action. Geneva survived the criticism and continued as a model Christian city, an example for Calvinist communities in Holland, Scotland, and eastern Europe.

Exporting Protestantism

Both Calvinism and Lutheranism soon won converts in other parts of Europe. Outside German lands, Lutheranism also took root in Scandinavia and some Baltic countries; by 1539, the rulers of Estonia, Finland, Sweden, Denmark, and Norway had all established it as the state religion. Calvinism was even more international. Students from lands as far away as Scotland and Hungary, and nearly everywhere in between, came to Geneva to study at its academy. They went out again, trained in the new theology which was a synthesis of humanism and biblical theology, to establish a new form of Christian polity, or organization. They did this by means of their learning and their influence in the circles that determined religious matters: the secular courts. Thus John Knox (c. 1514–1572) in Scotland and Jean Bodin (c. 1530–1596) in France were among the proponents of a Calvinist political theory—one that granted people the right to resist a ruler who did not uphold true (i.e. Protestant) religion.

Who's Who

The Calvinists

Ulrich (also Huldrych, or Huldreich) Zwingli (1484–1531) A Swiss humanist, cleric, and reformer. In 1519, Zwingli preached a series of commentaries on the New Testament and spoke out against certain Catholic practices. This was seen as the start of the influential Swiss Reformation.

John Calvin (1509–1564) Born in France, he became a major Protestant reformer and theologian. He created an important "theocracy" in Geneva and became the figurehead of Reformed theology, contributing hugely to the doctrine and organization of the Protestant Church.

John Knox (c. 1514–1572) Originally a Scottish Catholic priest, he joined the Reformation as a Protestant reformer, traveled to Europe, and came under the influence of Calvin. Returning to his homeland, he founded the Church of Scotland in 1560.

Girolamo Zanchi (1516–1590) A Protestant theologian, scholar, and originally an Augustinian canon. He worked with Zacharias Ursinus to formulate a Reformed Confession.

Theodore Beza (1519–1605) Born in France to a Catholic family, he became a Greek scholar and Protestant theologian. Upon Calvin's death in 1564, he was chosen as leader of Europe's Calvinist movement.

Zacharias Ursinus (1534–1583) A Protestant theologian. With K. Olivian, he produced the Heidelberg Catechism (a manual of faith).

Jacobus Arminius (1560–1609) A Dutch Reformed theologian who took issue with some central Calvinist doctrines, and in doing so created a movement called Arminianism.

Apart from their differences in Eucharistic doctrine, the issues that would divide Lutherans and Calvinists most distinctly at the end of the sixteenth century would be political. Lutheranism became associated with ABSOLUTISM, the principle that the ruler of a state holds full authority over religious matters within it, while Calvinism became associated with revolutionary movements that sought to overturn "impious," mostly Catholic, rule. Ironically, neither of these ideologies matches the teachings of Luther (who tended to distrust his princes, even though he advocated obeying them) or Calvin, who saw impious rulers as instruments of God's wrath and thus a punishment to be endured.

The absolutist principle, as applied by King Henry VIII (1491–1547; r. 1509–1547), was responsible for planting Protestantism in English soil. Henry's wish to obtain an annulment of his marriage to his first wife, Catherine of Aragon (and so, he hoped, sire by a subsequent marriage a son to succeed him), and the refusal of Pope Clement VII (1478–1534; r. 1523–1534) to grant him that annulment, finally led Henry to declare himself head of the Church in England in the Act of Supremacy (1534). Although Henry himself remained a steadfast Catholic (he had been declared "Defender of the Faith" by a previous pope for a refutation of Lutheran teachings), the break with Rome clearly gave English reformers an opportunity to bring their country into the Protestant fold. This was not accomplished smoothly. During the reigns of Henry's first two successors, Edward VI and Mary I (r. 1547–1553 and 1553–1558 respectively), the pendulum swung drastically back and forth, with Protestants gaining ascendancy under Edward and Catholicism restored under Mary. Not until the reign of Elizabeth I (1533–1603; r. 1558–1603) did the Church of England (or Anglican Church) become established as a distinctive branch of Christianity, with a liturgy derived largely from Catholic forms and doctrines (including justification by faith) greatly influenced by the Continental reformers.

The Reformation and Liturgy

In some respects, the emergence of Protestantism represents a more substantial turning point in liturgy and religious practice than it does in doctrine. Obviously these are vitally connected: the reduction of the sacraments from seven to two (baptism and Eucharist) was determined by the doctrinal principle that an authentic sacrament had to be "instituted" by Jesus, and that later additions did not count as sacraments. And eliminating the concept of "merit" changed, in a single stroke, the motivations behind a number of Catholic religious practices. (See Chapter 12.)

But Protestantism also changed the character of liturgy in other ways. For one thing, worship was now in the language of the people, rather than the Latin of the educated clergy, and was thus understandable by everyone. For another, removing the barriers between clergy and laity symbolized the inclusion of lay people in the church. Distributing the Eucharist in both "kinds" (see Chapter 6) was another way of making the doctrine of "the priesthood of all believers" a reality for the entire community.

The Protestant churches would also be known for their HYMNODY. Hymns written by Luther and other reformers are sung to this day (even in Catholic

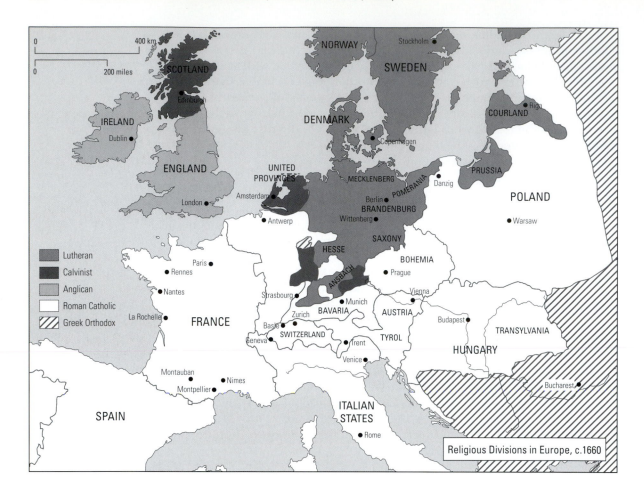

Religious Divisions in Europe, c.1660

churches), to settings very close to those heard in Luther's Wittenberg. One of these hymns, whose words and music were written by Luther himself, conveys eloquently the confidence and spirit of defiance with which the reformers were imbued:

> *A mighty fortress is our God,*
> *A bulwark never failing;*
> *Our helper he amid the flood*
> *Of mortal ills prevailing. ...*

In the following centuries the tunes of Lutheran hymns, called chorales, would inspire some of the greatest religious music, culminating in the cantatas and passions (settings of Christ's Passion) of Johann Sebastian Bach (1685–1750). A more restrained hymnody is found in Calvinist churches; but here, too, there is a discernible break with late-medieval precedents (see Chapter 6). The Psalms, many of them expressions of the hope of a besieged Israel enduring the punishments of the Babylonian empire, became the laments and declarations of loyalty by people who also experienced persecution by hostile forces—in this case, the Catholic Church. And this theme of loyalty despite oppression persisted even in those states where Protestantism became dominant.

Religious Imagery

As for the visual arts, many Protestants regarded these with suspicion. Under Catholicism, the use of imagery in churches had reached a high level of artistry, and beautiful sculpture and stained glass were considered powerful aids to devotion. The reformers saw dangers in concentrated devotion to such images; it was too easy to confuse the "sign" of the created artifact with the divine object of devotion, which should be God alone. The veneration of relics (see Chapter 13) was one practice that the reformers uniformly considered idolatrous. Accordingly, relics and pilgrimages to see them were abolished in the lands that became Protestant.

But attitudes toward artistic creation itself varied within the Protestant ranks. Wittenberg, home of two artists named Lucas Cranach (the father was a pharmacist and mayor as well as an artist; the son was mainly an artist), became home to a tradition of vibrantly colored altarpieces, some of which remain in the churches for which they were painted. Understandably, much of this work is focused on biblical scenes, and selected episodes at that. St. Peter, for example, is more often depicted as just one among many than as the leader of the apostolic group.

The Calvinists took a more severe stance toward images, interpreting the Second Commandment as a prohibition of all religious images. Accordingly, Calvinist leaders forbade the creating of biblical images, and in some well-publicized cases destroyed images already in churches, including stained-glass windows. As a result, Calvinist churches took on a distinctly austere appearance, establishing a tradition that expanded through Holland, Scotland, and, later, New England in the subsequent centuries.

Key Terms

ABSOLUTISM A political doctrine that grants secular rulers absolute control over religious (and other) affairs in their territories.

ACCIDENT The appearance of any material thing, irrelevant to its true nature and purpose.

ANABAPTIST A member of a Protestant sect that emerged in Germany in 1521; its adherents insisted on believers' (adult) baptism and moral purity in the community.

ANTINOMINIANISM The rejection of law as a norm in the Christian life, based on the idea that Christ abolished legalism.

AUGSBURG CONFESSION The 1530 declaration of Lutheran beliefs, presented at the Diet (council) of Augsburg; it became the basis for later Lutheran teaching.

CONSUBSTANTIATION The Lutheran Eucharistic doctrine holding that bread and wine take on properties of Christ's body and blood, but still remain bread and wine.

EDICT OF WORMS The 1521 decree of the Holy Roman Empire condemning Luther; this was an early point in the emergence of Protestantism.

HYMNODY The composing and performing of hymns; in some branches of the church, an important expression of faith.

MARBURG ARTICLES A set of 15 statements intended to unify Lutherans and Zwinglians in 1529; their disagreement over the Eucharist prevented concord.

MARBURG COLLOQUY The 1529 debate between Luther and Zwingli about the Eucharist; an early point of rupture within Protestantism.

SACRAMENTARIANISM The Eucharistic doctrine teaching that the bread and wine are purely symbols of Christ's body and blood.

SCHMALKALD LEAGUE A federation of Protestant states formed for protection against the Catholic Holy Roman Empire.

SUBSTANCE What any given thing ultimately is, beneath changeable appearances.

TRANSUBSTANTIATION The Catholic Eucharistic doctrine holding that bread and wine are transformed into the body and blood of Christ.

WITTENBERG CONCORD The 1536 joint statement on the Eucharist by Lutheran and Reformed theologians; the accord failed soon thereafter.

CHAPTER 17

Protestant Orthodoxy
Developments in Scholasticism

The Diet of Augsburg in 1530 marks the beginning of a process known in modern parlance as CONFESSIONALIZATION: the shaping of religious communities around explicit statements of belief, or CONFESSIONS. The confession presented at Augsburg by the Lutherans was the first of these—which are also variously designated as "catechisms," "articles of faith," and "formulas." Each of these documents was, for a time and a particular community, authoritative. As a reflection of their authority, the communities that subscribed to them also became known as "confessions." Instead of "churches" (an ambiguous term), "religions" (inaccurate since all were Christian), or "denominations" (a later phenomenon), "confessions" is the appropriate term for the different Christian communities of the early-modern period.

As these statements of doctrine multiplied, the need to support each one intensified. Scriptural evidence was a must; so was some measure of methodological coherence—presenting each doctrine in the same way. In time, Patristic evidence and philosophical reasoning entered the picture, and before the end of the sixteenth century each of the confessions was engaged in the defense and systematizing of its doctrines. Much of this took place at Protestant universities, either reorganized as such or newly established; the practitioners were trained theologians. Thus the Scholastic tradition that the early reformers rejected so harshly returned—in a different form, of course. The effect, in the long run, was to re-intellectualize the faith, or substantial parts of it; and here is where many felt it broke with the original reformers and their emotional piety. But let us look first at the beginnings of the process.

The "Re-Scholasticizing" of Christian Teaching

The second half of the sixteenth century was as tumultuous as the first, but in a different way. The Peace of Augsburg, promulgated by the Holy Roman Empire in 1555, allowed each ruler to determine the religion of his territory, and the

Catholic Church, despite its condemnation of Protestant doctrines at the Council of Trent (to be discussed in Chapter 18), began to recognize that the movement begun by Luther and other reformers was not going to go away. Divisions had formed between lands and confessions, and chaos rather than order seemed to be gaining the upper hand. Within Protestantism itself discord reigned, and concord was often nothing more than a distant hope. The Lutherans had split after Luther's death into adherents of different parts of his work, the radicals calling themselves "genuine Lutherans" and the moderates calling themselves "Philippists," after Luther's colleague Philip Melanchthon. The Calvinists were in somewhat better shape, but deviations from Calvin's teaching were right around the corner—so that historically "Calvinism" has come to mean something quite different from Calvin's own theological work, Calvinists having more revolutionary tendencies than their conservative namesake. Both branches, however, were successful in gaining the patronage of their rulers, an understandable phenomenon when we consider the political power of churches.

But freedom from the Roman Church came with a price. Many of the cultural functions that had been served by that church now needed to be replaced with local talent; and institutions that had belonged to the ecclesiastical realm, and thus were separate from the state, now needed to be reestablished within the secular world. One such function was moral discipline. The Catholic Church, through its penitential system, had operated a very efficient program of moral control, giving the faithful supernatural incentives to be loyal to church and ruler and moral in all their actions. And the threat of prosecution by the Inquisition

School Life in the Late Sixteenth Century, 1592. Engraving.

Social programs of Reformers included education for all. Many schools were in abandoned and secularized monasteries.

discouraged most people from straying into heresy. The new Protestant states could no longer depend on such institutions, as their theologians had dispensed with the penitential system, and the Inquisition held no jurisdiction outside the Roman Church. Thus one finds institutions of moral control being created in the Protestant states: a disciplinary agency was established in Wittenberg in 1539 to investigate and punish breaches of public morality. And in Geneva, the Consistory (see Chapter 16) quickly became a busy and effective regulator of public morals. In fact when we think of Calvin's Geneva, the image of a stern judicial body usually comes to mind. This institution was re-created, with various adaptations, in all the countries where the Calvinist tradition found a home.

Protestant Education

Education was another area that underwent a revolution of sorts at this time. The medieval system of cathedral schools and universities had trained applicants for high offices in both church and state; and arts, medicine, law, and theology faculties at the universities—which had been chartered by the papacy—served the mission of preserving a balance between the sacred and secular realms of church and civil government, and maintaining order within each realm. With Protestantism, all that changed; for there was a total break with both the Roman "church" and the Holy Roman "state."

In Protestant states, of course, just as in Catholic ones, there was an urgent need for an educational system: to train clergy, lawyers, other professionals and, at a lower level, to provide basic schooling for the general populace—at least enough to ensure harmony within the ranks of people whose religion, without any choice on their part, had suddenly and radically been changed. With the advent of printing and the spread of literacy, this last requirement loomed larger than it had in previous centuries. Education was to be the foundation of the new Protestant culture.

Some rulers had it easy: their domains already had universities, which they were able to secularize and put to a new political and social use. Such was the case with Tübingen, a great center for humanism founded in 1477, which became a bastion of Protestant theology after the duke of Württemberg (the territory in which the university was located) became Protestant in 1534. Heidelberg followed a couple of decades later, as did Greifswald. The process was similar to the one that converted other Catholic institutions, such as monasteries and cathedral schools, to state agencies. The ruler's responsibility was limited to installing the faculty that could carry out the religious and moral reforms required by the conversion to Protestantism.

Other rulers needed to found their own institutions of higher learning. These included such universities as Königsberg (1544), whose most distinguished alumnus was Immanuel Kant; Jena (1558), later to be Karl Marx's alma mater; and Geneva, founded under Calvin's auspices in 1559 and the mother of a plethora of Reformed academies elsewhere in Europe. There were also a number of new institutions that have not survived into the modern era, such as Helmstedt, founded in 1575 by the Duke of Braunschweig (or Brunswick) in Lower Saxony. In these cases the advantage was that the ruling power had a clean slate on which to create an educational program: a prince could appoint whom he wanted and

Mattäus Merian,
*A View of
Heidelberg*, 1620.
Copper engraving,
colored later.

*A center of late-
medieval piety
and learning
before the
Reformation,
Heidelberg became
home to a number
of Protestant
theologians in
the late 16th and
17th centuries.*

teach what he wanted. The disadvantage, at least from the prince's standpoint, was that he needed the collaboration of the resident intellectuals to frame and implement an educational program that could both replace the Catholic system and, it was hoped, surpass both it and rival Protestant programs. Thus the spirit of competition rather than collaboration, which comes to the surface whenever we hold one school as superior to another, was born.

But what was actually taught? When we compare Protestant education of the sixteenth century with its Catholic counterparts from the fifteenth, we find the same basic skills still emphasized. The medieval higher education curriculum, consisting of trivium (grammar, rhetoric, and logic) and quadrivium (arithmetic, music, geometry, and astronomy), together known as the seven "liberal arts," remained largely in place. Certain of these subjects were given different rationales, and the relation of each to the others might change from school to school, but the overall impression is one of continuity.

It is in the higher disciplines, theology in particular, that the picture begins to change dramatically. The medieval approach to theology had a distinct style: it was philosophical in character, being heavily indebted to Aristotle, and followed a pattern from creation to the sacraments borrowed from Peter Lombard (see Chapter 10) and the Nicene Creed. Such a system, with its heavy use of the historical tradition of the church, was out of place in the new Protestant program, where the scriptural canon was supposed to be the only valid basis for doctrine. And it was obvious, given the many disputes about the meaning of biblical passages, that the bible could not teach itself; instruction was needed to ensure uniformity within the confessions. Hence a new form of teaching arose, which became known as PROTESTANT SCHOLASTICISM or PROTESTANT ORTHODOXY.

The first of these terms may seem self-contradictory, since Protestantism saw itself as a rebellion against Scholasticism. In point of fact, the need to clarify and institute Reformation teachings required some systematizing of a church's beliefs; and the clergy in the parishes needed resources they could turn to for preaching and pastoral advice. So the fact that there had to be some standardized method of instruction required a "scholastic," or academic, treatment of doctrine. And the "Protestant" part? That was in the method of exposition, as well as in the content taught.

If the basic unit of medieval Scholastic method was the *quaestio* (see Chapter 12), in Protestant Scholasticism the fundamental passage was the *locus* (*loci* in the plural), or "place." There has been a lot of speculation about the origin of this term, but it is most likely drawn from ancient Roman rhetoric, where it meant an example or a pertinent text, something used as evidence in an argument. To a greater extent than was possible with the medieval *quaestio*, the early Protestant *locus* allowed biblical texts to speak for themselves. The author's task was to collect and arrange these texts in an effective way.

The "*loci* method," as this style of theology is called, is almost as old as the Reformation itself. In 1521 Philip Melanchthon, professor of Greek at Wittenberg, had issued a modest manual of doctrinal topics, originally called *Theological Outlines* but soon renamed *Loci Communes*, or *Commonplaces*. This work would go through two major revisions; and literally dozens of editions, in Latin, German, and a few other languages, would appear before the century's end. In Zurich, Zwingli issued in 1525 a work in *loci* form called *Commentary on True and False Religion*; this was the first comprehensive manual of Reformed theology. Catholic opponents of the Reformation followed with manuals, such as the *Enchiridion* of Johann Eck (1525 and many later editions), which countered Protestant doctrine, *locus* by *locus*.

Two texts that stand as foundation documents of the Protestant confessions are arranged in *loci*: the Augsburg Confession of 1530, Lutheranism's core statement of its central beliefs, and the *Institution of Christian Religion* (1536) by John Calvin, a work that would go through five editions, in both Latin and French, and serve as the core teaching of Reformed faith for decades. (It took on the plural form *Institutes* only in later editions.) The Augsburg Confession was made up of twenty-eight "Articles," some of which became subjects of intense religious disputes. And although the *Institutes* consisted at first of only six chapters, it would eventually grow into a massive tome in four books, addressing every possible topic in Protestant theology. But despite its bulk, Calvin insisted to the end that it was merely an aid to understanding Scripture: a study guide, of sorts, to the Bible.

Later generations of theologians had more ambitious goals for their writing. Although they tended to keep the *loci* method as a theological style, in the second half of the sixteenth century these treatises became more and more comprehensive, including arguments from the church fathers augmenting the scriptural prooftexts and counter-arguments against both Catholic and rival Protestant teachings. And despite the reformers' professed distaste for philosophical speculation, as time went on their treatises contained increasingly complicated and subtle arguments about philosophical matters such as human freedom and necessity, the existence and attributes of God, and whether knowledge is a single or multiform phenomenon or of various kinds.

Later Developments

Protestant Scholasticism developed gradually, and there is no point that we can identify as its origin. Although the *loci* method is found in works by the earliest

Peter Martyr, 16th century. Engraving.

Part of the second generation of Reformers, Peter Martyr sought to integrate philosophical elements into an evangelical tradition that had started out being suspicious of classical thought.

reformers, Protestant Scholasticism truly began to take shape in the second half of the century, possibly with Pietro Martire Vermigli, known as Peter Martyr (1500–1562), and Theodore Beza (1519–1605), both influential Protestant theologians.

Vermigli was a biblical exegete and a preacher, but he also wrote a number of works defending the use of Aristotle in the Protestant curriculum and identified the boundaries separating faith from understanding. (See "Peter Martyr on the Mass.") Born in Florence and educated at a monastery near Padua, Vermigli had acquired an intimate knowledge of Aristotle and Augustine (he was a member of the Augustinian order) and was an accomplished preacher, well known in various Italian cities. While serving in Naples he came upon some works by Zwingli and Bucer which he found highly persuasive; and by 1542 he was on his way first to Zurich, where Zwingli had done his most influential work, and then to Strasbourg, where he became Bucer's protégé. In 1547 he went to England to teach theology at Oxford and, with Bucer (who taught at Cambridge from 1548 until his death), was one of the formative figures in the English Reformation (see Chapter 16). On the accession of the Catholic Queen Mary in 1553, Vermigli was imprisoned and then exiled. He remained on the Continent, preaching in Zurich, a successor to Zwingli, one of the thinkers who had started him on his path as a Reformer.

Beza, the leader of the Geneva community after Calvin's death, was a prodigious author of treatises on grace, PREDESTINATION, and the covenant (the bond uniting the church community to God)—many of the concepts commonly associated with Calvinism. In fact, Beza was responsible for as much of Calvinism as Calvin was. Born in Vézelay, southeast of Paris (a famous pilgrimage center, once reputed to hold relics of Mary Magdalene), and educated in law and arts at Paris, Beza later became an accomplished biblical scholar. First at Lausanne, and after 1558 in Geneva, he became one of the leaders of French-speaking Protestantism, both in Switzerland and in his native France, whose Protestants (called Huguenots for an uncertain reason) followed Reformed teachings. Beza's "Huguenot Psalter," a joint effort with Clément Marot (1496–1544), in which the Psalms were translated into French verse, became a source of support and solidarity among the persecuted French Protestants.

Less colorful perhaps, but also important, are Zacharias Ursinus (1534–1583) and Girolamo Zanchi (1516–1590), both formulators of Calvinism who were instrumental in its international expansion. Ursinus had been a student of Melanchthon's at Wittenberg, but his later training included work with Calvinist leaders, whose ranks he joined. With the patronage of the Palatinate Elector Frederick III (1515–1576), a convert to Calvinism, Ursinus composed in 1562 the

Peter Martyr on the Mass

Peter Martyr was a Protestant theologian who wished to bring the wealth of the Patristic tradition to life, while pointing out the errors of the Catholicism of his day. Here the learned polemicist discusses terms for the eucharistic rite.

The Greek Church called the holy supper *leitourgia*, meaning a common or public work (*commune opus publicumque*). Nor is it limited to holy things; it is applied also to profane actions that are public. And who knows not that the administration of the Lord's supper is something related to Christian people? For as many as are present are to participate in it and to communicate together. Let me not skip over this point: the etymology of this word brings a final argument against private masses. Moreover, the word not only applies to the Lord's supper, but is attributed to other holy functions, as in the Acts of the Apostles ch. 13, *leitourgounton auton*. Some have translated this "while they sacrificed", when they should have said, "while they served or acted publicly", namely in that holy office which they certainly performed in preaching the Gospel. This holy function had different names among the Latins. Sometimes it was called communion, sometimes the Lord's supper, sometimes the sacrament of the body of Christ or the breaking of bread. And our fathers often called it what the Greek fathers did, great mysteries (*tremenda mysteria*) and *synaxis*. I will pass over the fact that they frequently called it by the name of sacrifice. This was not (as our adversaries foolishly think) because the body and blood of Christ is offered to God for a sacrifice on behalf of living and dead; although the fathers did not dislike that kind of talk, affirming that Christ's body and blood was offered to God. But what they understood by those words, if read with care, is clearly expressed, namely that thanks were given to God, who had delivered his Son to death on the cross for our sake.

The most ancient fathers called the holy supper by those names; but they never mentioned mass. For if you read Irenaeus, Tertullian, Cyprian, Hilary and the like, you never find that word in them with such a meaning. Augustine twice uses it, namely in his sermon *de tempore* 237, where he mentions the mass of those who were to be instructed before baptism. In that place he exhorts men to forgive injuries to each other. For, he says, we must come to the mass of those to be instructed, where we will pray, forgive us our debts as we also forgive our debtors. Again, in the sermon *de tempore* 91, he writes these words: "In the history to be read at masses". Some doubt whether those sermons were of Augustine's writing, but to me they seem to be the style and opinion of Augustine. If any conjecture is allowed, I think this name mass began to be used about that time, though not frequently. For if it had been a word much in use, Augustine especially would have it more often since he framed his language to the common man.

(From Peter Martyr, "Abridgement against the Bishop of Winchester," in J.C. McLelland and G.E. Duffield, eds., *Life, Early Letters, and Eucharistic Writings of Peter Martyr.* Montreal: Sutton Courtenay Press, 1984.)

Heidelberg Catechism, a work that became the norm for teaching Reformed belief in the Palatinate province of western Germany, and later in Holland where Calvinism was taking a strong hold, and in parts of England. Ursinus's defense of this catechism brought him into conflict with a number of other theologians, mainly Lutherans, and in explanation of his position he composed a *Commentary* to the Catechism that stands as one of the most thorough defenses of Calvinist teaching.

Zanchi was a colleague of Ursinus's at Heidelberg, though originally an Italian Augustinian who had first been attracted to Protestantism by the work of Pietro Martire Vermigli and others. A biblical scholar at Strasbourg, Zanchi in 1563 became a preacher of Reformed doctrine in Italy before being appointed professor of dogmatics at Heidelberg. He is best known for his defenses of the sacramentarian conception of the Eucharist (see Chapter 16) and of the doctrine of predestination. In both categories Zanchi must be regarded, with Ursinus, as one of the architects of Reformed thought in the second half of the sixteenth century.

Some Protestant theologies departed drastically from the received Reformation teachings. One of these is associated with Arminius (Jacob Harmansz; 1560–1609), a Dutch theologian and self-appointed corrector of Calvinist teachings. In Arminius's system, original sin is relative rather than absolute; the human will is capable of doing good; the atonement on the cross was meant for all humanity, not just the elect (as stipulated in the doctrine of predestination; and the believer cooperated with grace, rather than being passive to its activity. (See "Jacob Arminius on Creation and Original Sin.") Arminianism was based on a far more optimistic view of human nature than Calvinism held (or Lutheranism, for that matter), and was thought to diminish Christ's atonement by making it merely auxiliary to human effort. In the early seventeenth century, Calvinist theologians were engaged in a relentless campaign against these teachings. Rulings like those of the Synod of Dort (held at Dordrecht in 1618–19) were efforts at consolidating Calvinist doctrine.

The most massive revision of Reformed theology was probably the *Institutes of Elenctic Theology* (1679) of François Turretin (or Turrentino) (1623–1687). Turretin, a broadly educated Genevan (and a loyal one too: he dedicates his book to his fellow citizens), was an heir to Beza and an opponent of Arminianism. This meant that he based his work on Calvin's thought, but emphasized various elements differently, so that his system is neither Calvin's nor a departure from it. By "elenctic theology" Turretin means one that proceeds by means of refuting falsehoods; "controversial theology" would be another name for it. But despite its polemical intention, Turretin's work is systematic in its approach, able to be read without referring to the "false" positions of his opponents. Turretin defends theology as a counterpart to philosophy, and states that in theology the role of reason is limited. Echoing Paul and Matthew's Gospel, Turretin states: "Reason cannot be the rule of religion; neither as corrupted because it is below faith, but also opposed to it" (*Inst.*, Topic I). In keeping with this principle, Turretin unfolds a program of what can, must, and cannot be *believed*, with doctrines of the church and the sacraments included in this picture. Hence if we think of Scholasticism as a heavily rationalistic enterprise, Turretin's work serves as a corrective to that assumption. His work is a rational system because it is logical and coherent, but he avoids reducing matters of belief to objects of rational analysis.

Among the Lutherans, any account of the development of Scholasticism would have to include the names of the political philosopher Hermann Conring (1606–1681) and Johann Gerhard (1582–1637). These thinkers, influenced by Melanchthon's work at Wittenberg, brought Aristotle into the arts curriculum and based the study of ethics and politics on the Greek philosopher's work. By the end of the sixteenth century, Lutheranism found itself in many places under abso-

Jacob Arminius on Creation and Original Sin

Jacob Arminius was a Protestant Scholastic theologian who broke away from Calvinism over the extent and implications of original sin. Here we see one of his typical expositions, with statements and invented questions intended to forestall critics of his position.

1. The creation of things out of nothing is the very first of all the external acts of God; nor is it possible for any act to be prior to this, or conceived to be prior to it; and the decree concerning creation is the first of all the decrees of God; because the properties according to which he performs and operates all things, are, in the first [*momento*] impulse of his nature, and in his first egress, occupied about nihility or nothing, when those properties are borne, *ad extra*, "outwards."

2. God has formed two creatures rational and capable of things divine; ONE of them is purely spiritual and invisible, and [that is the class of] *angels*; but the OTHER is partly corporeal and partly spiritual, visible and invisible, and [that is the class of] *men*....

8. "God not only foresaw the fall of the first man, but by his own will he [*dispensavit*] ordained it."

1. Original sin is not that actual sin by which Adam transgressed the law concerning the tree of knowledge of good and evil, and on account of which we have all been constituted sinners, and rendered [*rei*] obnoxious or liable to death and condemnation.

2. QUERIES.—Is original sin only [*carentia*] the absence or want of original righteousness and of primeval holiness, with an inclination to commit sin, which likewise formerly existed in man, though it was not so vehement nor so inordinate as now it is, on account of the lost favor of God, his malediction, and the loss of that good by which that inclination was reduced to order? Or is it a certain infused habit (or acquired ingress) contrary to righteousness and holiness, after that sin had been committed?

3. Does original sin render men obnoxious to the wrath of God, when they have been previously constituted sinners on account of the actual sin of Adam, and rendered liable to damnation?

4. Adam, when considered in this state, after sin and prior to restoration, was not bound at once to punishment and obedience, but only to punishment.

(Jacob Arminius, "Certain Articles," in *Writings of James Arminius*, trans. James Nichols. Grand Rapids, MI: Baker Book House, 1956.)

lutism (see Chapter 16). This meant that the education of princes and their counselors was central to protecting the interests of the church. Hence a thinker such as Conring, being well trained in Aristotelian political thought (which clearly defined the limits of legitimate rule), was among the most influential shapers of Lutheran culture.

Gerhard was a Wittenberg graduate who later taught theology there and at the universites of Marburg and Jena. His work includes polemical writings in defense of Protestantism against the post-Trent Catholic Church, a number of biblical studies, and a nine-volume system called *Loci Theologici* (1610–22), a title reminiscent of Melanchthon's standard text (see Chapter 16.). This was the most thorough presentation of Lutheran doctrine, but in its use of philosophical—especially Aristotelian—method it came suspiciously close to the medieval *summa*, or Scholastic compendium. Gerhard's system remained influential through the seventeenth century, but the pendulum would eventually swing back from this rationalist extreme to a more emotional form of religion, called Pietism (see Chapter 19).

While all these Protestant theologians had been painstakingly constructing their new systems of belief, the Catholic Church had recovered from the initial shock of the Reformation and was renovating and reinforcing itself in a variety of ways which will be examined in the following chapter.

Key Terms

CONFESSION A statement of belief, often publicly presented; it affirms doctrines and points of difference from other traditions. Also an admission of wrongdoing.

CONFESSIONALIZATION A political process by which early modern states took on particular collective identities as Lutheran, Calvinist, or Catholic.

PROTESTANT SCHOLASTICISM (PROTESTANT ORTHODOXY) Extended systematic exposition of all doctrines within a given Protestant tradition, prevalent in the late 16th and 17th centuries.

PREDESTINATION The doctrine, usually associated with Calvinism, that each person's salvation or damnation has been determined by God and that one can do nothing to change it.

CHAPTER 18

Reformation-Era Catholicism

Reaction and New Religious Orders

Although it has long been traditional to refer to the Reformation as a purely Protestant phenomenon, the Catholic Church, too, underwent reformation during the sixteenth century—a series of momentous changes in both doctrine and practice. Some of these changes were responses to the reformers' challenges, while others were prompted by developments and issues that had appeared decades before Luther burst onto the scene—such as the invention of printing and the question of whether the church should be ruled by the pope or by councils.

Those scholars who have recognized the importance of this period in Catholic history have been divided over how to describe it. The most common label, "Counter-Reformation," suggests that the major developments within Catholicism during this period were intended purely to combat the Reformation. An alternate term, "Catholic Reform," does exactly the opposite by implying that the Catholic Church underwent its own internal reform without any attention to the Protestant presence at the time. Most recently, historians have chosen the neutral term "Early Modern Catholicism" to describe events within the Roman Church from the fifteenth century to the end of the eighteenth. Other scholars claim that what this term gains in objectivity, it loses in precision. This is a debate that will probably continue for decades. Our preference here is for the term "Reformation-era Catholicism," since it indicates that something "reformational" (whether internal or "counter") was going on in the Roman Catholic Church at the same time that the Reformation proper, the emergence of Protestantism, was taking place.

The Church Counterattacks

In the first decade after the initial challenges by the reformers, the Catholic Church attempted a number of counterattacks. In response to claims that the Roman Church did not have jurisdiction over all of Western Christendom, and even that St. Peter was never in Rome (an argument that would have seriously sabotaged the authority of the papacy), Catholic theologians launched a war of pamphlets and treatises intended to prove on historical grounds that Peter was indeed the first Bishop of Rome, and that obedience to him and his successors was part of the culture of the church from the earliest days. More important than such purely historical work, however, was the theological argument that care for the "flock" of Christ's faithful had passed from Jesus to Peter, and that this succession (which had continued to the contemporary papacy) was clearly indicated in the New Testament and recognized by the early church fathers. Moreover, their argument went, disobedience to that authority was always regarded as heresy, and punished in the past as such. Hence the denial of church authority was an act of disobedience which put the reformers in the same company as heretics convicted and punished centuries before.

Similarly, the reformers' claims that the ritual "works" of the church were merely human inventions without basis in the New Testament met with a swift rebuttal. The Catholic defenders produced passages from the Bible indicating that practices such as prayers for the dead and veneration of saints were not only approved, but required acts for the faithful to perform. As to the authority of the theological tradition, especially the later Scholastics whose works the reformers rejected so vehemently, the response of Catholic apologists such as Johann Eck (1486–1543) and Johannes Cochlaeus (1479–1552), two of a veritable legion of "controversialists," was that the tradition was necessarily a continuous one, and that the body of the church's teachings was both always expanding, and yet always rooted in Scripture. Thus the fact that there were seven sacraments by 1215 but only two commanded in the New Testament was proof, they claimed, that what was *implicit* in the Bible became *explicit* over time in the teachings of the church. (And as far as the teaching duty of the church was concerned, the reformers seemed to have taken up that role themselves, not eliminated it as they claimed.)

The Catholic response to the Reformation gave particular weight to a few of the reformers' claims, and by exposing what appeared to be contradictions in these arguments, they felt they were hanging their opponents out to dry. For example, when the reformers insisted that Scripture alone was to govern the formation of doctrine, the Catholic apologists insisted that there was no such thing as Scripture alone: the text is never removed from its setting, the church; and belief is never separate from practice. The Catholic theologians saw the New Testament as the product, rather than the cause, of the church's work. That is, if the Reformers wanted to adhere to Scripture alone, how did they explain how Scripture—at least the New Testament—came to be? And when the Reformers claimed that "faith alone" was sufficient for salvation, how could they reconcile that with the customs that began developing in the first decades of the church's history? And the reformers' denial of the validity of human traditions in religion generally did not mesh well with what the Catholics saw in Wittenberg: a mini-"Rome," headquarters for enforcing orthodoxy and an antithesis of the papacy. Moreover, what was going on in Wittenberg was being duplicated, with important differences, in Zurich, Geneva, Strasbourg, and elsewhere, so that wherever one turned in the Protestant world one got a different answer. By contrast, the teachings of Catholicism were uniform and unanimous; what they taught in Paris was the same as what they taught in Louvain and Cologne. Since inconsistency was one of the defining marks of heresy, the Catholics observed, this was a serious charge.

Thomas More and Desiderius Erasmus

Most of the spokesmen for this reaction are lost in historical obscurity, but their numbers did include such luminaries as Thomas More (1478–1535) and Desiderius Erasmus (1466–1536). At one time lord chancellor to Henry VIII, Sir (later St.) Thomas More was condemned to death by Henry for treason in refusing to acknowledge him as head of the church in England (see Chapter 16). In 1528 More had been assigned, by the Bishop of London, the task of refuting Protestant writings as an antidote to heresy in England; and over the next five years he produced a number of works attacking the arguments of reformers, notably those of William Tyndale (c. 1494–1536). More is a puzzling character: a convivial humanist and friend of Erasmus, author of *Utopia* and other works that helped put England on the map as a center of learning, he defended the study of Greek against opponents at his own alma mater, Oxford (which later became a world center for Greek studies). And he also defended the authority of the Roman Church and its traditions against early English Protestants, whom he condemned as heretics (and some of whom died for their beliefs), as well as against his own king. He is linked in martyrdom with St. John Fisher (1469–1535), Bishop of Rochester and fellow-opponent of Henry's break with Rome.

Erasmus was one of the outstanding figures of Reformation-era Catholicism. Of illegitimate birth (his father was said to have been a priest), he attended school in Gouda, where he came into contact with the ideas of the Brethren of the Common Life, or Devotio Moderna (see Chapter 12). While still in his teens he was entered (by his guardians) into the Augustinian monastery at Steyn. There he learned about the sacramental system, the programs of works and merits that supposedly brought grace. He also learned about companionship, for which he would have a lifelong gift, a valuable quality when one is dependent on the patronage of the rich. He continued his education at the University of Paris, where he suffered under austere living conditions (the rector of his college, Montaigu, was a Devotio adherent) and an academic climate too arid for his liking. Erasmus coined the term *philosophia Christi* ("Philosophy of Christ") for his idea of piety: one that emphasizes charity, moral refinement, and devotion—rather than rationality and empty observance of "works," which he satirizes unmercifully in some of his writings. He

Hans Holbein the Younger, *Sir Thomas More*, c. 1530. Oil on panel. Frick Collection, New York.

Sir Thomas More gave up a statesman's career to defend the Catholic Church and its teachings; he died a martyr in the defense of Roman authority.

is often called a proto-Protestant, and some of his thought anticipates that of the reformers; but the differences between Erasmus and the Protestants, especially on the doctrine of grace and the role of works, outweigh the similarities. Although Erasmus was a witty humanist who had written a number of satirical works critical of the clergy and of Scholasticism, in the end he defended the church and its religious practices, quite earnestly in the late 1520s and especially in the 1530s, when the Reformation was in full swing. (See "Erasmus' Examination Concerning Faith" and "Erasmus' *The Praise of Folly*.")

Erasmus' *Examination Concerning Faith*

Erasmus, editor and scholar of the Patristic tradition, was also a commentator on the foibles of the church and the academic world. Here we witness part of a dialogue in which the church of the Creed is distinguished from the Roman Church.

AULUS. Why is the Father alone called God in the Creed?

BARB. Because, as I said, he is absolutely the author of everything existent and the fountainhead of the whole deity.

AULUS. Speak more plainly.

BARB. Because nothing can be named that does not come originally from the Father; for this very fact, that Son and Holy Spirit are God, is admittedly due to the Father. Therefore the principal authority, that is, ultimate causality, is in the Father alone, because he alone is without beginning. The Creed, however, can be so understood that the name "God" is not peculiar to a Person but generic, for subsequently distinction is made by the terms "Father," "Son," and "Holy Spirit": one God, the "natural" word comprising Father, Son, and Holy Spirit, that is, three Persons.

AULUS. Do you believe in the Holy church?

BARB. No.

AULUS. What's that you say? You don't believe in it?

BARB. I believe the Holy church, which is the Body of Christ, that is, a certain congregation of all those persons throughout the world who agree in gospel faith, who worship one God the Father, who place their whole trust in his Son, who are guided by his same Spirit: in a congregation from whose fellowship anyone who commits mortal sin is cut off.

AULUS. Why do you shrink from saying "I believe *in* the Holy church"?

BARB. Because St. Cyprian taught me that we must believe in God alone, in whom we trust absolutely. But the church, properly so called, though it consists of none except the good, nevertheless consists of human beings, who can change from good to bad, deceive and be deceived.

(From *The Colloquies of Erasmus*, trans. Craig R. Thompson. Chicago, IL: University of Chicago Press, 1965.)

The roster of Catholic spokesmen also includes Johann Eck, a Scholastic and professor who opposed Luther in some of the momentous encounters of the early Reformation, and Tomasso de Vio, Cardinal Cajetan (1469–1534), a Dominican and scholar of Aquinas's work, who debated with Luther at Augsburg and predicted even then that Luther was going to found a completely new church. This list could be expanded many times over without approaching completeness.

Erasmus' *The Praise of Folly*

Erasmus's satire spared no one, least of all the pompous churchmen of his day. His character Folly is here poking fun at the Scholastic questions about the Incarnation and the various types of philosophy found in the universities.

But these are common and threadbare; these are worthy of our great and illuminated Divines, as the world calls 'em! At these, if ever they fall a thwart 'em, they prick up:—as, whether there was any instant of time in the generation of the Second Person; whether there be more than one Filiation in Christ; whether it be a possible Proposition that God the Father hates the Son; or whether it was possible that Christ could have taken upon Him the likeness of a Woman, or of the Devil, or of an Ass, or of a Stone, or of a Gourd; and then how that Gourd should have Preach't, wrought Miracles, or been hung on the Cross; and, what Peter had Consecrated, if he had administered the Sacrament at what time the Body of Christ hung upon the Cross; or whether at the same time he might be said to be Man; whether after the Resurrection there will be any eating and drinking, since we are so much afraid of hunger and thirst in this world. There are infinite of these subtile Trifles, and others more subtile than these; of Notions, Relations, Instants, Formalities, Quiddities, Ecceities, which no one can perceive without a Lynceus his eyes, that could look through a stone-wall, and discover those things through the thickest darkness that never were.

Add to this those their other Determinations, and those too so contrary to common Opinion that those Oracles of the Stoicks, which they call Paradoxes, seem in comparison of these but blockish and idle:—as, 'tis a lesser crime to kill a thousand men than to set a stitch on a poor man's shooe on the Sabbath-day; and that a man should rather chuse that the whole world with all Food and Raiment, as they say, should perish, than tell a lye, though never so inconsiderable. And these most subtile subtilties are rendred yet more subtile by the several Methods of so many Schoolmen, that one might sooner wind himself out of a Labyrinth than the entanglements of the Realists, Nominalists, Thomists, Albertists, Occamists, Scotists. Nor have I nam'd all the several Sects, but onely some of the chief; in all which there is so much Doctrine and so much difficultie, that I may well conceive the Apostles, had they been to deal with these new kind of Divines, had needed to have pray'd in aid of some other Spirit.

(From Erasmus, *The Praise of Folly*, ed. P.S. Allen, trans. John Wilson. Oxford: Clarendon Press, 1925.)

New Religious Orders

Reaction was not the only form of response from the Catholics. Initiatives from within to reform the church were already under way when the Reformation was in its early days, and took such forms as the founding of the Theatine order (1524) and a new interest among the laity in spiritual life, a subject that had previously been confined largely to those within the religious life. Many of the clergy, especially the rank-and-file members, recognized that there were things wrong with the church, but felt they were not so far gone that they could not be repaired. Thus some of the same figures whom we just met as antagonists of the Protestants were not blind defenders of the old church, but advocates of reform from within.

J. Weirix, *Ignatius Loyola*, 16th century. Copper engraving.

The founder of the Society of Jesus translated the values of Spanish chivalry and military culture into an organization that would serve the Roman Church.

Erasmus was among the first to point out the flaws in monastic life, and Thomas More was a supporter of reform in the church as well as an opponent of its enemies. In Germany, humanist theologians such as Johannes Cochlaeus (1479–1552) and Georg Witzel (1500–1573) sought a solid basis for correcting flaws in the church at the same time that they condemned the "schismatics" who broke with it. In the Catholic view, somewhat paradoxically, basic loyalty to the church was considered a prerequisite for advocating reform.

Ignatius Loyola and the Jesuits

In no event of the Reformation era is this more obvious than in the founding of the SOCIETY OF JESUS by a group of seven university students, led by Ignatius Loyola (1491–1556). Loyola was a nobleman and a soldier, a Spaniard and a Catholic, who would probably have continued to occupy his place in aristocratic society had he not been gravely wounded in 1521. During a long period of recovery from his injury he experienced a number of religious impulses and mystical insights, which made him resolve to devote his life to the glory of God. First, he commenced a program of serious study, initially in Spain and later in Paris, where he met a number of like-minded fellow students. Assuming the role of their spiritual leader, he led them through a series of exercises—reflections, meditations, and other intellectual and spiritual practices— which became the foundation of a new program of pastoral care. Ignatius and his companions then embarked on a mission to Jerusalem, to convert the Muslims there. When this failed (thwarted by the outbreak of war, they did not reach their destination) they began a personal "crusade" to invigorate the Catholic Church. Vowing obedience to the pope, and chartered as an order to fight for the church, the Society of Jesus took shape in the years 1539–41.

This was a new form of religious order. Like cenobitic monasticism (see Chapter 7), it was a highly organized group, with a constitution, an internal hierarchy, and a fixed headquarters in Rome. Like the mendicant orders of the thirteenth century, the Jesuits (as they are commonly called) were engaged in the world for the edification of the laity. From the start the Society was a missionary organization without boundaries, extending into Protestant Germany and even into non-Christian lands such as the Americas, China, and Japan—always with the same zeal to win adherents to the church. Their methods included sessions using "Spiritual Exercises," educational programs that included dramas (for memorization) and humanistic study (for mental refinement). A distinctive aspect of the Jesuits' approach was their willingness to engage with secular culture. The clearest example of this last feature may be the way in which the missionary Matteo Ricci (1552–1610) and his fellow Jesuits studied Chinese astronomy, introduced Western telescopes and other instruments to the Chinese, and gradually gained the confidence of Chinese intellectuals, only then introducing the subject of religion. Compared with earlier missionary efforts, the Jesuit

Chinese mission was remarkably thorough and patient; and the result was that Christian and Chinese cultures came together as a unity, at least for a while.

The Society's missionary activities were also directed within the Catholic Church itself. Thus we find Jesuits embarking, like their mendicant predecessors of the thirteenth century (see Chapter 12), on preaching tours of cities and towns where religion had grown lax, and building schools in places where only a nominal faith was present. Because of low literacy rates throughout Europe, even at the end of the sixteenth century, there was much of this internal missionary work to be done. And the Jesuit ethos was not a leisurely one: there was a concern for efficiency and thoroughness that marks the work of the Society to this day. The growth of their membership itself is a testimony to the new religious culture. In time, however, the Jesuits' high success rate drew critics, who suspected that they would resort to shady tactics to accomplish their goals—in fact, the word "jesuitical" became a synonym for "sinister"; and the order was for a time shut down. But that would take place in a later century.

In Europe, and in the New World also, the Society swiftly became a dominant presence. Jesuit schools appeared in France and Germany, offering a schooling that matched or excelled that of the newly secularized Protestant institutions. It was a diet heavy in the Latin classics, the ancient trivium (see Chapter 17), and theological study, a program that resembled Protestant education in content but that differed in the prominence given to the church in the students' cultural education. In Jesuit teaching—as in their preaching—the church was considered the true vehicle for civilization, an object of uncritical obedience. In Protestant educational systems, especially within the Lutheran world, it was the state that held this kind of authority. The difference may have seemed minor from the layperson's perspective, but the principles underlying both systems were as different as one could imagine.

Teresa of Ávila and John of the Cross

The Jesuits were not the only sign of a spiritual revival within the Catholic Church. In Spain there was a remarkable resurgence of interest in the religious life, led by Teresa of Ávila (1515–1582) and John of the Cross (1542–1591), both later canonized. Teresa, daughter of an affluent family with Jewish roots, entered a Carmelite convent in her native Ávila at the age of twenty. (See "St. Teresa of Ávila.") However, she found it spiritually unsatisfying, since many of the other nuns (most, like herself, from the privileged classes) had not abandoned their worldly values. Turning to devotional literature, Teresa cultivated an intense life of prayer; and at about the age of forty she began having visions and experiences that seemed to bring her closer to God. In 1562, acting on these experiences, she founded a convent of her own, which she led for twenty years. This was a reform version of her order, and was known as the DISCALCED (or Barefoot) CARMELITES, the term representing the austerity of its religious life. The nuns wore no shoes (considered a luxurious indulgence); remained strictly enclosed within the convent walls; and refused potentially corrupting endowments and contributions. The reform spread from Ávila to more than a dozen other sites in Spain and eventually included men's houses. Teresa's experiences and spiritual counsel are recorded in a (1562–65) *Life* (in which her mystical "attacks" are captured in powerful language), the *Way of Perfection* (c. 1565), and the *Interior Castle* (1577), in which the soul is depicted as a mansion in which one moves through a series of stages, or "rooms," to reach the innermost chamber in which union with God is possible.

Teresa's younger contemporary John of the Cross was, unlike her, a child of poverty; but he, too, found spiritual value in the ascetic life. (See "St. John of the Cross.") Ordained a priest but longing for a life of solitude, he joined the Carmelite

---

St. Teresa of Ávila

St. Teresa of Ávila, also known as Teresa of Jesus, was a Carmelite nun who brought reform to her order by calling for stricter observance; symbolic of her convent's austerity was the fact that the nuns wore no shoes, and hence became known as "discalced" (barefoot) Carmelites. Here she describes her family background, highlighting the qualities of virtue and piety.

If I had not been so wicked it would have been a help to me that I had parents who were virtuous and feared God, and also that the Lord granted me His favour to make me good. My father was fond of reading good books and had some in Spanish so that his children might read them too. These books, together with the care which my mother took to make us say our prayers and to lead us to be devoted to Our Lady and to certain saints, began to awaken good desires in me when I was, I suppose, about six or seven years old. It was a help to me that I never saw my parents inclined to anything but virtue. They themselves had many virtues. My father was a man of great charity towards the poor, who was good to the sick and also to his servants—so much so that he could never be brought to keep slaves, because of his compassion for them. On one occasion, when he had a slave of a brother of his in the house, he was as good to her as to his own children. He used to say that it caused him intolerable distress that she was not free. He was strictly truthful; nobody ever heard him swear or speak evil. He was a man of the most rigid chastity.

My mother, too, was a very virtuous woman, who endured a life of great infirmity: she was also particularly chaste. Though extremely beautiful, she was never known to give any reason for supposing that she made the slightest account of her beauty; and, though she died at thirty-three, her dress was already that of a person advanced in years. She was a very tranquil woman, of great intelligence. Throughout her life she endured great trials and her death was most Christian.

We were three sisters and nine brothers: all of them, by the goodness of God, resembled their parents in virtue, except myself, though I was my father's favourite. And, before I began to offend God, I think there was some reason for this, for it grieves me whenever I remember what good inclinations the Lord had given me and how little I profited by them. My brothers and sisters never hindered me from serving God in any way….

When I saw that it was impossible for me to go to any place where they would put me to death for God's sake, we decided to become hermits, and we used to build hermitages, as well as we could, in an orchard which we had at home. We would make heaps of small stones, but they at once fell down again, so we found no way of accomplishing our desires. But even now it gives me a feeling of devotion to remember how early God granted me what I lost by my own fault.

(From *Complete Works of St. Teresa of Jesus*, trans. P. Silverio de Santa Teresa, ed. E. A. Peers. London: Sheed & Ward, 1946.)

BIOGRAPHICAL PROFILE

Teresa of Ávila (1515–1582)

As a young girl growing up in the Spanish city of Ávila, Teresa developed an ardent religious faith. Her commitment to Christ and the church was such that, at age twenty-two and in spite of the strenuous objections of her father, she joined a convent of Carmelite nuns not far from Ávila. During her early years in the convent, Teresa began to study devotional literature seriously. More importantly, she began experiencing religious visions, even claiming to see Christ himself. Teresa was initially not sure that these visions were genuine (they would continue throughout her life). She feared that Satan or some demon might be deceiving her, trying to capture her soul for perdition. As a result, she sought the help of various spiritual advisors, but to no avail. In fact, she relates how one of her confessors suggested that if what she was seeing in her visions was a devil, she could frighten the devil away by simply directing an obscene gesture toward it; but such an action Teresa could not, in good conscience, undertake. Finally, though, Teresa did receive counsel from some friars whose judgment she had come to trust. With their guidance, she concluded that her visions were not the result of demonic pranks; she came to believe that she was actually communing with the divine.

As she continued with the Carmelite sisters, Teresa became convinced that they were leading lives that were far too easy for nuns who had dedicated their lives and souls to Christ. She therefore left the Carmelites (though not without some contention with her sisters and other Catholic authorities), and in 1562 founded and headed a new convent. Her nuns wore sandals rather than shoes, for which reason they were called the "Discalced" (barefoot) Carmelites. Teresa here began working for religious and monastic reform, an effort in which she was joined by another future saint, John of the Cross; as a result, a separate order of Discalced Carmelites was founded for men.

Perhaps more important than her reform efforts, however, were Teresa's mystical encounters. Throughout her life, she spent much time in prayer and meditation, continuing to see visions and encountering the presence of God in mystical union. These experiences became the absolutely firm confirmation of her faith, and she wrote much about them, recording the content of her visions along with devotional meditations and guidance for her readers concerning how to attain mystical states. Probably her most widely read work is her autobiography, known as *The Life of Teresa of Jesus*. She also wrote *The Way of Perfection* and the mystical work *The Interior Castle*. Teresa was so greatly revered that she was not only canonized by the Catholic Church in 1622 but also declared a Doctor of the church, an honor given to only two other women in history, Catherine of Siena (1347–1380) and Thérèse of Lisieux (1873–1897).

Teresa of Ávila, 16th century. Copper engraving.

monastery in Medina. Here he met Teresa of Ávila and came under her spell. At this time Teresa was establishing a Discalced Carmelite house at Medina, and John immediately joined her movement. He established a male order of Discalced Carmelite friars and became their leader. Repeatedly in trouble, like Teresa, with church superiors for his insistence on the need for reform, John was actually kidnapped twice by members of the Carmelite order who imprisoned and beat him. During this period of suffering he wrote works such as *The Dark Night of the Soul* (c. 1585) and *The Spiritual Canticle* (finished in 1578) (both posthumously

St. John of the Cross

St. John of the Cross and St. Teresa of Ávila raised the Carmelite Order to unique prominence in the golden age of Spanish Catholicism. John also wrote religious poetry and prose commentaries on his verse. Here he explicates a stanza of his poem about the "dark night" of the soul, a period of emptiness that precedes mystical union.

On a dark night, Kindled in love with yearnings—oh, happy chance!— I went forth without being observed. My house being now at rest.

1. In this first stanza the soul sings of the happy fortune and chance which it experienced in going forth from all things that are without, and from the desires and imperfections that are in the sensual part of man because of the disordered state of his reason. For the understanding of this it must be known that, for a soul to attain to the state of perfection, it has ordinarily first to pass through two principal kinds of night, which spiritual persons call purgations or purifications of the soul; and here we call them nights, for in both of them the soul journeys, as it were, by night, in darkness.

2. The first night or purgation is of the sensual part of the soul, which is treated in the present stanza and will be treated in the first part of this book. And the second is of the spiritual part; of this speaks the second stanza, which follows; and of this we shall treat likewise, in the second and the third part, with respect to the activity of the soul; and in the fourth part, with respect to its passivity.

3. And this first night pertains to beginners, occurring at the time when God begins to bring them into the state of contemplation; in this night the spirit likewise has a part, as we shall say in due course. And the second night, or purification, pertains to those who are already proficient, occurring at the time when God desires to set them in the state of union with God. And this latter night is a more obscure and dark and terrible purgation, as we shall say afterwards.

(From *Complete Works of St. John of the Cross*, trans. P. Silverio de Santa Teresa, ed. E. A. Peers. London: Burns, Oates, & Washburn, 1934.)

published), which are richly poetic meditations on the unavoidable sufferings in this life and their power to enlighten the faithful. In other works, notably *The Living Flame of Love* and *The Ascent of Mount Carmel*, John stands out as one of the most provocative mystics of the early-modern period, at times writing with an expressive power found elsewhere only among the Cistercians of the twelfth century.

The Council of Trent

By far the most important event of Reformation-era Catholicism was the Council of Trent, which met in Trento, northern Italy, in three phases between 1545 and 1563. Called by Pope Paul III (1468–1549; r. 1534–1549) at the beginning of his pontificate, this council was a dozen years in organizing and almost two decades in meeting; thus it spanned a period from the early, reactionary, generation of Catholic clergy who saw only threats to their church in the Protestant movement, to a more moderate generation who saw merit in some of the reformers' ideas.

No Council was more trouble to assemble. The years of preparation included meetings, mostly in Germany, between Catholic and Protestant theologians, at which some notable progress was made. The purpose of these meetings was to identify points of difference and clarify confessional positions, and it was a blessed (but temporary) event when a breakthrough occurred, such as agreement

---

St. Francis de Sales

St. Francis de Sales (1567–1622) popularized the devotional life with a number of works, the best-known of which is the Introduction to the Devout Life. *By means of character sketches personifying various devout types, and by addressing his audience in the manner of pastoral care, Francis provides religious instruction for his readers in an accessible and agreeable way.*

You wish to live a life of devotion, dearest Philothea, because you are a Christian and know that it is a virtue most pleasing to God's Majesty. Since little faults committed in the beginning of a project grow infinitely greater in its course and finally are almost irreparable, above all else you must know what the virtue of devotion is. There is only one true devotion but there are many that are false and empty. If you are unable to recognize which kind is true, you can easily be deceived and led astray by following one that is offensive and superstitious.

In his pictures Arelius painted all faces after the manner and appearance of the women he loved, and so too everyone paints devotion according to his own passions and fancies. A man given to fasting thinks himself very devout if he fasts, although his heart may be filled with hatred. Much concerned with sobriety, he doesn't dare to wet his tongue with wine or even water but won't hesitate to drink deep of his neighbor's blood by detraction and calumny. Another man thinks himself devout because he daily recites a vast number of prayers, but after saying them he utters the most disagreeable, arrogant, and harmful words at home and among the neighbors. Another gladly takes a coin out of his purse and gives it to the poor, but he cannot extract kindness from his heart and forgive his enemies. Another forgives his enemies but never pays his creditors unless compelled to do so by force of law. All these men are usually considered to be devout, but they are by no means such. Saul's servants searched for David in his house but Michol had put a statue on his bed, covered it with David's clothes, and thus led them to think that it was David himself lying there sick and sleeping. In the same manner, many persons clothe themselves with certain outward actions connected with holy devotion and the world believes that they are truly devout and spiritual whereas they are in fact nothing but simulacra and phantoms of devotion.

Genuine, living devotion, Philothea, presupposes love of God, and hence it is simply true love of God. Yet it is not always love as such. Inasmuch as divine love adorns the soul, it is called grace, which makes us pleasing to his Divine Majesty. Inasmuch as it strengthens us to do good, it is called charity. When it has reached a degree of perfection at which it not only makes us do good but also do this carefully, frequently, and promptly, it is called devotion. Ostriches never fly; hens fly in a clumsy fashion, near the ground, and only once in a while, but eagles, doves, and swallows fly aloft, swiftly and frequently. In like manner, sinners in no way fly up towards God, but make their whole course here upon the earth and for the earth. Good people who have not as yet attained to devotion fly toward God by their good works but do so infrequently, slowly, and awkwardly. Devout souls ascend to him more frequently, promptly, and with lofty flights. In short, devotion is simply that spiritual agility and vivacity by which charity works in us or by aid of which we work quickly and lovingly.

(From *Introduction to the Devout Life*, trans. John K. Ryan. New York: Harper, 1966.)

on the doctrine of justification (see Chapter 15) reached at Regensburg in 1541. (Other differences remained unresolved at this meeting.) Some German territories imposed moratoriums on religious debate, in the hope that the Council would finally settle all issues. And some Catholic theologians, especially the reactionaries, campaigned zealously for a chance to attend, looking forward to signing Protestantism's death warrant. Few of these actually attended, but they made sure, in voluminous pre-Council indictments of Reformation teachings, that their opinions would be represented. The Protestants, on the other hand, professed not to want to attend the Council, sensing (probably rightly) that the jury was rigged beforehand. In the end, it was Italian clergy—familiar only at second hand (if at all) with religious affairs north of the Alps—who dominated the Council.

Thus we are not surprised to see certain themes from the Catholic controversialists in the decrees of the early sessions. For example, the decree of the fourth session (April 1546), which affirmed the combined authority of Scripture and tradition in the life of the church, is a direct rebuke to Luther's claim to stand by "sola scriptura"—and an obvious echo of the controversialists' argument that the text is never removed from its context, the practicing life of the church. Likewise, when the sixth session in January 1547 issued its ruling on justification, it recognized the sovereignty of grace in the salvation of the believer, but also asserted the necessity of works as a vital form of cooperation with such grace. Many of these issues were carried forward into the second phase, which gave new force to such notorious features of the church as the Index of Prohibited Books and the Inquisition.

With the third phase of the Council, the tone shifted from reaction to reform, and it was here that what became known as "Tridentine Catholicism" (from the

---

Who's Who

Sixteenth-Century Catholic Reformers

Tommaso de Vio (1469–1534) Also known as Cardinal Cajetan. A Dominican, scholar, and interpreter of Thomas Aquinas, he debated with Luther at Augsburg and argued for Catholic reform at the Fifth Lateran Council (1512–1517).

St. John Fisher (1469–1535) Bishop of Rochester, distinguished apologist, and friend of Erasmus. He paid for his strong defense of Catholicism: he was found guilty of treason by Henry VIII and executed.

St. Thomas More (1478–1535) A staunch Catholic campaigner in the face of the Lutheran Reformation. As Chancellor of England, he opposed Henry VIII's petition for divorce and was found guilty of treason and executed.

Johann Eck (1486–1543) A German theologian and scholar. He was an opponent of Luther in the early stages of the Protestant Reformation and continued to organize support for Catholicism all his life.

St. Ignatius Loyola (1491–1556) From a wealthy Spanish family, this former soldier had a profound spiritual experience that led him to dedicate his life to renewal within Catholicism. He went on to found the Jesuit Order (Society of Jesus).

St. Teresa of Ávila (1515–1582) A Spanish mystic and Carmelite, she went on to found an order based on a reformed version of Carmelite practice.

St. John of the Cross (1542–1591) A Spanish mystic and Carmelite who worked with St. Teresa of Ávila to reform the order. His mystical poetry ranks as some of the finest writing in Spanish.

BIOGRAPHICAL PROFILE

Vincent de Paul (c. 1580–1660)

Vincent de Paul's life is a Catholic success story from the early modern period. Born circa 1580 into a peasant family in Pouy, France, where shepherding sheep rather than men was the typical vocation, Vincent received his early schooling among Franciscans, who saw enough potential in the boy to encourage him to pursue advanced studies. He enrolled at the University of Toulouse, paying his way by serving as a tutor to the children of a wealthy family. His life after graduation and ordination reads partly like a saint's life, partly like an adventure story. His first assignment as a priest was as rector of a small parish, an undertaking he willingly renounced when he learned that another candidate wanted the post. In 1605 he embarked on a voyage in the Mediterranean in search of an inheritance, during which he was captured by pirates and sold into slavery in Tunisia. Sold off as mere property by a fisherman to an alchemist, and in turn to a French convert to Islam, Vincent experienced the degradation of slavery. While in captivity, however, he gained the ear of one of the wives of his owner, who herself later converted to Christianity.

Once free and back in France in 1607, Vincent fell under the influence of Pierre de Bérulle, the founder of a new religious movement known as the Oratory, intended as a mission for French priests and aimed at improving their work with the laity. De Paul then experienced a period of doubt, which was resolved by his decision to dedicate himself to Jesus Christ as mirrored in the persons of the poor. That is, Vincent saw the poor as Christ personified, one to whom all his energies should henceforth be dedicated. His compassion and charity were directed particularly to poor boys who might have had a calling to the priesthood—an echo of the notice that the Franciscans took of him as a boy.

Vincent had a way with the rich as well as with the poor. His great opportunity arose while he served as tutor to the children of the noble De Gondi family; he managed to draw both husband and wife into charitable work. Furthermore, moving to Châtillon-les-Doubles, he converted the local count, de Rougemont, to his cause, and established groups known as "confraternities of charity." Madame de Gondi and the Comte de Rougemont became essential supporters of his work, while Admiral de Gondi made him Almoner to the King's Ships, essentially the chaplain to sick and suffering sailors in the French Royal Navy. His success in raising the social consciousness of the nobility and bourgeoisie was remarkable, and he served on a religious commission headed by Queen Anne of Austria (then regent in France). He was also the priest chosen to administer the last rites to King Louis XIII.

Vincent's work as a founder of charitable institutions that served the poor and the sick achieved its greatest fulfilment in 1625 with his hand in the creation of a "congregation" of preachers to be sent into villages and poor districts. Called the Congregation of Priests of the Missions, its emphasis lay in humility, clarity, and simplicity—qualities often lacking in the loftier institutions of Counter-Reformation Catholicism. The "mission" extended to priests as well. Members of the Congregation served as examples of good pastoral care to those priests needing reminders, and they offered them retreats in which to receive further instruction and inspiration. The Congregation also offered a retreat for laity, many of them from the upper classes—intended to sharpen their spiritual sensitivity and their sense of responsibility for the poor.

In 1634 Vincent founded a comparable women's order known as the Sisters of Charity. This was intended both to assist in the work of the Congregation and to take on its own responsibilities in the world. These included

caring for sick soldiers, establishing orphanages in cities for abandoned babies, and feeding the poor through the establishment and operation of soup kitchens. As with the Congregation, many of the French elite joined this order.

Vincent de Paul died in 1660 and was canonized in 1737.

Sebastien Bourdon, *St. Vincent de Paul*, 1649. Oil on canvas. St. Etienne du Mont, Paris.

Gianlorenzo Bernini, *Saint Teresa*, Cornaro Chapel altarpiece, S. Maria della Vittoria, Rome. Marble.

Saint Teresa of Ávila described her mystical experience in terms of an angel from heaven piercing her heart with a flaming golden spear. She was canonized in 1622.

Latin name for Trent) was inaugurated. Under the leadership of a new pope (Paul IV, 1476–1559, r. 1555–1559), the Council worked for ways to renew the church, ordering that bishops actually live in their dioceses (previously they had often drawn incomes from churches they never visited); that seminaries be founded for priests' education; and for active pastoral care, including religious instruction, to be a priority of parish life. Here were born the CATECHISM as a standard means of religious instruction, and a renewed emphasis on the sacraments as a source of grace and of contact with the divine (rather than as some magical and misunderstood ways to avoid punishment in the afterlife); and on parasacramental rites such as indulgences and veneration of saints and relics.

The Arts and Reformed Catholicism

In its concern to engender increased piety and orthodoxy among the faithful, the Council paid considerable attention to the arts. Church music came in for special scrutiny, for by the early sixteenth century it had become very elaborate, with complex polyphony (the interweaving of two or more melodic lines) which often obscured the words—and hence the religious message—of the music. Florid vocal writing and the use of musical instruments other than the organ were also deplored. The composer who best met the Council's requirement for more spiritually uplifting music was Giovanni Pierluigi da Palestrina (c. 1525–1594). Although polyphonic, Palestrina's choral works are relatively simple, with a soaring quality that evokes eternal bliss. Other composers, notably the Spaniard Tomás Luis de Victoria (c. 1548–1611), also produced fine religious music in this style. In the seventeenth century, all serious music, including religious works, would again become highly elaborate—exemplified in Italy by the compositions of Claudio Monteverdi (1567–1643). By this time, however, the Catholic Church was ready to accept, and even promote, a more extravagant artistic style.

This ornate BAROQUE style, which would spread throughout most of Europe, found expression in the visual arts as well as music, and nowhere more so than in Catholic churches. The undulating curves, dizzying perspectives, and ornate gilded altars of baroque church interiors designed by such architects as Francesco Borromini (1599–1667) and Gianlorenzo Bernini (1598–1680) were intended to overwhelm worshipers with the glory of God and the majesty of the church founded by Christ. (Best known for his dramatic, often sensual sculptures, Bernini was intensely devout and is known to have practiced Ignatius Loyola's Spiritual Exercises.) Magnificent altar-pieces, painted by such masters as Caravaggio (1573–1610) and Peter Paul Rubens (1577–1640), rendered the sacred images of Catholicism with total con-viction—giving a sense of mystery by the flickering candlelight and heady incense. Whereas in Protestant countries the word was the favored medium for transmitting the truths of Christianity, the Catholic Church made sure its message would reach everyone including those who could not read, appealing to the senses and the emotions as never before.

Tridentine Catholicism was to last for four centuries, until the First Vatican Council (1869–70)—and much of it lasted even longer. Having been goaded into action by the rise of Protestantism, the Catholic Church succeeded, not in revers-ing Protestantism's gains but in strengthening itself from within, so as to with-stand further threats for centuries to come. It is one of those unanswerable historians' questions whether a council such as that of Trent would have taken place without the reformers' challenges. Reforms would probably have come about, but much later than 1563.

Until fairly recently it was customary, even in academic circles, to think of the medieval Catholic Church as uniform and rigid (scholars used to speak of the "medieval monolith"). But the Catholic Church of the late-sixteenth and seven-teenth centuries was actually more authoritarian than its medieval counter-part—thanks to the renewed vigor of the papacy, the sustained program of diocesan supervision, and the other innovations examined in this chapter. As the church entered the seventeenth century, its heightened emphasis on discipline and devotion made it virtually invulnerable.

Key Terms

BAROQUE A 17th-century cultural movement associated with Counter-Reformation Catholicism, characterized by exuberance in painting, music, and architecture.

CATECHISM A comprehensive manual of religious instruction in question-and-answer form, usually for the young.

DISCALCED CARMELITES A reformed Spanish branch of the medieval Carmelite order with a strong devotional and mystical strain; their austerity is indicated by "discalced" (literally, "shoeless").

SOCIETY OF JESUS (JESUITS) A religious order founded in 1534 by Ignatius Loyola and a band of followers; it emphasized pastoral care and "recovery" of the faithful from Protestantism.

CHAPTER 19

The Challenge of Rationalism

Skepticism and Faith
in the 17th Century

The doctrinal divisions and upheavals of the sixteenth century seriously undermined the certainties of the Christian faith; and by the seventeenth century, in some quarters, religious certainty seemed more like an elusive dream than an attainable reality. Yet the basic human need for certainty never diminished. We all want to know which accepted truths are absolute, which are merely relative, and which are not true at all. Without some such understanding we are left floating in a realm that is potentially illusory.

The outstanding explorer of certainties of the seventeenth century was René Descartes (1596–1650), a French mathematician also considered the first truly "modern" philosopher. In his *Meditations* (full title of second edition [1642], *Meditations on First Philosophy, in which the Existence of God and the Distinction between Mind and Body are Demonstrated*) Descartes set about discovering what he could know with absolute certainty.

He first arrived at the certainty of his doubting, a form of thinking, and of his own existence, which he expressed in the famous statement *"Cogito ergo sum"* ("I think, therefore I exist"). From this point he proceeded to work his way systematically through a series of propositions with led him finally to certainty of the existence of God—a revival of the ontological argument (see Chapter 10).

Descartes' ultra-cautious reasoning, so strongly influenced by his mathematical training, was characteristic of his period, which has been described as an age of SKEPTICISM. This period was inaugurated by Michel de Montaigne (1533–1592), the author of an influential collection of *Essays* and the *Apology for Raymond Sebond*, a work influenced by the Greek Skeptic philosopher Pyrrho (c. 365–275 B.C.E.).

It was also an age of RATIONALISM, a school of thought that maintains that human reason, unaided by sensory observations, can arrive at truth, including religious truth. This philosophy has much in common with mathematics, and so it was no accident that Descartes, being a mathematician, used a rationalist approach in his search for religious certainty. The advantage of this approach is that it has no gray areas: every stage of the process is clear and every conclusion logical. The disadvantage is that anything that cannot be deduced through reason alone is left out of the picture, and this includes most of what constitutes religion: Scripture, revelation, faith, practice, tradition, and a supra-rational essence that separates religion from other forms of understanding.

Jansenism

Into the midst of rationalist explorations came a religious movement that proved to be as controversial as it was radical. The movement, called JANSENISM after a Dutch theologian named Cornelius Jansen (1585–1638), flourished especially in France and was centered at the convent of Port Royal. It emphasized human sinfulness to a degree not seen in the Catholic tradition for centuries. It stressed the more rigorous predestinarian qualities of the teachings of St. Augustine, arguing that the efficacy of the sacraments largely depended on the moral character of their recipients.

The strongest supporters of Jansenism were members of the influential Arnault family and their friend Jean Duvergier de Hauranne (1581–1643), Abbé de St. Cyran, who was a friend of Jansen's. Angélique Arnauld (1591–1661) was a girl of eleven when she became abbess of Port Royal des Champs, near Paris, having been induced by her family to take the veil two years earlier. In 1608, while listening to a Lenten sermon by a visiting Capuchin friar (the Capuchins were a branch of the Franciscan order), Mère Angélique experienced a conversion. Now dedicated to serving God, she decided to reform the convent (which had lapsed from the Cistercian rule under which it had been founded) along stricter lines. Although the Cistercian superior general at the time supported her, his successor from 1625 onward did not approve of her efforts; and in 1626 the abbey (now relocated in Paris) placed itself under the jurisdiction of the Archbishop of Paris, a secular bishop, and adopted the name Daughters of the Blessed Sacrament.

The association between Port Royal and Jansenism came about largely through the influence of the Abbé de St. Cyran, who became Port Royal's spiritual director in 1636. As already noted, St. Cyran was a friend of Cornelius Jansen. It may have been at Louvain (in present-day Belgium) that he became acquainted with Jansen. At any rate, they later studied theology together in Paris, concentrating on Patristic writings, especially those of St. Augustine. The two friends kept up a steady correspondence for many years, while Jansen worked on the book, *Augustinus*, which would later bring his ideas before the public. In the meantime St. Cyran made a number of enemies with his zeal for reform and for a reinvigorated penitential system, among them the increasingly

P. de Champaigne, *Jean Duvergier de Hauranne, Abbot of Saint-Cyran*, c. 1646–1648. Oil on canvas. Château de Versailles, France.

Patron of a conservative Catholicism, the abbot presided over the Port Royal convent and sought to reform religious practice along severe lines.

influential Jesuits and Cardinal Richelieu (Armand Jean Duplessis, Duc de Richelieu; 1585–1642), minister of state to Louis XIII (1601–1643; r. 1610– 1643). In 1638 Richelieu had St. Cyran arrested for heresy and deviating from the teachings of the Council of Trent. From prison St. Cyran sent moving and instructive letters to a number of followers, including Jane Frances de Chantal (1572–1641), founder of the Order of the Visitation; as well as essays and treatises that reached beyond his acquaintances to such thinkers as Blaise Pascal (1623–1662), the renowned scientist and mathematician, whose *Pensées* have some right to being included in the Jansenist canon.

Jansenists versus Jesuits

In 1640, two years after its author's death, Jansen's *Augustinus* was published. It is a treatise on sin and grace, every bit as forceful as those of St. Augustine himself or any of the reformers of the sixteenth century. The work revives controversies of the early fifth century (called Pelagian, after a heretic named Pelagius, c. 360–c. 431), which turned on whether, and to what extent, human faculties played a role in a believer's salvation. The targets of Jansen's book were the Jesuits and particularly the followers of Luis de Molina (1535–1600), whose *Concord of Free Will with the Gift of Grace* (1588) states that grace works because God already knows whether the recipient is going to cooperate with it. The Jansenist response was that if God grants grace, then it is the grace alone, without any cooperation from the recipient, that completes the work of salvation.

With the publication of *Augustinus*, Jansenism began to gain momentum, encouraged by Mère Angélique and various members of her family. (The Abbé de St. Cyran died in 1643, shortly after his release from prison.) Now reestablished at its country home of Port Royal des Champs, near Versailles, the abbey

---

Who's Who

Pioneers of New Thinking

Cornelius Jansen (1585–1638) Catholic theologian and advocate of a radical Augustinianism, born in the Netherlands. The reform movement called Jansenism is named after him.

René Descartes (1596–1650) French "Rationalist" philosopher who stressed the importance of human reason in the knowledge of all things, including the matter of God's existence. He was author of the statement *Cogito, ergo sum* ("I think, therefore I am").

Blaise Pascal (1623–1662) French theologian, scientist, writer, inventor (of the barometer, hydraulic press, and syringe), and Jansenist sympathizer. A profound spiritual experience led him to Jansenism, which he defended staunchly against the Jesuits.

Charles Wesley (1707–1788) and John Wesley (1703–1791) English brothers and zealous evangelists. Charles was a priest and leader of a group of Oxford University religious scholars who later became known as Methodists. John was a priest and Oxford academic who co-founded the Methodist movement. *See also* chapter 21.

George Whitefield (1714–1770) English evangelist and early Methodist, who was associated with the Wesleys at Oxford. His visits to America played a major role in the First Great Awakening (the American Christian revival movement). *See also* chapter 21.

attracted visitors, both laymen and clergy, who used it as a place of retreat and study. Prominent among the Arnauld contingent was Antoine Arnauld (1612–1694), a younger brother of Mère Angélique, who became associated with Port Royal right after his ordination in 1641. Arnauld's first contribution to controversy was his 1643 work *On Frequent Communion*, a defense of St. Cyran's work and an attack upon Jesuit claims that frequent communion was beneficial to the penitent person. Arnauld countered by claiming that *not* receiving the Eucharist on a frequent basis (weekly, for example) might be more helpful for piety since it would increase the desire for the sacrament. This angered the church hierarchy, who felt that each new reception of the Eucharist added merit (see Chapter 13) to the recipient.

Another of Mère Angélique's brothers, Robert Arnauld d'Andilly (1588–1674), managed to combine allegiance to Jansenism with government service. With Cardinal Richelieu as his patron, Robert Arnauld had the attention of the royal court, which he criticized for its luxury and corruption. By the 1650s Jansenism had become more than a theological program; it was a reform movement with the Jesuits as the prominent and obvious opposition. Tensions were high. The pope at the time, Innocent X (1574–1655; r. 1644–1655), condemned five of Jansen's teachings in the bull *Cum occasione* of May 1653, though did not mention the *Augustinus* or indict the movement in general. At about the same time a French duke who was sympathetic to the Jansenists was denied the Eucharist by a priest loyal to the Jesuits. Nothing could have caused a greater scandal: a veritable flurry of letters and pamphlets inundated church and court, a tempestuous episode that ended with Antoine Arnauld, the chief agitator, being censured by the Sorbonne for his failure to yield to the church's will. Innocent's successor, Alexander VII (1599–1667; r. 1655–1667) was as unsympathetic to the Jansenists as Innocent had been, but recognized the political value of an accord between the quarreling French camps. At the end of 1657 it was decided that the king, Louis XIV, was to be the mediator of the church's strictures against the Jansenists.

But the papacy hardly needed to devise measures against the Jansenists after *Cum occasione* and Antoine Arnauld's expulsion from the Sorbonne. Arnauld moved from Paris to Port Royal des Champs where he was joined by Pascal. Introduced to the Port Royal community by his father, and familiar with Jansenism from his own reading of St. Cyran and Arnauld, Pascal became an ally of the movement, although never an ordained member of it himself. (His sister, however, became a Port Royal nun.) Pascal's support took a literary form, a series of *Provincial Letters* published in parts between 1656 and 1657.

In imaginary letters, alternately scathing and satirical, Pascal exposes what he sees as the flaws of Jesuit practice, especially in the realm of penitential custom and moral instruction. The Jesuit method was depicted as one in which there was a mitigating factor in every sin and an exception to every rule. Thus there was no act, however sinful it might appear, that did not have any of a number of exonerating excuses, nor any rule that needed to be applied absolutely. The Jesuit method of pastoral care came out looking like a program aimed at minimizing the importance of contrition and the extent of the effects of original sin on human freedom and goodness—exactly the opposite of what the Jansenists emphasized. As a result of Pascal's refined polemics, the Jesuit pastoral method came to be labeled "laxist," its opposite being the "rigorist" methods of the Jansenists. It was perhaps inevitable that a later pope, in this case Innocent XI (1611–1689; r. 1676–1689), would reverse the anti-Jansenist cycle begun with Innocent X's *Cum occasione*, and issue a condemnation of the Jesuits. In a decree of March 4, 1679, Innocent XI identified sixty-five propositions found among the "lax" moralists. The Jesuits were not named (remember that the Jansenists had not been cited in *Cum occasione*), but their teachings were clearly implicated. Suspicion of Jesuit tactics, so pervasive that the order's name itself became synonymous with trickery and casuistry, would last for another century—culminating in the Jesuits' being officially suspended from activity by Clement XIV (1705–1774, r. 1769–1774) in 1773. (True to their reputation, the Jesuits continued working nevertheless, though not as Jesuits, and the ban was lifted in 1814.)

Jansenism lived on, despite occasional attempts by its opponents to invoke the papal condemnation against the movement as a whole. With the help of Clement IX (1600–1669; r. 1667–1669) a truce of sorts was achieved between the feuding factions. But tensions flared again with the work of Pasquier Quesnel (1634–1719), whose *Réflexions morales* (1687–94) offered a Jansenist, or suspiciously Jansenist-sounding, interpretation of the New Testament. So controversial was this work, though ostensibly only a commentary on the biblical text, that QUESNELISM became the name for the new wave of Jansenist thought. Exiled to Brussels because of his views, and in particular his refusal to come out against Jansenism, Quesnel met up with Antoine Arnauld, and together they defended, through their writings, Jansenist doctrine. Quesnel's work was condemned twice by Clement XI (1649–1721; r. 1700–1721); and the movement gradually lost support, even that of other opponents of the Jesuits. Port Royal was suppressed in 1709, its few remaining nuns dispersed to other convents, and, in 1711, its buildings were razed. Remnants of Jansenism survived in Holland and Italy to the end of the eighteenth century, but by then it had become, in effect, a schismatic sect.

The issue at the heart of the dispute between Jesuits and Jansenists was a more profound one than Pascal's satire of confessors' practices might suggest. Was the Augustinian correlation of absolute sinfulness and absolute grace the correct formula in understanding the human condition and humanity's relation to God, as the Jansenists insisted; or was humanity in some way responsible for restoring itself to grace, just as it had been for its fall from a primordial innocence—as the Jesuits held? More subtly, the issue was whether the absoluteness of grace was compromised by human effort, or whether human awareness of the divine work of redemption demanded some form of active response. These were questions that went back to Augustine and Pelagius, even to Peter and Paul. They had also been at the heart of theological debates between Catholics and Protestants in the sixteenth century—a fact that complicated matters. Were the Jansenists, in their denial of the possibility of cooperating with grace, more Calvinist than Catholic? Many of the tenets of the *Augustinus* would have found agreement among the participants of the Synod of Dort (see Chapter 17), not too many decades before. The decrees of the Council of Trent that upheld the doctrines of merit and of cooperating grace, and which condemned the radical doctrines of sin and salvation as an absolute gift, had already settled the issue in the Jesuits' favor. Whether they were authentically Augustinian or not, the teachings of the Jansenists were too similar to those of the Protestants to be completely at home within the Catholic Church.

Pietism

Among Protestants, too, the seventeenth century was a time of new movements. Within the camp of university-based academics, new systems of faith—and definitions of the relation of reason to experience and emotions—began to take shape, and Johann Gerhard and Hermann Conring (see Chapter 17) were among the leading thinkers who addressed these issues. These were largely academic questions, however; and whatever answers one produced had hardly brought anyone closer to God. In reaction to these intellectualizing tendencies, the Lutheran confession was reinvigorated by the birth of PIETISM, a movement intended as a revival of the original Reformation impulse. (The parallel is significant: Catholic Scholasticism was what Lutheranism saw itself as a corrective to, and Pietism emerged as an antidote to Protestant Scholasticism. In both cases, differences in theological methods, as well as beliefs, shaped the new movements.)

"Pietism," like many other terms that we now take as merely descriptive, was a highly charged term in the seventeenth century, and it is not clear whether the original Pietists applied it to themselves. The name may come from *Pia Desideria*, the title of a book published in 1675 by Philip Jacob Spener (see below). In any case, the name is apt: it is a religion of piety rather than of orthodoxy, of feeling rather than of reason. The movement saw itself as a return to original Lutheranism, just as Luther saw his work as a return to the work of Paul and the Gospels. Before examining Pietism itself, we should look briefly at the context in which it emerged.

The first half of the century had been dominated by the Thirty Years' War (1618–48), a series of religious and political wars involving various states of the Holy Roman Empire and, eventually, Sweden and France. While Central Europe was in the throes of this conflict, Lutheran theologians were wrestling with the issue of the nature of divine grace and how it works. Some of these theologians returned to the spirit of the earliest reformers by emphasizing the impact on the human heart of the divine action in grace. (This was in marked contrast to the dominant ways of Protestant Scholasticism; see Chapter 17.) Among them was Johann Arndt (1555–1621), a Wittenberg graduate, who wrote *True Christianity* (1606) in which he asserts that Christ's work is primarily in the heart of the believer, which is in turn transformed by grace. (See "Johann Arndt.") This was in sharp contrast to the dominant view among Lutherans at the time, which was that the justification of the sinner was a mere declaration by God (through Christ's atonement) that the believer's sins would not be held against him. Such a view, known as the FORENSIC DOCTRINE, was the divine equivalent of a judge acquitting a guilty defendant: the person remains guilty, and is innocent only by virtue of the "forensic" declaration. Arndt's position was that grace is an active element in the heart of the believer, and cannot but help to transform the person who possesses it.

Popular though Arndt's *True Christianity* was, it did not stimulate many other books until the last quarter of the century, when Philip Jacob Spener (1635–1705) appeared on the scene. Spener was from Alsace, and an ordained Lutheran pastor. During a visit to Switzerland, he became acquainted with the teachings of Jean de Labadie (1610–74), a Reformed pastor who emphasized a

Johann Arndt

Johann Arndt (1555–1621), one of the founders of Pietism, emphasized a pious life of active charity. Here is an excerpt from his book True Christianity *in which he stresses that purity of heart is proportional to love of God and neighbor.*

The aim of our charge is love that issues from a pure heart and a good conscience and sincere faith (1 Tim. 1: 5).

In this verse, the apostle teaches us of the highest and noblest virtue, love, and he tells us many things about it. First, he says it is the sum of all the commandments, for love is the fulfillment of the law (Rom. 13: 10), in which all the commandments are contained and without which all gifts and virtues are fruitless and impure.

In addition, he says that true love is to proceed from a pure heart. By this he means that love for God arises from a heart pure from all worldly love (1 John 2: 15–17 …). He, who has [such] a heart [is] purified of all creaturely love, so that he does not commit himself to any temporal thing, regardless of its name, or set the peace of his heart on it, but only on God (Ps. 73: 25–26 …). His love proceeds from a pure heart. Again, it is a pure love if it proceeds in pleasure and joy (Ps. 18: 2–3 …).

Third, the apostle teaches us that love is to proceed from a good conscience. The false love of an evil conscience loves neighbor for the use or benefit that can be gained from that love. True love will not knowingly attack a neighbor with words or deeds, or oppose him secretly or openly. It will not bear hatred, envy, wrath, or anger in its heart, so that the man's conscience will not speak against him in his prayers before God.

In the fourth place, love is to come from undefiled faith that one does not use against his belief and Christianity, that does not deny God in secret or openly, that continues in tribulation or in good days, or in misfortune or good fortune. This is the whole of the verse in 1 Timothy 1: 5. We wish now to look at each section of the verse.

(From *Pietists: Selected Writings*, ed. Peter C. Erb. New York: Paulist Press, 1983.)

quietly devotional life, and he became aware of the need for a similar renewal within Lutheranism. As a minister in Frankfurt from 1666, he introduced elements into church life that he felt could bring about this renewal. One of them was called "Collegia pietatis," semiweekly devotional meetings in his own home. But his most influential work was a book, known as *Pia Desideria* (*Pious Desires*), published in 1675.

In this work, the classic text of Pietism, Spener presents a comprehensive program for revitalizing the Lutheran Church. His ideas included the Bible-reading "collegia" that he had already begun (also known as the "*ecclesiolae in ecclesia*," or "little churches within the church"), an emphasis on the corruption due to original sin, a renewed focus in preaching on word and sacrament, an end to the "heresy hunting" of dogmatic disputations, and greater emphasis on a holy life as compared to academic pursuits. None of these is a new notion, of course, but their restatement at this time, when the German laity were accustomed to a formal and intellectual norm in church practice and preachings, had an impact. And to ensure that these teachings were correctly understood and properly disseminated, the Pietists were influential in founding the University of Halle

(1694), an institution that became the intellectual and spiritual headquarters of the movement. (It was later united with the University of Wittenberg.)

Pietism had other leaders besides Spener, who took it to new heights. These figures include August Hermann Francke (1663–1727), Gottfried Arnold (1666–1714), and Count Nicholas von Zinzendorf (1700–1760). Zinzendorf established a Pietist colony, known as Herrnhut, on his family estate. Many of those he took in were from Moravia, in the east, some descended from the followers of John Huss. (See Chapter 15.) Members of this group went to the West Indies, South Africa, Greenland, and Labrador, beginning in the 1730s. Some went to Pennsylvania about the same time to expand their social experiment; there, they founded Moravian College in Bethlehem, Pennsylvania, in 1742. Still known as Moravians, from the territory they originally came from, they remain an active missionary church, building schools and churches, and emphasizing community life and service to others.

The Lutheran tradition generated not only communal movements, such as the Moravians, but also an imposing mystical tradition. Jacob Boehme (1575–1624), a German farmer's son, who worked first as a shepherd, then as a shoemaker, claimed to have been directly guided by God in his writings. In such texts as *Morgenröte* (*Dawn*; 1612) and *The Way to Christ* (1623), Boehme presents a sprawling body of teachings asserting the direct divine inspiration of the soul, identifying God as the raw material of the universe, and associating Christ with the illumination of this "abyss." Revelation, furthermore, is not an action by God, but the coming to life of God in the soul. Boehme was too idiosyncratic to be absorbed easily by the church, and it is not surprising that his work was suppressed more than once. Baffling though popular, Boehme's spirit would fully flourish in Germany during the era of the Romantics.

Bethlehem, a Moravian Settlement in Pennsylvania, 1799. Engraving. Private Collection.

A community that traces its origins to Nicholas von Zinzendorf, Bethlehem was a Pietist enclave in the religiously tolerant climate of colonial Pennsylvania.

Johann Friedrich Starck

In its efforts to reinvigorate the affective element in Lutheranism, Pietism displayed a liturgical creativity similar to that of its sixteenth-century predecessors. Here is a hymn of resurrection by Johann Friedrich Starck (1680–1756), the author of an influential Pietist prayerbook.

1. "Rise from your graves, ye dead!" Thus shall the call be sounded,
   Which on the latter day shall find us all astounded;
   Which to the faithful flock promise rare delight,
   And fill the trembling hearts of sinners with affright.

2. "Rise from your graves, ye dead!" Your sleep at last is over,
   Ye blessed of the Lord, no more without shall hover.
   The garments are prepared, the crowns are for you stored;
   Enter into the joy and comfort of your Lord!

3. "Rise from your graves, ye dead!" Come from your earthly cover;
   Ye wicked all the pangs of hell shall now discover
   Ye once rejected me, I hold you nothing worth;
   Wailing and gnashing teeth shall be your lot henceforth.

4. "Rise from your graves, ye dead!" Lo, here are bone and tissue,
   Flesh, sinew, hand, eye, foot! from earth and air they issue.
   That wherewith you have served the Lord is glorified,
   That wherewith you have sinned, consumed and cast aside.

5. "Rise from your graves, ye dead." Ye faithful now shall glory
   In halos like the sun, undimmed, untransitory.
   Immortal bodies with immortal souls shall blend,
   Ye shall enjoy the rest of saints that hath … end.

(From *Pietists: Selected Writings*, ed. Peter C. Erb. New York: Paulist Press, 1983.)

Pietism in English Dress

Despite its unmistakably German and Lutheran origins, Pietism had an impact beyond its confessional and national borders. The English theologian William Law (1686–1761) had read a number of Pietist works, and their influence is evident in his 1726 treatise *On Christian Perfection* and also in *A Serious Call to a Devout and Holy Life* (1728), one of the classics of English devotional literature. (See "William Law.") Law had absorbed the teaching of the late-medieval mystics; and like the adherents of the Devotio Moderna in the fifteenth century, he identified Christianity with simple faith and humble charity. He spent most of his life as spiritual counselor to some pious women, offering consolation and instruction of a sort very similar to the work of the collegia in Germany. In *A Serious Call* Law presents a number of human types, identifying the best ones with habits of daily prayer and religious reading, and recommending the custom of praying for others and a manner of life in contrast with the ways of the world. It is anomalous in being an ascetic manual for the lay Protestant (as opposed to Catholic) reader; but it was perhaps this rarity that accounts for its astounding popularity through the eighteenth century.

A more recent German influence is observable in Law's *The Spirit of Love*, published in two parts in 1752 and 1754. This work is a triad of imaginary dialogues between three religious figures, with the names Theogenes (child of God), Eusebius (pious), and Theophilus (lover of God). The work offers a critique of Deism (see Chapter 20), a religion that conceives of God only as a creator, which Law (via Theophilus) calls a great absurdity. The full state of being is to have Christ in human form, says Theophilus; and only then can the divine nature be fully manifested. In *The Spirit of Love* Law comes quite close to the mysticism of Jacob Boehme, whom he had begun reading twenty years earlier. The idea that the truth of Christianity is not known in external actions or historical events, but is known inwardly by the believer, is common to both writers, both of whom are eager to protect religion from the attacks of skeptics and Deists. Their work will echo in various forms during the next century.

Influenced by the German mystical tradition, Law was, in turn, an influence in the beginnings of Methodism. While still at Oxford, John and Charles Wesley (see Chapter 21) were attracted to the work of William Law, whom John and possibly Charles, too, visited at his semi-monastic retreat in King's Cliff, in Northamptonshire. A different form of influence came after the brothers returned from Georgia, for it was the Moravian Peter Böhler (1712–1775) who led each of them to a conversion experience; and John Wesley's visit to the Moravians' Herrnhut in 1738 helped to strengthen his faith and decide on the character that his ministry would take.

William Law

William Law's A Serious Call to a Devout and Holy Life *was a classic of English spirituality, broadly influential, and one of the texts that helped inspire the Wesleys in their work. Law here describes a character whom he calls "Miranda" ("Admirable"), regarding her as a role model for any readers who might wish to identify with her qualities.*

Miranda (the sister of Flavia) is a sober, reasonable Christian: as soon as she was mistress of her time and fortune, it was her first thought how she might best fulfil everything that God required of her in the use of them, and how she might make the best and happiest use of this short life. She depends upon the truth of what our blessed Lord hath said, that there is but "One thing needful," and therefore makes her whole life but one continual labour after it. She has but one reason for doing or not doing, for liking or not liking anything, and that is, the will of God. She is not so weak as to pretend to add what is called the fine lady to the true Christian; Miranda thinks too well to be taken with the sound of such silly words; she has renounced the world to follow Christ in the exercise of humility, charity, devotion, abstinence, and heavenly affections; and that is Miranda's fine breeding.

While she was under her mother, she was forced to be genteel, to live in ceremony, to sit up late at nights, to be in the folly of every fashion, and always visiting on Sundays; to go patched, and loaded with a burden of finery to the Holy Sacrament; to be in every polite conversation; to hear profaneness at the playhouse, and wanton songs and love intrigues at the opera; to dance at public places, that fops and rakes might admire the fineness of her shape, and the beauty of her motions. The remembrance of this way of life makes her exceeding careful to atone for it by a contrary behaviour.

(From *A Serious Call to a Devout and Holy Life*. London: Everyman's Library, 1906.)

In Chapter 21 we shall look more closely at the Wesleys and the world in which they lived and worked—the European Enlightenment—and at the secular ideas that presented Christianity with yet more challenges.

Key Terms

Forensic doctrine   A view of justification associated with Lutheranism, holding that each believer is granted salvation by divine declaration and with no individual effort.

Jansenism   A strict form of Catholicism dominant in France in the 17th century; it emphasized a radical doctrine of original sin and the necessity for grace.

Pietism   A late 17th- and 18th-century revival within Lutheranism, characterized by extraliturgical devotions and preaching focused on love.

Quesnelism   A strict form of Catholicism in the late 17th and early 18th centuries, emphasizing human sinfulness and denying any goodness in human actions outside of the church.

Rationalism   A 17th-century philosophical movement striving to limit all truth to that which can be proved deductively.

Skepticism   A 17th-century philosophical movement questioning all beliefs and subjecting them to rational proof; also (more rarely) the denial that anything at all can be known with certainty.

Early American Religion
Between Reformation and Enlightenment

It would be hard to overemphasize the role that religion played in the beginnings of American culture. Many of the original Thirteen Colonies were founded by religious refugees; for the absolutist system then prevailing in Europe (see Chapter 16) did not mesh well with the proliferating reform movements and dissident sects circulating there. Although the Protestant Reformers had all invoked freedom of conscience in breaking away from Rome, their followers—once they achieved political control—made little allowance for such freedom for others. The principle of *cuius regio, eius religio* ("in a [prince's] country, the [prince's] religion"), granting to each ruler the right to determine religious practice in the territory, caused many believers in unofficial faiths, and certainly the most devoted adherents, to go into exile. If the Bible narrative had assured them that wanderings in the wilderness were preferable to slavery to a hostile ruler (the Exodus account of the Jews' sufferings in Egypt was very popular among early-modern religious exiles), it also promised them a land of their own, in which the freedom to worship God according to what they saw as divine mandates would be forever protected.

The Spread of Religious Diversity

In such a spirit, and with such hopes, bands of pious folk began making the voyage across the Atlantic. Two groups of English Calvinist Protestants—Puritans, who wished to reform the Church of England from within, and Separatists, who had broken away from it—established settlements in Massachusetts, at Plymouth (1620) and Massachusetts Bay (1630) respectively. There, they created THEOCRATIC colonies, governed by religious leaders. The story of the Plymouth settlers, who had first moved to tolerant Holland but left because they did not wish to lose their English identity, has become one of the cornerstones of American folklore. The Puritans' mission has been described as an "errand into the wilderness," a phrase that conjures up images of the medieval missionaries, although these settlers (much later dubbed Pilgrims) saw themselves as latter-day Jews. The Torah narrative of Jewish exile and the Psalms were close to their hearts, and in this intensely Calvinist culture, one of the highest compliments was to be called a "good Jew."

The freedom of religion that the Puritans established for themselves in the Massachusetts Bay Colony (present-day Boston and environs) was not something that they were prepared to extend to others. One victim of their intolerance was Roger Williams (c. 1603–1683). Williams had been an Anglican priest, then became a Puritan and, finally, a Baptist, one of the heirs of the sixteenth-century Anabaptists, who rejected infant baptism and insisted on full commitment in adulthood—with stringent expectations of behavior. Forced to leave the Massachusetts Bay Colony, for political as well as religious differences, he founded the colony of Rhode Island in 1635 and America's first Baptist Church in 1639.

Elsewhere along the Atlantic coast, people of different Christian persuasions and nationalities also founded colonies. In 1638 some Lutherans from war-weary Sweden settled along the banks of the Delaware River, where they created a colony called New Sweden. This was taken over in 1655 by Dutch from New Amsterdam (present-day New York City), traders who had brought the Dutch Reformed variety of Calvinism to American shores. English Quakers (properly the Society of Friends)—who, like other Protestant "Dissenters," were perennially on the wrong side of the law in Stuart England—found a haven in Pennsylvania, a colony obtained from the Crown in 1681 by William Penn (1644–1718), the Quaker son of a family to whom the Stuarts owed a favor. In Pennsylvania people of all faiths were welcome, and persecuted sects from central Europe, such as the Mennonites (a breakaway group from the Reformed faith), also settled there. Immediately to the south, English Catholics—also victims of discrimination in their homeland—had previously founded the colony of Maryland (1632), naming it after Queen Henrietta Maria, the French Catholic wife of the reigning monarch, Charles I (see below). The oldest English colony, Virginia (1607; following an abortive settlement in 1585, in present-day North Carolina), was settled by Anglicans, whose church at Jamestown was the site, in 1619, of the first representative assembly in the New World. A mixture of peoples, including some French Huguenots and German Protestants, as well as the English, were among the first settlers of the Carolinas and Georgia.

To the north and south of these mainly British colonies, other European colonists were perpetuating the Catholic faith. Catholicism had been a force on the North American continent before the first Protestants ever considered their voyages. Spain had had a strong presence in Florida and Mexico since the early sixteenth century. The Spanish and Portuguese also controlled vast regions south of Florida and down into South America. A Jesuit-dominated state in Paraguay was the setting for roundups, beginning in 1607, of Natives to protect them against kidnapping by Brazilian slave traders. The Portuguese colonization of Brazil had begun in the mid-1500s and continued with the division of the coastal lands into twelve autonomous regions, each with its own "captain," reaching its high point with the creation of São Paulo as a trading post. These are not major points in religious history except for the Christianization that came with contact, the initial encounter of Native and European peoples. (The Christianization of Latin America will be looked at in more detail in Chapter 29.)

In Canada, meanwhile, the establishment of the French settlement of Quebec in 1608 was followed by the arrival of Roman Catholic missionaries, including the Jesuits in 1625. French settlement extended from Quebec and Montreal (another missionary base, established in 1642) through the Great Lakes and along the Mississippi to New Orleans: much of this territory, later named Louisiana after the French king Louis XIV (1638–1715; r. 1643–1715), still bears names of missionaries and the saints they venerated: Père Jacques Marquette (1637–1675) was the namesake of a Jesuit university (1864); St. Paul, Minnesota, was an early outpost that Marquette explored; and St. Louis, Missouri, is named for King Louis IX of France (1215–1270; r. 1226–1270), canonized in 1297 for his leadership in the Crusades. Missionary efforts would in time extend westward from the Mississippi as well, following the paths of the explorers Lewis and Clark through the vastness of the 1803 Louisiana Purchase.

Religious diversity prevailed as the Americas were explored and claimed. Within the colonies that would join together to shake off British rule in the 1770s, religion was a part of the culture and organization, some colonies being more tolerant of confessional diversity than others. What we think of as "Quaker Philadelphia" consisted, by 1700, of interwoven strands of Lutheranism, Calvinism, and Anglicanism, while also learning to tolerate Catholicism in its midst in the early eighteenth century. New York, proverbially focused on commerce rather than piety, was religiously the most diverse city in the Thirteen Colonies, if not the world. Therefore, separating the religious and political lives of people when the colonies organized into a nation after the American Revolution of 1775–83 became a pragmatic necessity. What is now known as separation of church and state is due largely to the genius of Thomas Jefferson (1743–1826), advocate of the VOLUNTARY PRINCIPLE, according to which no person is bound involuntarily to a religion. Originally intended to preclude any form of established religion, this principle came to mean that anyone could practice whatever form of religion he or she chose.

Old England and New

Without a rebellious spirit and a strong collective will, English religious minorities might never have crossed the Atlantic. The Stuart monarch James I (1566–1625; r. 1603–1625), successor to Queen Elizabeth I (see Chapter 16), wished to strengthen Anglicanism within Great Britain (a term adopted at the beginning of James's reign, when England, Wales, and Scotland were united under his rule). Accordingly, he condemned both Puritanism and Catholicism at a conference in Hampton Court Palace in 1604 attended by Anglican bishops and Puritan leaders. The Catholics did not take well to this action, and in 1605 a small group of them mounted the Gunpowder Plot, an attempt to blow up the Palace of Westminster, where Parliament sat, and so preserve Catholics' rights in the kingdom. It failed.

So did the Puritans' attempts to reform the Church of England by instituting a "pure" form of worship (the source of their name, originally a pejorative term used by their enemies), based on Calvinist doctrines and free of "popish" (Roman Catholic) rituals and government control. The Scottish Presbyterians (Calvinists) rose up in 1638 against the attempts of the Archbishop of Canterbury, William Laud (1573–1645), to introduce the Church of England into Scotland. The Scots felt they had already formed a federation, or covenant, with God, and replacing it with one tying them to the English Church was no improvement in matters (irrespective of the Scottish origins of the reigning Stuart dynasty).

Laud also dealt severely with Puritanism in England, backed by King Charles I (1600–1649; r. 1625–1649), who was suspected of having Catholic sympathies. This issue, combined with Charles's high-handed treatment of Parliament (which he was empowered to summon or dissolve at will), precipitated the English Civil War. Following armed hostilities between Charles's army and the Scots, and between Catholics and Protestants in Ireland (then an English possession), war between the king and Parliament, which was dominated by Puritans, broke out in 1642. Seven years of intermittent fighting ended in 1649 with victory for the Parliamentarians under their Puritan leader Oliver Cromwell (1599–1658), and the execution of Charles I.

The English Civil War was mainly a religious conflict rather than a political (or secular) one, and so resembles more closely the Protestant-Catholic wars of the sixteenth and seventeenth centuries (such as the Thirty Years' War; see Chapter 19) than the American and French Revolutions of the late eighteenth century. The crucial issue was not the independence of religion from the state, nor whether civil rights should override religious duties, but the very "Reformational" notion that a Christian society (however one defined "Christian") was still possible. This was an ambition that dated back to Charlemagne; in some senses it was the ambition of all Christian societies of the medieval and early-modern periods. The English Puritans had the opportunity to try, in the Commonwealth that they established in 1649. But eleven years of Puritan rule, led by Cromwell and then briefly by his son Richard, brought yet more internal strife and resentment from non-Puritan English; and it was with some relief that the country welcomed the restoration of the Stuart monarchy under Charles II (1630–1685) in 1660.

In New England, too, the Puritans had only mixed success in creating a "godly commonwealth." Having fled intolerance in their homeland, they now had the chance to be intolerant on their own terms. Difficulties emerged early, with the "heresy" of Anne Hutchinson (1591–1643), who saw Christianity as a covenant of grace rather than of works, and, later, with the Salem witch trials in the 1690s. Laws against Quakers were also enacted; one Quaker woman, Mary Dyer, was hanged for her beliefs. Even so, the Calvinist experiment in New England had a fairly long run and left an indelible mark on American civilization.

Calvinist thought germinated and thrived in American soil, nurtured by ideas that the land had indeed been given by God for a new and purer form of worship. Echoes of the biblical account of the Jews' liberation from Egypt are found in their narratives and survive today in certain place names, such as New Canaan in Connecticut. Having supposedly entrusted themselves to divine care, the Puritans felt they were under divine protection in the New World, and that their own history was one with the history of human salvation.

For over a century Puritan literature in New England was devoted to the theme of the perfectly ordered Christian commonwealth, while the organization of the colony tried to bring the religious ideals to realization. Clerical dynasties such as those of the Mather family (Richard [1596–1669], his son Increase [1639–1723], and grandson Cotton [1663–1728]) rose up, prolific authors who left such works as Cotton Mather's *Magnalia Christi Americana*, an account of recent events presented as salvation history—a chronicle of the triumph of the church throughout the world. (See "Cotton Mather.") Other leaders of the movement left cities rather than books as their creations: Thomas Hooker (1586–1647) was the founder of Hartford, Connecticut, and John Davenport (1597–1670) of New Haven—originally an independent colony. It was a great age for Christian polity building, and the Puritans felt that the power of God, rather than the force of human initiative, was on their side. This proved to be a powerful assumption, as it sustained them through decades in a harsh and unfamiliar world while they built cities, churches, and schools that survive to this day.

By the early 1700s, however, questions about adaptation to new influences had begun to arise. The seventeenth and eighteenth centuries' developments in philosophy and science made their way, somewhat slowly, to the New World, calling for some kind of response. Enlightenment skepticism toward the supernatural

Title page to *Tryals of Several Witches* by Cotton Mather, 1693.

Out of concerns for a pious and orderly community, many Puritans were suspicious of deviant behavior, especially witchcraft. The trials of the 1680s demonstrated the closed culture of some colonial communities.

and optimism in the progress of reason were a direct attack upon the worldviews at the foundation of New England culture. Entrenched resistance to advances in thought would keep the many colonists stuck in their Reformation-era worldview—behind, rather than ahead of, the world they had left in Europe and reluctant to depart from the orthodoxy of the Calvinist theologians who had shaped

---

Cotton Mather

Cotton Mather (1663–1728) was the third-generation heir to a Puritan dynasty in New England, who interpreted his forebears' "Errand into the Wilderness" as a response to a divine call that remained incumbent on his own generation. (He helped found Yale University because by his standards Harvard University had become too religiously lax.) In this excerpt from his 1702 Magnalia Christi Americana *he offers a commentary on the condition of Boston, c. 1700.*

We are a very Unpardonable Town, if after all the *help* which our God has given us, we do not ingenuously enquire, *What shall we render to the Lord for all his Benefits?* Render! Oh! Let us our selves thus answer the Enquiry; *Lord, we will render all Possible and Filial Obedience unto thee, because hitherto thou hast helped us: Only do thou also help us to render that Obedience!*

Mark what I say; if there be so much as one *Prayerless House* in such a *Town* as this, 'tis Inexcusable! How Inexcusable then will be all *Flagitious Outrages?* There was a Town, ['twas the Town of *Sodom!*] that had been wonderfully saved out of the Hands of their Enemies. But after the *help* that God sent unto them, the Town went on to Sin against God in very prodigious Instances. At last a provoked God sent a *Fire* upon the Town that made it an Eternal Desolation. Ah, *Boston,* beware, beware, lest the Sins of *Sodom* get footing in thee! And what were the Sins of *Sodom?* We find in Ezek. 16.49. *Behold, this was the Iniquity of* Sodom; *Pride, Fulness of Bread, and Abundance of Idleness was in her*; *neither did she strengthen the Hand of the Poor and the Needy*; there was much Oppression there. If you know of any *Scandalous Disorders* in the Town, do all you can to suppress them, and redress them: And let not those that send their Sons hither from other Parts of the World, for to be improved in *Virtue,* have cause to complain, *That after they came to* Boston *they lost what little Virtue was before Budding in them: That in* Boston *they grew more Debauched and more Malignant than ever they were before!*...

And Oh! That the *Drinking-Houses* in the Town might once come under a laudable *Regulation.* The Town has an *Enormous Number* of them; will the *Haunters* of those *Houses* hear the Counsels of Heaven? For *You* that are the *Town-Dwellers,* to be oft, or long in your *Visits* of the *Ordinary,* 'twill certainly expose you to Mischiefs more than ordinary. I have seen certain *Taverns,* where the Pictures of horrible *Devourers* were hang'd out for the *Signs*; and, thought I, 'twere well if such *Signs* were not sometimes too too *Significant:* Alas, Men have their Estates *devoured,* their Names *devoured,* their Hours *devoured,* and their very Souls *devoured,* when they are so besotted, that they are not in their Element, except they be Tipling at such Houses. When once a Man is bewitched with the *Ordinary,* what usually becomes of him? He is a *gone Man*; and when he comes to Die, he'll cry out as many have done, *Ale-Houses are Hell-Houses! Ale-Houses are Hell-Houses!* ...

(From *Magnalia Christi Americana,* ed. Kenneth B. Murdock. Cambridge, MA: Harvard University Press, 1977.)

their original purpose. The development of American religious sentiment ran parallel to the course of Christian thought in the Old World.

Jonathan Edwards: America's First Theologian

Out of the bewildering blend of philosophical and theological proposals of the eighteenth century emerges Jonathan Edwards (1703–1758), one of the most profound religious thinkers of all time. Edwards was not really the first theologian of the American colonies, of course: there had been Puritan thinkers of some

Jonathan Edwards, 18th century. Mezzotint. Private collection

A student of seventeenth-century Calvinism and early eighteenth-century philosophy, Edwards was one of the most creative religious thinkers in the American tradition.

merit in seventeenth-century New England. But he was unquestionably the most original and influential. A graduate of Yale and president of Princeton, Edwards was first and foremost a preacher in the Calvinist tradition of his ancestors. (He was a member of a Puritan preaching dynasty, the grandson of Solomon Stoddard [1643–1729], author of *A Treatise Concerning Conversion*.) Yet he was also a preacher fully acquainted with the new currents of his age, a man who read Locke and Berkeley and corresponded with leading scientists and scholars. For most of his career he was the minister of the church in Northampton, Massachusetts (Stoddard's old church), where he wrote his classic *Treatise Concerning Religious Affections* (1746) and other works. In 1749 his congregation dismissed him because of the qualifications he had set for church membership. For Edwards, a person could be considered a member of the church only after having experienced a fairly intense CONVERSION. This was a standard that most of his parishioners did not meet, and so they fired him. He remained unbowed by this setback, and continued to write in support of an experiential piety.

Edwards achieved his goals not just in books, but forcefully in sermons. His style of preaching is most colorfully exemplified in his 1741 sermon "Sinners in the Hands of an Angry God," in which he likens the individual to a hideous spider hanging literally by a thread over the flames of hell. Only when a person knows the extent of his or her sin, Edwards insists, can that person recognize that it is grace and grace alone that keeps him or herself from damnation. (See "Jonathan Edwards.") The dynamics of sin and grace are, of course, familiar themes going back to St. Augustine. But presenting them during an age of general skepticism calls for both boldness and originality; and when assessing Edwards's thought it is essential to consider how he presents his ideas. In many of his theological works he displays an originality not often found among his contemporaries; and in many of his sermons he presents relatively traditional material in bold new forms.

Edwards's originality is found in the way he juxtaposes emotion and rationality in a systematic arrangement that is as current with Enlightenment-era confidence in the progress of reason as it is loyal to Reformation-era insistence that the human condition is something revealed, not discerned by the intellect. Piety and progress thus coexist rather than conflict with each other.

Partially in response to Enlightenment challenges to Reformation-era and orthodox Protestant teachings, Edwards locates religious understanding not in the intellect, but in the emotions; here it would be exempt from the empiricists' criteria for truth. One knew the fact, and certainly the extent, of original sin in the heart, not the mind; and it was there also that one felt the working of grace. A person's conversion experience was as real as any experience of the senses, but it took place in a different organ. From this it may seem that conversion is known by the believer alone, and that no one else would be aware of such an inner change. But this is not entirely true. In Edwards's view, a person who has genuinely experienced conversion would start to show certain "marks of true religion," displaying a virtue and religious affection that could not be feigned. Thus the man or woman of true religion is indeed outwardly different from others; in this way another person—a pastor, for example—could judge the sincerity of someone's religious assertions. It becomes easy to see why Edwards's theological program was so strongly resisted by his contemporaries.

Jonathan Edwards

Jonathan Edwards (1703–1758) was the most original American theologian of his time and surely its most fiery preacher. His sermon Sinners in the Hands of an Angry God *is a classic of Calvinist homiletics. In this excerpt Edwards explains why humans are at constant risk of being cast into hell.*

II. They *deserve* to be cast into hell; so that divine justice never stands in the way, it makes no objection against God's using his power at any moment to destroy them. Yea, on the contrary, justice calls aloud for an infinite punishment of their sins. Divine justice says of the tree that brings forth such grapes of Sodom, "Cut it down, why cumbreth it the ground," Luke 13: 7. The sword of divine justice is every moment brandished over their heads, and 'tis nothing but the hand of arbitrary mercy, and God's mere will, that holds it back.

III. They are *already* under a sentence of condemnation to hell. They don't only justly deserve to be cast down thither; but the sentence of the law of God, that eternal and immutable rule of righteousness that God has fixed between him and mankind, is gone out against them, and stands against them; so that they are bound over already to hell. John 3: 18, "He that believeth not is condemned already." So that every unconverted man properly belongs to hell; that is his place; from thence he is. John 8: 23, "Ye are from beneath." And thither he is bound; 'tis the place that justice, and God's Word, and the sentence of his unchangeable law assigns to him.

IV. They are now the objects of that very *same* anger and wrath of God that is expressed in the torments of hell: and the reason why they don't go down to hell at each moment, is not because God, in whose power they are, is not then very angry within them; as angry as he is with many of those miserable creatures that he is now tormenting in hell, and do there feel and bear the fierceness of his wrath. Yea, God is a great deal more angry with great numbers that are now on earth, yea, doubtless with many that are now in this congregation, that it may be are at ease and quiet, than he is with many of those that are now in the flames of hell.

So that it is not because God is unmindful of their wickedness, and don't resent it, that he don't let loose his hand and cut them off. God is not altogether such an one as themselves, though they may imagine him to be so. The wrath of God burns against them, their damnation don't slumber, the pit is prepared, the fire is made ready, the furnace is now hot, ready to receive them, the flames do now rage and glow, the glittering sword is whet, and held over them, and the pit hath opened her mouth under them.

V. The *devil* stands ready to fall upon them and seize them as his own, at what moment God shall permit him. They belong to him; he has their souls in his possession, and under his dominion. The Scripture represents them as his "goods," Luke 11: 21. The devils watch them; they are ever by them, at their right hand; they stand waiting for them, like greedy hungry lions that see their prey, and expect to have it, but are for the present kept back; if God should withdraw his hand, by which they are restrained, they would in one moment fly upon their poor souls....

(From *The Sermons of Jonathan Edwards: A Reader*, ed. W. H. Kimnach et al., New Haven, CT: Yale University Press, 1994.)

The Great Awakening

The difference between persons of differing intensity of conversion showed itself in various ways. In the decades of Edwards's ministry, the Colonies experienced the GREAT AWAKENING, a revival movement that reached from north to south and drew in Presbyterian, Congregationalist, Dutch Reformed, Baptist, Lutheran, and even some Anglican churches—the last in the form of George Whitefield (1714–1770), one of the founders of Methodism. The leaders of the movement were a father-and-son team, William (c. 1673–1745) and Gilbert (1703–1764) Tennent. An Irish-born Presbyterian, William Tennent founded, in 1736, a school called the "Log College," a rudimentary seminary which his son Gilbert and another influential preacher, Samuel Blair (1712–1751) attended. In opposition to the more relaxed form of Christianity then prevailing in the Colonies, the Tennents placed remarkable emphasis on conversion, the experience of grace as a transforming force. This is a conversion within a church, not from one religion to another; it was in fact the standard definition of the term before the modern era, when changes from one church to another became easier and then common. Just as Edwards refused to consider his Northampton parishioners true members of the church without such an inner transformation, so these other preachers of the Great Awakening set new levels of involvement as criteria for calling oneself a Christian.

The leaders themselves were converts in this sense—having experienced conversion either through each others' influence or spontaneously; so they claimed to know whereof they preached. Graduates of the Log College of the Tennents and the Yale of Edwards formed an energetic missionary movement. Notable among them were the youthful missionaries David Brainerd (1718–1747) and Eleazer Wheelock (1711–1779), who preached the need for conversion, describing from their own experience the signs and products of the divine activity within them.

Who's Who

Puritan Preachers and Revivalists

Solomon Stoddard (1643–1729) Grandfather of Jonathan Edwards (*see below*). Part of a well-known family of Calvinist Puritan preachers who stressed the importance of attaining grace through conversion, he authored *A Treatise Concerning Conversion*.

William Tennent (c. 1673–1745) and Gilbert Tennent (1703–64) Irish-born father and son, and leaders in the Great Awakening revival movement in North America. Presbyterian pastors who placed great stress on the state of grace.

Jonathan Edwards (1703–1758) Grandson of Solomon Stoddard (*see above*). A thinker whose work synthesized Calvinism with Enlightenment philosophy.

Samuel Blair (1712–1751) Irish-born Presbyterian preacher, educated at William Tennent's Log College, Nashaminy. Founded a school for classical studies.

David Brainerd (1718–1747) Presbyterian preacher and missionary, he spent some time living in a wigwam with Native Americans and was responsible for a large number of conversions.

The timing of the Great Awakening was auspicious, since new political ideas as well as philosophical notions were then engaging the colonists. Establishment, or governmental, imposition and regulation of religion was an increasingly hot issue as troubles with Britain increased. In achieving independence, the former colonies, now states, were parts of a religiously pluralistic confederation, in which any hint of religious establishment would feel like a restraint of the liberties just received. Most Americans (as they began to call themselves) were suspicious of Anglican establishment, as existed in England; but they differed on whether any other church might become the official religion of the States, and if so, which one and how might that be determined? That the States were pious communities was beyond doubt, but exactly how their religious life fit with their political structure would remain in doubt until the separation of church and state became a constitutional fact with the passing of the Bill of Rights in 1791.

But these were issues of polity, and did not directly impact on piety, without which the churches would lose their reasons for being, government or no government. It was the preachers of the Great Awakening who, somewhat stridently to be sure, kept the attention of the faithful focused on their own experience of the divine. By stressing the personal and voluntary element of religious life, the Great Awakening helped to shape American religious life through the nineteenth century.

Key Terms

CONVERSION Changing from one religion or spiritual state to another; within Christianity, making or renewing one's dedication to Christ and the work of the church.

GREAT AWAKENING An American revival movement of the early 18th century, stressing repentance and conversion.

THEOCRATIC Divinely ruled; under theocratic governance a state is ruled by clerical authorities and its principles are determined by religious priorities.

VOLUNTARY PRINCIPLE The notion that membership of a church must have an element of personal choice to be meaningful; a reaction against the imposition of any one religion by a higher authority.

Samuel King, *Portrait of the Reverend Ebenezer Stiles*, 1771. Oil on canvas. Yale University Art Gallery.

PART FIVE

From Enlightenment to Modernity

Divisions within the Christian Church were exacerbated in the late seventeenth and eighteenth centuries. New branches of Protestantism appeared. Some were forms of the same confession, such as Pietism within Lutheranism. Other branches emerged as almost entirely new churches; Methodism, starting as a reformed form of Anglicanism, soon took on a life of its own. Within Catholicism, new devotional orders and forms continued along the lines established at the Council of Trent (1545–1563). Schools and universities taught the principles of faith to growing numbers of students.

The world was by now increasingly secularized. Old assumptions that church institutions and practices were ordained by God, that questioning them was a form of impiety, were gradually yielding to the belief that all human institutions were subject to scrutiny and change. Revealed religion came in for the most trenchant analysis: a body of beliefs that once were thought to be truer than rational reason itself was now cast aside by many as the stuff of myth and superstition. Conversely, however, Christian authors, philosophers, and theologians also embarked on campaigns in defense of church traditions.

The world was changing in other ways too. More than ever before, Europeans were colonizing Asia, Africa, and the Americas. Missionaries were spreading the Christian Gospel, although it was often received in indigenous religious cultures as an unwelcome interloper.

In North America, colonies founded as religious enterprises in the seventeenth century were roused to new levels of religiosity during the eighteenth century's First Great Awakening. In the last quarter of that century, American religious divisions were set aside in the interests of shaping a nation in which all religions could enjoy freedom and tolerance.

Contact with other religions forced theologians and religious scholars to acknowledge the validity of such faiths without abandoning their claims to Christianity being the true faith. In the twentieth century, this would become one of the most urgent intellectual tests faced by the Christian Church.

1700	
1721	Boston clergyman Cotton Mather publishes *Christian Philosopher*.
1730	Matthew Tindal publishes the Deist treatise *Christianity as Old as the Creation*.
c. 1738	The Great Awakening religious revival sweeps through North American colonies.
1739	John Wesley founds the first Methodist chapel, in Bristol, England.
1741	Jonathan Edwards preaches his sermon "Sinners in the Hands of an Angry God."
1742	Pietists found Moravian College in Bethlehem, Pennsylvania.
1750	
1773	The Jesuit order is officially dissolved by Pope Clement XIV.
1779	David Hume's *Dialogues concerning Natural Religion* is published posthumously.
1789–94	The French Revolution leads to attacks on the church.
1790	The first American Roman Catholic bishop, John Carroll, is consecrated.
1791	The American Bill of Rights establishes the separation of church and state.
1794	William Paley's *Evidences of Christianity* is published.
1795	The London Missionary Society is founded.
1799	Friedrich Schleiermacher publishes *Speeches on Religion to its Cultured Despisers*.
1800	
1801	By the Concordat with Pope Pius VII, Napoleon restores Catholicism in France.
1814	The Jesuit order is officially reauthorized.
c. 1820–40	The Second Great Awakening occurs in the United States.
1829	In Britain the Roman Catholic Emancipation Act gives Catholics near equal rights.
1830	Joseph Smith founds the Church of Jesus Christ of Latter-Day Saints (Mormons).
1833–41	The Oxford Movement is founded with the publication of *Tracts for the Times*.
1838	In his *Divinity School Address* Ralph Waldo Emerson rejects institutionalized religion.
1840	David Livingstone makes his first visit to Africa for the London Missionary Society.
1844–45	In America both the Methodist and Baptist Churches split over attitudes to slavery.
1846	Former Tractarian John Henry Newman becomes a Catholic priest.
1848–49	Europe is swept by revolutions; Pope Pius IX is briefly driven out of Rome.
1850	
1854	A papal bull decrees that the Virgin Mary was born without sin: the Immaculate Conception.
1864	In the *Syllabus of Errors*, Pius IX condemns aspects of modern thought and society.
1864	Newman publishes his autobiographical essay *Apologia pro Vita Sua*.
1865	William Booth founds the Christian Mission in London, origin of the Salvation Army.
1869–70	The First Vatican Council ends with a declaration of papal infallibility.
1870	Rome becomes Italy's capital; the pope withdraws to the Vatican.
1871	Charles Darwin publishes *The Descent of Man*.
1872	Octavius Frothingham publishes his influential Unitarian work *The Religion of Humanity*.
1873	German scholar Julius Wellhausen argues that the Bible is a composite work of many human hands.
1873	Chancellor Bismarck launches the *Kulturkampf* against the Catholic Church in Germany.
1884	Frederick Temple's Bampton Lectures accept Darwin's work as compatible with Christian faith.
1889	In *The Social Aspects of Christianity*, Richard T. Ely calls on churches to work for the poor.
1891	Leo XIII's encyclical *Rerum Novarum* asserts the value of work and opposes exploitation.

Enlightenment Religion
Adaptations in an Age of Progress

The transition from the "early modern" to the "modern" period is as difficult to trace as those terms are to define. We may see the modern period of Western history as beginning in the nineteenth century, in which case the eighteenth century can be considered as a period of development leading up to it. And so it was: between the last of the rationalists and the beginning of the idealists, the European mind underwent a profound change. In many respects, it is not the Reformation but this period, known as the Enlightenment, that marks the true turning point in Western religious thought, for only now did questions about biblical authority and the progress of rational humanity challenge traditional views of revelation and sinfulness. But for many this period is more difficult to grasp and characterize than the Reformation.

The Enlightenment was an era in which people were often highly conscious of their participation in a pivotal moment in history, and of the significance of that moment. They saw their time as one of progress, and if they could not know what lay ahead in the next century—one in which royal dynasties based on ideas of divine right were overthrown, and many of the church's own properties secularized—they certainly had a sense of where they were coming from. They considered previous generations to be mired in superstition and fable, whereas they had certainty. Thinkers in the Enlightenment period saw themselves as agents of the shift from faith to knowledge, and for them no purpose could be clearer or more important.

The Enlightenment itself was preceded by a period of preparation, the era of the seventeenth-century rationalists (see Chapter 19). These thinkers, of whom Descartes is probably the best known, counted as knowledge only what they could know with complete certainty—the same certainty available in mathematics. So high a standard of truth obviously left out many teachings of religious traditions, based as they were on legends and unverifiable narratives.

We need to be careful when we describe the Enlightenment within the context of religious history, because it was not primarily a "religious" phenomenon at all. If anything, it was a movement that developed in opposition to traditional religion, or at least to its claims of inherited truth and its dependence on divine revelation. Thus it might be technically more accurate to use the term "post-Enlightenment religion" for the ways in which Christianity adjusted its methods in the wake of Enlightenment challenges. But "Enlightenment Christianity" may be just as accurate, so long as we take it to mean the tradition during the Enlightenment period, but not necessarily a religion of the movement itself.

Empiricism

John Locke

Godfrey Kneller, *John Locke*, 18th century. Engraving.

Locke's thought underlay political revolutions in England and America, and philosophical ones within Anglo-American religious traditions.

The desire for rational certainty that began with the skepticism of Descartes (see Chapter 19) reached a new level of sophistication with the thought of John Locke (1632–1704), a politically active and intellectually versatile thinker, whose ideas on government were influential among the American founding fathers. Locke was concerned with the origin and validity of ideas, a topic he explores in the *Essay Concerning Human Understanding* (1690). Ideas, for Locke, come from sense experience and nowhere else. They are not implanted in our souls before birth, nor do they come from intangible beings. The mind at birth is like a blank sheet, which receives and records sense experience. Thought is the processing of the recorded impressions.

Locke applied his exacting epistemology to religion in *The Reasonableness of Christianity as Delivered in the Scriptures* (1695). Predictably, he reduces the value of the supernatural elements in Christian belief, retaining instead the moral element as the genuine essence of Christianity. True doctrines, according to Locke, are rational ones, and the biblical teachings that bear on law and morality are supremely rational and thus valid. They have been revealed because certain rational doctrines benefit from the corroboration of revelation.

Deism

Locke was not the first thinker to regard the natural as being more true than the supernatural. Before him, Edward Herbert, Lord Cherbury (1583–1648), had argued that religious understanding did not depend on revelation from supernatural sources. And in a 1730 work titled *Christianity as Old as the Creation*, Matthew Tindal (1655–1733) argued that the natural world, being itself perfect, has no need for redemption or supernatural illumination. NATURAL RELIGION, locating God within nature rather than beyond it, was, in his view, the only valid way to seek an understanding of the divine. Influenced by the writings of his contemporary

Isaac Newton (1642–1727), Tindal holds that the basic truths of Christianity are already present in nature—hence the meaning of his title. This school of thought, which includes Newton and less well-known authors such as John Toland (1670–1722) and Thomas Woolston (1670–1733), is known as Deism. Its name derived from the Latin for "god," *deus*, Deism holds that the divine is within nature, an impersonal structure or energy within a material world that alone is knowable. Unlike THEISM (from the Greek *theos*), which sees deity as a personal and supernatural being, Deism rejects the supernatural and any claim to know a reality beyond what lies before our senses. Deism is thus closely intertwined with empiricism—the theory that all knowledge is derived from experience—and indeed may be called its theology, though we might be more precise in calling it a "deology."

Idealism: Bishop Berkeley

Both empiricism and Deism are English schools of thought, and so is the school that arose as a critique of materialist philosophies. Among the opponents of Deism we would include the Irish-born Anglican Bishop (of Cloyne, in Ireland) George Berkeley (1685–1753), a leading advocate of Idealism. Building on Lockean assumptions about ideas, Berkeley contests Locke's division of ideas into two categories: those that can change of their own accord and thus possess the power to inform the knower, and those that cannot be manipulated at will by the subject. According to Locke, the second category contains material objects in the outside world. According to Berkeley, there are no material objects outside of perception; their being is only in being objects of perception. Being, in Berkeley's view, is either being perceived or perceiving.

This is not very good news for the material world. The divine realm fares a bit better from the bishop's work. If things, for Berkeley, are merely complexes of ideas, then they are grasped by the sensations ("affections") of the human spirit—and by God. God is the perfect understander of ideas, whose observance of all things guarantees their continued existence. For example, you cannot know *absolutely* that this book will continue to exist after you've put it away; but Berkeley's God will continue to be aware of it. Hence it will not vanish into thin air when no one is looking at it. However, at that point the book still lies beyond human knowledge, since that is formed only by material experience.

Continuity and order thus have a place in Berkeley's thought; the world is not entirely dependent on the human senses. Natural laws, the product of God's will to connect and order beings (that is, things that exist) are in place; though of course, being out of view, they have a different reality for us than objects in the material world. Indeed, Berkeley feels that God's ideas are the only independent reality, the only things that can exist perfectly without being perceived by subjects. God may not be knowable to us in this rather severe epistemology, but what we can know is the product of God's ordering energy.

Joseph Butler and William Paley

In his *Analogy of Religion* (1736), the Anglican theologian Joseph Butler (1692–1752) attempted to overturn the arguments of Matthew Tindal and his fellow Deists. Butler appeals to certainty, or the lack of it, in our empirical understanding of the natural world. If the only form of certain knowledge is what we draw from our sense experiences, Butler argues, then the laws and points of connection that give coherence to those experiences are only "probable": that is to say, hypothetical and awaiting verification. (The term originally meant "subject to proof," not our sense of "likely.") Natural religion, according to Butler, is a probable truth, not itself a certainty. Similarly, the claims of revealed religion are equally probable, and so whether the deity is natural or supernatural is a matter of working out mutually exclusive sets of chosen assumptions. The contest between revealed and natural religion is, in the end, a tie. But rather than letting it go at that, Butler sees the un-disprovability of Christianity as a strong factor in its favor over natural religion. Biblical revelation serves as "documentation," of sorts, for natural religion, which by itself is uncertain and insufficient. In arguments reminiscent of Scholastic defenses of revelation, Butler locates absolute certainty in revelation because of revelation's divine source, and relative or incomplete certainty in human understanding, given its contingent and fallible source. Whatever one may think of such arguments in a world made skeptical by twentieth-century philosophy, it is worth noting that Butler's *Analogy* became a standard apologetic work for decades following its publication.

Other authors found their way into university courses and from that platform influenced generations of educated believers. William Paley (1743–1805) was an Anglican cleric whose book *Evidences of Christianity* (1794) popularized the argument (for God's existence) from design, which drew on the writings of David Hume, discussed later in this chapter. Paley is responsible for the classic example of the watch on the beach. The argument, in brief, is that the observer of nature is like a shipwreck survivor on a presumably deserted island. If such a person is walking along the beach and sees a watch in the sand, then it would be impossible to deny that someone else, somewhere, had made the watch. Similarly, when the student of nature observes the clocklike regularity of the heavens and the orderliness of nature, it is impossible to deny that there has been a designer and maker.

Who's Who

The Natural Religion Debate

Edward Herbert (1583–1648) Herbert, or Lord Cherbury, paved the way for Deism. A poet and philosopher, he believed that religious understanding was not dependent on supernatural revelation.

John Locke (1632–1704) Formidable English philosopher and great supporter of religious tolerance (except of Roman Catholics). His ideas on valuing the natural over the supernatural held great sway with American colonists.

Matthew Tindal (1655–1733) A major figure of Deism. Author of *Christianity As Old As the Creation*,

Tindal believed that all rational beings shared a fixed law of Nature.

George Berkeley (1685–1753) Irish-born Anglican bishop and philosopher. A leader in the Idealist movement, opposed to Deism.

Joseph Butler (1692–1752) Anglican theologian and Bishop of Durham. An opponent of Deism, Butler nevertheless believed passionately in a natural theology where humans found a morality within their own natures.

The system of nature is no more the product of happenstance than a watch is. The argument was an influential one, and for a century Paley's *Evidences* was a standard text in religion.

The drawback to this argument, at least from a Christian perspective, is obvious: one can arrive at some proof for the *existence* of God, but there is no provision for the next step, to a knowledge of the *type* of God found in biblical revelation. Thus empirical religion was stuck, so to speak, in Deism, and the traditional attributes of God were simply not forthcoming.

Methodism: John and Charles Wesley

An original form of religion did emerge in the eighteenth century, and like much of eighteenth-century culture it combined novelty with tradition. This movement, METHODISM, was launched by John (1703–1791) and Charles (1707–1788) Wesley, both dedicated priests of the Church of England. Their work was mainly pastoral, intended to restore vitality to worship, and it began when they were students at Oxford and members of a society called the "Holy Club." The emphasis of early Wesleyanism, as the new movement was called ("Methodist" was more a term of reproach), was on preaching and hymnody, with John doing most of the preaching and Charles serving as music director. Together, and with their mother Susannah, the Wesleys worked to revitalize a system of worship which, in the opinion of many people, had become formal and sterile.

The Wesleys' efforts were so successful that they irritated the Anglican hierarchy, but the brothers considered themselves good Anglicans and did not wish to break away from the church. Instead, they continued with a highly effective missionary thrust throughout England. Stories of John's travels, of riding for days and composing sermons on horseback—he delivered 40,000 sermons during his career—became part of Wesleyan lore and surely added fascination to this new movement. Large segments of the middle and working classes, alienated by the aristocratic character of the Established Church, found a congenial home in the emotionally charged services offered by the Wesleyans.

The tenor of Methodist piety is grounded in the experiences of the Wesleys themselves, John especially. In a well-known passage from his *Journal*, John Wesley describes having his heart "strangely warmed" on May 24, 1738, when listening to a reading from Luther's Preface to Paul's Epistle to the Romans. Interpreting this feeling as a sample of divine grace, Wesley embarked on a program aimed at arousing the same emotional experience in others. Thus, from the start, the emphasis of Wesleyanism was more on practice than on dogma—a relatively new departure for a religious reform.

The movement became most popular in North America, which the brothers visited in 1735. Not only the Wesleys but other like-minded missionaries traveled through the American Colonies, some becoming notable figures in the history of Methodism. An early friend of the Wesley brothers at Oxford, George Whitefield went with them to Georgia and became a one-man revival movement, traveling throughout the American South and "planting" churches wherever he went. Although Methodism is an English movement in origin, it was the adopted tradition of a vast number of early Americans, and might be considered a typically

John Wesley,
c. 1736.
Oil on canvas.

John Wesley is here
seen preaching to
a group of Native
Americans during
a visit to Georgia.

American denomination, for many of the same sociological reasons that account for its success in England. The emphasis of Methodism on an emotional experience of God and its egalitarian leanings are two factors in its popularity in the American Colonies.

Philosophical Critiques

Among the intellectual aristocracy in both Europe and America (and among intellectual members of the aristocracy itself) the Wesleyans' intuitive, personal approach to divine truth had relatively little appeal. As we have seen, they generally approached the subject in a coolly rational way, preferring such cautious beliefs as Deism and Theism. Indeed, Deism may be considered the philosophical solution to questions of God's existence and Theism its theological counterpart. Which of the two schools had greater influence on the course of religious thought is an open question, though beyond doubt the challenges of the Deists were more provocative than the defenses of their Theist opponents. Philosophy influenced theology during the Enlightenment, rather than the other way around, as during the Middle Ages and the Reformation.

David Hume

Among the most influential figures in this area was the Scottish philosopher David Hume (1711–1776). A person of broad intellectual range, Hume was best known in his day as an historian (his *History of England,* completed in 1762, is a classic), for few people took seriously his epochal *Treatise of Human Nature* (1740). Hume's great epistemological achievement was to recognize the role of the imagination in creating complex impressions. With the imagination, one could have certainty of relations, notably causality, that are not themselves tangible.

The *Treatise* had a substantial impact on the possibility of knowledge of God. If one could be certain of the laws of causality, then one might be able to arrive at a knowledge of the first cause of the material world. This is the topic of *Dialogues concerning Natural Religion*, published in 1779 after Hume's death. There are three participants in the dialogue. One, named Demea, is an uncritical believer, who sees human reason as limited and thus in need of divine revelation. His approach is quickly dismissed as unproductive. The two others are Philo and Cleanthes, who want to reach a knowledge of God by means of causal reasoning, but they reach a deadlock because there are two possible kinds of causation. On one hand, it is possible to see the order, structure, and complexity of nature as a masterly artifact, proof that there was a designer crafting the whole system. On the other hand, everything within the natural realm here and now must have a cause, and that in turn must have had a cause, and so on in a presumably infinite regression. If we choose the "designer" model, then we have a transcendent deity—which might in turn be the product of other causes. (According to Hume and others, the problem with the notion of causality is that it never stops.) And if we take the second option, we have an immanent, or internal, cause—which is thus necessarily natural rather than divine (or supernatural). This is a serious philosophical dilemma, which Hume leaves unresolved.

F. Becker, *Immanuel Kant*, c. 1768. Oil on canvas. Schiller National Museum, Marbach, Germany.

Kant advocated a religion of "reason alone," and saw the progress of humanity as marked by the rejection of the mythical and irrational.

Gotthold Lessing and Immanuel Kant

In Germany such authors as Samuel Reimarus (1694–1768) and the play-wright Gotthold Lessing (1729–1781) chipped away at uncritical assumptions about the authority of biblical revelation. Reimarus wished to substitute for revealed religion a religion of reason, while Lessing held that biblical revelation had been an elementary "textbook" in the education of humanity, which had been gradually, and now finally, illuminated by reason. Like a textbook in any subject, it is meant to be superseded and no longer consulted once the student has mastered the subject. Humanity, in Lessing's view, has mastered the material of the biblical "primer," and can dispense with it.

In 1781 the German philosopher Immanuel Kant (1724–1804) first issued his *Critique of Pure Reason* (revised 1786), the first of three massive works that changed the way we think about perception and thought, action, and aesthetic judgment. Philosophically, Kant is the heir to the British empiricist tradition: he credited Hume for waking him from the "dogmatic slumbers" of his early years. (Kant was raised in an earnestly Pietist environment, where the dogma was strong, no matter how deep the slumber may have been.) In Kant's thought, we have an affirmation that all knowledge is drawn from nature, and that concepts such as God, freedom, and immortality are ultimately unknowable. All that offers certainty is what falls within the category of pure reason.

One of Kant's most readable and illuminating statements is an essay titled "What Is Enlightenment?" (1784). Kant answers this question by defining Enlightenment (*Aufklärung*) as a shaking off of primitive impediments and moving from a belief-ridden past to a progressive and independent future. "Dare to know!" he demands of his readers, echoing a Roman slogan: have the courage to cast off the crutch of faith and walk with your unaided understanding. This was quite a controversial statement—one that sent more than one theologian "back to the drawing board," as we shall see when we look at developments in the early nineteenth century. Before leaving the Enlightenment, however, we should look at another aspect of the religious culture of this period.

Religious Expression in Music

In contrast to the seventeenth century, with its flowering of baroque religious painting, sculpture, and architecture, especially in Roman Catholic countries (see Chapter 18), the eighteenth century produced little visual religious art of great importance. To be sure, some fine churches were built—some in the frothy rococo style, a development of the baroque especially popular in Austria and other Catholic German states, and others, later in the century, in a more restrained classical style. This latter style, dating from the Italian Renaissance, drew upon the ancient Greek temple, with its columns and pediments, and proved to be applicable for almost every type of building, especially churches. The typical white-frame eighteenth-century New England meetinghouse, for all its chaste simplicity, can, ironically, trace its ancestry back to pagan Greece.

The interiors of such churches depart not only from the ancient Greek model but also from traditional Christianity in placing not an altar but a pulpit at the center, thus reflecting the emphasis on preaching that characterizes evangelical Protestantism. The spoken word continued to dominate Protestant worship during the eighteenth century, with sermons often lasting two hours or more.

It is safe to say, however, that few of these sermons ever approached the spiritual power of the great religious music of this period. For eighteenth-century religion found its most eloquent artistic expression in music. Supreme in this respect was the music of Johann Sebastian Bach (1685–1750), whose use of Lutheran chorales was mentioned in Chapter 16. Some of the passages in Bach's two settings of gospel Passion narratives (the *Saint Matthew Passion* and *Saint John Passion*) have been known to move even atheists to tears. Especially effective is Bach's use of shimmering strings around the words of Christ, creating a sort of aural halo. In his capacity as cantor (director of music) at St. Thomas Church, Leipzig, Bach also produced more than two hundred religious cantatas (works for singers and orchestra including arias, choruses, and orchestral passages) for performance at Sunday services. A devout Lutheran, Bach demonstrated the breadth of his Christianity in his great *Mass in B Minor*, which he wrote for a Catholic German prince and which stands as one of the pinnacles of all religious music.

Bach's contemporary George Friedrich Handel (1685–1759), who was born in Germany but spent most of his life in England, also wrote many fine sacred works, including numerous anthems and oratorios. The latter often have a strongly operatic flavor (Handel also excelled as a composer of numerous operas), but his best-loved and greatest oratorio, *Messiah* (1742), contains arias and choruses of transcendent spirituality.

By mid-century the extravagant baroque style in music, as in architecture, was being supplanted by a simpler classical style, which typically features a clear, single melodic line supported by harmonizing chords—"homophonic," as contrasted with "polyphonic." In the music of Wolfgang Amadeus Mozart (1756–1791) this style was brought to perfection. The six hundred-plus works that Mozart composed in his short life include relatively few religious pieces; yet the phenomenal ease with which he produced one masterpiece after another has led some people to conclude that he was quite literally divinely inspired. Some of Mozart's church music—for example, his great *Mass in C Minor* (1783) and *Requiem* (1791)—is permeated by profound seriousness; but the dominant mood elsewhere is more often one of pure joy, typified by his (anything but) *Solemn Vespers* (1780). This wonderfully flowing music, settings of five psalms and the Magnificat (the Virgin Mary's praise of God), combines the serene elegance characteristic of the Enlightenment with a cheerful, confident piety.

One should not forget that at this time relatively few people had access to such splendid music. An anthem sung by the church choir, psalms, and hymns constituted religious music for the vast majority. The singing of hymns continued to be a prominent part of Lutheran services—the earlier chorales augmented during the seventeenth century by hymns written by Paul Gerhardt (1607–1676), many of which were set to music by his friend Johann Crüger (1598–1662). Isaac Watts (1674–1748) contributed hundreds of hymns to English-speaking denominations, as did John and Charles Wesley (though congregational hymn singing would not be adopted fully by the Anglican Church until the early nineteenth century). Within the Reformed tradition the solemn settings of the Psalms dating back to Calvin's day continued to be an integral part of worship; heirs of the English Puritan tradition (see Chapter 20) will be familiar with "Sternhold and Hopkins," the musical Psalter that dominated services in New England for centuries.

The rich affirmation of biblical and liturgical traditions that we find in the realm of music stands in stark contrast to the cool skepticism toward the revealed

J.S. Bach, from Bach's *St. Matthew Passion* (chorale "Wenn ich einmal soll scheiden"), 1727–1736.

Bach's religious music stands as a monument to the creative inspiration behind the Christian message.

and the supernatural that we find in such eminent Enlightenment philosophers as Locke, Hume, and Kant. There seems to be a disjunction between religious thought and religious life and practice; and this separation will have repercussions over the next two centuries, as theologians occupy one world and the guardians of the religious culture of the laity another. The thirteenth and fourteenth centuries, when Scholasticism was at its most intellectual and popular religion at its most anxious, provide a parallel case. With regard to the eighteenth century it is essential to become familiar with the artistic and philosophical expressions of religion in this period before attemping to assess its full meaning.

Key Terms

METHODISM A denomination that grew out of revival within the Anglican Church associated with John and Charles Wesley; it focuses on emotional piety and centers around the sermon.

NATURAL RELIGION In Enlightenment thought, a belief holding that nature presented sufficient evidence of the existence of God.

THEISM Belief in the existence of God; during the Enlightenment, a view of the divine as an abstract metaphysical principle rather than a supernatural personal agent.

The Dawn of Modern Religion
The West and its Missions

Enlightenment thought, with its optimism about progress linked to skepticism toward revealed religion and "superstition," ushered in a new era in Christian thought and practice. Rather than back down in the light of Enlightenment critique, much of the Christian tradition emerged with new vigor, new methods of theological thought, and new impulses to spread Christianity in areas in which it had previously been unknown or imperfectly understood. The dawn of the nineteenth century is known as the beginning of the "modern" era in Christian history.

In the sixteenth century, the Polish astronomer Nicolaus Copernicus (1473–1543) had caused an upheaval in Christendom when he challenged the traditional belief that the earth stood at the center of the universe. Some two hundred and fifty years later, in the preface to his *Critique of Pure Reason* (1781), the German philosopher Immanuel Kant (see Chapter 21) dubbed his own approach to philosophy a "Copernican turn"—meaning that he was offering a radically new perspective on metaphysics. Considered by many people to be the most important philosopher since Aristotle, Kant's impact was felt most evidently in the realms of epistemology and ethics. But he had almost as great an impact on religion.

Johann Gottlieb Fichte (1762–1814) was a philosopher whose work reflects this "turn." For Fichte, philosophy is a "doctrine" of science or knowledge; however, this does not mean that it is the study of other sciences or other forms of knowledge. Rather, it is the "science" of knowledge itself. Fichte's great contribution to thought lay in identifying three principles: the absolute "I" asserting itself, the "I" being negated by the "not-I," and the reconciliation of these contradictory propositions in a mutually limiting and interdependent unity. (See "Johann Gottlieb Fichte.") These three forms of identity and its negation, expressed as *thesis*, *antithesis*, and *synthesis*, would take fuller shape in the thought of Hegel (see below) and, later, Karl Marx (1818–1883), and in various theological systems as well. Fichte's own philosophy of religion is found in his 1798 essay *On the Ground of Our Belief in a Divine World Governance*, in which God is identified with a moral ordering of the world (another idea that would prove highly influential in the next century). In his *Instructions for a Happy Life* (1806), he wrote

Johann Gottlieb Fichte

One of the great philosophers of his time, Johann Gottlieb Fichte (1762–1814) was influenced by Immanuel Kant, and visited him in Königsberg in the hope of becoming his protégé. In the spirit of the "critical" school of philosophy that Kant had founded, Fichte in 1792 wrote (and dedicated to Kant) his Attempt at a Critique of All Revelation. *In this excerpt Fichte acknowledges the impossibility of empirical certainty about religious matters, but asserts that belief is a secure and valuable possession.*

It has now been proved sufficiently that there is no objective certainty about the reality of any ideas of the supersensuous but only a faith in them. All faith developed so far is based on a determination of the faculty of desire (on a determination of the higher faculty in the case of the existence of God and the soul's immortality; on a determination of the lower by the higher in the case of the concept of providence and revelation) and in turn facilitates this determination reciprocally. It has clearly been shown that no further ideas are possible in whose reality a direct or indirect determination by the practical law would move us to believe. So the only question remaining here is whether a faith is not possible which does *not* arise through such a determination and does *not* facilitate it in turn. In the first case, it must be easy to decide whether the faith actually exists *in concreto*; namely, it must follow from the practical consequences that this faith must necessarily produce as a way of facilitating the determination of the will. In the latter case, however, where no such practical consequences are possible, it appears difficult to determine anything solid about it, since the faith is something merely subjective, and it fully appears that nothing is left for us to do but to believe every honest man at his word when he says to us, I believe this, or I believe that. Nevertheless, it is perhaps possible to ascertain something even about this case. For it is surely not to be denied that a person often persuades others, and just as often himself, that he believes something when he simply has nothing against it and leaves it quietly in its place. Nearly all historical faith is of this kind, unless it happens to be based on a determination of the faculty of desire, such as the faith in the historical element in a revelation, or the faith of a professional historian, which is inseparable from respect for his occupation and from the importance that he is bound to place on his painstaking investigations, or the faith of a nation in an event that supports its national pride. Reading about the events and activities of beings who have the same concepts and the same passions that we have is a pleasant way of occupying ourselves; and it contributes something to the increasing of our enjoyment if we may assume that people of this kind actually lived, and we assume it all the more firmly the more the story interests us, the more similarity it has to our events or our way of thinking. But we would also have little objection, especially in some cases, if everything were mere fiction. Even if it is not true, it is well concocted, we would think. How, then, is one to come to some certainty about oneself in this matter?

(From *Attempt at a Critique of all Revelation*, trans. Garrett Green. London: Cambridge University Press, 1978.)

that the particular character of life lies in turning toward the Eternal—something to be embraced in the happy life.

Another shaper of the new style of thinking was Friedrich W. J. von Schelling (1775–1854), an early disciple of Fichte's, who later in his career came under the influence of the Lutheran mystic Jacob Boehme (1575–1624; see Chapter 19). Schelling was concerned with the unity of paired counterparts, such as the ideal and the real, subject and object, and spirit and nature. Nature, in his thought, is spirit made visible; spirit is invisible nature. Taking up questions left by Fichte, Schelling describes the "I" that is a subject as identical with the "I" that is an

Friedrich von Schelling

Friedrich von Schelling (1775–1854) was a contemporary of Hegel's and a leading Idealist philosopher, who taught at a number of German universities, among them Munich and Berlin. In this excerpt from Ages of the World *(1815) Schelling presents the "thesis" and "antithesis" of the idea of God.*

Everyone recognizes that God would not be able to create beings outside of itself from a blind necessity in God's nature, but rather with the highest voluntarism. To speak even more exactly, if it were left to the mere capacity of God's necessity, then there would be no creatures because necessity refers only to God's existence as God's own existence. Therefore, in creation, God overcomes the necessity of its nature through freedom and it is freedom that comes above necessity not necessity that comes above freedom.

What is necessary in God we call the nature of God. Its relationship to freedom is similar (but not identical) to the relationship that the Scriptures teach is between the natural and the spiritual life of the person. What is understood here by "natural" is not simply the by and large "physical," that is, the corporeal. The soul and the spirit, as well as the body, if not born again, that is, elevated to a different and higher life, belong to the "natural." The entirety of Antiquity knows as little as do the Scriptures of the abstract concept of nature.

Even this "nature" of God is living, nay, it is the highest vitality, and it is not to be expressed so bluntly. Only by progressing from the simple to the complex, through gradual creation, could we hope to reach the full concept of this vitality.

Everyone agrees that the Godhead is the Supreme Being, the purest Love, infinite communicativity and emanation. Yet at the same time they want it to exist as such. But Love does not reach Being [*Seyn*] from itself. Being is ipseity [*Seinheit*], particularity. It is dislocation. But Love has nothing to do with particularity. Love does not seek its own [*das Ihre*] and therefore it cannot be that which has being [*seyend seyn*] with regard to itself. In the same way, a Supreme Being is for itself groundless and borne by nothing. It is in itself the antithesis of personality and therefore another force, moving toward personality, must first make it a ground. An equivalently eternal force of selfhood, of egoity [*Egoität*], is required so that the being which is Love might exist as its own and might be for itself.

Therefore, two principles are already in what is necessary of God: the outpouring, outstretching, self-giving being, and an equivalently eternal force of selfhood, of retreat into itself, of Being in itself. That being and this force are both already God itself, without God's assistance.

It is not enough to see the antithesis. It must also be recognized that what has been set against each other has the same essentiality and originality. The force with which the being closes itself off, denies itself, is actual in its kind as the opposite principle. Each has its own root and neither can be deduced from the other. If this were so, then the antithesis would again immediately come to an end. But it is impossible *per se* that an exact opposite would derive from its exact opposite.

(From *Ages of the World*, trans. Jason M. Wirth. Albany, NY: SUNY Press, 2000.)

object, since it becomes an object of thought. Thinking *about* the "I" makes it an object of thinking, while the "I" still remains the subject of the activity of thinking. In matters of religion, Schelling sees God in two forms: as ground and existence. What this means is that God fully exists and there can be nothing outside of God, but there is still a possibility for humans, in their freedom, to act in either a good or a bad way. Thus human freedom requires the *possibility* of evil action, even though this seems incompatible with the divine nature. As the *ground of existence*, God may be seen as the potential for perfect being—but not its actualization. When persons act badly, they are unaware of the perfection of God; they act in this realm of potentiality (or ground), since only God has complete knowledge of perfection. (See "Friedrich von Schelling.")

The identification of God with a metaphysical Ideal was crucial to the philosophy of Georg W. F. Hegel (1770–1831), whose *Phenomenology of Spirit* (1806) attempts to unfold the development of mind from consciousness through reason to "spirit," "religion," and "absolute knowledge," which for Hegel is manifested in revealed religion, art, and philosophy. Hegel is sympathetic toward Christianity in an unconventional way, seeing it as having essentially the same content as philosophy. As such, Christianity for Hegel represents the highest level of development for religion generally. And philosophy serves as proof that there is a continuous dialectical process of God, love, spirit, and substance. The Hegelian legacy in theology is seen most clearly in the work of F. C. Baur (1792–1860), a New Testament scholar at the University of Tübingen who saw the contrasting positions of Peter (insistence on works of the Law) and Paul (grace as freedom from law) as thesis and antithesis respectively, resolved in the experience of the Catholic Church.

The Beginnings of Liberal Theology

Friedrich Schleiermacher

Modern Protestant theology has a birth date, one of the most precise and least questioned moments in the history of Western religious thought. In 1799 Friedrich Schleiermacher (1768–1834), a Calvinist German pastor and theologian, published a small volume called *On Religion: Speeches to its Cultured Despisers*. (See "Friedrich Schleiermacher.") These were not actual speeches, but essays; and the intended readership went far beyond the enemies of religion, cultured or not. Schleiermacher's intention was to redefine religion in such a way as to draw the educated and skeptical back into the tradition. Recognizing that reassertions of transmitted doctrines would make no claim on the enlightened intellects of his day, Schleiermacher located religion within feeling. According to Schleiermacher, there is in all persons a sense of the Infinite, and oneness with the Infinite is the highest form of religious experience.

In Schleiermacher's comprehensive theology, titled *The Christian Faith* (originally published 1822; 2nd ed., 1830), the foundation of religion is the experience of "absolute dependence," the sense that one's existence is completely contingent. Such a feeling is profoundly disorienting, since the human will operates on the assumption that a person is independent and free. Thus there is a fundamen-

Friedrich Schleiermacher

Friedrich Schleiermacher (1768–1834) is said to have inaugurated modern liberal Protestant theology with the 1799 publication of his On Religion. *In this excerpt from the fifth of these "speeches," Schleiermacher identifies the uniqueness of Jesus Christ.*

When, in the mutilated delineations of His life I contemplate the sacred image of Him who has been the author of the noblest that there has yet been in religion, it is not the purity of His moral teaching, which but expressed what all men who have come to consciousness of their spiritual nature, have with Him in common, and which, neither from its expression nor its beginning, can have greater value, that I admire; and it is not the individuality of His character, the close union of high power with touching gentleness, for every noble, simple spirit must in a special situation display some traces of a great character. All those things are merely human. But the truly divine element is the glorious clearness to which the great idea He came to exhibit attained in His soul. This idea was, that all that is finite requires a higher mediation to be in accord with the Deity, and that for man under the power of the finite and particular, and too ready to imagine the divine itself in this form, salvation is only to be found in redemption. Vain folly it is to wish to remove the veil that hides the rise of this idea in Him, for every beginning in religion, as elsewhere, is mysterious. The prying sacrilege that has attempted it can only distort the divine. He is supposed to have taken His departure from the ancient idea of His people, and He only wished to utter its abolition which, by declaring Himself to be the Person they expected, He did most gloriously accomplish. Let us consider the living sympathy for the spiritual world that filled His soul, simply as we find it complete in Him.

If all finite things require the mediation of a higher being, if it is not to be ever further removed from the Eternal and be dispersed into the void and transitory, if its union with the Whole is to be sustained and come to consciousness, what mediates must not again require mediation, and cannot be purely finite. It must belong to both sides, participating in the Divine Essence in the same way and in the same sense in which it participates in human nature. But what did He see around Him that was not finite and in need of mediation, and where was aught that could mediate but Himself? "No man knoweth the Father but the Son, and He to whom the Son shall reveal Him." This consciousness of the singularity of His knowledge of God and of His existence in God, of the original way in which this knowledge was in Him, and of the power thereof to communicate itself and awake religion, was at once the consciousness of His office as mediator and of His divinity.

(From *On Religion: Speeches to its Cultured Despisers*, trans. John Owen. New York: Harper, 1958.)

tal conflict at work in Schleiermacher's thought: the need for freedom and autonomy in contrast to the apparently undeniable awareness of dependence and limit. In Schleiermacher's system, the conflict is resolved by another feeling, that of redemption. Such a feeling signals the individual's liberation from limit and dependence. Now this is hardly the form of redemption one finds in the theological tradition, yet Schleiermacher significantly draws on the biblical and confessional texts to support his position. Thus the declared task of *The Christian Faith* is to defend the character of the Christian experience of redemption on psychological and anthropological grounds rather than on an external body of teachings.

H. Lips, *Friedrich Schleiermacher*, late 18th century. Engraving.

Schleiermacher found the essence of religion in his feeling of dependence; he found a corresponding feeling of support in the role of the Christian community.

The historical teachings are used as evidence that dependence and redemption are in fact trans-historical experiences. Sometimes they are expressed mythically, as in the biblical narratives, and sometimes in other ways. Schleiermacher, like the philosopher Arthur Schopenhauer (1788–1860), was part of the first generation of Western academics to discover and appreciate Eastern religious traditions, and thus he saw the dynamic character of Christian life as but one form—the supreme one, to be sure—of universal human experience.

A text that served as an unofficial blueprint for nineteenth-century Protestantism is Schleiermacher's *Brief Outline for the Study of Theology* (1810; 2nd ed., 1830), a product of his teaching activity at the newly established University of Berlin. The first part of the study of theology, in Schleiermacher's program, is philosophical: the definition of basic principles for apologetics and polemics. The second part, substantially larger, concerns historical theology in its main forms: exegesis of texts and church history. In Schleiermacher's view, historical understanding of the tradition is a necessary condition for any further development of Christianity. The third and final part concerns practical theology, which we might easily equate with ministry if Schleiermacher did not stipulate that a "scientific spirit" needed to be added to "ecclesial interest" in this segment of the discipline.

Educational Advances

The belief that Christianity was the perfect form of human experience, combined with confidence that it was destined to absorb all of humanity—a belief called triumphalism (see Introduction)—was now entering its heyday. The language of the kingdom of God was not secularized, since it was held in dialectical opposition to the present kingdom; but the image of the divine kingdom was seen as an ideal toward which the world, led by the church, was moving.

Such optimism about the course of history bore certain resemblances to the progressive character of Enlightenment thought, and nineteenth-century liberal theology can indeed be seen as the payoff, in religious terms, of the tradition begun with the British empiricists of the previous century. Emphasis on transcendent, mythical, supernatural elements was reduced in favor of emphasis on the knowable. Even more significant in this trend is faith in the progress of culture and its institutions. The idea that social institutions could transform society on a broad scale, which in the eighteenth century had been a philosophical notion entertained mainly outside academic circles, became in the nineteenth century the engine driving the creation of great new universities such as Berlin, Göttingen, and Bonn in Germany, the University of London, in England,

BIOGRAPHICAL PROFILE

Søren Kierkegaard (1813–1855)

Reacting against the direction of Hegelian philosophy and a culture of easy Christianity, the Danish thinker Søren Kierkegaard must be considered one of the most profound writers of the nineteenth century. Although the Russian novelist Fyodor Dostoyevsky and, to some degree, the German philosopher Friedrich Nietzsche are prominent figures in the development of what would become known as existentialist philosophy, Kierkegaard is considered by most to be the true father of existentialism, especially through his influence upon Jean-Paul Sartre. Kierkegaard foreshadowed existentialism in his belief that the individual is a work-in-progress, responsible for creating and maintaining his or her own identity.

Kierkegaard's life was marred by much personal unhappiness. He had a distant relationship with his melancholic father, an extremely austere Lutheran, and his mother and several siblings all died before he reached twenty-one. Moreover, because of a physical ailment that deformed his posture, Kierkegaard suffered much ridicule as a child and even later as an adult. Not surprisingly, his romantic life, too, was quite tragic: he ended his engagement to Regine Olsen in order to pursue his writing with total devotion. Upon later reflection, Kierkegaard felt he could have led a most contented life had he married Regine, but then he would not have been able to attain all his intellectual and literary goals.

Ignoring the rational approaches to God recently adopted by Kant and Hegel, as well as Schleiermacher's feeling-based approach, Kierkegaard considered God to be accessible only through a radical type of faith. His approach was not very different from the one espoused by the church Father Tertullian, who believed in the truth of Christianity not because it was rational or helped him feel God's presence, but because it was absurd. For Kierkegaard, God is a being not just quantitatively infinitely greater than humans but one who is qualitatively different in being absolutely transcendent. Thus, to know God requires faith—a veritable leap of faith—in a being ultimately and completely unknowable. Kierkegaard's emphasis on God's transcendence would later be adopted as a centerpiece of the theology of Karl Barth and other Neo-Orthodox theologians.

Kierkegaard's philosophy of religion contrasted greatly with the state-supported Lutheranism of his native Denmark and most of European Christianity. Kierkegaard excoriated the "bourgeois" brand of Christianity which in his view had abandoned such key Christian concepts as sacrifice and suffering in the interests of faith alone. His reaction against the Christianity practiced in his day was so strong that, on his deathbed, he refused communion from a Lutheran minister because this priest of the state church represented to him all that was wrong with Christianity. Despite this repudiation, Kierkegaard remains one of the most important thinkers in the history of Christianity as well as a philosopher of no little repute.

His greatest works—*Either/Or, Fear and Trembling, Philosophical Fragments, The Concept of Dread*, and *The Sickness unto Death*—remain standard reading for modern theologians and philosophers alike.

N.C. Kierkegaard, *Søren Kierkegaard*, 1838. Drawing.

numerous institutions in the United States, such as Cornell, Johns Hopkins, and Chicago, where the university movement gained momentum in the late nineteenth century. All of these institutions were organized around carefully defined disciplines, with the common purpose of advancing understanding through research. In branches of study ranging from philology to physics, the aim of study was the improvement of culture—not the wistful contemplation of superior but long-past eras. Thus it was entirely in keeping with this mentality that theology, too, should move forward and contribute to the betterment of the world.

Julius Wellhausen and Rudolf Bultmann

Thus we can set the work of the influential Christian thinkers of the nineteenth century within a progressive and "scientific" academic setting, with Schleiermacher and Adolf Harnack (1851–1930) at Berlin and Albrecht Ritschl (1822–1889) at Göttingen, where the biblical scholar Julius Wellhausen (1844–1918) also taught. Wellhausen was a Hebrew Bible scholar who, working from such evidence as the different names for God given in the Bible, along with linguistic peculiarities and differences in the conception of God, presented a theory holding that the Hebrew Bible was a composite work drawn from a number of sources, and that the Pentateuch itself (the first five books), traditionally thought to have been penned by Moses alone, is a compilation of texts from different regions and ages. Wellhausen's theory is known as the DOCUMENTARY HYPOTHESIS: "documentary" because it tries to identify four different source-documents: "J," named for its use of the TETRA-GRAMMATON (the holy name YHWH) for God; "E," for the source using the less specific term "Elohim," for God; "P," for the "Priestly" source (found most clearly in Leviticus); and "D," for the Deuteronomist, the author or compiler of the fifth book.

Wellhausen's work, first published as articles in 1876–77, hit the theological establishment like a thunderbolt. Holy Scripture, which tradition had regarded as divinely revealed, now proved—or so it seemed with the amount of scholarly research that underlay the hypothesis—to be a human book like any other. Thus, what had appeared to be supernatural and unfathomable, both in content and origin, turned out to be an epic narrative with all of the edifying and culture-forming characteristics of great literature—and nothing more. However, instead of compromising religious belief, the documentary hypothesis was welcomed in

Who's Who

Protestantism in Modern Germany

Friedrich Ernst Daniel Schleiermacher (1768–1834) German Calvinist theologian and pastor. He believed that religion lies in a sense of the absolute, which all humans can find within themselves.

Albrecht Ritschl (1822–1889) German Protestant theologian and academic. He believed that we achieve religious understanding through faith, and not through reason.

Julius Wellhausen (1844–1918) German biblical scholar. Wellhausen held that the Pentateuch was a collection from four different sources.

Adolf Harnack (1851–1930) Outstanding German theologian and historian, author of a formidable body of religious scholarship. He opposed the metaphysical aspects of Christianity, and this brought him into conflict with many conservative Christians.

Rudolf Bultmann (1884–1976) An academic specializing in New Testament studies who sought to make Christianity meaningful to a modern world. His questioning of the historical value of the gospels made him a controversial figure in the 1940s–50s.

many circles as a way of bringing the Bible back to life and giving it a relevance in human terms that it could no longer claim in divine ones.

What began with Wellhausen was completed with the work of Rudolf Bultmann (1884–1976) in the first half of the twentieth century. Bultmann was a New Testament counterpart to Wellhausen, a scholar of impeccable training who set about disentangling "mythic" elements from the enduring message that, in his opinion, was the essence of Christian faith. In a prodigious body of work, Bultmann proceeded, in his own term, to DEMYTHOLOGIZE the New Testament— that is, to separate the "mythical" elements that could no longer claim credibility from the underlying message, or KERYGMA (Greek for "announcement") of Jesus' and his followers' work of proclamation.

Fundamentalism

Dominant though it was for several decades, this "historical-critical" trend in theology did not go unchallenged. Theological faculties throughout Europe sounded the call to battle stations after the appearance of Wellhausen's work, and continued to resist attempts to reduce the Bible to culturally conditioned terms. In the process they elevated the sacred canon, in all of its linguistic and textual peculiarities, to a uniquely lofty status, one it had not always occupied. The reaction reached its climax in the United States with the rise of FUNDAMENTALISM, a school of thought inaugurated by certain graduates of Princeton Theological Seminary with the appearance, beginning c. 1909, of a number of tracts titled *The Fundamentals*, which gave the movement its name. Fundamentalism shared certain features with the movement it opposed, at least insofar as it began from certain unproven assumptions about the nature of religion and the form of the divine will. There the similarities end. In the Fundamentalists' view the Bible, as a divinely inspired text, was true historically (so much for Darwin's discoveries) and eschatologically (thus rejecting claims of a divine kingdom to be realized in this world). The Fundamentalists saw the historical-critical scholars' denial of biblical "inerrancy" as the prideful boasting of fallible reason over revelation. On the other hand, biblical theology in earlier centuries did not subject the Scriptures to historical truth tests before interpreting them allegorically; the allegorical meaning, rather than the literal meaning, could be the primary one. Fundamentalists continued, and continue still, to go to war against science. In that respect it is certainly contrary to the nineteenth-century academic culture of the theology it opposes.

Missionary Christianity in the Late Nineteenth Century

Liberal Christianity's trust that the divine plan for humanity was being realized in the historical realm gave a renewed sense of purpose to the work of the church. Just as the late nineteenth century was a period of colonial expansion by the European powers, so it was also a time for redoubled missionary endeavors, since Westernizing, Christianizing, and "saving" had all somewhat fuzzily come to

Missionaries in Africa, from *Missionary Scenes* (pub. by Scholz, Basel), c. 1850.

"The reverend and Mrs Townsend arrive at Ijaye, Nigeria, to do the Lord's work among the benighted heathen, who are amazed...."

mean the same thing. English missions to Japan and China in the 1850s were followed, toward the end of the century, by missions to Korea, the Philippines, and Indonesia. India, which already had a British presence of long standing, became the sometimes reluctant host to a series of missionary campaigns that multiplied Protestant numbers in India by a factor of ten.

Africa

In Africa, parts of which had already embraced an Islam brought by Arabs in the 1840s, the English expeditions continued, Henry Morton Stanley (1841–1904) succeeding David Livingstone (1813–1873) in exploration and evangelization. After his famous encounter with Livingstone in 1871, Stanley, who had based himself in Uganda, appealed to his fellow Britons for aid in the missionary endeavor. Uganda soon became a missionary field for Anglicans as well as French Catholics—only decades after beginning the difficult transition from indigenous tribal religion to Islam. The crucial element in the success of these missions was the king, Mutesa I (r. 1852–1884), who was at least tolerant of the missionaries' work. His son and successor Mwanga II was not, however; and the latter's intolerance led to an Anglican bishop's being speared to death in 1885. Some of Mwanga's newly converted Christian subjects objected to his predilection for boys (of which his conquests were as numerous as his father's wives), and in retaliation, Mwanga had thirty-two of his young Christian male subjects burned at the stake. Other Christian Ugandans also suffered for their faith. Mwanga was finally driven into exile; economic development began; and the church ended the century with an established position in Ugandan culture.

Europe's gradual banning of the slave trade in the 1830s removed some of the economic rationale for a colonial presence in sub-Saharan Africa, which nonetheless remained very strong there. A Christian presence also remained especially in hospital and schools. Of course, instruction in European-based languages (English, German, and Afrikaans, a variant of Dutch) and the system of apartheid (legal separation of the races) served as convenient means for driving home the message that there was a hierarchy of races, and that the white was destined to dominate the black. Many African clergy held out no greater hope for their subordinate populations than that of the chance to find fulfilment in a segregated world.

This was the dilemma for the native peoples who were the focus of the missionaries' efforts: Accept the education and health care that the Europeans offered, and tolerate baptism and Christian teachings as the price to pay for cultural improvements, or refuse religious instruction and thereby relinquish things that would improve the quality of life. In actual fact the second option was often no option at all, since the church had already made its inroads during colonial administrations and the native peoples had little choice in becoming Christians.

So far we have spoken of missionary work as an abstraction, a project that "the church" undertook among the "uncivilized" or "unChristianized" peoples. We now shudder at these last two terms, aware of different levels of culture in the non-Christian world. But the dynamics of contact between native peoples and European culture and Christianity remain somewhat hidden. We should recognize

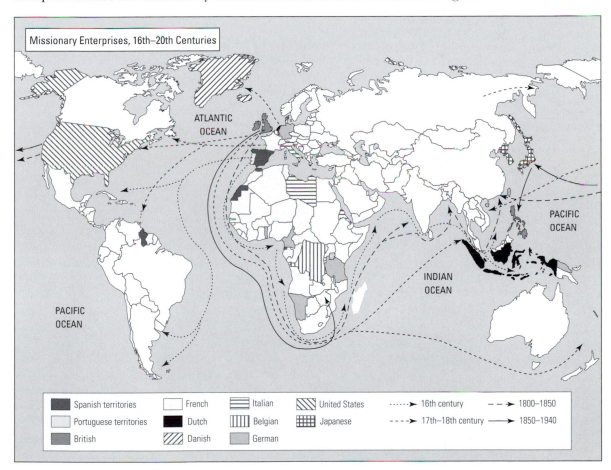

Missionary Enterprises, 16th–20th Centuries

that missionary activity was undertaken by organizations formed from Christian denominations either on a national or regional level. These organizations tended to mirror those within the mercantile companies that explored and exploited new regions for natural resources. As such, many of them were also structured in the interests of the greatest efficiency, as if there were a spiritual profit that could be measured like material gain.

India

India provides a useful example. By 1700, the indigenous Hindu and Islamic populations had encountered trading expeditions from Holland, England, France, and Portugal, with the French and English East India Companies in open competition. By 1800, English Protestantism had made an established presence there, the work primarily of the Baptist missionaries William Carey (1761–1834), Joshua Marsham (1768–1837), and William Ward (1764–1823), who found refuge in a Danish colony near Calcutta named Serampore. These three made the Bible available in a number of local languages; Carey's translation of the New Testament into Bengali became one of the pillars of Bengali literature. The founding of a college at Serampore offered a Western education that for its time was astonishingly cross-cultural, with instruction in Asian literature as well as the history and the precepts of Christianity.

The Church of England maintained a fairly high profile in India, featuring missionaries such as Henry Martyn (1782–1813), whose work included biblical translations and revisions into Arabic, Persian, and Urdu; and Thomas Middleton, who was the first Anglican bishop in India and the founder of an Anglican

H. Room (engraver J. Cochran), *Religious Missionaries in China*, 1840s. Engraving.

This shows a missionary and scholar, the Reverend James Legge, with three students at the London Missionary Society's Theological Seminary in Hong Kong.

seminary, Bishop's College, in Calcutta. Many of these clergy were university-trained and scholarly, yet most worked tirelessly to bring their religious message to the native people. Due to the expansion of British influence and industry on the subcontinent in the mid-nineteenth century, the cultural landscape became a blend of European and Indian elements.

China

China proved less hospitable to Christian overtures. Culturally insular by tradition and Confucian in their thinking, the Chinese of the eighteenth and early nineteenth centuries were resistant to outside influences of any sort. By the beginning of the 1840s, however, diplomatic treaties had paved the way for a European presence in a number of port cities, among them Hong Kong, Guanghou (Canton), and Shanghai. Here and elsewhere along the coast, missionaries in the 1850s began preaching in the footsteps of the traders. The vast Chinese population presented an irresistible challenge to every branch of European and American Christianity, so that Anglicans were soon joined at the very least by Methodists, Presbyterians, Baptists, and Congregationalists arriving from Holland, Germany, Canada, and the United States. Naturally some expeditions were better run and more successful than others, though in the end Christianity left only a trace in Chinese spiritual life, which remained steadfastly faithful to Confucianism. In the long run the West may have been the greater beneficiary of such contacts than China was; access to Chinese literature, philosophy, and Confucianism proved highly stimulating to European intellectuals at the end of the nineteenth century.

The United States

The United States entered the arena in the final decades of the century, building on momentum gained from earlier missionary efforts, both Protestant and Catholic, among Native Americans. Protestant missionaries from a dizzying array of denominations were able to win new converts without ever leaving the continent. The first such efforts had accompanied the westward expansion of European-Americans. The next frontier for these missionaries was Mexico—predominantly Native but already, of course, Catholic. Missions to South America and the Caribbean soon followed. Methodists, Baptists, and Presbyterians saw the need to convert the Native Americans of Latin America not so much because they were Catholic but because their conversion by Catholic missionaries had been superficial. To the north, most of the Natives had been beyond the reach of early French Catholic missionaries, but in 1876 an organized Episcopal missionary expedition was started; it brought Christianity, and in many cases literacy and much-needed health care, to the Eskimo population. Even farther north, Alaska had been a missionary field for Orthodox priests from Russia in the late eighteenth and early nineteenth centuries; churches and cemeteries on Kodiak Island and the Kenai Peninsula (south of present-day Anchorage) continue as reminders of this Orthodox presence. But it was a Presbyterian missionary, Sheldon Jackson (1834–1909), who brought a Western European religion, together with a school (which survives as Sheldon Jackson College), to the Native people of Alaska after the United States purchased the territory in 1867.

A milestone in the maturing of nineteenth-century Protestant evangelization was the World Missionary Conference held in Edinburgh, Scotland, in 1910. With more than 1,200 in attendance, the meeting had as its slogan "The Evangelization of the World in Our Generation." Led by an industrious American, John R. Mott (1865–1955), the conference participants devoted attention to consolidating their efforts and building on the work of the past century. It was thought that the streamlining of efforts, clear formulations of purposes and principles, and deeper commitments from the participating denominations would accelerate the expansion of Christianity through the world. The momentum was interrupted by World War I and almost lost during World War II, and so there is some irony in the fact that missionary activity was at its peak just when its leaders were resolving to take it to new heights.

Albert Schweitzer and Missionary Work under Attack

The missionary enterprise in the twentieth century is represented not by an organization but by individuals, notably Albert Schweitzer (1875–1965), one of the most creative minds of modern times. Born into a cultured Protestant family in Alsace, Schweitzer was a trained musician and musicologist, a theologian (and the author of *The Quest for the Historical Jesus* [1906, trans. 1910]), and a physician. In any of his academic careers he could have been a dominant figure; yet in mid-career he abandoned the scholarly life and moved to Africa, where he built a hospital in Lambarene in Gabon, and lived and wrote among the poor. It was in many ways a life committed to the religious ideals dominant at the time, a twentieth-century version of monastic withdrawal or the work that women religious did among the sick and poor during the plague years of the later Middle Ages. In 1952 Schweitzer received the Nobel Peace Prize.

By the time Schweitzer died, Christianity was on the defensive in many parts of the world; and missionaries, in particular, were being roundly criticized for imposing the Christian faith on peoples who already had religions of their own. Even the Roman Catholic Church, heretofore so firmly convinced of the truth of its doctrines and practices, was undergoing some major soul searching, as we shall see in Chapter 28. Before we consider these twentieth-century trends, however, it is necessary to look at some other aspects of Christianity as it evolved during the nineteenth century.

Key Terms

DEMYTHOLOGIZE To identify the durable religious meaning in the New Testament text by separating it from outmoded "myths"—a theological program associated with R. Bultmann.

DOCUMENTARY HYPOTHESIS A theory in biblical scholarship that regards Scripture as a compilation from a variety of sources rather than a unified divine revelation.

FUNDAMENTALISM A form of Protestant thought that emerged in early-20th-century America, stressing in particular biblical inerrancy and the divinity of Jesus.

KERYGMA Literally, "message"; the meaning of the biblical text beneath various layers of supposed myth.

TETRAGRAMMATON The four-letter unutterable name of God, often transliterated YHWH.

Challenges to the English Church

The Oxford Movement and Evolution

Since the Reformation, Christianity had been continually challenged by new ideas in philosophy and new movements for reform—some of which led to the formation of new churches. During the nineteenth century, as we saw in the last chapter, Protestantism had undergone some major theological mutations, notably in Germany and the United States. In Britain, too, important changes were afoot, but these would differ significantly from those on the Continent and elsewhere, partly because they were triggered by political issues.

The Established Church

When, in 1837, Queen Victoria (1819–1901; r. 1837–1901) ascended the throne of the United Kingdom of Great Britain and Ireland, she also became head of the ESTABLISHED CHURCH of England. Also known as the Anglican Church (see Chapter 16), the Church of England had been the official religion of the English nation and its colonies since the sixteenth century. In keeping with its Reformation-era origins, it did not owe allegiance to the pope, and yet it remained more liturgically rich than its more severe Continental Protestant counterparts. From the beginning, the Anglican Church saw itself as a middle way between Roman Catholicism and Protestantism, incorporating the sacramental life of the Roman Church but without its polity and the independence of the Protestant Churches but without their abandonment of the historical tradition. It was a difficult balance to maintain, but the English Church managed to do this fairly successfully for a number of centuries. There were, to be sure, signs of discontent within it. We have seen (in Chapter 21) how, in the eighteeenth century, the Wesleys and others brought a more evangelical and emotional kind of Christianity into the church, appealing to many people who found traditional Anglicanism too formal—and too closely associated with the aristocracy. This eventually resulted in the formation of the separate Methodist Church. By and large, however, the Anglican Church and its flock seemed content with the status quo.

Nevertheless, there were many persons in the 1820s and 1830s who felt that the church should be disestablished—or at least that its dominance should be reduced. The problem was, first, that many British subjects were not members of the Church of England. A number of aristocratic families, and untold numbers of ordinary people, had never relinquished their allegiance to Rome—while being loyal Britons in all other respects. In Scotland (which had been joined with England in 1707 to form Great Britain) most people belonged to the official (Presbyterian) Church of Scotland and were not subject to Anglican polity, although some Scots belonged to the (Anglican) Episcopal Church of Scotland. In Ireland, however, it was a different story. Ireland had been an English possession since the twelfth century. Since the Reformation, various English rulers had tried to impose Anglicanism (or, in Cromwell's case, Puritanism) on the steadfastly Roman Catholic Irish; and although by the early nineteenth century attempts at conversion had generally been abandoned, the (Anglican) Church of Ireland enjoyed a privileged position, being supported financially by Roman Catholic tenant farmers. Thus, the ethnic and religious diversity within the British Isles made the idea of an established church seem somewhat untenable.

Around 1830 this began to change. The repeal of the 1673 Test Act in 1829 freed applicants for government positions from declaring allegiance to the English Church; and the Roman Catholic Relief (or Emancipation) Act of the same year removed most of the existing restrictions on that religion, enabling Catholics, for example, to serve in Parliament and in the Civil Service. Some distinguished Catholic schools were also founded during this time.

The Oxford Movement

Possibly the most notable phenomenon of Victorian-era Anglicanism was a movement begun in Oxford in the 1830s by a number of clerical academics who sought renewal within the Church of England. There was surely a need for such renewal; but the form that it was to take was unclear at the time.

John Keble and Edward Pusey

The founders of the Oxford Movement included John Keble (1792–1866), a churchman after whom Oxford's Keble College is named, and Edward Bouverie Pusey (1800–1882), a prominent scholar and theologian (his translation of Augustine's *Confessions* remains one of the standard versions). The circumstances that launched the movement were some attempts, or at least perceived attempts, to reduce the number of bishoprics in the Anglican Church. In 1833 Parliament tried to suppress ten bishoprics in Ireland, and it was Keble's protest against this move, in what is known as the "Assize Sermon" on July 14th of that year, preached at the Oxford University church, St. Mary's, that set the revival in motion. In this sermon, Keble did more than criticize the government's action against the Irish bishoprics; he asserted the church's divine origins, in the person of Jesus Christ, and the validity of the apostolic succession (see Chapter 5).

Keble's sermon was followed, in the same year, by the first of a series of pamphlets, written by various like-minded Anglicans, as well as Keble himself, called

Richard Doyle (?),
*Edward Bouverie
Pusey*, 19th
century. Etching.

*Pusey, theologian
and leader of the
Oxford Movement,
is shown walking
at the head of a
group of his
disciples (called
here "satellites").*

Tracts for the Times. These tracts were essays, some long, some short, on a variety of topics relating to the Church of England. Over the next eight years, the authors reconceptualized the Anglican Church, stressing its links with the Roman Catholic Church and its continuity with the medieval and ancient Christian traditions. While reaffirming that the Scriptures contained everything necessary for salvation, the Tractarians also insisted on the authoritativeness of the interpretation of these writings by the early church fathers.

The ideas of the Oxford Movement also appeared in other writings. The title of one of Pusey's works, *The Church of England, a Portion of Christ's One Holy Catholic Church, and a Means of Restoring Visible Unity* (1865), can serve as a summary of the movement's political stance. Putting the Church of England under the sovereignty of a monarch, he claimed, was equivalent to claiming Constantine as the founder of the Byzantine Church. Historically and theologically, Pusey contested, such an assertion must be regarded as senseless. Just as the mission of the church is spiritual and not political, so must its nature be understood as spiritual and divine.

The writings of the Tractarians also signaled a shift in relations with the larger Christian community. Whereas previously the Church of England had carefully steered a middle course between Catholicism and Protestantism, in the Oxford Movement it seemed to be creating an alliance with Catholicism. It also found new affinities with the ancient Greek tradition. These decades in England saw a flowering of classical, and particularly Greek, scholarship; and the philosophical spirit of the Greek Patristic tradition must surely have resonated in the minds of Anglican clerics, some of whom made important scholarly contributions in this area.

Effects of the Oxford Movement

The movement affected religious life and practice as well as theological concepts; and indeed in this respect its presence continues to be felt in Anglican liturgy. At the same time that the Tractarians were exploring the Patristic tradition, Europe in general and England in particular were rediscovering the Middle Ages. This cultural trend, part of the Romantic movement in the arts, expressed a nostalgia for the supposedly idyllic life of medieval times, long before the mechanization of the Industrial Revolution and before the splitting of Christendom in the Reformation. It manifested itself in many ways, but above all in a proliferation of churches built in a Gothic style. The two trends, one religious, one cultural, fed each other, and produced, within churches, a richly embellished form of worship. Beautifully embroidered vestments, the use of incense, the chanting rather than speaking of parts of the liturgy are legacies of these two movements. The practice of private confession was also revived.

Another legacy of the Oxford Movement was the revival of religious orders within the Anglican Church. Monasticism had been suppressed by Henry VIII after the break with Rome. Now, spearheaded by Pusey, this tradition was reinstated. In 1845, with his encouragement, the first Anglican community of nuns, the Sisterhood of the Holy Cross, was founded in London; other communities, mainly women's, soon followed. In addition to their devotional practices and their work embroidering liturgical vestments, nuns undertook badly needed social work among the urban poor, caring for the sick and destitute and running schools for children.

The Oxford Movement was larger than Keble and Pusey and the other Tractarians. That series of pamphlets ceased publication after eight years, in 1841, with ninety essays published. But the Oxford Movement itself persisted for much of the nineteenth century (though not without some opposition from the evangelical wing of the church). Among its other members was Alexander Forbes (1817–1875), a Scotsman whose appointment as Bishop of Brechin in 1847 brought new visibility to the Oxford Movement, since none of its members had yet risen to that rank. With the rapidly industrializing city of Dundee under his care, Forbes began social welfare and education programs to benefit the urban poor, helping to expand this dimension of the renewal movement. This program would also include Henry Scott Holland (1847–1918). Although at the beginning and end of his career, Holland was an Oxford scholar—returning to Oxford in 1910 as Regius professor of divinity—he spent almost three decades as a canon at St. Paul's Cathedral, in London. During his years at the cathedral he worked for social reform, founding the Christian Social Union, a pioneering social welfare agency.

Many other clergymen and theologians contributed to the Oxford Movement, but ironically the most famous of these eventually left the Anglican Church to become a Roman Catholic. His career deserves to be considered in some detail.

John Henry Newman

One of the leading intellectuals of the nineteenth century, John Henry Newman (1801–1890) gave little indication in his early life of the remarkable career he would pursue in later years. The son of a banker, he was reared in the evangelical tradition of the Church of England. At Oxford, he did not graduate with honors but obtained only a second-class degree in 1820. He went on to become ordained in 1824, and in 1828 became Vicar of St. Mary's in Oxford. Only later in 1833, when hearing John Keble speak from the pulpit at St. Mary's, denouncing Parliament's actions as a "national apostasy" and calling for a renewal of spiritual purpose within the church, did Newman find a sense of purpose in his own work.

A program of literary work, which includes an essay on *The Prophetical Office of the Church* (1837) and editorship of a leading periodical, reached a turning point in 1841, when he wrote the provocative *Tract No. 90*, modestly titled "Remarks on Certain Passages in the Thirty-nine Articles." The points of the essay, supported by scrupulous analysis of the Articles (the confessional statement of the Church of England, adopted in the sixteenth century) were not basically in disagreement with the teachings of the Catholic Church. The differences between the Roman Catholic and Anglican communions were, in Newman's opinion, matters of organization only. A century before ecumenical inclusiveness became an occupation of the churches, Newman's tract argued for unity in faith between Catholics and Anglicans.

John Henry Newman, 1888.

Newman revitalized Catholicism in England and as a creative thinker gave it new intellectual credibility.

This Tract, which caused an uproar in Anglican circles, launched Newman on a new and meteoric but controversial career. In 1843 he resigned his position at St. Mary's. Two years later, after a long period of study and reflection, he was received into the Roman Catholic Church by a traveling Italian priest. Within six months he was in Rome, where he was ordained a priest in May 1846. In 1849, having returned to England, he established near Birmingham a religious house, or "Oratory," dedicated to St. Philip Neri (1515–1595), founder of the Congregation of the Oratory and a helper of young men in need of spiritual guidance. Newman's interest in education was enhanced when he was appointed first rector (1852–1859) of the new Catholic University of Ireland (now University College Dublin). His insights into the nature of education, and the role of religion in modern university life, are lucidly, even at times wittily, preserved in *The Idea of a University* (1852; 2nd ed., 1858). (Today, Newman's renown as an educator is commemorated on university campuses worldwide in Newman Centers and Clubs for Catholic students.) Newman was made a cardinal in 1879. He died at his Oratory in August 1890.

Newman's influence was greater in his books than in his administrative work. In *An Essay in Aid of a Grammar of Assent* (1870) he offers a study of the epistemology of religious belief, a philosophical work of a high order, and as subtle in argument as anything in English. In contrast to the empiricist tradition of the eighteenth century, Newman here defends the place of the conscience within humans, and identifies faith as an act of conscience. Conscience for Newman is what leads persons to states of awe, reverence, and fear, and it is in the conscience that piety, or the fear of God, is located. Like other religious writers of the time, Newman defends religion as experience, and so bypasses questions of the existence and attributes of God, or the meaning of the revealed status of Scripture. Those were veritable minefields in that skeptical age, and Newman, no less than Schleiermacher (see Chapter 22), manages to avoid them. In his 1845 study *An Essay on the Development of Christian Doctrine*, Newman applies a doctrinal variant of the scientific evolutionary theory to the body of Christian teaching, interpreting the doctrine of the church as an evolving organism, shedding the old and adding the new, rather than as a fixed body of beliefs progressively coming into view. (The theory of evolution of species actually antedated Darwin, its leading proponents at the beginning of the century being Georges Cuvier [1769–1832] and Jean Baptiste de Lamarck [1744–1829].) Newman became aware of this evolutionary character of Christian doctrine in his study of the development of Christology (the study of Christ's Person, or nature) during the period of the early ecumenical councils—research published as *The Arians of the Fourth Century* (1833; 3rd ed., 1871).

In his *Apologia pro Vita Sua* (1864), Newman offers an account of the organic development of his own work as well as a defense of his evolution from Anglican to Roman Catholic. In the course of this extended autobiographical essay, which, like all of his work, is meant to instruct the greatest number of people, Newman sees the Roman Church as the necessary culmination of the development of the previous centuries. His own progress in religion, in other words, paralleled the evolution of Christianity itself. (See "John Henry Newman.")

The Oxford Movement

John Keble (1792–1866) Oxford University academic and leader of the "Tractarians." He campaigned to hold back the increasing liberalization of the Church of England and to retain high-church influences. Keble College, Oxford, is named after him.

Edward Bouverie Pusey (1800–1882) Another "Tractarian" leader and Oxford academic with a particular zeal for high-church practices. In 1845, he helped to found the first Anglican sisterhood.

John Henry Newman (1801–1890) Theologian, academic, and later Cardinal. A leading figure of the Oxford Movement and a major "Tractarian," he converted from Anglicanism to Roman Catholicism in 1845. His beliefs had a significant influence on the Roman Catholic Church in the 20th century.

Alexander Penrose Forbes (1817–1875) A leading "Tractarian" in Scotland and Bishop of Brechin from 1848.

Henry Scott Holland (1847–1918) Canon of St. Pauls and theological academic at Oxford University. As co-founder of the Christian Social Union, he tried to apply Christian teaching to everyday social ills.

John Henry Newman

John Henry Newman's Apologia pro Vita Sua *(1864) is a record of his progress toward Roman Catholicism. In this passage he describes points in his religious development, noting that Calvinism and Law's "Serious Call" played roles in the process.*

Calvinists make a sharp separation between the elect and the world; there is much in this that is parallel or cognate to the Catholic doctrine; but they go on to say, as I understand them, very differently from Catholicism,—that the converted and the unconverted can be discriminated by man, that the justified are conscious of their state of justification, and that the regenerate cannot fall away. Catholics on the other hand shade and soften the awful antagonism between good and evil, which is one of their dogmas, by holding that there are different degrees of justification, that there is a great difference in point of gravity between sin and sin, that there is the possibility and the danger of falling away, and that there is no certain knowledge given to any one that he is simply in a state of grace, and much less that he is to persevere to the end:—of the Calvinistic tenets the only one which took root in my mind was the fact of heaven and hell, divine favour and divine wrath, of the justified and the unjustified. The notion that the regenerate and the justified were one and the same, and that the regenerate, as such, had the gift of perseverance, remained with me not many years, as I have said already.

This main Catholic doctrine of the warfare between the city of God and the powers of darkness was also deeply impressed upon my mind by a work of a very opposite character, Law's "Serious Call."

(From *Apologia pro Vita Sua*. London: Everyman's Library, 1912.)

Evolution

Charles Darwin

In some ways, the most influential figure of Victorian-era religion in England was not Newman, or any other churchman for that matter, but the renegade naturalist Charles Darwin (1809–1882). In *The Origin of Species by Means of Natural Selection* (1859) and particularly in *The Descent of Man* (1871), Darwin challenged religious anthropology as thoroughly as biblical scholarship was debunking assumptions about sacred revelation. In his study of the relations of species, Darwin offered the hypothesis that each species in the animal kingdom had its origin in some other one, and that adaptation to the environment—rather than creation by a divine hand—was the reason for the differentiation observable in nature. This would have had little impact on religious thought had it been limited to lower life forms, but according to Darwin's theory, all life—human included—had evolved from the same organic base. Thus humans were part and parcel of the expansion of life into various forms, and no longer a separate category of God's creative work.

The effect of this theory on religious belief was enormous. In a single blow, it overthrew generations of belief that God had created and ordered all beasts according to a divine plan, and that some primordial Adam and Eve had been placed at the apex of this creation and made in God's own image. The Darwinian hypothesis threatened nothing less than the entire Christian sense of order, and seemed to put the church in a dilemma between rejecting the new discoveries and thus appearing hostile to science, or adapting in response to the new developments, and thus jeopardizing the sacred truths of the Christian faith.

Separating Nineteenth-Century Science from Religion

The dilemma was resolved by separating religious truths from scientific facts, thus isolating Scripture from science; see, for example, the work of theologians such as Frederick Temple (1821–1902), Headmaster of Rugby School, Bishop of

George Richmond, *Charles Darwin*, 1840. Watercolor. Down House, Kent, England.

The naturalist's researches into the development of species challenged adherents to the biblical creation narrative, while also prompting a sense of evolutionary development within Christianity itself.

Exeter, and a president of the Devonshire Association for the Advancement of Science, Literature, and the Arts. Many such organizations were founded in England toward the end of the century, some with quite distinguished members. In his lectures to this group, Temple, a churchman of genuine distinction who would go on to be Archbishop of Canterbury, reconciled religion and science by offering a religious rationale for scientific study. Echoing a theological view that extends back to Scholasticism and the Reformation, Temple maintained that closer study of nature could deepen awareness of God's work.

In 1884 Temple gave the Bampton Lectures at Oxford, an important center for original theological work. Speaking on the relation between religion and science, Temple acknowledged evolution but viewed it from a religious perspective, seeing the developing of life in its countless forms as the unfolding of a divine plan. To Temple, there was nothing about science that actually contradicted Genesis—although we should remember that the Bible's "truth" was not a literal one. Temple's Bampton Lectures were a scientifically astute restatement of the argument from design (see Chapter 21), and are considered the point at which Christians in England could begin to feel comfortable with evolution.

The reluctance of Temple and his fellow Anglican bishops to reject scientific investigation as false, or to capitulate and reduce Christian teachings to a set of moral precepts, helped the Church of England to survive its encounter with evolution and the scientific tradition that accompanied it. Thanks in part to Temple's initiative as an educational reformer, science found a solid place in education, at both the secondary and university level; and public institutions continued to thrive as forums for religious and scientific discussion. The Bampton Lectures were followed, in 1888, by the Gifford Lectures, delivered in Scottish universities, which became the platform for a highly distinguished roster of religious and philosophical thinkers during the twentieth century and into the twenty-first. Whether through university sponsorship (as in the Bampton and Gifford Lectures), ecclesiastical patronage (particularly through schools), or civic initiative (the community societies), the challenges facing religion became, in Britain, topics for broad public engagement.

Key Term

ESTABLISHED CHURCH The church authorized by secular sovereignty to be the religion of the state; usually used of the Church of England.

Nineteenth-century America

Religious Diversity and Revivalism

The European absolutist principle, formalized at Augsburg in 1555 and reinforced in the Westphalian Peace of 1648, which gave the ruler of a country the right to dictate religion, was not going to a be a working model for the young American republic. The religious diversity of the colonies (now states), their repudiation of anything that smacked of monarchy, and anxieties over the churches' influence in political life led (as noted in Chapter 20) to the constitutional principle of separation of church and state. Religion was to be a matter of private choice and individual exercise; it was among the first of the freedoms guaranteed in the Bill of Rights. Hence the idea that a region could be identified with a single confession, as had been the case in Europe, was an impossibility in the new states. This did not mean that there were not dominant religious traditions in given regions; but this was through historical happenstance, not law. Formally if not actually, all of the American states, some of them previously "monoreligious" colonies, became multireligious civil communities.

It was a difficult transition for many churches, which had previously not had to share public space with all other religious groups that wanted to set up shop in a community. Religious leaders who may have seen their form of Christianity as the only path to salvation found themselves restraining their rhetoric out of courtesy toward their fellow citizens who belonged to other churches. The irony of the Reformation and its aftermath—the proliferation of a bewildering number of competing, indeed mutually exclusive, claims to truth and salvation—met its most severe challenge in early-nineteenth-century America. For whereas in Europe each religion had been shielded from most of its competition, in America the competitive spirit seemed to be working at full force.

During the colonial period most forms of Christianity in North America had been provincial in the extreme: they had origins and ties with hierarchies and authorities back in Europe, but were for practical purposes relatively independent and disorganized. Clerical training and ordination were under colonial auspices, and the churches were in close enough touch with each other to form their own administrative structures.

Formalizing American Protestant Denominations

These haphazard arrangements needed to be formalized, and the decades after the Revolution saw a number of measures designed to set the American churches firmly on native soil. For example, in 1789 the Protestant Episcopal (Anglican) Church in the United States of America was formally organized, its first bishop, the former Tory Samuel Seabury (1729–1796), having been consecrated by a Scottish Episcopal bishop five years earlier. Seabury had actually been a loyalist during the Revolution and was imprisoned for a while by the patriots; he couldn't later be consecrated by a Church of England bishop because he could not now take the oath of allegiance to the British Crown. But the Scottish Anglicans didn't require this formality, so the apostolic succession was preserved.

The first American Roman Catholic bishop, John Carroll (1735–1815), was consecrated (in England) in 1790 in the chapel at Lulworth Castle, Dorset, which was the first Roman Catholic Church built legally in England (in 1786, by special permission of George III) since the Reformation.

Soon American editions of prayer books and Bibles began to appear, symbols of autonomy. Declarations from American-based bishops and other church leaders became more authoritative for Americans than those from European ones. And styles of worship developed to suit the new social and political milieu.

Despite its resolute refusal to adopt an official church, the United States saw itself as a Christian nation and, in particular, a predominantly Protestant one. The force of conviction that had led the sixteenth-century reformers to break from the "tyranny" of Rome seemed to echo in the colonists' rejection of British rule and their creation of their own social and religious world. But with the new opportunities came new problems. Did citizenship relate primarily to a state, or to the nation? Was American identity merely political, or cultural as well, so that one could speak of American "ways" and not only of American government structures? Did the values of independence and freedom enshrined in the Declaration of Independence impose on all individuals an obligation to respect others' choices? These and other questions had not been part of the mainstream of Western political thought, but they were urgent matters as the new nation sought to define itself.

Many of the questions bearing on national identity bore on religious identity as well, for the American religious consciousness developed alongside the national one. The questions surrounding national citizenship were echoed in questions of church identification: was one a Christian, or a Methodist? Did a person's religious values determine his or her activity in public life, or only private morality? If a person

Richard Upjohn, *Trinity Church*, Warsaw, New York, 1854.

Part rustic, part Gothic, church architecture such as this demonstrated how certain denominations saw themselves bridging old traditions and pioneer communities.

belonged to a church that saw itself as the only path to salvation, then did he or she follow the dictates of that religion and try to impose it on others, or observe the nation's principle of freedom of religion and let the neighbor follow a path to supposed damnation? Many of these questions continue today to emerge occasionally as flash points of public debate in liberal democracies.

The various American Protestant Churches—now called DENOMINATIONS—began to see themselves less as mutually exclusive religions than as parts of the Christian Church as a whole, but collaborating in the shaping of a religious nation. Their heightened sense of common faith was augmented by an awareness that the differences between them were more historically than theologically conditioned: cultural variants were present but subsumed within a shared purpose.

The coexistence of denominations may not have resulted in competition among churches, but it did call for a voluntary element which has been considered one of the defining marks of American religion. The fact that Protestant Christians were often presented with a range of churches within a given community meant that each person or family was able to choose a religion to which to belong. With choice came a higher possible level of commitment, as we saw in the early church and in movements aimed at "conversion" within Christianity. Religion, we recall (see Chapter 4), can be either natural or voluntary: one either is born into a tradition or chooses it. In the case of American Protestantism, these two modes coexisted, since most Americans of the early nineteenth century were born into Protestant families, and yet were free to choose from a variety of options. Jonathan Edwards's call to conversion, along with the other voices of the Great Awakening (see Chapter 20), echoed in the religious life of the new nation.

Expanding Frontiers

Around 1900 the historian Frederick Jackson Turner (1861–1932) offered an interpretation of American culture that has had a powerful influence in U.S. historiography. Generally referred to as the "frontier thesis," Turner's point was that a pioneering spirit has always informed the American imagination. Whereas the densely populated European communities of the early-modern period were confined to a relatively stationary existence, the vast North American continent was a rich source of challenges and opportunities. Hence expansion across an ever-receding frontier was from the outset an integral element of the culture.

Although religion did not form part of Turner's area of study, his thesis applies to nineteenth-century religious history as well. An impulse to extend the frontier marking the boundary between Christian and Native culture was part of the colonial imagination as early as the seventeenth century. Early missionary efforts to bring Christianity to the Native Americans included translations of the Bible into indigenous languages, creation of schools for their instruction, religious and otherwise (Harvard College had an "Indian annex" almost from its founding, in 1639), and itinerant expeditions by well-trained preachers. In the eighteenth century Jonathan Edwards was for a while a missionary among Native Americans; so was his protégé David Brainerd and also Eleazer Wheelock, the founder in 1754 of a charity school for Native Americans. Later, this became part of Dartmouth College (1769), of which Wheelock was the first president. Two Baptists from New

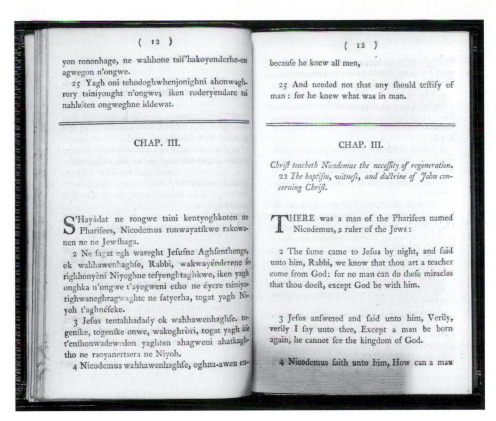

(12)

yon rononhage, ne wahhone tsif'hakoyenderhe-on agwegon n'ongwe.

25 Yagh oni tehodoghwhenjonighni ahonwaghrory tsiniyought n'ongwe; iken roderyendare tsi nahhóten ongweghne iddewat.

─────────────────────

CHAP. III.

S'Hayàdat ne rongwe tsini kentyoghkoten ne Pharifees, Nicodemus ronwayatſkwe rakowanen ne ne Jewfhaga.

2 Ne fagat egh wareght Jefufne Aghfenthenge, ok wahhawenhaghfe, Rabbi, wakwayénderene ſerighhonyèni Niyoghne tefyenghtaghkwe, iken yagh onghka n'ongwe t'ayegweni etho ne éyere tsiniyotighwaneghragwaghte ne fatyerha, togat yagh Niyoh t'aghnéfeke.

3 Jefus tentahhadady ok wahhawenhaghfe. togenfke, togenfke onwe, wakoghròri, togat yagh àfe t'enfhonwadewedon yaghten ahagweni ahatkaghtho ne raoyanertsera ne Niyoh.

4 Nicodemus wahhawenhaghfe, oghna-awen en-

(12)

becauſe he knew all men,

25 And needed not that any ſhould teſtify of man : for he knew what was in man.

─────────────────────

CHAP. III.

Chriſt teacheth Nicodemus the neceſſity of regeneration.
22 The baptiſm, witneſs, and doctrine of John concerning Chriſt.

THERE was a man of the Phariſees named Nicodemus, a ruler of the Jews :

2 The ſame came to Jeſus by night, and ſaid unto him, Rabbi, we know that thou art a teacher come from God: for no man can do theſe miracles that thou doeſt, except God be with him.

3 Jeſus anſwered and ſaid unto him, Verily, verily I ſay unto thee, Except a man be born again, he cannot ſee the kingdom of God.

4 Nicodemus ſaith unto him, How can a man

Two pages from a Mohawk Bible, 1864. John Rylands Library, University of Manchester.

In this version of the Bible, the Mohawk language is printed on the left pages and an American English translation on the right pages.

England, Shubael Stearns (1706–1771) and his brother-in-law Daniel Marshall (1706–1784) took their preaching to the South, establishing Baptist Associations in North Carolina and Georgia. Marshall, the founder of the Georgia association, spent two years as a missionary among Native Americans.

Once the republic was established and denominational headquarters in operation, the church's move westward began in earnest. Church buildings formed part of the original fabric of frontier towns. Recognizing the value of churches to a community, the founders of towns, almost as general policy, would set aside a section of land for building churches. If the town was organized around a central square, one side of the square might be reserved for this purpose. Elsewhere a centrally located parcel of land, perhaps a few blocks square, would be made available, usually at much reduced prices, to the first ecclesiastical takers. In one town a block might be divided to accommodate a church, a cemetery, and a church-run school; in another, a parcel of land might be sold to a denomination at preferential rates on the condition that a church costing a certain sum would be built within a five-year period. Since the settlers were accompanied by other lay members of their own denominations, there was little likelihood that a Presbyterian Church, for example, would dominate a community settled mostly by Methodists. Thus by tracing the pattern of church building in the American West, we can learn something about the expansion of the various denominations.

Colleges were another important part of the churches' presence on the frontier. The westward expansion of the denominations is prominently documented in such institutions as Ohio University in Athens, Ohio (1804; originally Presbyterian, now nonsectarian); Illinois Wesleyan (1850); Oberlin College in Ohio (1833; originally Congregational, now nonsectarian); and Loras College in Iowa (1839; Catholic). The list could be multiplied many times, but the point is the same: higher education came to the American West with religion, and its original purpose was to preserve the religious and moral values of the established eastern communities. Religious instruction was a part of the curriculum, as was compulsory chapel—sometimes daily but at least weekly—almost everywhere for most of the century.

Religious Settlement and Cultural Change

With the waves of immigration that began in the middle of the nineteenth century, the cultural composition of the United States, and especially the West, where land was cheap, began to change. Churches began to appear that preserved the language and rituals of the regions from which most of their members came; it was not hard to find Lutheran churches offering German and English services back-to-back, or colleges such as Hope and Calvin, both in Michigan, that tried to preserve the history and traditions of Calvinist Holland, as well as its language. Some of the most visible denominations of twentieth-century America had their origins in these immigrant communities: one thinks of the Lutheran Church-Missouri Synod, founded by Germans in the 1830s (and German-speaking, or at least bilingual, for a century thereafter), or the Christian Reformed (Calvinist) Church, created by Dutch immigrants to Michigan and devoted to Holland as their cultural homeland. A trace of New Amsterdam's Dutch Reformed tradition (see Chapter 20) remains in New York's Collegiate School for boys (now nondenominational), founded in 1628. As we saw in Chapter 20, the New Sweden colony on the Delaware River was ephemeral. Its church, Gloria Dei, became Episcopalian in the 1850s; and its founding families had long since assimilated into the English culture of the Quakers and Anglicans who followed them up the river. In the mid-nineteenth century, however, many thousands of Swedes and other Scandinavians came to the United States, settling primarily in Wisconsin, Minnesota, and Iowa, and establishing a strong Lutheran presence in these states.

The Midwest during the nineteenth century was a far more ethnically diverse area than many people suppose. In the popular imagination (fed by films), the settling of the western territories was achieved almost entirely by descendants of the original (mainly British) colonists, while the eastern cities became more and more cosmopolitan, receiving boatloads of new citizens from Germany, Ireland, Italy, eastern Europe, and eventually everybody from everywhere. In fact, although the initial settling of the land beyond the Appalachians had begun as an expansion movement by the mature settlements along the East Coast, by the 1880s the Midwest had become a cultural "melting-pot" (to use the popular but misleading term for this mixture, in which the "ingredients" generally remained easily identifiable) of daunting proportions. The Europeans who braved the harsh conditions of the frontier had to set aside any religious and ethnic prejudices brought with them from the Old World in order to achieve the political freedom and economic prosperity that had drawn them to the New. At the same time, however, they needed to retain a sense of their own identity, and in this respect, their churches played a crucial role.

Thus we see, in midwestern American cities, the establishment of parishes for the various ethnic constituencies. For example, in Iowa City, Iowa, separate Catholic parishes were formed for the Irish, German, and Czech populations of that small city (the state capitol only from 1846 to 1855). In larger cities, such as Chicago, separate Polish and Italian Catholic churches appeared. Many of these took on the responsibility for preserving ethnic traditions at a time when the pressure on their parishioners to "Americanize" was heaviest. To the implicit question, "How am I still Irish [or Italian, or Spanish, etc.]?" the church answered, in effect: "This is your home. We will keep language and folkways alive, so far as we can. The U.S. Constitution allows us, the church, the freedom to help you, the citizen, achieve a fusion of who you were—or who your ancestors were—and who you now are, as citizen and as Christian."

In far too many ways to list, religious institutions helped the new settlers of the nineteenth century negotiate the conflicts between their ethnic identity and their new citizenship, in which ethnic backgrounds did not matter. To an extent unprecedented in Europe, the ethnic churches in America sponsored events intended to enhance pride in cultural identity (often through national religious festivals and observances with special meaning to particular ethnic religious traditions: Czech, Polish, or Greek, for example). Their civic cultures, meanwhile, promoted observances equally remote, from a cultural angle at any rate, from their religious lives. What meaning would Thanksgiving, with its New England origins, have for New Yorkers or Southerners? Or how could St. Lucia, with its Swedish origins, ever become a truly American holiday? These were all variants on the century-old question of what it meant to be an American. The freedoms guaranteed by the Constitution would guarantee that this was a question without easy or obvious answers.

The Second Great Awakening

While the religious character of the United States was becoming more and more diverse, it was also undergoing periodic waves of intensification—at least among Protestants. This was not a new phenomenon: in the 1730s the first Great Awakening (see Chapter 20) had spread through most of the Thirteen Colonies. A similar revival movement took place a century later. (Some historians have spoken of a third and fourth awakening; we must wait to see if those are regarded as legitimate movements.) We have an incomplete picture of American religious life in the nineteenth century if we ignore the enthusiasm that swept over American college campuses in the 1820s and 1830s. Documents from this period are full of reports of students swooning before the rhetoric of visiting preachers; and within a few years such pious enthusiasm became a cause more for concern than for rejoicing. But whatever its benefits or drawbacks, this movement extended across the frontier and dominated American religious life for decades.

The origins of the Second Great Awakening are as elusive as those of the first, possibly more so. The movement seems to have originated at Yale, particularly under the presidency of Timothy Dwight (1752–1817; president of Yale from 1795 until his death), who was a grandson of Jonathan Edwards and a formidable religious writer in his own right. From those Congregationalist origins, in which Dwight was joined by protégés such as Lyman Beecher (1775–1863), Asahel Nettleton (1783–1844), and Nathaniel William Taylor (1786–1858), there arose a movement of preaching and conversion that swept through North America. The Second Great Awakening was an academic phenomenon before it spread to the Protestant public at large, but in both of these phases it testified to the need for emotional expression by a generally straitlaced populace.

The Phenomenon of the Revivalist Tradition

The Second Great Awakening was followed by many other waves of REVIVALISM, a phenomenon that has remained endemic in the United States ever since. Essentially, revivalism is a form of missionary work within Christianity itself; its message is the need for intensified commitment to Christ. The nineteenth-century revivalists were itinerant preachers, active mostly on the western frontier, who considered it their mission to warn people against sin and exhort them to repentance. Revivals were major events in rural America, arranged months beforehand and eagerly attended by almost the whole community. Unlike a conventional sermon, the revivalist's message involved the audience, as loud acclamations and dramatic gestures of penitential self-abasement became part of the event. A standard feature of revivals was the "anxious bench," a seat near the front, where those who were moved to make public renunciation of their sins awaited their opportunity.

The beginnings of the revivalist tradition can be seen in the camp meetings organized by the Presbyterians James McCready (1758–1817) and Barton Stone (1772–1844) in Kentucky and North Carolina in the early years of the century. Stone founded his own church, which he called simply the Christian Church, perhaps as an indication of its inclusiveness. Thomas Campbell (1763–1854) and

---

Who's Who

The Revivalists

James McCready (1758–1817) Presbyterian preacher and an early revivalist. With Barton Stone, he organized camp meetings in North Carolina and Kentucky during the early 1800s.

Thomas Campbell (1763–1854) and Alexander Campbell (1788–1866) Father and son were Presbyterians, originally from Ireland. They arrived in the U.S.A. in the early 1800s and founded the Disciples of Christ church. This merged with Barton Stone's followers in Kentucky to form a flourishing movement—the Christian Church (Disciples of Christ), still very active today.

Barton Stone (1772–1844) Presbyterian preacher and co-organizer of revivalist camp meetings with James McCready. Stone founded his own Christian Church, which later merged with that of the Campbells.

Charles Grandison Finney (1792–1875) American traveling revivalist preacher and theology professor (Oberlin College, Ohio). Famous for pioneering an evangelical preaching style and revivalist traditions that included very long religious meetings.

his son Alexander Campbell (1788–1866), both also originally Presbyterians, but born in Ulster, came to the United States in the early 1800s and to advance their ministry founded a church of their own, known as the Disciples of Christ; it later merged with Stone's group, and today their church, now quite mainstream and stationary, is called the Christian Church (Disciples of Christ).

The Influence of Charles Finney and Dwight Moody

In Charles Grandison Finney (1792–1875) we have an orator in the same class as Edwards, and a figure whose influence in American religious practice matches Edwards's place in theology. A lawyer by training and for a while president of Oberlin College, in Ohio, Finney was largely responsible for making revivalism a continuing dimension of American religious life. Finney saw revival as a constant need; and it was he who defined revival as a natural and necessary element of religion. For Finney, the life of a congregation is cyclical; it swings from piety to backsliding and back again; and it is the function of the revival to return the members of a church to a renewed faith. Awareness of sinfulness and consequent repentance are thus integral to the Christian life, and needed, Finney felt, to be ritualized in the revival meeting.

Finney's influence is perhaps most clearly seen in Dwight Lyman Moody (1837–1899), an unordained independent Christian, founder and planner of a number of institutions, among them what is now Moody Bible Institute (1889), in Chicago. Moody's impact was broadest, however, in a number of "crusades" he led throughout the United States (and also in Britain), beginning in the 1870s. A Moody revival, often held under a big tent (our use of this term for an all-inclusive gathering comes from the revivals), was a major event for a town, an extravaganza far beyond any traditional church services. There was original choral music; the oratory was enthusiastic and unstoppable; the anxious bench was always

A Moody and Sankey Meeting at the Agricultural Hall, 1876. Engraving.

"'Crazy Moody,' as he was called when he gave up 1,200 dollars a year as a clerk in a boot store, is now known as 'Brother Moody,' and has come among us to evangelise England and to convert heathen as degraded as cannibals...."

occupied; and many felt purified, or at least closer to God, from the experience. More diligent church attendance—to Moody it did not matter which church it was—inevitably followed. (See "Dwight Lyman Moody.")

Moody had followers and successors; for Finney had been right in identifying a constant need for the revival experience. Reuben Torrey (1856–1928) was a helper and successor to Moody, the first president of the Bible Institute and a crusader in his own right; so was J. Wilbur Chapman (1859–1918). From Chapman it is a short step to the baseball player-turned-evangelist Billy Sunday (1862–1935), whose personal story and oratorical histrionics moved many. With another Billy, Billy Graham (b. 1918), we have a continuation of the revival in technological society, with international broadcasts and a media center capable of sending the Graham gospel message to every corner of the world. Graham is a continuation of

Dwight Lyman Moody

Dwight Lyman Moody was one of the most energetic revivalists of his time, and the founder of boarding schools in New England and a Bible college in Chicago. In this excerpt from the sermon What Will You Do with Jesus, *Moody compares the vacillating Christian of his day with Pilate at Jesus' trial.*

Pilate wanted to get rid of the responsibility. And others told him that He had disturbed the whole country and that if he released Him he would not be a sincere friend of the people. And so he was forced into a decision. He had to decide whether he would receive Him or reject Him. There may be some here tonight that have not received Christ. But you have got to decide some time. You must either decide to receive Him or reject Him. Pilate was vacillating, and so he said he would call upon them to decide. He thought they would all want Christ released rather than Barabbas. Christ had given life, Barabbas had taken life. Barabbas was not only a thief, but he was a murderer, and he thought, surely the Jews would rather have him out for execution than the Son of God. But they insisted upon having Barabbas released, and then he said, "What shall I do with Jesus who is called Christ?" and the cry went up, "Let Him be crucified." Then Pilate, washing his hands, said, "I am innocent of this just man's blood." And they cried out, "His blood be upon us and our children." There are a great many men now like Pilate, they think they can shift the responsibility. But bear in mind that God gave Himself up freely for us all. God sends Him to each one of us, and we must decide what we will do. We must either reject Him or receive Him. The trouble with Pilate was that it was not for his earthly interest to decide in favor of Christ. Instead of deciding it like a man he was vacillating, and wanted to be popular with the people. This vacillating man gave way. Instead of deciding what he knew was right he let the public influence him. How many men do you think would become Christians inside of forty-eight hours if it were not for public opinion? How many men are convinced that God can save them from sin, that He can redeem them from the curse of the law, but are withheld from acknowledging it from fear of public opinion, from fear of what professed friends may say? There are more men lost for the want of decision than for anything else. Pilate thought that Christ would perhaps cross his path again, and he could then show some kindness to Him. But it was the last time that he ever saw Him. It may be that the Son of God is coming to-night, and to you for the last time. The question is "What will you do with Him?" May God help us to decide what we shall do with him.

(From *To All People*. New York: E. B. Treat, 1877.)

the revivalist tradition, but without the regional flavor of the nineteenth-century tent meetings.

Having traced the outlines of Christian expansion in nineteenth-century North America—especially among Protestant denominations—and the burgeoning of revivalism, we must now look at the ways in which the Roman Catholic Church endeavored throughout that century to deal with the political and intellectual movements that often threatened to undermine it.

Key Terms

DENOMINATION Any of the various forms or sects of Christianity.

REVIVALISM A form of Christianity centered around waves of conversion and repentance sweeping through regions; it is characterized by passionate preaching, "tent meetings," and emotional affirmations of faith.

Roman Catholicism
Confronting the Modern World

The essentially conservative stamp that the Council of Trent placed upon Roman Catholicism (see Chapter 18) did not dampen a creative impulse within the tradition. Ritual, always strong within Catholicism, was enhanced by the intensely dramatic surroundings and embellishments that now attended it. As we noted in Chapter 18, baroque artists, architects, and composers collaborated to overwhelm worshipers with a sense of divine mystery and power, and the presence of the church within culture.

In quieter ways, too, the seventeenth century was an age of intense devotion, as one sees in the mysticism of such women as Margaret Mary Alacoque (1647–1690), advocate of the devotion to the Sacred Heart of Jesus, and Jeanne Marie Bouvier de la Mothe Guyon (1648–1717), whose *Short and Very Easy Method of Prayer* (1685) brought a threefold program of mental prayer (consisting of meditation, the "prayer of simplicity," and "active contemplation," a type of disciplined passivity) to a lay public.

The eighteenth century saw the foundation of new religious orders, such as the contemplative Redemptorists, founded in Italy by Alphonsus Liguori (1696–1787). This order—like the Lazarist Fathers and the Sisters of Charity, both founded by Vincent de Paul (c.1580–1660)—were missionary orders, in the broad sense of the term, dedicated to revival and renewal within the Catholic Church.

All of these developments, however, were changes within Catholicism; at the same time, changes in the larger outside world were driving the church and secular society farther apart. The revolutions of the late eighteenth century (fueled by ideas that had been circulating since the English Civil War; see Chapter 20); the rise of industrialism in the early nineteenth century; the various revolutions of 1848: all of these posed threats to the authority of the Catholic Church. The nineteenth century was a far different world from the seventeenth, a fact that the Catholic hierarchy recognized slowly and with difficulty. Even when it did, the response was defensive and divisive, rejecting the changes in the secular world, rather than constructively seeking a way to bring the church more into step with the world around it. The result was a Catholic Church that by the mid-nineteenth century had clearly adopted a reactionary posture toward the outside world. In fact, the effort to stay the same in a changing environment made it even more reactionary than it had been in the sixteenth and seventeenth centuries. By the end of the nineteenth century, Catholicism and modernity were aligned in opposing camps.

A Reasonable Pope: Pius VII

The Catholic Church entered the nineteenth century under a very dark cloud: the French Revolution. One of the main targets of the extreme revolutionaries had been the church—not only its hierarchy but also its beliefs. Following the 1790 Civil Constitution of the Clergy, which placed the church under state administrative control, the extremists in 1793 launched a policy of dechristianization and began promoting a cult of Reason, complete with picturesque pageants, as the approved religion. Later this was replaced by a deistic "Worship of the Supreme Being." Things seemed to be taking a turn for the better in 1801, when the new government of France, led by First Consul (soon to be emperor) Napoleon Bonaparte (1769–1821; r. 1804–1814) made peace, of a sort, with the papacy. The CONCORDAT of 1801 formally acknowledged Roman Catholicism as the official religion and provided for state support of the clergy, but it gave the state many powers over the church—powers that Napoleon increased the following year, without papal consent.

The pope during this period, Pius VII (1740–1823; r. 1800–1823), was a negotiator as well as a moderately progressive spirit, one who wished to preserve the tradition even amidst drastically new social circumstances. Pius VII was also responsible for the restoration of the Jesuit order. In his bull *Sollicitudo omnium ecclesiarum* of August 1814, the pope granted the general of the order (which had never actually dissolved, despite its ban) and his successors all means necessary to revitalize their work for the church.

Pius VII was followed by two unremarkable popes and then by Gregory XVI (1765–1846; r. 1831–1846), whose reign was marked by political unrest in the Papal States (Italian territories owned by the papacy since 754) and who helped to develop the doctrine of papal infallibility, which would become a key issue (see below) later in the century. Meanwhile, the uneasy peace that Europe had experienced since the Napoleonic wars was about to be shattered, while philosophical, theological, and scientific developments would present yet more challenges to Catholicism. The man who would lead the church through the next three tumultuous decades was determined to hold the line against any further threats to papal authority.

A Reactionary Pope: Pius IX

The man who took the name Pius IX (1792–1878; r. 1846–1878) was the dominant figure of nineteenth-century Catholicism. He remains a highly controversial one. To conservative Catholics he was the leader who guided the church through a difficult phase of the modern era. To liberals within and outside the church, he was the pontiff who resisted modernity with declarations that today seem as stubborn and wrongheaded as the flat-earth notion of the Middle Ages. If one views Pius's pontificate as neutrally as possible, as an attempt to preserve the Catholic tradition amid a torrent of change in the political, economic, and scientific realms, it would have to stand as a heroic—if not entirely successful—effort. Such was surely the pontiff's understanding of his role.

The epileptic son of a noble Italian family, Giovanni Mastai-Ferretti was ordained a priest in 1819 and became a cardinal in 1840. At the beginning of his career, he had a reputation for progressive ideas, but his pontificate was soon torn by conflict as he sought to maintain control of the Papal States just as nationalist revolutionaries such as Giuseppe Mazzini (1805–1872) and Giuseppe Garibaldi (1807–1882) were trying to unify the various Italian territories into an independent nation. By the end of 1870, all the Papal States, including Rome, were part of the new Italian state. Pius himself was confined, during the last eight years of his life, to the Vatican complex, where he ruled like a monarch but considered himself a prisoner. Some of his attitudes toward the secular world must be seen as the result of his embattled political life.

Revolutionary Ferment

To understand this crucial period in papal history, we need to set it within an even broader context. Although the revolutions of 1848 did not achieve their egalitarian goals, they certainly ushered in many political changes. In France, the February Revolution brought a new government: the so-called Second Republic (1848–1852), whose president, Prince Louis-Napoleon (1808–1873), proclaimed a new empire four years later, with himself as Emperor Napoleon III (r. 1852–1870; his cousin Napoleon II, son of the great Napoleon, never reigned). In Germany, a series of upheavals led to the brief formation, in 1848, of a constitutional assembly, held in Frankfurt, which attempted to create a coalition government of previously independent states, but failed to do so. (One participant in the Rhineland uprising of 1848 was Karl Marx, whose pamphlet *The Communist Manifesto*, a collaboration with his friend Friedrich Engels [1820–1895], had just been published.)

Nationalistic uprisings in the multiethnic Austrian Empire, notably by the Hungarians, were followed by an insurrection of working men and students in Vienna—events that drove the autocratic chancellor, Prince Clemens von Metternich (1773–1859), into exile in England. On the abdication of Emperor Ferdinand I (1793–1875; r.1835–1848), Franz Joseph (1830–1916; r. 1848–1916) ascended the throne which he would occupy for the next sixty-eight years. The Austrian presence in northern Italy was attacked by nationalist Italians, who proclaimed a (short-lived) Roman Republic in February 1849. No period for centuries could have been a more tumultuous one during which to ascend to the papacy.

Amid such revolutionary fervor, Pius IX's reactionary stance is perhaps understandable. The papacy was, in effect, a monarchy, an endangered species; a divinely privileged order in an era that saw such claims as aristocratic fictions.

Moreover, it was a source of religious teachings at a time when such teachings were being scornfully dismissed by many people as sinister myths. Pius had learned from the pontificate of Pius VII that true democracy was compatible with Christianity; and he remained convinced that any democracy that drove out Christianity was a false one. As to the papacy, it was structurally different from secular states; the charge given to Peter needed to be kept by Peter's successors, and neither divided nor delegated. Pius IX retained his power by acting like a ruler of state, even as the papal territories were being reduced by Italian nationalist forces. (The fact that Pius had enlisted the help of French and Austrian troops did not endear him to the Italians.)

Pius IX's Attacks on Protestantism and Progress

The first sign that this pontificate was going to be a tumultuous one came on December 8, 1854, with the bull *Ineffabilis Deus*. In this declaration Pius IX elevated to official dogma the belief, held for many centuries, that the Virgin Mary had herself been born without original sin, thus making her an exception to the human condition. This doctrine, called the IMMACULATE CONCEPTION, placed Mary in a special category, farther from the general lot of humanity and closer than ever before to the Trinity. It hardly needs stating that this bull accentuated differences between the Roman Church and the various form of Protestantism. As if that weren't enough, on the following day, December 9, 1854, Pius issued an "allocution," or papal address delivered in a secret consistory, to the effect that no salvation was possible outside the Roman Church. Boniface VIII (c. 1234–1303; r. 1294–1303) had said the same thing, but there were fewer forms of Christian faith outside the Roman Church in 1300. In 1854 Pius's declaration explicitly repudiated every form of Protestantism, as well as Orthodoxy.

A discernible stridency entered papal rhetoric during these years. This can be seen in such documents as the 1863 encyclical (circular letter) *Quanto conficiamur moerore*, a condemnation of heresy every bit as harsh as the condemnations issued during the Reformation era. In itself, such a declaration seems inexplicably hostile; but when viewed alongside the developments within Protestant theology in the nineteenth century (see Chapter 22), it can be interpreted as an attempt by the pope to protect

Theodor Breitweiser, *Portrait of Pope Pius IX*, 19th century. Oil on canvas. Lobkowicz Collections, Nelahozeves Castle, Czech Republic.

Reviled by later generations for his rejection of nineteenth-century progress, Pius IX also defended Catholicism against secular threats and crises.

the transcendent and revealed truths of Christianity against the tendency, in the popular theological liberalism of the day, to reduce religion to the human and cultural.

Opposition to the perceived secularization of culture reached a high point in 1864, when Pius IX issued his *Syllabus of Errors*, condemning most of the dominant modes of modern thought. (See "Pope Pius IX" and "Pope Pius IX's *Syllabus of Errors*.") This document, which caused a furor in liberal circles, identified the "errors" of the time, in political and social thought, in ethics, regarding Christian matrimony, regarding the primacy of the Roman pontiff, and in other matters of concern. All told, there were eighty assumptions or attitudes that came under condemnation. Some of the ideas that Pius attacked had already become accepted

Pope Pius IX

Pius IX enjoyed a long and highly popular reign; lay Catholics saw him as the defender of the faith against all the sinister developments of modern culture. In this popular Catholic biography of the pope, John G. Shea describes the nature and purpose of the Syllabus of Errors.

But with the shadow of a great wrong thus announcing its coming, Pius IX. was still the great Pope. On the 8th of December, 1864, he published the Encyclical *Quanta Cura* condemning a host of erroneous doctrines which he had from time to time censured, and of which a summary, or syllabus, was appended. There was nothing new to Catholics in this; but when modern liberalism and infidelity were confronted by this mass of sound Catholic doctrine, which struck at some favorite crude theory of the time, all rose in arms. The Pope whose declining power made him but yesterday one of whom they spoke with a kind of pity, became suddenly the great enemy of human progress, a man of boundless power and influence. The Encyclical and Syllabus have ever since been an inexhaustible topic; generally misunderstood and misrepresented, few stopping to think that it is one thing to condemn a general proposition as false, and another thing to set forth which is the true doctrine; and that this is a series of condemnations of errors propagated among Catholics, which it was the duty of the Pope to condemn.

The first articles of the Syllabus, or summary of the principal errors of our time condemned in the Consistorial Allocutions, Encyclicals, and other Letters Apostolic of our Holy Father Pope Pius IX., refer to pantheism, naturalism, and absolute rationalism. The next to moderate rationalism, which claimed too much for human reason, or excluded revelation. Then the prevailing indifferentism and latitudinarian ideas of the day are condemned, which seek to make men believe that the existence of the true church and adherence to it are unnecessary for salvation. The condemnation of socialism, communism, secret societies, the Bible societies, clerico-liberal societies is formally renewed. The next topic is a series of errors concerning the church and its rights. The Syllabus in fact lays down that the church is a true and perfect society, absolutely free, enjoying her own peculiar and constant rights, conferred upon her by her divine founder, and that it is not competent for the civil powers to define what the rights of the church are, or the limits in which they shall be exercised. It lays down, moreover, that the church in the exercise of its authority does not depend on the permission or consent of the civil government, and the episcopal power includes no part dependent on the State.

(From John G. Shea, *The Life of Pope Pius IX*. New York: Thomas Kelly, 1878.)

throughout the Western world; others were well on their way to acceptance; but all were equally censured. The Roman Church, so it appeared, had declared itself the opponent of all modern and progressive ideas. And the Catholic faithful, who had to live in the secular world while still remaining good Catholics, were expected to choose their allegiances. The laity, as never before, found themselves being asked to vote for the church or for secular progress. It was not an easy choice.

Pope Pius IX's *Syllabus of Errors*

In the Syllabus of Errors *(1864), Pope Pius IX expressly condemns whole categories of modern thought. In these articles he identifies a number of modern political "errors."*

VI. Errors About Civil Society, Considered Both in itself and in its Relation to the church.

39. The State, as being the origin and source of all rights, is endowed with a certain right not circumscribed by any limits.—Allocution "Maxima quidem," June 9, 1862.

40. The teaching of the Catholic Church is hostile to the well-being and interests of society.—Encyclical "Qui pluribus," Nov. 9, 1846; Allocution "Quibus quantisque," April 20, 1849.

41. The civil government, even when in the hands of an infidel sovereign, has a right to an indirect negative power over religious affairs. It therefore possesses not only the right called that of "exsequatur," but also that of appeal, called "appellatio ab abusu."—Apostolic Letter "Ad Apostolicae."

42. In the case of conflicting laws enacted by the two powers, the civil law prevails.—Ibid.

43. The secular Power has authority to rescind, declare and render null, solemn conventions, commonly called concordats, entered into with the Apostolic See, regarding the use of rights appertaining to ecclesiastical immunity, without the consent of the Apostolic See, and even in spite of its protest.—Allocution "Multis gravibusque," Dec. 17, 1860; Allocution "In consistoriali," Nov. 1, 1850.

44. The civil authority may interfere in matters relating to religion, morality and spiritual government: hence, it can pass judgment on the instructions issued for the guidance of consciences, conformably with their mission, by the pastors of the church. Further, it has the right to make enactments regarding the administration of the divine sacraments, and the dispositions necessary for receiving them.—Allocutions "In consistoriali," Nov. 1, 1850, and "Maxima quidem," June 9, 1862.

45. The entire government of public schools in which the youth of a Christian state are educated, except (to a certain extent) in the case of episcopal seminaries, may and ought to appertain to the civil power, and belong to it so far that no other authority whatsoever shall be recognized as having any right to interfere in the discipline of the schools, the arrangement of the studies, the conferring of degrees, in the choice or approval of the teachers.—Allocutions "Quibus luctuosissimis," Sept. 5, 1851, and "In consistoriali," Nov. 1, 1850.

(From Encyclical *Quanta Cura*: www.reformation.org/syllabus.)

The First Vatican Council

Pius IX was not content with declaring war against materialistic ideas or Protestant dogmatics. He saw himself as the defender of the faith in an age of turmoil. The previous great challenge to the Roman faith had been met by the Council of Trent, and Pius was resolved to face the next such challenge with a similar council. Held at the Vatican, it therefore became known as the Vatican Council—later as the First Vatican Council, to distinguish it from the one held in 1962–65. Unlike Trent, it was a short council, lasting only from 1869 to 1870, but it had an extraordinary effect on the life of the church.

The First Vatican Council, 1869–1870. Engraving.

This scene depicts a meeting in July 1870 "proclaiming the dogma of Papal Infallibility at Rome."

In its tone the council was no great departure from Pius's work of the preceding thirty years. Most of the cardinals in attendance had been appointed during his pontificate and shared at least some of his attitudes. All, it seemed, shared a skepticism toward the growing of materialism in society and in political thought, and most felt that preservation of the tradition, rather than adaptation, was the key to preserving the faith.

Vatican I differs from its predecessor, Trent, in the political slant of its deliberations and rulings. Many of its discussions would have been meaningless in any century before the nineteenth, a number of its assertions unnecessary in an age when divine ordering of the world went unquestioned. Questions about the sig-

nificance of the council began from the moment it was announced. Did the calling of a council mean that the Roman Church also was now also a parliamentary democracy, with bishops as the "regional representatives" contributing to policy? Was this pope going to forge constructive alliances with the rapidly changing secular society? This would continue the process begun in 1851 when Pius forged a concordat with Spain, the first of a number of strategic alliances that solidified the church's power just as its geographical territory was contracting. Or would the meeting serve to strengthen an already entrenched resistance to modernity and secularism—a stance that had also been firmly in place since the 1850s? Hopes and apprehension alike ran high on the eve of the first meeting, on December 8, 1869.

Debates about procedure and the initial drafting of a statement of faith took up the first month, but the going got no easier when substantive issues came to the table. The statement of faith reads like the *Syllabus of Errors*: it is a list of the things that the church deemed erroneous to deny—such as the earth's having been created for the glory of God, or the Bible's having been inspired by God. Other early documents debated at the council included disciplinary and regulatory measures, some of which provoked serious disagreement. One argument concerned the proposal that the Catechism of the Council of Trent be used throughout the church; German bishops resisted this because the catechism of the Jesuit Peter Canisius had been used in their dioceses since the sixteenth century. A Hungarian bishop defended the Germans, expressing the fear that sermons also would eventually be dictated by Rome. No action was taken on this question, because another issue appeared; and this one would take up the rest of the council's time.

Papal Infallibility

The issue was papal infallibility, and it would prove to be one of the most controversial issues for the rest of the nineteenth century and most of the twentieth. (See "The Doctrine of Papal Infallibility.") It was not simply about whether the pope could err (in some respects all popes had), nor was it a completely new idea: experts in canon law in the aftermath of the Gregorian Reform (see Chapter 11) had come close to the council's position; and Gregory XVI, as noted above, had developed it further. The issue was whether the pope, in certain circumstances, could make pronouncements that would remain unchallenged over time—could make statements, in other words, that could not be disputed. The qualifications for infallible pronouncements were these: the pope needed to be speaking *ex cathedra* (literally "from the [bishop's] chair")—that is, as the heir of St. Peter; and he needed to be defining matters of faith or morals. Under these conditions the statements of the pope could be considered binding and "irreformable," or incapable of improvement.

If the *Syllabus of Errors* was a declaration of war against modernism and secularism, the infallibility doctrine was a declaration of war against dissenters within the church. Instead of putting an end to controversy, however, the doctrine ignited it—immediately. Advocates of the measure succeeded in putting it at the top of the council's agenda, an action that drew criticism even from their allies, as it seemed to place undue importance on the issue. These cautious advocates

The Doctrine of Papal Infallibility

The First Vatican Council, called by the conservative Pope Pius IX, was the epicenter of conflict over papal authority in the church. The doctrine of infallibility, issued amid controversy, seemed to give the papacy unprecedented power in matters of faith and ethics.

... We, adhering faithfully to the tradition received from the beginning of the Christian faith—with a view to the glory of our Divine Saviour, the exaltation of the Catholic religion, and the safety of Christian peoples (the Sacred Council approving), teach and define as a dogma divinely revealed: That the Roman Pontiff, when he speaks *ex cathedra* (that is, when—fulfilling the office of Pastor and Teacher of all Christians—on his supreme Apostolical authority, he defines a doctrine concerning faith or morals to be held by the Universal Church), through the divine assistance promised him in blessed Peter, is endowed with that infallibility, with which the Divine Redeemer has willed that His church—in defining doctrine concerning faith or morals—should be equipped: And therefore, that such definitions of the Roman Pontiff of themselves—and not by virtue of the consent of the church—are irreformable. If anyone shall presume (which God forbid!) to contradict this our definition; let him be anathema.

(From Vatican Council, Session IV, in Henry Bettenson, ed., *Documents of the Christian Tradition*. New York and London: Oxford University Press, 1947.)

insisted that it was "inopportune" to push the question so hard. The outright opposition was based on a number of arguments, such as the negative effect such a definition would have on non-Catholic churches, the absence of historical precedent, even the incorrect claim that it was already an article of faith. Further reservations about the definition came in the form of proposed alternate wording; altogether 200 changes were suggested. More politicking and debating followed until the final votes were cast, on July 18, 1870—while a thunderstorm raged so severely that extra lamps were needed in the chamber and some voices were hard to hear. In the end all but two bishops (one of them an American, Fitzgerald, of Little Rock, Arkansas) approved the definition. The others who had opposed the definition expressed their views privately but voted with the majority for the good of the church.

The most determined opponents to the new dogma formed a schismatic church, known as the Old Catholics (one of several groups of that name), which took hold in Germany, Austria, and Switzerland for a few decades but never drew large numbers away from the Roman Church. For the majority of laypeople, the definition of papal infallibility may have been a welcome event in the face of the change and doubt that were convulsing the secular world. Regardless of the implications for the clergy, a strengthening of the authority of the papacy was seen as a strengthening of the church generally. This was one "monarchy" that was not going to change or topple.

Nevertheless, the papacy was still vulnerable to political events. The Franco–Prussian War had begun the same month, July 1870, and Italy was involved from the start. The Italian king, Victor Emmanuel (the second of Sardinia, the first of Italy; 1820–1878; r. as king of Italy 1861–1878), had wished to keep the peninsula as unified as possible, and thus hoped to have the support of the papacy. Pius resisted; but without the continuing support of French troops, now occupied in fighting Prussia, such resistance was futile. For a short time, the Vatican became

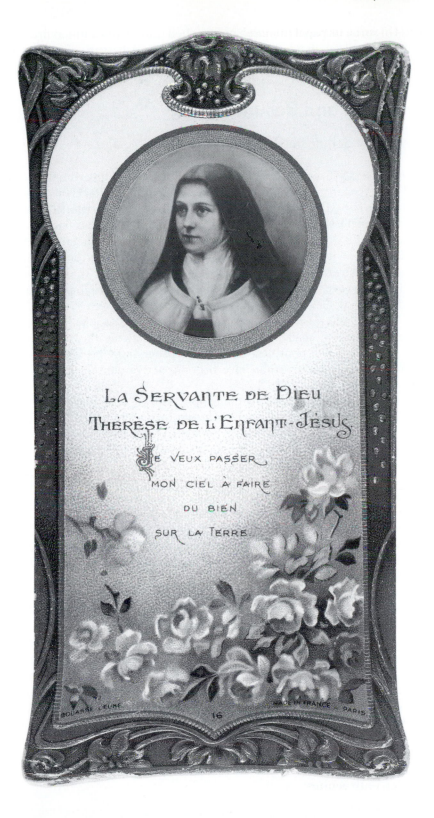

La Servante de Dieu
Thérèse de l'Enfant-Jésus

Je veux passer
mon ciel à faire
du bien
sur la terre.

*Thérèse of Lisieux,
c. 1900.
Photograph and
tribute.*

*Thérèse of Lisieux
(1873–1897)
became a
Carmelite nun
aged 15 but died of
tuberculosis at 24.
Her* Story of a Soul
*(published
posthumously,
1898) recounts
how the most
ordinary
individual can
attain sainthood
by following her
"little way" of
simple, childlike
Christianity. She
was canonized in
1925 and in 1947
was associated
with Joan of Arc as
patron saint of
France.*

a fortress of sorts, its papal monarch entrenched until, amid cannon fire, a flag of surrender was raised above the dome of St. Peter's. A gesture of independence had been made, and reality accepted.

Regrouping and Resuming

The Revival of Scholastic Theology

On February 8, 1878, Pius IX was pronounced dead by the cardinal who would succeed him, Vincenzo Gioacchino Pecci (1810–1903; r. 1878–1903), who would take the name Leo XIII. An avid student of Thomas Aquinas's thought, Pecci was considered a moderate when elected pope, and as Leo XIII he was on much more cordial terms with the secular world than his predecessor had been. Nevertheless he was determined not to lessen the authority of his office, and some of his early pronouncements against political and ideological threats appear just as conservative as Pius's. However, his approach to the problem was more intellectual. It was he who declared, in his encyclical *Aeterni Patris* of August 4, 1879, that Thomas Aquinas (see Chapter 10) had far surpassed all other Scholastic theologians; and he established an academy in Rome for Thomistic studies. This would be the first of a number of pontifical institutes—others may be found in Louvain and Toronto, for example—that have become active centers for research on Scholasticism generally.

From these institutes emerged a philosophy known as NEO-SCHOLASTICISM or NEO-THOMISM. In some ways the renewed attention on Thomas diverted attention away from the infallibility controversy, for such a formula was not generally recognized in the thirteenth century (Thomas's period), even though in some circles it would have been considered compatible with the church's teaching. In other ways Leo sought to bring the medieval philosophical worldview into full engagement with the secular world of the late nineteenth century. Thomas, we remember, granted a great deal of power to human rationality, yet insisted that this faculty was insufficient for understanding the world—and certainly God—completely. And it was Thomas who made the most constructive use of that pagan Greek philosopher and scientist Aristotle. Who better than the "angelic doctor" (as Thomas was called) to make the best use of modern science, while yet reminding the modern world of science's limitations?

More broadly, the revival of Scholastic theology as a living organism rather than an antiquated curiosity helped the Catholic Church to systematize and structure its teachings. Theological faculties could operate on a common foundation, and philosophical rigor became a regular test of theological arguments. Divisions of theology into separate areas such as fundamental, moral, and sacramental ensured that clergy understood the current dogmatic questions, had traditional sources available for their own study, and knew the connections between various issues. It also prompted academic theologians in seminaries and universities to undertake serious research into current issues, working with Scholastic materials for answers to urgent current problems. In many ways the intellectual tradition of Catholic theology reached its current plateau in the final two decades of the nineteenth century.

The century that began with a new theological system in Protestantism, and the creation of elaborate systems, Hegelian and otherwise, ended with Catholicism organizing its own system. Like its Protestant counterparts, Thomism was intended to mediate the conflict between the otherworldly beliefs of the church and the very worldly demands of the secular realm. But unlike Protestant liberalism, Thomism tempered its enthusiasm about the progress of culture with an implicit, but essentially conservative, conviction that the thirteenth century and its great Dominican friar had already worked out all the important issues that would face the modern world.

Key Terms

CONCORDAT An agreement; specifically, one between the Vatican and a European state, identifying political and ecclesiastical jurisdictions in secular society.

IMMACULATE CONCEPTION The Roman Catholic doctrine that the Virgin Mary was free of sin even at the point of her own conception; despite long historical tradition, this was first promulgated in 1854.

NEO-SCHOLASTICISM (NEO-THOMISM) A theological movement originating in a late-19th-century revival of the ideas of Thomas Aquinas; it was the dominant school of Catholic thought in the early 20th century.

Antoni Gaudí (and others), *Sagrada Familia*, Barcelona, 1893–1930.

PART SIX

The Twentieth Century and Beyond

Modernity has tested the adaptability of the Christian tradition. The rise of science and the triumph of technology over nature have brought challenges at every turn. Weakened by issues such as Darwin's theory of evolution or the advent of revolutionary communism, the Christian Church turned its attention to social problems and the healing of a suffering world. For example, the Vatican made pronouncements on the economic situation of the working classes and American Baptists articulated a vision of the Gospel in which the divine kingdom can be realized here in our world. Modern as these positions may have seemed at the time, they were echoing sentiments voiced in the fourth century by Constantine and his defenders, and in the ninth century at Charlemagne's court.

Two world wars and decades of other regional wars have brought untold suffering to a world once confident of the inevitability of progress. The scientific discoveries that held promise for improving life on earth have proved devastatingly potent in worsening it; many churches that had subscribed to a belief in scientific progress found themselves having to rethink their position after two world wars. Pessimistic or apocalyptic pronouncements about society, technology, and government have proved a potent counterweight to the power politics of states and the application of technology for its own sake.

In their opposition to war and right-wing political regimes, different confessions have come together on a united front while in other respects remaining in opposition; the aftermath of the Holocaust drew thinkers from all walks of church and academic life to reevaluate Christianity's relation to Judaism. Only a few decades after the kinship of these faiths became explicitly acknowledged in terms such as the "Judeo-Christian Tradition," the rise of Islam as a presence in global politics led to an extended conceptualization of the Western religious tradition as a Jewish-Christian-Islamic triad. Despite the growing secularization, resilience, and flexibility that Christianity has demonstrated in modern times, it enters a most uncertain twenty-first century.

1900		
	1905	Pope Pius X's encyclical *Acerbo Nimis* calls for improved religious education.
	1905	Separation of church and state in France.
	1908	The Federal Council of the Churches of Christ in America is formed.
	c. 1909	Princeton Theological Seminary promotes fundamentalism, asserting the Bible's divine truth.
	1910	World Missionary Conference is held in Edinburgh, Scotland.
	1914	Many German theologians support the German Emperor at the start of World War I.
	1917	Walter Rauschenbusch delivers lecture series *A Theology for the Social Gospel*.
1925	1922	The papal bull *Ubi Arcano* encourages the Catholic Action movement.
	1929	Pope Pius XI and Italian dictator Benito Mussolini sign the Lateran Treaty.
	1932	Reinhold Niebuhr publishes *Moral Man and Immoral Society*.
	1937	Papal encyclical *Mit brennender Sorge* criticizes aspects of Nazism without condemning it.
	1937	Pastor Martin Niemöller is sent to a concentration camp for preaching against Hitler.
	1939	Eugenio Pacelli, architect of the 1933 concordat with the Nazis, becomes Pope Pius XII.
	1945	Pastor Dietrich Bonhoeffer is hanged by the Nazis.
	1947	Discovery of the Dead Sea Scrolls.
1950	1948	The World Council of Churches is established.
	1950	Pius XII's encyclical *Humani Generis* condemns much of modern science, including evolution theory.
	1952	Alsatian missionary and theologian Albert Schweitzer is awarded the Nobel Prize for peace.
	1957	Martin Luther King sets up Southern Christian Leadership Conference to campaign for civil rights.
	1961	The Russian Orthodox Church joins the World Council of Churches.
	1962	The Second Vatican Council initiates radical change in the Catholic Church.
	1965	Pope Paul VI declares that Jews were not responsible for the death of Christ.
	1968	World Council of Churches recognizes human rights as a vital issue.
	1968	The South African Council of Churches denounces apartheid as hostile to Christianity.
	1968	The papal encyclical *Humanae Vitae* says Catholics must not use artificial contraceptives.
	1970	The Catholic *Decree on Ecumenism* calls for dialogue between Christians of all churches.
	1970	Publication of the *New English Bible*.
	1970	British Methodist Church votes to allow women as ministers.
1975	1971	Peruvian Catholic priest Gustavo Gutiérrez publishes *A Theology of Liberation*.
	1976	Episcopal Church in the United States approves the ordination of women.
	1978	Polish Archbishop Karol Wojtyla elected Pope John Paul II, first non-Italian pope since 1522.
	1980–89	Churches play a role in the overthrow of communism in eastern Europe, especially Poland.
	1984	The Vatican rejects liberation theology, warning against Marxism and materialism.
	1986	The Vatican condemns liberal views on divorce, homosexuality, contraception, and abortion.
	1988	John Paul II confirms his opposition to women priests in the apostolic letter *Mulieris Dignitatem*.
	1994	The Church of England ordains its first women priests.
	2002	Child sex-abuse scandal rocks confidence in US Catholic hierarchy.
	2002	Dr. Rowan Williams named the new Archbishop of Canterbury.
	2002	Pope John Paul II canonizes Juan Diego, Native American recipient of the 1531 Marian revelation.

CHAPTER 26

Social Christianity
The Dawn of the 20th Century

For the West, the nineteenth century was a period of momentous change: in politics, industry, science, and religion. In a meaningful sense, this period began and ended not with the years 1800 and 1900 but with the Napoleonic wars (from about 1803, closely following the French Revolutionary wars, to 1815) and the outbreak of World War I in 1914. Between these two prodigious conflicts, two new nations, Italy and Germany, were formed and another, the United States, was temporarily split asunder by civil war. The Industrial Revolution, which began during the previous century, continued to transform the way people worked, used money, and lived. Modern science—physics, chemistry, and medicine—came into being. To some people, notably the growing ranks of the prosperous middle class, it seemed an age of steady progress; to others, it was an age of exacerbated social injustice, slavery and women's rights being highly contentious issues. Undeniably, it was a time of extraordinary ferment.

In the realm of philosophical and religious ideas, too, great changes were taking place. Many of the religious ideas current in 1900 had not been thought of a century earlier. A radically changing world forced Christians to reexamine their faith to take these changes into account—or at least respond to them in some way. In some cases the response was positive and constructive; in others, negative and obstructive.

Perhaps nowhere did churches face greater challenges than in the United States, where the Civil War (1861–65) and its aftermath, coupled with decades of immigration, had created social problems on an unprecedented scale.

The Civil War and its Aftermath

The problems that the Christian Churches faced in 1900 had been long in the making. The fact that the newly industrialized economy was unable to absorb the supply of labor available from the 1840s to the 1890s is recognizable only in hindsight: the growth of slave labor before the Civil War, and the waves of immigration in the decades following it, called for a more efficient and industrialized economy than any nation at the time could offer. In fact, the Reconstruction that followed the Civil War placed such a drain on the nation's resources that absorption of the new immigrants was more difficult than it might otherwise have been. All of this meant more work—or more opportunity—for the Christian churches already active in social causes.

The recently abolished institution of slavery had produced an unquantifiable amount of human misery, which had been reinforced in many instances by Christian clergy who informed the slaves that their lot was divinely ordained and assured the slaveholders that the divine ordering of society had endowed them with the heightened responsibility of ownership of others. Slavery had had opponents throughout the colonies, especially among the Quakers, even in the South. For example, a prosperous Virginia colonist named Thomas Dew (c. 1600–1691), renounced slavery upon becoming a Quaker in 1672; yet one of his descendants, Thomas Roderick Dew, thirteenth president of the College of William and Mary, in Virginia, was in the 1830s and 1840s one of its boldest defenders, arguing, among other things, that Southern society, with slavery, was more egalitarian than northern society without it. Dew based his position on the idea that Southern society had only two classes, black and white, and that all whites were therefore equal. Such arguments did not prevail against the rhetoric of the Rev. Henry Ward Beecher (1813–1887), whose sister Harriet Beecher Stowe (1811–1896) wrote the anti-slavery novel *Uncle Tom's Cabin* (1852), or of fiery abolitionists such as Lucretia Mott (1793–1880). And when oratory failed to prevail (Lincoln himself, we must remember, was not an abolitionist before 1863, when he issued the Emancipation Proclamation), armed conflict eventually did.

The dislocation that followed the war was profound and far-reaching. Vast populations of freed slaves, trained only in agricultural labor and promised "forty acres and a mule," which most never received, migrated to the industrialized North, which was unable to train or accommodate them. African-American neighborhoods were created and grew, though their level of prosperity remained shamefully low. Much of the Southern preaching that had consoled African-Americans before the Civil War was echoed in the consolatory oratory of post-Civil War black churches. Much of the worship among these communities affirmed a faith in an

A Prayer for Deliverance, c. 1863. Library of Congress, Washington, D.C.

Union and Confederate armies in the Civil War both considered their cause a holy one. This shows a religious service within the Ninth Massachusetts Infantry Division near Washington, D.C.

M. Jackson, *Sunday Chapel Meeting*, from *The Illustrated London News*, December 5, 1863.

Slaves here attend Sunday chapel on a South Carolina plantation under the watchful eye of their master and his family. A slave's duty to accept his or her subordinate place was a regular theme of such sermons.

otherworldly reward, paid for in advance by bitter sufferings in this life. That freedom was not, as expected, an unmixed blessing was becoming abundantly clear in city after city. And northerners, seeing the wretchedness of their new neighbors, began to wonder whether their struggle to free the slaves had been the wisest and kindest course.

The Social Gospel

The need to address the social problems of the day served, toward the end of the nineteenth century, to draw most of the Christian denominations closer together. The American religious establishment had been fully engaged in social issues since the beginning of Reconstruction, the rebuilding of the nation after the Civil War. But some of the origins of this work extend back to the first half of the century, especially in New England, and the rise of Unitarianism and of the idealistic philosophy of Transcendentalism.

Unitarianism

The idea of UNITARIANISM, whose roots go back to the Reformation era, espouses belief in God as one Person and Jesus as merely a spiritual leader, thus rejecting the doctrine of the Trinity, or indeed any formal creed. As it developed in nineteenth-century America, this liberal denomination increasingly emphasized the essential goodness of human nature. Thus it was closely allied to Transcendentalism, a philosophy that flourished in the North in the early- and mid-1800s and that asserted the ability of the human soul to grasp the truth. This philosophy was exemplified by Ralph Waldo Emerson (1803–1882), a onetime Unitarian minister and one of the leading intellects of his time. Both movements informed the creation of Brook Farm, near Boston, a utopian community (1841–1847) which attracted many intellectuals including, for a while, Emerson himself.

Later in the century, Unitarians such as Octavius Brooks Frothingham (1822–1895) kept the tradition alive with the forming of a Free Religion Association centered around a "religion of humanity." Frothingham's 1872 book *The Religion of Humanity* served as a foundation for the Unitarian movement; it is an eloquent affirmation of human perfectibility with no need for supernatural intervention or revelation. Among mainstream Protestant clergy in the 1880s the need for social activism was recognized with contributions by A. J. F. Behrends (1839–1900) and Washington Gladden (1836–1918). Perceiving that industrialization was an opportunity for new forms of social inequality to become embedded in American life, Behrends in *Socialism and Christianity* and Gladden in *Applied Christianity* (both 1886) adopted, and encouraged in their readers, a critical stance against the injustices posed by monopolistic businesses and in favor of increased governmental vigilance against the greed of the few. Richard Theodore Ely (1854–1943) followed in 1889 with a work titled *The Social Aspects of Christianity*, a work that calls not just individual Christians, but churches as a whole, to more active work on behalf of the poor and vulnerable.

Walter Rauschenbusch

The idea of a divine kingdom, so ubiquitous and yet so fluid during the nineteenth century, becomes a powerful image for social change during its final decades. In countless works of this period, God's realm is conceptualized in historical rather than eschatological terms: that is, as something to be realized here on earth, not in a separate supernatural sphere. Combined with the idea of development—drawn mainly from contemporary research on evolution—the metaphor of a kingdom of God began to be seen as a realizable goal. In 1892 a Baptist minister named Walter Rauschenbusch (1861–1918), along with two other Baptist ministers, formed a society called the "Brotherhood of the Kingdom." This group, which attracted many followers, met to discuss ways of implementing the kingdom, "the most splendid idea," said Rauschenbusch, "that has ever enriched human thought." Their work came to broad public notice with publications such as *Christianity and the Social Crisis* (1907) and *Christianizing the Social Order* (1912), both by Rauschenbusch, and Samuel Zane Batten's (1859–1925) *The Social Task of Christianity* (1911).

Walter Rauschenbusch's *A Theology for the Social Gospel* (1917) is thus the unmis-

Walter Rauschenbusch, 1915.

A careful reader of the German liberal tradition, Rauschenbusch applied concepts such as kingdom and kinship to the sufferings of people in the cramped conditions and slums of newly industrialized cities.

Walter Rauschenbusch

Walter Rauschenbusch (1861–1918) is the author most prominently associated with the Social Gospel movement, and its most articulate theorist. In this excerpt from A Theology for the Social Gospel *(1917), Rauschenbusch applies the metaphor of the Kingdom of God to a social ideal.*

In the following brief propositions I should like to offer a few suggestions, on behalf of the social gospel, for the theological formulation of the doctrine of the Kingdom. Something like this is needed to give us "a theology for the social gospel."

  1. The Kingdom of God is divine in its origin, progress, and consummation. It was initiated by Jesus Christ, in whom the prophetic spirit came to its consummation, it is sustained by the Holy Spirit, and it will be brought to its fulfillment by the power of God in his own time. The passive and active resistance of the Kingdom of Evil at every stage of its advance is so great, and the human resources of the Kingdom of God so slender, that no explanation can satisfy a religious mind which does not see the power of God in its movements. The Kingdom of God, therefore, is miraculous all the way, and is the continuous revelation of the power, the righteousness, and the love of God. The establishment of a community of righteousness in mankind is just as much a saving act of God as the salvation of an individual from his natural selfishness and moral inability. The Kingdom of God, therefore, is not merely ethical, but has a rightful place in theology. This doctrine is absolutely necessary to establish that organic union between religion and morality, between theology and ethics, which is one of the characteristics of the Christian religion. When our moral actions are consciously related to the Kingdom of God they gain religious quality. Without this doctrine we shall have expositions of schemes of redemption and we shall have systems of ethics, but we shall not have a true exposition of Christianity. The first step to the reform of the churches is the restoration of the doctrine of the Kingdom of God.

  2. The Kingdom of God contains the teleology of the Christian religion. It translates theology from the static to the dynamic. It sees, not doctrines or rites to be conserved and perpetuated, but resistance to be overcome and great ends to be achieved. Since the Kingdom of God is the supreme purpose of God, we shall understand the Kingdom as far as we understand God, and we shall understand God so far as we understand his Kingdom. As long as organized sin is in the world, the Kingdom of God is characterized by conflict with evil. But if there were no evil, or after evil has been overcome, the Kingdom of God will still be the end to which God is lifting the race. It is realized not only by redemption, but also by the education of mankind and the revelation of his life within it.

(From *A Rauschenbusch Reader*, ed. Benson Y. Landis. New York: Harper & Row, 1957.)

takable product of an American religious movement. (See "Walter Rauschenbusch.") Delivered as a series of lectures at Yale, the work attempts to provide the ideas that can keep the social program alive. In his opening words, "We have a social gospel. We need a systematic theology large enough to match it and vital enough to back it," Rauschenbusch's call was for a socially committed theology. His underlying assertion was that the work of the Brotherhood and the activities of the socially engaged clergy, who saw the New Testament message as a command to heal society's ills, cannot be dismissed as something peripheral to theology. By constructing a theological system to shape and theorize the work of his activist peers, Rauschenbusch makes a strong claim for attention by the theological mainstream.

In Rauschenbusch's hands, the Social Gospel is coherently but creatively systematized under some of the standard theological categories. The human condition, for example, is understood as sin; but sin's manifestations include "despotic governments," "war and militarism," "landlordism," and "predatory industry and finance." Moreover, these forms of sin are transmitted down the ages by culture's "idealization of evil," its tendency, in Rauschenbusch's view, to elevate the "horrid" and suppress the beautiful. Thus instead of a beneficent social order, modern civilization labors under the rule of a "Kingdom of Evil"—language that would be echoed later by Reinhold Niebuhr (see Chapter 27). Sounding at points more like a prophet than an academic lecturer, Rauschenbusch delivers a pessimistic diagnosis of the condition of modern civilization.

But Rauschenbusch also offers a solution: the replacement of the Kingdom of Evil with a Kingdom of God, which he defined as "humanity organized according to the will of God." Such a kingdom is God's will for the world, and thus the goal toward which the church should be moving. The personal example of fulfilling the ideal of the kingdom is Jesus Christ, described as a distinctive personality, one who lived for others as well as himself, and in that life initiated a new process in the world's history. Setting aside the traditional Christological questions of humanity and divinity, Rauschenbusch identifies Jesus' uniqueness as his ability to experience God in a new way and to present to his companions a kinder and more loving image of God than the Hebrew prophets were able to conceive.

In Rauschenbusch's program, the Kingdom of God is no mere dogmatic concept or pious ideal, but a historic force at work in humanity, a redemptive energy capable of saving humanity by expanding to embrace, in the end, all persons. But such a force must first be noticed, then cultivated, and finally extended. In a persuasive insight, Rauschenbusch notes that the language used to describe redemption throughout Christian history is always taken from the life of society: sacrifice, death and rebirth, penance, and so on, each understood in a time-bound way. The terms reflect the experience of the time. Thus for early twentieth-century America, he insists, the social crisis must provide the terms for the work of redemption. Hence it is necessary to think in terms of kingdoms, of evil, and of God, and to address issues of economic injustice, racial inequality, and war. (It is worth noting that these lectures were delivered the same month, April 1917, that the United States declared war on Germany and entered World War I.)

Social Religion and Academe

A Theology for the Social Gospel received a fair amount of notice in academic circles, but never became the unifying American theological program that the Brotherhood might have hoped it would become. Most of the attention it did receive was not from theologians, but from sociologists, often enlisted by church groups and seminaries to analyze the conditions of American life and identify possible means to improve them. Richard Ely, whom we encountered earlier in this chapter, was himself a political economist with little apparent taste for dogmatic abstractions. Such early sociologists as Albion W. Small (1854–1926) and

Children Receiving Salvation Army Handouts, London, c. 1900.

Children from London's East End are seen queuing for "Farthing Breakfasts" provided by the Salvation Army.

Charles R. Henderson (1848–1915), both of the University of Chicago, came to their academic field with ministerial training behind them, and a religious viewpoint is found in the work of other sociologists in the first decades of the century—and arguably also of that discipline. More public social thinkers, such as Scott Nearing (1883–1983) at the University of Pennsylvania, author of *Social Religion* (1913) and other works, found themselves promoting a religious approach to social concerns.

Bonds between religion and the American academic establishment were probably never so close as in the early decades of the twentieth century. The minister-sociologists who shaped that discipline at U.S. universities saw their mission as the improvement of society, and not just the analysis of groups; many conceived of sociology as a professionalization (but not necessarily a secularization) of work previously done by individual churches and religious organizations. The churches themselves took part in this work. In 1908 the Federal Council of the Churches of Christ in America (later absorbed into the National Council of the Churches of Christ in the USA) was formed; this organization included various religious bodies subscribing to the Social Gospel. The Council supported, morally and materially, the work of social reconstruction; it issued declarations and study documents; occasionally it called for strikes against unjust working conditions. As an institutional base for the Social Gospel, it represents the culmination of a process begun in Reconstruction, taken up to a large extent by universities and various philanthropic bodies (one thinks of the YMCA and the Salvation Army), as well as continued by the churches. Its work would itself to some extent be taken over by the World Council of Churches (see Chapter 28). And the Social

Gospel, activist program and theology alike, would be reincarnated in the liberation theology of the later twentieth century.

Catholicism and Social Teachings

The Catholic Church, meanwhile, had taken a prominent stand on social issues of the time. The encyclical *Rerum Novarum,* issued by Pope Leo XIII (1810–1903; r. 1878–1903) in 1891, was a bold step for a church that had often been identified with the ruling classes. *Rerum Novarum* was in many ways a radical document: the church until then had not addressed social and economic conditions so directly, and in this encyclical it did so in a more constructive manner than it had in the preceding decade (see Chapter 25), when facing the mounting tide of materialistic culture. Recognizing that the Industrial Revolution had brought new attitudes to resources and work, Leo acknowledged that two very deeply divided classes had been created. Without using the specific terms, the encyclical saw the capitalist class as oppressing, in varying degrees, the relatively powerless laboring class. The pope recognized the urgency of the social question, but also saw it as a problem that could be solved only by the Gospel. For Leo XIII, work and the worker both have a dignity that needs to be protected. Through labor the individual is fulfilled and perfected, and it is thus a contradiction of the nature of work to allow it to oppress and degrade those performing it.

At the same time, *Rerum Novarum* affirmed the right to own property; indeed, it insisted upon the necessity of personal ownership. Thus, what a person earns rightfully belongs to that person, and can encourage labor as a means of self-fulfillment. On the other hand, achieving wealth at the cost of the dignity of workers has no legitimacy, and hence the use of property to exploit others— through harmful working conditions or other means—is a violation of the nature of property. It is noteworthy that, with its paired affirmation of the value of work and of property, the encyclical directly counters two of the principles of Marxism, then an ideology on the rise. The dignity of labor and the worker, set in the Christian context of *Rerum Novarum*, counters the Marxian claim that labor is a form of oppression that can be eliminated only through revolution. Where communism saw work as a restriction of freedom, the papal document saw it as a form of fulfillment. Similarly, asserting the legitimacy of privately owned property counters the belief, going back to the French socialist Pierre J. Proudhon (1809–1865), that "property is theft" and that the only legitimate form of ownership is communal. The Catholic position sees property as an object of stewardship, a care that protects the beneficial qualities of the things of this world. Worldly goods, even when privately owned, have a divinely ordered function; and their proper use is always guided by a knowledge of that end.

Such a view is consistent with certain elements of Scholastic theology (see chapters 10 and 13), and it is no surprise that Leo XIII was the main agent in the revival of Thomas Aquinas's thought. Leo's encyclical *Aeterni Patris* of August 1879, issued soon after he became pope, identified Thomas as the Scholastic "doctor" *par excellence*; and it was Leo who began the monumental edition of Thomas's works, known as the Leonine edition, which has been one of the foundations for Thomistic studies since the 1880s.

Leo's successor, Pius X (1835–1914; r. 1903–1914), also faced the rising trend of secularism and attempted to remedy it in his 1905 encyclical on the teaching of Christian doctrine, *Acerbo Nimis*. Pius's approach was to underscore the need for religious instruction, a subject that had been on the agenda of the church since the sixteenth century. Seeing much of the Catholic population as religiously ignorant, Pius realized that the more visible materialist ideologies of the day would capture the loyalties of the people if the church continued to ignore its own educational mission. Thus he proposed a number of measures to form part of a reform initiative. These included at least an hour of instruction for boys and girls each Sunday and holy day; confirmation preparation extending over a number of days; religious classes for students in secular schools; catechism instruction for all parishioners; first communion instructions each Lent; and the establishment of the Confraternity of Christian Doctrine (C.C.D.), in which clergy and laity would work together to educate the young in each parish.

The *Kulturkampf* in Germany

On the political front the Catholic Church had earlier found a new opponent in the form of the German Empire. Created in 1871, largely through the efforts of the Prussian statesman Otto von Bismarck (1815–1898), this political entity included most of the Germanic states apart from Austria. Many of these were predominantly Catholic, whereas the empire was dominated by Prussia, a traditionally Protestant northern state. However it was not the Protestants, per se, but the National Liberal party—Chancellor Bismarck's main supporters—who opposed the Catholics, represented by the Center party. The conflict between Bismarck and the National Liberals, on the one hand, and the Catholic Church/Center party, on the other, was triggered by the defection of some German Catholics from Rome after the promulgation of the doctrine of papal infallibility (see Chapter 25) and a consequent dispute over the role of these "Old Catholics" in German Catholic education. It quickly escalated into a major church–state struggle, known as the *Kulturkampf* (literally "culture conflict"). In 1873 Bismarck pushed through the parliament a series of repressive measures called the "May laws," which, in addition to placing state controls over Catholic schooling and the appointment of priests to benefices, also made marriage an exclusively civil proceeding. This desacramentalizing of matrimony brought a sharp rebuke from Pope Pius IX (see Chapter 25) in his encyclical *Quod Nunquam* (1875).

Bismark responded to this by, among other things, outlawing the Catholic religious orders. Some Catholic bishops who led the opposition to the May laws were imprisoned. Eventually these extreme measures antagonized so many Germans —even including some Protestants—that the government had to back down. Beginning in 1880, various mitigating laws were enacted, and Catholic life was once again integrated into the life of the German state. Relations with the Vatican, broken off in 1872, were restored in 1882, and theological faculties for Catholic clergy were established at German universities and seminaries. In 1886–87 there were laws declaring a political "truce" between Catholics and Protestants in Germany, amounting to a declaration of failure on Bismarck's part.

The stridently reactionary Catholicism of Pius IX might have been odious in the eyes of Chancellor Bismarck, but the people really had the last word in this matter; and their last word was a refusal to abandon their religious life and practice.

Nationalism and religion remained closely connected in Germany, and by the end of the century it was felt in some circles that political history and the course of religion had both come to a final point, with Protestant Germany the perfect culmination of ecclesiastical and national history. Such a view found expression, in varying degrees of clarity, in writers such as Adolf von Harnack (see Chapter 22), and Ernst Troeltsch (1865–1923), who would prove to be one of the most influential thinkers of the early twentieth century. Troeltsch, trained as a Reformed theologian and a professor of theology at Heidelberg, moved, in 1915, to Berlin where he taught philosophy at its university. He is best known for his massive study *The Social Teaching of the Christian Churches* (1912; English ed. 1931), in which he introduced the distinction between "church-type" (mainline and established) and "sect-type" (or radical and separatist) forms of Christianity, both of which he contrasts with an individualistic "mystic" type. But a triumphalist tone is evident in another of Troeltsch's works, *Protestantism and Progress* (1906; English ed. 1912), in which he distinguishes an "older" (i.e. Lutheran) form of Protestantism from a more progressive "newer" one (which he associates with Calvinism) and credits the latter with being instrumental in creating the modern world.

Destiny seemed to be favoring the German Empire when shots fired in Sarajevo, in 1914, signaled the beginning of World War I. For many Germans, the conflict was a chance to demonstrate the supremacy of their culture, both political and religious; and the churches, especially the Protestant confessions, fell in behind the state in this war. In a famous wartime declaration on August 1, 1914, the first day of the war, a group of ninety-three distinguished German intellectuals and theologians, including Harnack, signed a declaration of solidarity and support for the German emperor in the struggle. When theologians support a particular side in a given war, they tend to see it in terms beyond the political or ideological; rather, their inclination is to see it as a contest between good and evil, more specifically between a divinely willed good and a sinister opposition. Thus the support of these theologians and academics was more than just politically significant. It was close to a spiritual alliance.

Key Term

UNITARIANISM A movement within the Reformation that denied the doctrine of the Trinity and held that Jesus was a human servant of a unified deity; it gained ground in the United States in the 19th century.

CHAPTER 27

The Crisis of War
The Recovery of Orthodoxy

World War I did not end as it should have. It was intended to be, in a popular phrase, the "war to end all wars"; but it came to an end without a resolution of the conflicts that had brought the powers to arms in the first place. The Fourteen Points, proposed by U.S. President Woodrow Wilson (1856–1924) in January 1918 as a foundation for an equitable peace, did provide the basis for a truce in some parts of Europe throughout the year and finally for the Armistice of November 11. But the German emperor, William II (1859–1941; r. 1888–1918), had abdicated the day before, leaving Germany with an untested republican government. In January of 1919 the leaders of the victorious Allied nations met in Paris to establish European harmony on the foundation of the Fourteen Points— with the conquered powers not represented. The German government was presented with a treaty that was the work of the "Big Four" leaders alone: Wilson for the U.S., Georges Clemenceau (1841–1929) for France, David Lloyd George (1863–1945) for Britain, and Vittorio Orlando (1860–1952) for Italy. Faced with the choice between signing the treaty or running the risk of continued attacks upon already diminished German borders, Germany capitulated. At the palace of Versailles, near Paris, the German foreign minister Hermann Müller (1876–1931) and colonial and transport minister Johannes Bell (1868–1949), representing a very divided German parliament, signed the treaty (which ultimately contained four hundred and forty articles) on June 28, 1919. Many of Wilson's Fourteen Points were omitted or compromised in the treaty.

Peace is always preferable to war (for democracies at least), but by the early 1920s this one was proving costly and unstable. Borders were redrawn, governments replaced, economies thrown into confusion. A wave of totalitarian governments came to power, beginning with the 1922 march on Rome by fascist blackshirts, led by Benito Mussolini (1883–1945), and ending in 1936 with the establishment of a military dictatorship in Spain, under General Francisco Franco (1892–1975), which was consolidated only after three years of civil war. In this period, too, Adolf Hitler (1889–1945) came to power in Germany (1933) and dictatorships sprang up in Turkey (1923), Poland, Lithuania, and Portugal

The Demolition of the Simonov Monastery, Moscow, 1927.

Church buildings were nationalized in Russia in 1918, immediately after the Revolution. A wave of demolition began in the 1920s under the Commissar of Anti-Religious Affairs. Marble from churches was used to construct Moscow's subway system.

(1926), Yugoslavia (1929), Austria and Estonia (both in 1934), and Greece (1936). Meanwhile in the newly formed Soviet Union, congresses of the Communist International (Comintern) sought to create a culture as different from that of imperial Russia as could be imagined. With the ratification of a new constitution for the USSR in 1923, followed early the next year by the death of Lenin (1870–1924) and the accession of Josef Stalin (1879–1953) as dictator, the Russians and their subject peoples were in for the most oppressive three decades of their long history.

The optimistic view of human progress, eagerly fostered by so many theologians in the nineteenth century, was being put to a crucial test in these postwar decades. Assumptions that the world was approaching a state of perfection under Christian hegemony were severely challenged by years of unprecedented human destruction followed by political and economic collapse. The world-affirming stance of much mainline religion, shaken by the aftermath of the war, was no longer so easy to subscribe to; and some important theologians found the need to regroup.

Theology Between the Wars

Karl Barth and Neo-Orthodoxy

The most influential and prolific of these theologians was Karl Barth (1886–1968), a Reformed pastor from Basel who would become the anchor of a new evangelical movement. Barth was trained in the liberal tradition of his day, but he found it profoundly unsettling, as it seemed to him to be more anthropology than theology: more about human experience than the relationship between humans and God. The memory of the prominent German theologians of his day pledging support for their nation, and doing so as a religious affirmation (see Chapter 26), struck him as a dangerous capitulation to secular power. His famous critique of Schleiermacher (see Chapter 22), an insistence that one cannot speak of God as if one were speaking about humanity "in a loud voice" (i.e. projecting human values upon God and then claiming to know God's will), was to be the watchword of a theological program that would include volumes of sermons and treatises and a multivolume constructive work called *Church Dogmatics* (1932–67), a theological system to rival the great medieval summas in scope and penetration. (Like Thomas Aquinas's *Summa Theologiae*, the work with which it is most often compared, it was left unfinished at Barth's death.) Barth's career as a writer began with an explication of Paul's Epistle to the Romans (*Der Römerbrief*; 1919), in which he insists that the divine word is qualitatively different from any human message, demanding an openness to the sort of proclamation one does *not* want to hear, not the sort that one does. (See "Karl Barth on *Romans*" and "Karl Barth's *Church Dogmatics*.")

In a series of lectures published in English in 1928 as *The Word of God and the Word of Man* (*Das Wort Gottes und die Theologie*; 1924), Barth again stresses the paradoxical and indeed "hostile" nature of divine revelation. Revelation does not corroborate the constructions of human reason, Barth insists; it more often confounds them and forces a choice between the two categories: Does one heed the word of God, recognizing its potential for being harsh and demanding, or the word of human culture, something more likely to be affirming and accommodating? For Barth the choice was obvious, and it was equally obvious to him that the Protestant theological establishment of his day had chosen the easier second path, thus abandoning their mission as bearers of divine revelation. It was a harsh indictment, and it had a substantial impact in both the German- and the English-speaking worlds. For the next four decades Barth would represent a prophetic stance within Protestant thought, writing at a furious pace and with passionate intensity of the divine judgment hanging over mid-century Christendom. He was the self-appointed guardian of the divine "No," the judgment of God that holds humanity forever accountable for original sin. And it is only when one has heard this "No" and been humbled by it that one can hear the "Yes" of the atonement on the cross.

Karl Barth on *Romans*

Karl Barth (1886–1968) inaugurated the "Neo-Orthodox" movement in Protestant theology with the publication of his exegesis of Romans *(1919). In this passage on* Romans *3:28 Barth emphasizes the difference between the human and the divine.*

For we reckon that a man is justified by the faithfulness of God apart from the works of the law. Our transference from the point of view of religion to the point of view of Jesus involves the transference from a well-established attitude towards the relation between God and man to a wholly different method of *reckoning*. All religions either *reckon* that human achievements in this world—some concrete human behaviour or disposition—constitute a claim to the favour of God and must be rewarded by Him (ii. 6); or else they *reckon* that human achievements are themselves the reward of God, since they are the tangible and recognizable products of a transformation of human behaviour that has been wrought by God. So all religions assume either that God will act or that He has acted; making the assumption quite apart from any consideration of the "Moment" when men stand naked before God and are clothed upon by Him. They do not consider before and after to be before and after the "Moment" when men are moved by God; or they suppose either that the "Moment" depends upon some previous behaviour or that it carries with it some subsequent behaviour; that is to say, they conceive of the "Moment" as in some way comparable and commensurable with human behaviour. Consequently, all religions admit the possibility of boasting of what men are and do and have, as though they were divine. In all religions it is therefore possible to disregard or to escape from the paradox of faith. From the point of view of Jesus, however, we must *reckon* otherwise: fundamentally there are no human *works* sufficiently significant to excite the favour of God; nor are there works so well-pleasing to Him that they become significant in the world. In Jesus everything that occurs in the world is bent under the judgement of God and awaits His affirmation.

(From *The Epistle to the Romans*, trans. Edwyn C. Hoskyns. London: Oxford University Press, 1933.)

Barth is the foremost representative of a movement called NEO-ORTHODOXY. The movement is a revival of the Latin tradition shaped by Augustine and the Protestant Reformers, particularly Calvin. In these authors Barth found the clearest sense of the difference between revelation and reason, and of the way the content of revelation works on a person. In answer to the nineteenth-century scholars who saw the Bible as only a set of human books, Barth insisted that this was only another form of exalting reason over revelation, and the presumption is

---

Karl Barth's *Church Dogmatics*

Barth's Church Dogmatics *(1932–67) is one of the great Protestant systems of the twentieth century, often taking a dramatically new approach to traditional theological themes. In this excerpt from the section on "The Doctrine of God," Barth sets strict limits to God's knowability by humans.*

How far is God known? and how far is God knowable? We have answered these questions in principle in the two previous sections. We may summarise our answer in the statement that God is known by God and by God alone. His revelation is not merely His own readiness to be known, but man's readiness to know Him. God's revelation is, therefore, His knowability. On the ground and in the sphere of this basic answer we now have to give a practical answer—a concrete description of the event between God and man which we call the knowledge of God and which as such is the presupposition, continually to be renewed, of all Christian doctrine, of Church dogmatics and therefore of the preaching of the church. We have to make this event and the form of the knowledge of God plain and understandable to ourselves. We do so by defining its limits. Since we are dealing with an event, limit is here to be understood in the sense of *terminus*. What happens when God is known becomes clear and understandable to us, and visible to us as a form, when we know the *terminus a quo* and the *terminus ad quem* of this event, the point with which it begins and the point with which it ends. Thus the title of this section might well have been "The way of the knowledge of God." But the nature of this way is determined by the points at which it begins and ends, and is thus determined by the limits of the knowledge of God. The way of the knowledge of God running between these two limits is the Christian doctrine presented so far as it rests on the knowledge of God and produces the knowledge of God. If we again ask how far this doctrine rests on this knowledge and produces this knowledge, and if we ask especially about the form of its knowledge, our questions will be more clear and precise if we ask about its limits.

The limit which is our concern in the first part of this section is the *terminus a quo*, the point of beginning and departure in the knowledge of God. We have said that knowledge of God is the presupposition of all Christian doctrine. But this means that it is the basis of the church and its confession, the basis of the faith of all those who, in the church and by the church, are called to fellowship with God and thus to their own salvation and the glorifying of God. Knowledge of God in the sense hitherto defined by us as the knowledge of God which is objectively and subjectively established and led to its goal by God Himself, the knowledge of God whose subject and object is God the Father and the Son through the Holy Spirit, is the basis—and indeed the only basis—of the love of God which comes to us and the praise of God which is expected of us.

(From *Church Dogmatics*, vol. 2. Edinburgh: T. & T. Clark, 1957.)

already condemned by the divine judgment of revelation itself. Other members of this movement include Emil Brunner (1889–1966), another author of a multivolume systematic theology. Brunner is better known, however, for his dispute with Barth over the possibility of a link between human reason and the divine mind. On the basis of close study of Calvin's work, Brunner argued that the term "image of God" in Genesis 1:27 and other biblical texts indicated that there was a point of connection between the human mind and the divine, and that God and the divine will were in some way knowable. Barth answered this essay with a 1934 tract entitled *No! Answer to Emil Brunner*, and argued that any point of connection that might have made God known to humans was completely lost in the Fall. Brunner was more correct in capturing Calvin's thought, but Barth was, by this point, defending his own system.

Reinhold Niebuhr

In the United States, the conservative strain represented by Neo-Orthodoxy was carried on by Reinhold Niebuhr (1892–1971) and a number of other theologians

---

Reinhold Niebuhr

Reinhold Niebuhr (1892–1971) was one of the most influential Protestant thinkers of mid-twentieth-century America, who provoked his audiences to look critically at much of what was taken as progress in society. In this commentary on the first humans landing on the moon, Niebuhr corrects the journalists who saw this event as a triumphant moment for civilization.

With all Americans I have a proper pride in the technical achievement of our first moon landing. It was a triumph of technology, teamwork, and discipline. Many speak of a "breakthrough" but one asks, breakthrough in what? The landing on the moon has been compared with the discovery of the new continent of America. But the moon is dead and barren of all natural and human life; and America was rich in all physical and historic possibilities.

But the chief reason for assessing the significance of the moon landing negatively, even while the paens of triumph are sung, is that this tremendous technical achievement represents a defective sense of human values and of priorities in our technical culture.

The same technology that gave us this triumph has created many of our problems. Our population at the beginning of the century was only twenty per cent urbanized; and now eighty per cent live in large cities. We have woefully neglected these urban centers. They are stinking with air and water pollution. Their inner cities are decaying. They are filled with Negro minorities, increasingly resentful, even in violent resentment, because they have been deficient in technical training and therefore subject to a much higher level of unemployment than the national average. The rich nation which can afford the technical "breakthrough" cannot offer the impoverished cities tax help to feed the hungry or educate the uneducated.

We are betraying our moral weakness in our very triumphs in technology and economics.

(From *A Reinhold Niebuhr Reader*, ed. Charles C. Brown. Philadelphia, PA: Trinity Press International, 1992.)

in his circle. Niebuhr was a child of the Germanic Midwest, raised in the missionary Protestantism of nineteenth-century pioneers, destined from youth for a life of preaching. From an initially unlikely academic post at Union Theological Seminary, in New York, Niebuhr embarked on a crusade of preaching, lecturing, and writing that accentuated sin and indicted the blindness of liberal theology which minimized the effects of sin. (See "Reinhold Niebuhr.") In prophetic works such as *Moral Man and Immoral Society* (1932), subtitled *A Study in Ethics and Politics*, Niebuhr presented a vision of the evil embodied in large groups, and saw Christianity as the worldview that could counteract tendencies toward social evil. Niebuhr's style was reminiscent of the revivalism of the earlier century (see Chapter 24), and it was no accident that he became associated with such movements as the YMCA and Chautauqua (a program of adult education, originally religious, named for the lake in New York State near which it started in 1874).

Social Problems and the Catholic Church

In Catholicism, too, theological systems were receiving renewed attention. A movement known as Neo-Thomism (see Chapter 25) gained momentum during these decades, making Thomas Aquinas the focal figure in a wave of scholarship on medieval Scholasticism. The potential for the theology of the thirteenth and fourteenth centuries to illuminate the issues facing the modern world was the impetus behind the founding of a number of institutes for Thomistic or medieval studies, and for a rich harvest of journals and book-length studies. The philosophic structure of Thomas's thought gave it a compatibility with modern science that other theological systems lacked (remember that Aristotle, whose methods served as a model for Thomas, was a formidable natural scientist). And his encompassing theological vision, reflected in the cycle of exitus-reditus (see Chapter 10), was more inclusive than other thinkers', presumably relevant for the whole world and not just the church. Catholic intellectuals such as Etienne Gilson (1884–1978) and Jacques Maritain (1882–1973) offered new Christian worldviews that were popular antidotes to the materialism and logical analysis being developed by philosophers such as Bertrand Russell (1872–1970) and Ludwig Wittgenstein (1889–1951). In a world of intellectual reduction and fragmentation, the Thomistic revival promised a grand picture—and a more optimistic view of human nature than Neo-Orthodoxy, with its emphasis on sin, could claim, or that logical Positivism, with its denial of the transcendent, could allow.

Pius XI's Calls for Social Reform

As we have seen (see Chapter 25), the Thomistic revival initiated by Leo XIII was accompanied by a social program intended to combat the materialistic and revolutionary spirits of the nineteenth century. The post-World War I decades appeared to the Catholic curia, or governing body, as only the worsening of an already tragic situation, and Pope Pius XI (Achille Rati, 1857–1939; r. 1922–1939) chose to address the times in a number of official documents. A liturgical historian with impeccable scholarly training, Pius XI saw the need for the church to become involved more constructively in society, and he also saw greater involvement by the laity as the means toward this. His bull *Ubi Arcano* (1922) gave an impetus to the CATHOLIC ACTION movement, a group of various lay-clerical organizations dedicated to advancing the church's social and religious work. In the diplomatic work of the church he made substantial strides in restoring damaged relations with a number of countries, including France (where church and state had been separated since 1905); Italy (in the Lateran Treaty of 1929, securing from Benito Mussolini the independence of the Vatican as a sovereign state); and, in 1933, Germany (see below).

But Pius was not one to make deals with such devils as Mussolini and Hitler and then turn silent when their sinister natures came to light. In 1931 he observed the fortieth anniversary of Leo XIII's great social encyclical *Rerum Novarum* (see Chapter 25) with one of his own, titled *Quadragesimo Anno* (May 15, 1931). Acknowledging his predecessor's boldness and recognizing that the social conditions of the worker had indeed improved in the decades since 1891, Pius went beyond merely defending the right of private ownership and encouraged the pursuit of even higher, yet more equitable, levels of material prosperity. One of the missions of the church that Pius identified in *Quadragesimo Anno* was the "redemption of the non-owning workers," the elimination of the virtual slavery of working completely for another, with no personal stake in the work being done. This can be accomplished by reconstructing society so as to bring out the dignity of all persons. Quoting Thomas Aquinas, Pius defined the social order as a harmonious arrangement of members united by a strong bond—that bond being, in

The Vatican Signs the Concordat with Hitler's Reich, March 1933..

Torn between protecting Catholics in Germany and Jews vulnerable to an anti-Semitic ideology, the papacy chose to protect its own: This decision has been hotly debated ever since.

Pius's view, the common good. Thus business and the professions are not just the means to individual self-realization, as Leo XIII had suggested; they are instruments for the creation and nurturing of the common good.

A sense of crisis in the economic realm is voiced even more sharply in the encyclical *Caritate Christi Compulsi* (May 3, 1932): on the one hand a condemnation of communism and the excesses of nationalism, and on the other a plea for the preservation of religious values amid the turmoil in the secular world. In Pius's view, only a spirit of prayer and reparation can cure society of its ills, and he calls for a period of mortification and prayer as a step toward such healing.

The political situation in Germany is the subject of another encyclical, *Mit brennender Sorge* ("With burning concern"), issued in German to the Catholic pastors of Germany on March 14, 1937, and meant to be read in all churches that Easter. After signing a concordat with the German government four years earlier, in 1933, the Catholic Church had become subject to a number of persecutions; but the terms of the concordat prevented the hierarchy from openly denouncing the government's policy. Thus the hierarchy faced a dilemma: denounce the increasingly brutal regime and violate the concordat, or honor the 1933 agreement and watch the Catholic Church suffer unprecedented degradation? *Mit brennender Sorge* was a middle path between this choice, a denunciation of the ideological claims which fell short of an outright condemnation of the Nazi regime.

In this encyclical, Pius excluded from the category of believers anyone who equates God with the world; who identifies God with the deities and forces of ancient Germanic myth; or who locates the ideal form of human values in any nation or people. True belief in God is possibly only through Christianity, Pius insisted, and in the church as the foundation of truth. The appeal to the faithful was poignant and prophetic, and would echo in Catholic ears in Germany for the following decade.

Nazism and the Churches

Pius's words were unable to reverse the tide. Nazism was in many ways an alternate religion, with its leadership demanding undivided loyalty and holding the power of life and death over the people. Crosses were removed from churches and replaced with swastikas, and ceremonies of "consecrating" the ever-present red, white, and black banners were major events of the new cult. German identity (or "Aryan" or "Nordic" in the language of the time), rather than the "slave" religion of Christianity, or the even more degrading ways of the Jews, was the new ideal; terms like "folk," "race," and "blood" entered the political vocabulary. The Nuremberg Laws of September 1935—followed by thirteen supplementary laws the following year, all designed to "protect the German Volk [people]"—denied citizenship to Jews in Germany; prohibited marriage and extramarital relations between German gentiles and Jews; and forbade Jews from employing non-Jewish women under the age of forty-five, lest "racial mixing" take place. It got worse with new laws in March 1938, when Jews had to wear an identifying yellow star, add "Sarah" and "Israel" to their names, and relinquish all property in excess of 500 marks. The licenses of Jewish physicians and lawyers were suspended. On the twentieth anniversary of the emperor's abdication, November 10, 1938, thousands of Jewish businesses, houses, and synagogues throughout Germany were vandalized in the notorious "Kristallnacht" ("night of broken glass").

The sequence of events thereafter is well known. The rounding-up of Jewish people in Germany and its numerous conquered nations began in 1939; concentration camps, mostly in the east and, so, intentionally off "German soil," were built to accommodate them. In January 1942 at a mansion in Wannsee, outside Berlin, the leaders of the Nazi regime decided upon a "final solution" to the "Jewish problem" and embarked upon a program of extermination that would claim nearly six million Jews, plus another five million people deemed undesirable by the leaders of the "Master Race," including non-Jewish Poles and other Slavs, Gypsies, homosexuals, political and religious dissidents, and people with physical or mental disabilities. Around the time that Hitler committed suicide, on April 30, 1945, Allied troops entering Poland and Germany were discovering the full horror of the "final solution" in such places as Buchenwald, Treblinka, and Auschwitz.

When the war finally ended in August 1945 with the surrender of Japan, it had claimed more than 90 million victims, with around 55,000,000 killed, 35,000,000 wounded, and upward of 3,000,000 lost without a trace. Half of the casualties were civilians.

The Christian churches of Germany, all of which suffered huge losses in clergy and faithful, were deeply divided by these events. In Germany a number of Protestant leaders were members of the Nazi party, and kept their ecclesiastical positions by forming an alliance known as the GERMAN CHRISTIANS. This movement saw no contradiction between Christian values and those of the Nazi party, and used the pulpit to encourage support for Hitler and his organization.

In opposition, a resistance church known as the CONFESSING CHURCH was organized; these clergy continued their work, despite the constant threat of persecution, throughout the war. They took their name from a confessional synod held in May 1934, and had originated in a "Pastors' Emergency League" formed in 1933 by Martin Niemöller (1892–1984), a Lutheran pastor who would be an outspoken opponent of Nazism and who would, along with the Jews he defended, find himself incarcerated in a camp. (His widow would later convert to Judaism.) Karl Barth and Emil Brunner would also join the Confessing Church—and lose their academic positions. Another member of this group was Dietrich Bonhoeffer (1906–1945), a promising young theologian who had studied at Union Theological Seminary, in New York (where he had worked with Reinhold Niebuhr), and later served as chaplain to the Lutheran community in London. In 1935 he returned to Germany, where he took an active role in the struggle against Nazism. He lost his life in punishment for a botched assassination attempt against Hitler.

In the United States, emigré theologians such as Paul Tillich (1886–1965) struck out in new directions (Tillich would be the architect of an existential theology that had broad impact in the 1960s and later), while native-born American theologians such as H. Richard Niebuhr (1894–1962), brother of Reinhold, would provoke serious reflection on the state of the world in a series of wartime essays in the magazine *Christian Century* entitled "Where Is God in the War?" True to the Neo-Orthodox standpoint, Niebuhr saw a divine judgment, and a harsh one, over-

BIOGRAPHICAL PROFILE

Paul Tillich (1886–1965)

Paul Tillich, born on the eastern border of Germany in 1886, called himself a child of the nineteenth century, but he would prove to be one of the more influential theologians of the twentieth. The son of a Lutheran pastor, he received a solid grounding in Greek and Latin before studying philosophy and theology at the universities of Berlin, Tübingen, and Halle. After service as a chaplain in the German army during World War I, Tillich taught theology at Berlin, at the time one of the great centers for that discipline. From there he moved on to Marburg, where he began work on his *Systematic Theology*, a modern "summa" that would be completed only decades later. Posts at other universities followed, but ended in 1933 with his dismissal from the philosophical faculty at Frankfurt by the Nazi authorities who had just won power.

Emigrating to the U.S. in late 1933, Tillich joined the faculty of Union Theological Seminary in New York, the home of Reinhold Niebuhr, the most influential American theologian at the time. Tillich became a popular lecturer both on-campus and off, and his sermons and public lectures brought new ideas to people seeking meaning in a world quickly becoming chaotic. With the rise of the Third Reich, German Protestant theology had split into two branches: the "German Christians," who supported the Nazi regime, and the "Confessing Church," which was dominated by Neo-Orthodox theologians under the influence of Karl Barth. Tillich's program of a "Theology of Culture" represents a third path, one in which culture is a medium for religious ideas. Alongside the secularized religious culture of the German Christians and the intensive dependence on scriptural revelation by Neo-Orthodox Christians, Tillich's views were considered a provocative new style of thinking.

Although many of his main ideas had their roots in his German past, his work and influence reached their peak in the U.S. Students came to Union Theological Seminary and neighboring Columbia University to study under him (1933–55); professorships at Harvard (1955–62) and Chicago (1962–65) followed in the 1960s; and his Terry Lecture

at Yale, published as *The Courage to Be* (1952), was for decades a standard introduction to twentieth-century existentialist religious thought. His advocacy of religious socialism, also conceived in Germany but developed in the U.S., was an antidote both to the materialism he witnessed among the upper classes in Europe and America and the misery he saw among the dispossessed. Visits to his beloved jazz clubs in Harlem brought him face-to-face with some of that misery.

From a vast array of concepts, two elements of Tillich's thought stand out. One is his identification of the "Demonic" in culture, not just the presence of evil but the objectification of that presence in symbols and mythic narratives—in other words, how evil becomes a force in human experience. For Tillich only an equally strong, or stronger, symbolization of the good can overcome the demonic: and this, he states, is the image of grace in Christian experience. The second feature of his work is a methodological one: the method of "correlation." What Tillich means is that certain questions seem to be universal in human experience, and that religious systems such as Christianity hold the valid answers to those questions. There is therefore a correlation between the questioning framework of human existence and the truth behind Christian revelation.

Tillich's influence was greatest outside confessional theological circles: philosophers of religion, students of culture in its various forms, and existentialist thinkers drew the most from Tillich, who was most eloquent when describing "boundary" situations (points in life demanding critical choices) and defining the religious as the realm of "ultimate concern" in contrast to the changeable and relative concerns of our secular existence. Tillich's main scholarly work was *Systematic Theology* (1951–63) and his more popular books included *Dynamics of Faith* (1957).

Paul Tillich, 1960.

hanging the world's events during those years; the pressing question was to whom that judgment was directed.

Pius XII's Controversial Legacy

Seemingly impervious to the storm raging around him, Pope Pius XII (Eugenio Pacelli, 1876–1958; r. 1939–1958) has posthumously drawn all the controversy he tried to avoid in his own lifetime. Pacelli was a Roman who entered the service of the Vatican curia in 1901, shortly after his ordination; in 1917 he bacame papal nuncio to Bavaria, and in the following years he drew up concordats with Bavaria, with Prussia, and, in 1933, with the new National Socialist (Nazi) government of Germany. He ascended to the papacy the same year that Hitler invaded Poland. Pius evidently felt himself bound by the concordats he had negotiated, even though the developments since 1933 could have been seen as a breach of faith on the German government's part. Pressed on all sides to condemn the Nazi aggression, and urgently so by Allied envoys to the Vatican during the war years, Pius maintained an almost eerie silence, fearful (so he claimed) that his vocal opposition would elicit only worse persecutions. His condemnations of war during this period failed to mention Germans or Jews, though he did lament the singling out of peoples for extermination on the basis of "nationality or race." The German capture of Rome in 1943 brought with it the roundup and deportation of the Jewish population of Rome, a community that predated the Diaspora (see Chapter 1) and Christianity itself. (Some of these people were descendants of Jews brought back as slaves by Roman forces in Palestine in the first century B.C.E.) Pius reportedly said nothing as the trucks drove past St. Peter's and the Vatican palace, with some of their doomed passengers calling out for help.

In the postwar years, Pius XII pursued matters that did concern him with various encyclicals including *Humani Generis* (August 1950), a call for renewed orthodoxy in Roman Catholic dogma. Rejecting as erroneous such scientific theories as evolution and new developments in philosophy and the social sciences, Pius asserts that Christian philosophy (by which he means Thomism) and Scripture (as interpreted by the MAGISTERIUM, the teaching office of the Roman Church) can be the only solid and satisfying sources of truth.

From the beginning of his papacy, Pius remained above the fray, the advocate of transcendent principles and protector of the church, which he was confident would survive the assaults of war and communism. In recent years, his efforts on behalf of the church during World War II have sparked moves among some conservative Catholics to have him declared a saint and a hero who saved the lives of thousands of Jews. Not surprisingly, this has provoked outrage among people of all faiths and proceedings for Pius's canonization are on hold. Whatever the outcome, the debate about Pius XII and his activities during the war will undoubtedly continue for many years: What did he, or did he not, know? What could he have done? What really were his intentions? The answer to this last question has been beyond human reach since October 9, 1958, when Eugenio Pacelli took his last breath.

With his passing, the Catholic Church was forced to look forward and face the realities of the postwar world; so, for that matter, were the other churches within the Christian tradition. All the old problems—such as social injustice and the divisions between churches—remained, and new ones were emerging. Once again, Christianity would be put to the test.

Eastern Orthodoxy

The Orthodox tradition followed its own course, when it could, in the twentieth century, preserving the ancient liturgy and devotions while other branches of Christianity were adapting to modernity. As a result, the Eastern Church appeared increasingly alien to the supposedly more progressive churches of the Latin tradition.

A church that has kept within its own borders for much of its history suffered severe blows during World War I and the Russian Revolution. The first and second Balkan Wars (1912 and 1913) raised but did not answer questions about the identities of Greece, Albania, Romania, Montenegro, and Turkey. Although these countries were engaged in political rather than religious conflicts, religious identity is so fundamental to the ethnic consciousness of the Balkan peoples that alliances between Catholic and Orthodox nations, or Orthodox and Muslim ones, created feelings of alienation rather than stability.

World War I continued the unrest, with Eastern (Russian) and Western (Austro-Hungarian) powers ready to take possession of states such as Serbia and Greece. It was the Russian Revolution, however, that posed the greatest challenge to the Orthodox Church. Ideologically driven by atheistic communism, the Leninist ideal of a dictatorship by the working classes based on an economic worldview brought the grand tradition of Christianity in Russia virtually to its knees.

With the assassination of the Russian royal family in July 1918 and the rise in its place of the Communist Party, Russia fell under the control of an atheistic government; the prohibition of all opposition groups in 1921 meant that clergy still loyal to the old regime were silenced, often by torture and death. In place of Christianity a substitute religion was erected in the form of political rallies and effigies of state leaders replacing church services and icons. The resemblance between Soviet agencies and the intricate ecclesiastical hierarchy of the Russian Church was obvious to any perceptive observer.

Orthodoxy went underground but did not die out. Migrations of peoples after World War I redrew the boundaries of Orthodoxy. Declining numbers of Orthodox monks also weakened an element of the tradition that had been powerful and influential beyond the Greek-speaking world. The fragmentation into various denominations, many of them indistinguishable in the West, made Orthodoxy something of a shadowy presence in the Western world. Simultaneously, however, as the Western world demonstrated more and more diversity, some of the more exotic elements of the Eastern tradition helped bring Orthodoxy into clearer focus. Its rich artistic tradition, evidenced by its icons but also in the liturgy, stood out from elements of Protestant and Catholic traditions that had become tediously similar and familiar.

As the years passed, what had been known as the Russian Church in Exile became a vibrant part of the American Church, its members no longer just Russians and Greeks, but converts via marriage and others drawn to an ancient and colorful branch of the Christian family. And to the extent that Orthodoxy sees itself as universal, a missionary element emerged and attracted others to the faith.

Beyond North America, Orthodoxy emerged and even flourished in some of the most unlikely places—if one thinks of it as grounded in Eastern European culture. In Africa, for example, an Orthodox community under native leadership appeared in Uganda and was officially recognized in 1946 as a branch of authentic Orthodoxy. Kenya followed, and a seminary was established in Nairobi in 1982. The spread of this tradition on the African continent remains a remarkable and still highly mysterious phenomenon.

One fundamental distinction between Orthodox and Western Christianity is found in the notion of the "filioque." This is the Latin term for "and the son," a reference to whether the Holy Spirit proceeds from the Father and Jesus Christ or from the Father alone. The Western tradition has held that the Holy Spirit proceeds from Father and Son alike, meaning that the experience of the Holy Spirit is contingent on recognizing Jesus as the second person of the Trinity. Orthodoxy eliminates the "filioque" so that the Holy Spirit is seen to proceed from the Father alone. This gives the tradition a close tie to Judaism, because something similar to the Holy Spirit is found in the Hebrew Scriptures.

The Eastern Block after 1989 experienced a religious revival. Catholics and Protestants in former East Germany saw their churches spring back to life and their long-suppressed clergy raised to new levels of influence. In the Orthodox tradition, the end of seven decades of oppression released a wellspring of religious expression. Contempt for the old regime and the veneration of ancestral practices have been factors in this: a martyred church has an immediate appeal to a people that suffered under a totalitarian system.

The change of regimes in Russia has brought with it a new sensitivity to interconfessional relations. The Russian Church of the 1990s has been aware, in ways its pre-Soviet predecessor never was, of other Christian traditions. Magadan, near Vladivostok in Eastern Russia, the site of one of Stalin's notorious prison camps, became a mission field for the Roman Catholic Church; and in a reversal of nineteenth-century relations between Russia and Alaska, the Catholic Archdiocese of Anchorage established an ecumenical center in Magadan serving the children and grandchildren of Catholic prisoners from the West. In Russia's western regions, more open lines of communication between the Orthodox and Lutherans in Finland led in the 1990s to a new "Finnish School" of Lutheran theology, one that, like Orthodoxy, stresses the transformation in Jesus Christ from the human

Memorial sculpture, Magadan, Siberia, 1990.

This sculpture stands on the site of one of Stalin's former internment camps.

to the divine. This school of thought has both engaged and enraged Lutheran theologians around the world; but it also marks the beginning of a potentially fruitful exchange of Lutheran and Orthodox ideas.

Although Orthodoxy largely remains a tradition unto itself, we should not conclude that the Eastern tradition has not had a voice in the mainstream of Christian thought. On the contrary, Western Christianity has been remarkably open to doctrinal and liturgical influences from the East. In terms of theology and philosophy, the Russian Nicolai Berdyayev (1874–1948) was a pathbreaker, an apologist for the "religion of spirit and personality," defining both as irreducible essences of the human person. He was also a skeptic about materialistic claims to human progress, holding instead that the dignity and freedom of the individual triumphed over the collective will to power. His eloquence in defending the individual spirit against purely materialist ideologies brought him into conflict with both political and ecclesiastical powers in Russia, yet gained him a significant audience in the West.

In the U.S., the Russian-born Georges Florovsky (1893–1979) was one of the first Orthodox clergy to enter the mainstream of American religious discourse. An early voice for ecumenism at Harvard and Princeton as well as at St. Vladimir's Seminary in New York, Florovsky never abandoned his conviction that Orthodoxy was a uniquely sacred church, one that could never be simply a variant on Christianity. Also at St. Vladimir's Seminary, John Meyendorff (1926–1992) trained more than one generation of Orthodox men. Born and trained in Patristic and Byzantine studies in France, Meyendorff also taught at Harvard and Columbia, and participated in the work of the World Council of Churches. Finally, a priest and professor at Holy Cross Greek Orthodox School of Theology in Brookline, Massachusetts, Stanley Harakas has addressed moral issues and elucidated the Eastern liturgy; in *Toward Transfigured Life* (1983) he sets out a foundation for an Orthodox moral theology. Modern in tone and applied to contemporary problems, Harakas's work draws from the Patristic tradition, demonstrating that a theological system can be anchored in the past but still speak clearly to the present.

Key Terms

CATHOLIC ACTION An early-20th-century European movement empowering lay Catholics in social and educational work.

CONFESSING CHURCH A branch of German Protestantism during World War II which opposed Nazism and its takeover of the Christian establishment.

GERMAN CHRISTIANS A group of German clergy who saw in Nazism the fulfillment of nationalist ideals; collaborators who "consecrated" Nazi banners and symbols.

MAGISTERIUM The teaching office of the Roman Catholic Church; the theologians and hierarchy who protect the dogmas held by the Catholic faithful.

NEO-ORTHODOXY A 20th-century Protestant movement reviving stringent Reformation-era conceptions of original sin and the harmful potential of human organizations.

Ecumenical Initiatives
The World Council of Churches and Vatican II

The aftermath of World War II was a wake-up call for most mainline churches in the United States and Europe. Amid the rubble of innumerable cities and the millions of dead, the religion that embodied the teachings of a martyred first-century peacemaker awoke from a nightmare a dozen years long. The most catastrophic war in history demanded rigorous soul-searching by all Christian leaders. Had Christendom and its most highly developed constituent nations failed to see and counteract the evils of fascism, or was the church an unwitting accomplice in the destruction? Were Christian attitudes toward the Jews at all responsible for the antisemitism that resulted in the deaths of millions of innocent people? If European civilization was a Christian culture in any real sense, then the churches were surely implicated in the events of 1933–45.

The Establishment of the WCC

While such questions hung in the air, some of the churches tried to take positive steps toward healing and reconciliation. Since the late 1930s plans had been mooted to combine the efforts of two ecumenical organizations, Life and Work, and Faith and Order, into one large organization; but these plans had been thwarted by the war. After 1945 there was a dire need for the churches' work: feeding, clothing, and educating the civilian victims of war. A commission for refugees, already under way by 1938, worked overtime during the war and afterward to help resettle Jews and other homeless people who had been collected into refugee camps.

In Amsterdam in 1948, the World Council of Churches (WCC) was established, with 144 churches making up its initial membership. With a General Assembly as its governing board, the WCC met at six- or seven-year intervals in Evanston, Illinois; New Delhi, India; Uppsala, Sweden; and elsewhere, a sequence reflecting its intercultural nature. Formally bound together only by their faith in Jesus Christ, the member churches shared in missionary work as much as postwar

World Council of Churches Assembly Meeting, Amsterdam, 1948.

Representing a range of the church hierarchy, leaders of European denominations and missionary churches founded the WCC to protect and extend Christianity.

reconstruction efforts, presenting Jesus as the hope for all humanity. Such evangelism, refined by WCC study groups focused on non-Christian nations, brought new waves of Christian contact to people in the developing world.

By the time the WCC met for the fourth time, at Uppsala in 1968, the organization had matured to a point that certain changes were required. The theme of the Uppsala meeting was renewal, and the WCC took this as an occasion for its own renewal, as well as the renewal of the church within culture generally. The year 1968 was one of ferment; intellectually, politically, and, as it turned out, religiously. A revolutionary spirit was in the air at the Uppsala meeting. "Renewal" at this conference meant change and adaptation to new secular realities—rather than revival of the old religion disregarding these realities. This may have been in keeping with the spirit of the time, but it was not in accord with the spirit of some of the churches, especially the Orthodox, the Russian branch of which (along with Bulgarian, Polish, and Romanian branches) had joined the WCC at the 1961 New Delhi meeting. In the ongoing negotiation between the past and the present that religion is always engaged in, it was evident to most that at the Uppsala meeting the present won the day, at least for the time being.

In the final decades of the century, the WCC became something of an ecclesiastical United Nations. At its headquarters in Geneva it hosted an array of special departments: Faith and Order, Mission Studies, Evangelism, Church and Study (all within the division of studies); and departments for youth, laity, education, and an ecumenical institute (within the division of ecumenical action). Conferences continue to be held and documents issued, all directed toward the goal of mutual understanding and constructive coexistence. Many theologians have spent time as visiting fellows at WCC headquarters, and WCC documents continue to attract public attention, even if some of the mid-century ecumenical enthusiasm has waned.

There have been some distinguished offshoots of the WCC. One of these is the International Congress of Luther Research, which has met at three- or four-year intervals since the 1950s. Led by an international Continuation Committee, the Luther Congress has been a meeting ground for the leading Luther scholars, both Protestant (mostly Lutherans) and Catholic, to assess each others' contributions to the literature; for younger researchers to share and test their ideas; and for all to examine Luther's enduring legacy in the modern world (see below). Recent meetings have seen more and more non-Lutherans participating, and under the canopy of Luther research some truly ecumenical discussions have taken place. An increasing number of participants from outside Europe and the United States have brought provocative questions to the forum. In particular, the question of the relevance of a sixteenth-century German monk in twentieth- and twenty-first-century Latin America and Asia invites serious reflection about the relation of cultural conditions to religious ideas.

Christians and Jews

In the wake of the Holocaust and in a spirit of inter-faith harmony, Christian theologians looked hard at relations between Christianity and Judaism, and came to a new awareness of affinities between the two traditions. With the aid of biblical scholars and experts on ancient history, Christian theologians came to appreciate in a substantial way Christianity's origins in first-century Judaism. Researches in Jewish sectarianism in the period of Roman rule revealed the extent to which the Jews were an anxious and divided people at this time and the need, out of historical accuracy as much as any conciliatory impulse, to see first-century Christianity as a sect within that milieu.

Just how close these Jewish–Christian affinities are was revealed by the discovery, in 1947, of the Dead Sea Scrolls (see Chapter 2). This discovery was partly responsible for the increased use, around this time, of the term "Judeo-Christian

Dead Sea Scrolls, c. 1st century.

This ancient collection of texts probably changed Christian understanding of the nature of belief more dramatically than any other discovery of the last millennium.

tradition," with its acknowledgment of the many aspects of belief, worship, and ethics held in common by these two religions.

Not everyone accepted this label, however. Jewish theologians in particular felt that the hyphenated term subordinated Judaism to Christianity, and bound the Jewish tradition too closely to the Christian one. It was one thing, they felt, for Christians to recognize the Jewish roots of their faith, but another thing entirely to imply that Judaism was incomplete without its Christian partner; and this is what they felt the "Judeo-Christian" term was doing. Marrying together the two religions as a single tradition was historically as well as theologically inaccurate, for it threatened to gloss over a long and painful history of exclusion and persecution. Thus there are few Jews who subscribe to the combined term.

Nevertheless, progress in reconciliation has proceeded at its own pace. The Lutheran Church, through numerous declarations and gestures, has repudiated certain writings by Martin Luther which, in keeping with the spirit of their time, accentuated the supposed "impiety" of the Jews. And the Catholic Church has followed suit, issuing its own official declarations of regret over its part in the persecutions of Jews.

The Second Vatican Council

The Catholic Church had a different set of problems. Details of concordats between the Vatican and various European nations, especially Germany, came to light in the years after the war, raising questions about papal self-interest and the Vatican's attitude to Jews. Was the Roman curia more concerned with preserving its power and property when it entered into alliances with the German government, promising, among other things, not to come out in opposition to German policies toward Jews? As to Protestantism, was it not time also to mend some fences in that area? Recent events had shown the appalling extremes to which prejudice could lead and had put doctrinal differences into perspective.

The death of Pius XII (see Chapter 27) in 1958 was followed by the election to the papacy of Cardinal Angelo Giuseppe Roncalli (1881–1963; r. 1958–1963), Patriarch (cardinal-archbishop) of Venice. Although Roncalli came from a peasant background, he had quickly distinguished himself as a scholar, obtaining a doctorate in theology in 1904 while still in his early twenties. During his career he proved himself an able diplomat and was active in humanitarian work. On becoming pope, he took the name John XXIII. Already almost seventy-seven at his election, Pope John was expected to be little more than a temporary preserver of the status quo; the COLLEGE OF CARDINALS often signals its expectations by the age of the man they elect to the papacy. No one could have imagined that this elderly and scholarly pontiff who wanted only to be a "good shepherd" would usher in a new era for the Catholic Church.

Yet a new era is exactly what John had in mind from the very beginning of his pontificate. Within three months he called for a synod of the Roman diocese, a general council of the church, and a revision of the code of canon law (see Chapter 11), the body of rules, put into systematic order in 1917, by which the Catholic Church ruled. The term associated with John's pontificate is *aggiornamento*, literally "updating," and it was applied to Catholicism in both practice and doctrine.

The Council, known as VATICAN II (1962–65), ranks with Trent (see Chapter 18) and Lateran IV in importance. It was an "updating" in a number of ways, most obviously in the substitution of the vernacular for Latin in the Mass, a step many Catholics regarded as long overdue. Eliminating the Index of Prohibited Books, an invention of Trent, was another step toward modernization; and new translations and editions of the Bible made the Scriptures more accessible to Catholics, who had tended to see Scripture as off-limits. And the laity were given a more active role in the affairs of the church, as teachers, in distributing the Eucharist, and as partners in ongoing consultations with the clergy. The ancient chasm between laity and priesthood, in other words, was being bridged in as many ways as possible without eliminating the essential distinction between the two.

Lay Involvement in the Catholic Church

Longstanding symbols of the separation of clergy and laity gave way to symbolic expressions of their closeness. Along with the Latin liturgy went the custom of saying Mass at the altar, placed at the east end of the church, while facing away from the people. Instead, the priest of the post-Vatican II church now celebrates Mass at a special communion table placed much closer to the congregation, and stands facing them. (However, provision was made, in some countries, for occasional celebrations of the Latin, or Tridentine, Mass where a significant number of parishioners desired it.)

New musical forms, ranging from the popular to the esoteric, have now been incorporated into the liturgy, as have new roles for the laity. Eucharistic ministers, lay people who distribute the communion elements (now in both kinds, another breakthrough) are found in churches; and altar girls outnumber their male counterparts in some parts of the Catholic world. Members of the laity now sometimes deliver the Eucharist to the sick in hospitals and provide other forms of pastoral care. Shortages of priests and increasing demands on their energy have stimulated some of this shift, but much of it would not have been possible without the turn toward the laity that the Catholic Church made during the Council.

Apart from liturgy, lay involvement in the life of the church has taken many other new forms. Cardinal Newman's suggestion, in an 1859 essay, that the laity be consulted in matters of faith (a suggestion not well received by the hierarchy in his day), has now been implemented with numerous committees and advisory boards within parishes and dioceses, in which the lay majority consults with their priests and bishops as to their own needs and desires. One diocese may feel that a

E. Lessing, *Pope John XXIII*, 1962.

By ushering in a new era for global Catholicism at the Second Vatican Council, this popular pope opened communication with other branches of Christianity and other religions.

*Opening Day of
Vatican II, 1962.*

*As the opening day
began, questions
abounded in
everyone's mind
about whether the
Catholic Church
could modernize
and become
relevant in the
secular society of
post-World War II.*

stronger adult-education program is necessary; a parish experiencing a wave of immigration may need a priest fluent in a new language for Masses and other services for the new members; a parish with an aging population might want to start a hospice. Again, some of this change has been made necessary by a shrinking priesthood; but it generally has been seen as a movement toward more vitality at the parish level.

One of the leading areas of lay involvement in the work of the church is the effort to bring new members into the Catholic fold. The Rite of Christian Initiation for Adults (RCIA for short) is a parish-level movement in which Church members are paired with prospective members, from other Christian churches, other religions, or no religious background at all, in order to help them learn about Catholicism. Throughout the process, sponsors (the members) and catechumens (the inquirers) meet weekly to discuss the week's biblical passages and aspects of the church's teaching; and rather than being authoritatively instructed as earlier generations were, today's initiates share in a partnership and thus feel part of the community before they have formally joined it.

A Dialogue Between Catholics and Protestants

Unexpected measures were also taken to minimize the divisions between the Catholic Church and other Christian denominations. The division of Christendom into Greek and Latin Churches, finalized in 1054 by the pope's excommunication of the Byzantine patriarch was made less glaring by revoking the excommunication. (They remain two churches, however, because the patriarch excommunicated the pope also—and that act still stands.) Protestants were no longer to be dismissed as heretics, but from Vatican II onward were to be regarded as "separated brethren." And serious dialogue with other traditions was begun and encouraged. Vatican II was attended by a large number of non-Catholic theologians and religious leaders, and their attendance was more than a gesture of goodwill: it was meant to be the beginning of lasting dialogue.

Among the various bodies established by the Council to implement its decisions was the Secretariat for the Promotion of the Unity of Christians. The Secretariat's 1970 *Decree on Ecumenism* called for ecumenical dialogue, so that Christians of all churches can understand their common beliefs and their differences. Such dialogue is not meant merely to point to a respectful appreciation of differences, but to "strive for a more complete communion" among Christian communities. While spelling out various rules for these ecumenical dialogues (some of which were shaped by input from Protestant dialogue partners), the authors of the decree seriously recognized that certain articles of belief were "negotiable"—subject to respectful disagreement—while others were held in common and thus outside of debates about possible modifications. For a church that had previously seen its way as the only true and valid one, this was an extraordinary step toward conciliation.

Hans Küng and Karl Rahner

There was more than ecclesiastical politics at work here. The theological style of the Roman Catholic Church was beginning to change also. Influential thinkers such as Hans Küng (b. 1928) and Karl Rahner (1904–1984) were theologians present at the Council, reconceptualizing Catholic and Christian identity in bold new ways. Küng's most important statement (*Justification: The Doctrine of Karl Barth and a Catholic Reflection*, 1957) was an inquiry into the Catholic and Protestant doctrines of justification—a stubborn sticking point for four hundred years. In this he found an essential base of commonality between the two faiths, enough to prompt other theologians on both sides of the divide to explore their shared convictions. Küng's book on justification was welcomed, in a generous preface, by no less than Karl Barth, as Protestant a thinker as one could have imagined in the late 1950s. On other topics, such as papal infallibility, Küng went a bit farther to the left than the Roman hierarchy would have wished, and in 1979 he was censured by his church and prohibited from teaching as a Catholic theologian (a decision subsequently moderated). This action has only served to increase his popularity among both Catholic and Protestant readers.

Less well known to general readers, but much more influential among academics and theologians, Karl Rahner was one of the most prolific theologians of all time, one whose work (such as the multivolume *Theological Investigations* and *Foundations of Christian Faith*, 1987) had as much impact on Catholic thought as the Council had on church life. Central to Rahner's thought is the sense that Christianity forms the essential structure of human experience. Dependence on a creator-divinity and freedom made possible by a redeemer-divinity are, in his view, universal givens of human experience, and organizing principles of all the great religions. While acknowledging their universality, however, Rahner holds that Christianity offers the most perfect expression of these principles. All believers of creative-redemptive religions are, in Rahner's term, "ANONYMOUS CHRISTIANS." That is to say, they really do believe in redemption through Christ, but are not yet aware of their redeemer's name. Thus, his theological program, which from one angle may appear conciliatory toward other religions can, from another view-point, appear like another form of apologetic theology (see Chapter 8). The very difficult job that Rahner was trying to do was to balance the distinctiveness of Christianity against the shared experience of all religions. Hence reading Rahner feels different from reading most of his predecessors, who were not concerned about extending their scope to include non-Christian religions. In some ways Rahner's thought is an updated Catholic version of Schleiermacher's theology of the early nineteenth century (see Chapter 22): "liberal" in the same sense, and built on appeals to common human experience rather than ideas of revelation—which will always be exclusive to the recipients of such revelation.

Progressive versus Conservative Forces

The Council and its theologians made progress in other areas as well. A 1972 doc-ument issued by the Secretariat for the Promotion of Unity of Christians identi-fied conditions under which members of other Christian denominations could participate in Catholic communion. This has proved as difficult an issue in the twentieth century as it was in the sixteenth, when disputes about the presence of Christ in the eucharistic bread and wine had solidified along confessional lines. Because the Eucharist has been the central experience in the Christian life, deciding who can and who cannot come together at the altar is tantamount to determining who is and is not a Christian. (Non-Catholics have always been welcome to attend and observe the Mass, but sharing in the Eucharist is a form of being "present" at the Last Supper and sharing in that mysterious oneness with Christ.) The 1972 document formulated certain principles that allowed any Christian who has a "serious spiritual need for the Eucharistic sustenance" and who believes in a sacramentally ordained clergy to partake of the "ecclesial com-munion" of the eucharistic sacrament. But only in the case of "urgent necessity" (left undefined in the document) can one who is outside of such ecclesial com-munion join in eucharistic communion.

As a result of discussions over the following decades, a number of churches that had their origins in Reformation-era divisions from the Roman Church have found themselves in "full communion" with it, in a coexistence that many theolo-gians on all sides deem the best of both worlds. Lutherans and Anglicans (Episcopalians) enjoy full communion with the Roman Church. The "separated" churches can retain their separate identity, organization, and history without being condemned as heretical, while sharing the sacraments with the church from which they broke away centuries before.

These developments, which have taken very different forms in the decades fol-lowing the Council, have been viewed by some Catholics as an over-liberal ten-dency within Catholicism and a compromise of its distinctive characteristics. A conservative reaction set in and by the 1980s this had gained considerable momentum in the United States, Germany, and some other places. The Latin liturgy, they argued, was intrinsically more profound, and thus holier, than the vernacular Mass ordered by the Council. And ecumenical initiatives, in seeking common ground with other denominations, were destructive to the integrity of Catholicism.

An organization known as Opus Dei ("the work of God"), founded in Spain in the 1920s, was one of the vehicles for this reaction. Its founder, Josemaría Escrivá de Balaguer (1902–1975), became an image of the pre-Vatican II church: hierarchical, aloof, and authoritative. In rhetoric reminiscent of the Council of Trent, members of Opus Dei protested the popularization of liturgy as a concession to an increasingly worldly laity, saw the various consultations as yielding to lay pressure for control, and rejected pluralism as an admission that Catholicism was not the one true faith. Through its publishing arm, Ignatius Press, Opus Dei has brought a number of influential European authors before an American readership: Hans Urs von Balthasar (1905–1988), Henri de Lubac (1896–1991), the Holocaust martyr Edith Stein (1891–1942), all right-of-center Catholics. In so doing, the organization has broadened the spectrum of viewpoints within American Catholicism.

Divisions between progressive and conservative branches of the same denomination also appeared in other churches. The Lutheran Church, a mixed family of denominations in the American scene, experienced upheavals in the early 1970s that led to the consolidation of mainline branches in the Evangelical Lutheran Church in America (ELCA)—with the conservative wing of American Lutheranism anchored by the Missouri Synod and its still all-male school, Concordia Seminary in St. Louis, Missouri. Episcopalians radically revised their *Book of Common Prayer* in 1979, breaking with a tradition reaching back to the sixteenth century, although many Episcopalians (along with members of other Anglican churches who also produced new editions of the liturgy) continue to use the traditional prayer book in their services. Anglicans also began ordaining women and even (in the United States) appointing them to the office of bishop. This was too much for some High church priests (spiritual descendants of the Oxford Movement; see Chapter 23), who moved to the Roman Catholic Church, where ordination of women appeared far less likely to happen. Others have remained within the Anglican fold in a prophetic role of sorts, challenging their more liberal colleagues to be more mindful of their shared tradition. As the century ended, controversy continued to focus on the ordination of women and the possibility of recognizing homosexuality as something other than an avoidable sin. The ordination of gay clergy, both men and women, was an issue animating much of the Protestant mainstream. Indeed, sexuality in its many aspects and guises would prove an increasingly contentious issue for Christianity as a whole as it entered the third millennium.

Key Terms

ANONYMOUS CHRISTIANS A term popularized by Karl Rahner for believers in a sovereign and merciful God who might not explicitly believe in Christ himself.

COLLEGE OF CARDINALS An assembly of the highest officials, below the pope, in the Catholic Church; the electoral body for the papacy.

VATICAN II A council of the Roman Catholic Church (1962–65) charged with modernizing ritual, organization, and relations with other faiths.

CHAPTER 29

Mainstreams and Margins
Colonialism and Liberation Theology

The near suicide of Western civilization during World War II was followed by a sober awareness of the fragility of cultures, their ideals, and the people who keep them alive. Wave after wave of mass murder—of Soviet people in Stalin's prison camps, of Chinese victims of the Cultural Revolution, and of Muslim people in the former Yugoslavia—offered sobering proof of the speed with which barbarism can undermine and corrupt the structure of a civilization. Business and science had made their contributions to the destructive efforts of nations. The cylinders of Zyklon B gas used in Nazi death camps and the uranium and plutonium bombs (each capable of killing hundreds of thousands at once) dropped on Hiroshima and Nagasaki were evidence that technology had a destructive potential just as powerful as its constructive one. And communism, which in the restructuring of Europe had taken over in the eastern third of the continent, appeared to many to threaten the cultural and spiritual lives of the survivors of those devastated regions. The ideological struggle that drew nations into war in the 1930s and 1940s had not diminished after 1945; in state and foreign affairs government departments worldwide, the war was still being waged.

In churches, too. The spectre of hostile ideologies, together with the potential for genocide endemic in ordinary people, provoked intensive reflection on the human condition, a state that no longer permitted much optimism. In the years following World War II, many churches became actively engaged in relocation and aid efforts for the millions of displaced persons; supported materially by the wealthier sectors of their memberships, and operated by some of their more energetic leaders, these efforts helped restore credibility to the churches along with helping their devastated beneficiaries. At its 1968 meeting in Uppsala, Sweden, the World Council of Churches (see Chapter 28) officially recognized that the conditions under which humanity now lived were a pressing issue. It was stating the obvious, but by stating it the WCC put human rights on the agenda of the world's churches.

Human Rights and Self-Governance

Human rights had already been decisive and divisive issues in the church for a century or more. The abolition of slavery was a religious issue before it became a political one. Protestant clergy such as Lyman Beecher (1775–1863) and his family (see Chapter 26) were instrumental in bringing the plight of African-Americans to public notice. In the decades before the Civil War, four mainstream American denominations split over the slavery issue. In 1844–45 the Methodists in the north became the Methodist Episcopal Church; in 1845 the Baptists became the American Baptist Missionary Union and the Southern Baptist Convention; and in 1861 both the Episcopalian and Presbyterian Churches broke into two: the former becoming the Protestant Episcopal Church and the Protestant Episcopal Church in the Confederate States of America, the latter becoming the Presbyterian Church in the United States of America and the Presbyterian Church in the Confederate States of America. (The Episcopalians reunited right after the war, in 1866; the Methodists rejoined in 1939; and the Presbyterian Church, U.S.A., combining its northern and southern branches, became a reality in 1983. The Baptists remain divided over questions such as biblical authority.)

Concern for the Native peoples of the Americas dates back to the earliest landings by European settlers. Already in the sixteenth century the Dominican Bartolomé de las Casas (1474–1566) had prepared lengthy descriptions of the

Théodore de Bry, *Spanish Cruelties*, from *Brevissima Relación* by Bartolomé de las Casas, 1598. Engraving. Bibliothèque Nationale, Paris.

Rampaging Spanish soldiers are shown hanging and burning the inhabitants of a Mexican village.

lives of the Native peoples in Spanish America, including accounts of the ways they were being mistreated by the conquistadores, and urged the king of Spain to order his colonists to be more compassionate in their treatment of the indigenous people. The requests went unanswered. The people continued to suffer as Spanish and Portuguese settlers established themselves in states and plantations and drew off the wealth of the land.

Independence for the Spanish and Portuguese colonies did not come until the early decades of the nineteenth century, but once the movement began, it spread quickly. Two Mexican priests, Miguel Hidalgo y Costillo (1753–1811) and José María Morelos y Pavón (1765–1815) were active in their country's struggle for freedom; both were shot as traitors before the viceroyalty of New Spain (founded in 1535) became the independent nation of Mexico in 1821. The viceroyalty of New Granada, formed in 1717 from colonies on the northern coast of South America, was split into several new independent states: Venezuela ("little Venice"; named after a coastal Native settlement built on stakes over the water, reminiscent of early Venetian buildings), which achieved freedom in 1811; Colombia (1819); and Ecuador (1830). Within the first three decades of the century Brazil, Uruguay, Paraguay, Chile, Peru, Bolivia, and Argentina also embarked on sometimes rocky paths toward independence and self-governance. The new states adopted various forms of government. Brazil became a monarchy in 1822. In Mexico, Agustín de Iturbide (1783–1824), who declared Mexico's independence in 1821, named himself emperor and in short order was driven into exile by General Antonto Lopéz de Santa Anna (1797–1876), and shot. Elsewhere dictatorships were set up. Simón Bolívar (1783–1850) was named dictator of Venezuela in 1811; and Bernardo O'Higgins (1778–1842), liberator of Chile, was named dictator of that coastal nation.

Despite independence, the nations of Latin America were still ruled mainly by people of European descent. Families of Spanish and Portuguese origin formed the governments, controlled the economies, and set both domestic and foreign policy. From Caracas to Buenos Aires, Europeans dominated and the Natives endured poverty and oppression. From the mid-nineteenth century onward, Europe and North America were fighting their own battles, literally and ideologically; and general ignorance of the conditions of the people kept attention away from the Latin American social structure. It was not until the mid-twentieth century that Europe and North America, sensitized to the brutalities of totalitarian governments, took a serious look at the Native peoples of the Americas.

From Colonial to Post-Colonial Culture

A number of Christian churches in Europe and the United States developed substantial programs designed to extend Christianity to parts of the world still largely uninfluenced by European and Anglo-American culture. Outside of the churches, many viewed this initial contact between Christianity and other world cultures as the first step in the "taming" and eventual "civilizing" of the rest of the world. In its more benign form, this meant bringing the rule of international law, egalitarian policies in education and human rights, and a modest measure of technological and medical infrastructure to peoples who may have lacked—and urgently needed—all three. A more sinister manifestation of this missionary zeal was the annexing of vast territories by nations, reducing native rulers to the status of local agents of a foreign power, and depriving native peoples of a full sense of ownership in their indigenous culture.

Imperialistic tendencies on the part of developed nations were curtailed by a number of factors. The "White Man's Burden" articulated by Western thinkers was too much to bear for societies themselves experiencing unprecedented immigration and the side-effects of industrialization. Aside from these partly external political and economic factors threatening the success of colonial ventures, cultural resistance by colonized peoples also impeded the spread of Christianity. Expansion of empire has its price, and even the most advanced of Western societies faced difficulty paying the bills. In most cases, the venture was worth the cost when the natural resources of the colonized nation returned sufficient revenue to justify the investment in "civilizing" the resident population. But once the natural resources lost their economic value (a virtual certainty among nations that had neither the capital nor the infrastructure to sustain the exploitation of natural resources in an economically viable manner), imperial interest was quick to wane or shift direction.

Once colonialism began to unravel, the process was slow because there were elements that the colonized peoples were reluctant to abandon, no matter how much they despised the occupying colonial power.

It is hard to identify the point at which the colonization enterprise reached its climax, since it began to deteriorate in some parts of the world almost as soon as it started in others. The American Revolution was certainly a major starting-point in the "de-colonization" process. The Founding Fathers built their case on the idea that a people governed by an external power should enjoy the same rights as the domestic subjects of that power; in other words, geographic distance does not diminish a subject's rights. The American colonies, founded in many cases out of religious fervor, formed a pluralistic religious culture in which any form of official establishment of religion would have alienated a majority of the populace. Thus, after independence was achieved and a constitution written, the first rights granted in the Amendments to the Constitution forbade any governmental sanctioning of religion while giving citizens freedom to practice religion in any legal way.

The European colonial enterprise had not yet crested when the American colonies achieved independence. Britain itself would achieve its widest colonial dominion a century later, and at its peak twenty percent of the world's land, and twenty-three percent of its population, would be bound to the British Crown. France, in the wake of her revolution of 1789–99, would embark in the 1830s on a process of colonization that by 1914 would encompass Southeast Asia and most of the northwestern African continent. Germany started still later with the Bismarck regime in 1871; by the outbreak of World War I, Germany would have control of four colonies in Africa and a Pacific archipelago. In all three cases the colonial populations, and the terrain they occupied, dwarfed those of the homelands.

Missionaries of various denominations followed their governments' officials into these regions, many with the sincere hope of converting the native peoples, but many others with an equally fervent wish to keep them docile while their resources were being exploited. The native peoples likewise submitted to missionary efforts equally if not more for the sake of education, healthcare, or economic and political stability as for religious reasons. Whatever the individual circumstances (which in most cases cannot be discerned at this distance), it is sufficient to note that the church—at least the number of baptisms—grew dramatically during these decades in which Christianity became a truly global religion.

However much the arrival of missionaries may have been linked to the European subjugation of African and Asian peoples, the Christian message they brought did not depart along with the colonial administrations. Church and state were separate enough, institutionally and conceptually, for indigenous peoples to accept Christianity more readily and durably than they accepted European hegemony. The church has retained a presence, sometimes major, sometimes minor, in all of the territories vacated by European powers. Whatever the native peoples understood about Christianity, enough seemed to be of positive value for them to include it in their perception of the world.

What accounts for this? The fact that Jesus himself was not European, but a member of a colonized people under an oppressive regime, must have given him an appeal that prevailed over the Europeans' claims to being a truly Christian civilization. An additional irony may have been that he was crucified by the imperialistic Romans, and that his message was one of solace for the oppressed, not one of solidarity with the oppressors. In many cases, such as in Latin America, what had begun as "conquistador" religion ended up, and thrived, as "liberation theology."

Liberation Theology

A phenomenon of the late twentieth and early twenty-first century, liberation theology is most closely associated with Latin America (though it is also concerned with other groups of people, as we shall see). In essence, it is a movement designed to involve the church in positive action on behalf of the poor of the developing world and other oppressed peoples. Since Vatican II (see Chapter 28) and the Second Latin American Bishops' Conference, held in Medellín, Colombia, in 1968, many clergy and laypeople have worked in and written about this movement.

The wave of religious literature calling attention to the conditions of the poor in Latin America was inspired by European thought as much as by the poverty of the people. Leo XIII's social encyclical *Rerum Novarum* (see Chapter 26) may not have been composed with Latin America in mind, but its message was as relevant to the southern hemisphere as to the northern. The same is true of *Quadragesimo Anno* (see Chapter 27), Pius XI's call for a more socially responsible economic system for persons to realize their full potential. Neither industrial capitalism nor communism had made sufficient inroads in Latin America for anyone outside to see the pertinence of these encyclicals; but within the system they resonated among the clergy and the people in their care.

Other tributaries leading into the stream of liberation theology are Hegelianism (see Chapter 22), the social teachings of Jesus, and the doctrine of redemption found in the Hebrew Bible (see below). One of the founders of the movement is the Peruvian Catholic priest Gustavo Gutiérrez (b. 1928). In *A Theology of Liberation* (1971; 2nd ed., 1988), Gutiérrez picked up Hegel's sense of history as a dialectical process between lords and servants; only through this process, Gutiérrez maintained, can humanity reach its full actualization in freedom. (See "Gustavo Gutiérrez.") That is to say, neither the master nor the slave is completely free, since the identity of each is determined by its relation to the other. If humanity is to advance, it must do so in such a way that master-servant relations are finally overcome. Often associated with Marxism on account of its concern for the oppressed and its advocacy of mobilized resistance, liberation theology actually owes its philosophical origins more to Marx's intellectual master, Hegel.

The social makeup of the first Christian community is another component of liberation theology. The fact that Jesus and his followers were workers and in some cases, outcasts, and that Jesus himself was subject to persecution ending in death, has normative religious value for liberation thought. The meaning of Jesus' teachings, especially the Beatitudes in the Sermon on the Mount (Matthew 5–7), can be fully recognized only by those who are meek, oppressed, and suffering. The marginal status of the disciples is not a mere historical condition, long since irrelevant to the message of the Gospel. Rather, it is an integral part of the message, and only if one can identify with that marginalized ancient audience can one grasp the meaning of the teachings. Thus the poor of Latin America share a strong kinship with those disoriented Jews under Roman domination in Palestine. It is a kinship so strong that the New Testament message presumably speaks across the cultures and becomes as powerful a force in the lives of Latin American Christians as it had been for first-century Jews. The inversion of the power structure is remarkable: the dominant class of Europeans in South America may have possessed all the economic and political power, but for that very reason, according to liberation theology, held no spiritual power. The indigenous peoples, on the other hand, being excluded from the power structure, therefore possessed the spiritual knowledge that was true power. The relation of powerless and powerful is reversed. And if God is still the author of history, which few Christians doubt, the reversal of the world's order is an eventual certainty.

A third element in liberation theology is the doctrine of redemption. Here, in fact, occurs a bold new understanding of divine action in history, one that reinforces the vitality of the biblical narrative. The divine work of redemption is only partly identified with the Cross. That symbol mainly represents God's solidarity with the oppressed, the willingness of the incarnate deity to suffer at the hands of a cruel temporal power. In other words, the crucifixion is just as much a form of reassurance to those who suffer as a liberating act itself. An equally if not more important redemptive event in liberation theology was the Exodus. Liberation theology, like Judaism, sees God's redemptive work as fully realized in history.

Gustavo Gutiérrez, 2001.

The liberation theologian is shown addressing a seminar.

The parting of the Red Sea and the liberation of the Jews from Egypt, followed seven centuries later by the restoration of the Jews to Jerusalem after the Babylonian Exile, show how God redeems the faithful. Wherever the pious are oppressed and enslaved to such an extent that they cannot properly worship God, then divine intervention overthrows the oppressors and restores the people to ideal conditions for the faithful life. To the liberation theologians of Latin

Gustavo Gutiérrez

Gustavo Gutiérrez is one of the leading liberation theologians, one of the first to see the Christian message through the lens of concern for the poor of Latin America. In this passage from A Theology of Liberation *(1971; 1988) he describes liberation as a three-fold process.*

Summarizing what has been said above, we can distinguish three reciprocally interpenetrating levels of meaning of the term *liberation*, or in other words, three approaches to the process of liberation.

In the first place, *liberation* expresses the aspirations of oppressed peoples and social classes, emphasizing the conflictual aspect of the economic, social, and political process which puts them at odds with wealthy nations and oppressive classes. In contrast, the word *development*, and above all the policies characterized as developmentalist (*desarrollista*), appear somewhat aseptic, giving a false picture of a tragic and conflictual reality. The issue of development does in fact find its true place in the more universal, profound, and radical perspective of liberation. It is only within this framework that *development* finds its true meaning and possibilities of accomplishing something worthwhile.

At a deeper level, *liberation* can be applied to an understanding of history. Humankind is seen as assuming conscious responsibility for its own destiny. This understanding provides a dynamic context and broadens the horizons of the desired social changes. In this perspective the unfolding of all the dimensions of humanness is demanded—persons who make themselves throughout their life and throughout history. The gradual conquest of true freedom leads to the creation of a new humankind and a qualitatively different society. This vision provides, therefore, a better understanding of what in fact is at stake in our times.

Finally, the word *development* to a certain extent limits and obscures the theological problems implied in the process designated by this term. On the contrary the word *liberation* allows for another approach leading to the Biblical sources which inspire the presence and action of humankind in history. In the Bible, Christ is presented as the one who brings us liberation. Christ the Savior liberates from sin, which is the ultimate root of all disruption of friendship and of all injustice and oppression. Christ makes humankind truly free, that is to say, he enables us to live in communion with him; and this is the basis for all human fellowship.

This is not a matter of three parallel or chronologically successive processes, however. There are three levels of meaning of a single, complex process, which finds its deepest sense and its full realization in the saving work of Christ. These levels of meaning, therefore, are interdependent. A comprehensive view of the matter presupposes that all three aspects can be considered together. In this way two pitfalls will be avoided: first, *idealist* or *spiritualist* approaches, which are nothing but ways of evading a harsh and demanding reality, and second, shallow analyses and programs of short-term effect initiated under the pretext of meeting immediate needs.

(From *A Theology of Liberation*, trans. Sr. Caridad Inda and John Eagleson. Maryknoll, New York: Orbis, 1971.)

America, faith in a redemptive deity is hope for another miraculous triumph over their European-stock masters. In Gutiérrez's pregnant phrase, political liberation is linked to God's creative work as humanity's "self-creation."

Gutiérrez learned this doctrine from the Hebrew Bible, of course, but it was with the help of German biblical scholars such as Johannes Baptist Metz (b. 1928) and Gerhard von Rad (1901–1971) that he recognized the centrality of the Exodus event in the redemptive work of God. Von Rad's research into ancient Israelite thought found that the faith of the Jewish people was in a God who performed mighty acts of salvation, and that the biblical narrative of the people and their normative religious documents are records of those deeds. The various sources of the Hebrew Bible (von Rad subscribed to Julius Wellhausen's Documentary Hypothesis, described in Chapter 22) represented the various episodes and interpretations of God's action in history. If the Christian faith was continuous with the Jewish witness, then it would hold that God would still act in redemptive ways within the course of human events. Liberation theology witnesses to the God who shows solidarity with the poor and acts on that solidarity by reversing the course of history.

Conflict with the Catholic Church

The potential for conflict between liberation theology and the church is obvious. The Catholic Church of the original Spanish and Portuguese settlers, inherited by their heirs, is indicted as a co-conspirator in oppression, while the Catholic Church of the Natives is the one true Israel awaiting God's liberating deed. The Catholic Church, and the Iberian and Roman establishments with which it was linked, did not take well to being identified with the Egyptians of Moses' time. In fact, to the extent that they saw liberation theology as a subversive movement, they condemned it all the more vehemently as false doctrine. Nor was it hard to locate biblical texts, such as the Passion narrative, that seemed to identify the ideal for humanity as submission to the social order, no matter how harsh it may seem. Since the Passion narrative could be cited in support of God's identification with the persecuted, it is understandable that liberation theology and its opposition achieved no resolution on matters of biblical interpretation.

While the liberation theologians explore and expound such doctrinal issues, the poor on whose behalf they write are experiencing the effect of this theology in their lives. In many parts of Latin America, but especially in El Salvador, Nicaragua, and Colombia, leaders of the movement have formed BASE COMMUNITIES — parishes that address the economic and spiritual needs of the people, which are organized along socialist lines but with the day ordered around the Mass and Catholic devotions. A priest or a member of the laity exercises a measure of leadership while maintaining some connection to the sacraments of the church. Many of these leaders have borne the same degree of suffering, even martyrdom, as the people they serve. Within these groups certain symbols take on a power that others rarely have in other cultures. The servitude of the Jews under Pharaoh, the Psalms' affirmations of devotion amid devastation, the prophetic words of Jesus on behalf of the meek and the persecuted: these themes have a power that people in secular and bourgeois societies can hardly fathom. Like the early Christians, the poor of Latin America find the truths of revelation more real, more true, than

Juan Luis Segundo's Critique of the Vatican's *Instruction*

The Instruction on Certain Aspects of the "Theology of Liberation" *drew a number of responses, including one from Juan Luis Segundo, a prominent theologian in the Liberation tradition. In this critique of the* Instruction *Segundo takes issue with the way Liberation theology is described, in particular its alleged Marxist orientation.*

Because something so important has been totally blown out of proportion by the sensationalism of the press and even passed over by the few theological studies I have seen, I hope the reader will allow me to make a brief analysis of the first paragraphs that begin the second part of the document.

Precisely because Christian faith has been reduced, according to the document, to an earthly humanism, it is incapable of exercising its power of discernment and of guarding Christians against the ideologies that falsely promise results in the search for liberation within history. The most notorious and most seductive of these ideologies is Marxism—perhaps because it foreshadows a possible victory of elements similar to Christian ideals (see IX, 10). What is decisive about this point is that what the document considers to be a fall into or "refuge" in ideology is explained as an *effect*, and not as the cause, of a desperate search for earthly results. So the arrival at such a point has, according to the document, a theological *cause*.

The "urgency of the problems" and "the feeling of anguish" (VI, 3) generate "impatience and a desire for results"; and this finally leads Christians to "turn to … Marxist analysis" (VII, I). "Their reasoning is this: an intolerable and explosive situation requires *effective action* which cannot be put off. Effective action presupposes a *scientific analysis* of the structural causes of poverty. Marxism now provides us with the means to make such an analysis, they say. Then one simply has to apply the analysis to the third-world situation, especially in Latin America" (VII, 2).

One can see then that a faith which exercises "discernment" as to how the aspiration for justice and the liberation from evil should be expressed will not be the captive of ideologies. The recourse to Marxism as the instrument of analysis or, as the document states, "taking refuge in it," is nothing more than an example—favored by historical circumstances—of how a faith weakened by and reduced to an earthly content is incapable of resisting ideological temptations.

Theologically speaking, it is of little importance that Marxist analysis itself or the relationship that liberation theology has with it either agrees with reality or deforms it, because the theological judgment does not depend on this fact. *Any ideological captivation of faith implies that faith has deviated.* Moreover, instead of hearing the voice of God in the search for liberation, humanity is merely listening to earthly urgencies to which it attributes the values proper only to the divine word.

Now we must place the emphasis where the document places it: in the reduction and deviation of faith to the earthly. What arguments form the basis of this negative judgment? From what theological perspective is liberation theology viewed so that it is (almost) fatally inclined toward an earthly reductionism? These are the questions that must be answered.

(From *Theology and the Church*, trans. John W. Diercksmeier. Minneapolis, MN: Winston Press, 1970.)

their own worldly sufferings. To give a modern voice to their sentiments, Latin American writers have produced an astonishing body of poetry and song, expressive of both piety and hope.

A counter-argument to liberation thought came in a September 1984 document from the Sacred Congregation of the Doctrine of the Faith, a Vatican agency headed by the conservative Cardinal Joseph Ratzinger (b. 1927). Titled *Instruction on Certain Aspects of the "Theology of Liberation,"* the document unambiguously identifies Christianity with liberation—and equally clearly states that this liberation is from sin—a personal, as opposed to a sociological, matter. While acknowledging the crucial role of the Exodus event in forming the people of God, the *Instruction* still warns against equating God's redemption with political events. It highlights the importance of social justice as a mission of the Catholic Church but warns against reducing the Gospel to a "purely earthly" message. And seeing Marx lurking in the shadows of liberation theology, the *Instruction* reaffirms its condemnation of materialist ideologies.

Whether the *Instruction* and similar Vatican documents have understood liberation theology correctly, the two parties were clearly locked into a conflict that has not proved easy to resolve. The conflict has brought to the surface the preexisting differences between "First World" and "Third World" churches, and raised questions of whether Rome can really be the center of the Catholic Church when most of its faithful live in the Southern Hemisphere. It has raised class issues, some of which were resolved in Europe during the revolutionary decades from 1789 to 1848. And it has raised obvious questions about whether Catholics outside Latin America can display solidarity with the poor of those regions while still being loyal to their own church—connected, as each parish necessarily is, with the hierarchical church.

Other Liberation Causes

The principles of liberation theology have found their way into the North American Christian community, drawing attention to injustices within that society. At the same time that thinkers such as Gutiérrez and the Jesuit Juan Luis Segundo (b. 1925) were shaping a religious and social program for the oppressed of Latin America, theologians in the United States were recognizing that the dignity of all persons was far from universally acknowledged. No one can study U.S. history of the 1960s without being aware of the work of Martin Luther King, Jr. (1929–1968), a Baptist preacher with a Ph.D. in theology from Boston University, or of his successor as champion of civil rights, the Chicago-trained minister Jesse Jackson (b. 1941). The African-American theologian James Cone (b. 1938) emerged from the segregated South to receive a Ph.D. from Northwestern University and assume a chair at New York's Union Theological Seminary. In works including *For My People: Black Theology and the Black Church* (1984) and *A Black Theology of Liberation* (1970), Cone sets before a mainline Protestant readership the realities of a struggle of race and class that did not end with the abolition of slavery. On the contrary, Cone argues, the struggle for the freedom of African-Americans only began with the Thirteenth Amendment, for the structure that had made slavery possible made the continued subjugation of the slaves' descendants not only possible but inevitable; however, this situation could be overcome by determined acts of will on the part of white society.

Feminist and "Womanist" Theologies

The Women's Liberation movement, another phenomenon that emerged in the 1960s, also had a religious dimension. Feminist theology took hold of the American academic mainstream in the 1960s and 1970s with a genuine vengeance. The former Catholic theologian and now radical feminist philosopher, Mary Daly (b. 1928), and the Catholic Rosemary Radford Ruether (b. 1936) had broken into the privileged ranks of Protestant male academics and built their lives' work around exposing the misogyny of the dominant society—its religious values included. In works such as *Beyond God the Father* (1973), Daly addresses the implications of the pronouns used for God and the meaning of the Christian idea that God took human form as a man. The results of her discussion are highly controversial, as she rejects both the maleness of God (in the form of Jesus) and the emergence of an alternate religion in which the "Goddess" becomes the projection of a feminine ideal through which her female followers can experience fulfillment. Rosemary Ruether is slightly closer to center within the feminist program, partly in her continued loyalty to the Catholic Church and partly in the extension of her concerns to the African-American and Jewish communities, both of which she sees as victims of institutionalized oppression. Rather than being concerned with the plight of women under the Catholic hierarchy, as Mary Daly is, Ruether is concerned with oppression as a structural problem of organized religion. And whereas Daly's work is bent on perpetuating and aggravating differences (evidenced in her exclusion of male participants from her seminars and conferences),

Who's Who

The Struggle for Liberty

Juan Luis Segundo (b. 1925) Jesuit and one of a group of South American "liberation" theologians who sought to improve the social and economic conditions in their homeland.

Gustavo Gutiérrez (b. 1928) Peruvian Catholic priest and one of the founders of the South American "liberation theology" movement. Author of *A Theology of Liberation*, his Marxist views include abolishing master-servant class systems.

Mary Daly (b. 1928) Radical former Catholic feminist theologian. Daly challenges what she sees as overbearingly male values at the center of mainstream religion—as far as arguing against God as "He."

Martin Luther King (1929–1968) African-American Baptist minister and leading campaigner for civil rights for American blacks. A pioneer in the struggle to stop white-black segregation in the U.S., he was assassinated in 1968.

Rosemary Radford Ruether (b. 1936) Catholic feminist theologian. Less radical about male dominion than Daly, she is more concerned with fighting the general oppression that can arise from the rigid structures of mainstream organized religion.

Jesse Jackson (b. 1941) African-American Baptist minister and politician who trained at Chicago Theological Seminary. A leader in the civil rights movement, he is regarded by some as the successor to Martin Luther King.

Ruether is concerned with conciliation and an ecumenical understanding that does not obliterate historical identities.

In the wake of these pioneers have come a number of other radical theological schools, including "womanist" and "mujerista" theologies. "Womanist" theology was a term coined by Alice Walker in the 1980s for emerging feminism among black women. It is also used by some African-American theologians (among others) to characterize this distinctive movement, which is more inclusive of men and male symbols than mainstream white feminism. Mujerista theology (from the Spanish *mujer*, "woman") is the feminist variant of Latin American liberation theology, born of the awareness that working-class women within the Latin American social structure are doubly oppressed. As the calls for compassion have increased in volume, however, the criteria for identification have risen above the level that most could meet. It takes a lot for members of the bourgeois American mainstream, whether straight or gay, male or female, to see themselves among the oppressed; in fact it requires, for the most part, so much imagination that the population with whom one wants to claim solidarity can then accuse its empathizers of insincerity.

At the end of the twentieth century, Latin American liberation, African-American, feminist, womanist, and mujerista theologies had failed to gain a place at the seminar table of American (and European) academic theology. With few exceptions, theological seminaries continue to favor the white, male, European world, both in their choice of subject matter and in their selection of participants in the dialogue. In time, perhaps, theological work will recognize these new movements as vital elements of a continuously evolving theological culture.

Rosemary Ruether, 2000.

A Catholic feminist thinker, Ruether's work has raised questions about the gendering of language and relations between Christianity, Judaism, and Islam.

Key Term

BASE COMMUNITY A primitive form of church, current in Latin America, which brings together the marginalized and stresses hope for some form of redemption.

Christianity at the Dawn of the Third Millennium

The digital clocks and computers, not to mention most other electronic devices, that made the successful transition from 1999 to 2000 foiled the expectations of many who thought the world was coming to an end at midnight of the last day of the old millennium. Apocalyptic expectations were overthrown as the world continued on its course with little disruption to its technological infrastructure. The fact that this infrastructure was completely modern, only decades old at the most, obscured similarities with the previous turn of the century. In 1900 all seemed new; the progress of science was taken as a fact and as a force that was mastering nature. On January 1, 2000, after a breathless wait and much preparation, much of the same optimism returned. The lessons of the twentieth century had been digested, and the next century and millennium would build on the achievements, and be guided by the errors, of past generations. Religious leaders and their followers, at least those not disappointed that the Kingdom did not come at the end of that December 31, entered with a sense of survivor's relief into the new millennium. Many took solace in the fact that apocalyptic expectations ran high at the turn of the millennium, with no Judgment Day awaiting on January 1, 2000.

As Paul Tillich and his contemporaries made obvious, however, the nineteenth century extended well beyond its conventional chronological boundaries. For some it ended with the sinking of the Titanic in April 1912, a catastrophe widely interpreted as a divine rebuke to claims of mastering nature. For others the century ended with the outbreak of World War I, the end of illusions of peaceful coexistence. The twentieth century, likewise, ended not with the change of calendars but with a drastic rearrangement of values and priorities: a rearrangement that reawakened Christianity and set before it a new task, just as it was laboring with seemingly intractable old ones.

On the morning of September 11, 2001, partisans of a branch of Islam that held all things American, Western, liberal, and secular as hostile to its own ideals seized control of four aircraft and inflicted damage unprecedented in American history: civilian life in the thousands, military personnel in the hundreds, eco-

C. Hughes, Catholic Worship, Kuito, Angola, 2000.

After Kuito Cathedral was bombed to pieces during the Angolan Civil War that began in 1992, Catholics have been forced to cram into this makeshift hall for Sunday worship.

nomic damage in the billions of dollars, and a vastly altered cultural landscape for all who had enjoyed the liberties of a tolerant democracy protected by conventional military force. With the crash of hijacked airplanes, the boundaries between Christianity and the world beyond it were redrawn. As generally happens, such redrawing involves strengthening alliances, exacerbating hostilities and clarifying differences. And, as is also usually the case, the difficulty of such work is proportional to its urgency.

Christianity and Other Religions

Not since the Holocaust has the relationship between Christianity and other religions been so urgent an issue for all major denominations. Relations between Christians and Jews remain strained in some parts of the world. On the other hand, the expression of regret by the Evangelical Lutheran Church of America for the antisemitism of Luther and its repercussions among his followers was welcomed by Jewish communities throughout the United States; and interfaith initiatives toward social justice have brought Christian churches and other religious groups together in many communities. The "melting pot" metaphor that had characterized American society and helped drive ecumenical efforts in the late twentieth century has given way to the "salad bowl" image, in which the quality of the final product is determined by the variety of ingredients rather than their tendency to blend into an undifferentiated whole. Such diversity can be achieved within the churches, by outreach to people from cultures in which Christianity is a minority religion; but it has value among the churches as well. This pluralistic principle at work in American society promotes the understanding of, and respect for, differences among peoples, rather than attempting to reduce all to a single cultural standard. Such "freedom of cultural identity" is an extension of what the Founding Fathers intended when granting freedom of religion and association to all citizens.

The bond that helped Christians and Jews recognize a common foundation provides a basis for including Islam in the family of Western religions. The third member of the monotheistic religions, Islam represented an intentional return to the "pure faith" of Abraham, and thus was as much a form (or variant) of Judaism as was Christianity. Affirmation of a single sovereign deity (Allah is cognate with the Hebrew El and Elohim, two of the biblical names for God); a protective covenantal bond with that God; and a sense of oneness exhibited through charity: these are some of the features of Islam that give it a family resemblance to Judaism and Christianity.

Even granting common historical origins, a program of reconciliation with the Islamic tradition will be a challenge. The emergence of Islam after Christianity had become the dominant religion of the Mediterranean has traditionally been seen as an "upstart" religion's rejection of the finality of revelation in Christ; and the Crusades, in turn, symbolized Christianity's rejection of Islam. Compounding the religious alienation that exists between the two faiths is a cultural separation far wider than that between Christianity and Judaism. Whereas Jews had occupied Christian Europe since its beginning, the Islamic tradition has developed in North Africa and the Near and Middle East, and finding common cultural foundations may be difficult.

C. Reyes,
A Multi-Ethnic Congregation at Sunday Worship, St. Mary of the Angels, London, 1984.

In the late twentieth century multiethnic communities expanded. Their various Christian denominations serve increasingly important roles in preserving harmony and common values.

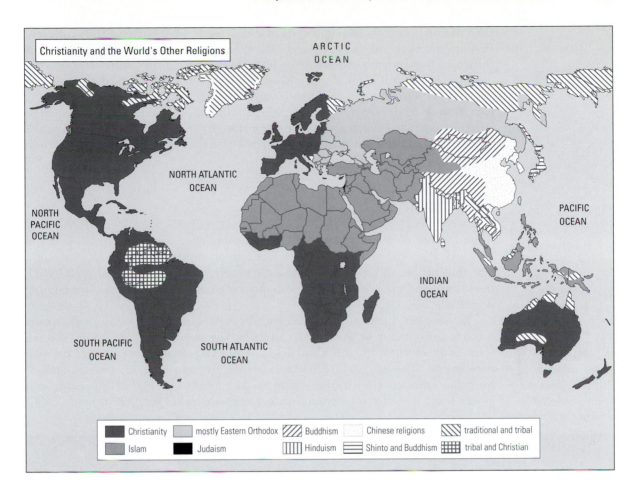

A Pluralistic Christianity

While global political realities are shaping the agenda for Christianity's dealings with other religions, the work of identifying commonalities and differences among the various Christian churches continues. The wave of ecumenical dialogues of the 1960s and 1970s experienced a reaction, with conservatives in each denomination reasserting confessional distinctiveness. In the intervening decades a more focused awareness of ethnic heritages and cultural traditions has given a premium to distinctiveness rather than assimilation. This general pattern has been mirrored in the religious realm: the national and ethnic particularities of parishes and denominations have been retrieved and set out in the interest of diversity. Some parishes, especially in urban areas undergoing demographic changes, have had a succession of identities: for example a given parish might originally have been Polish, later became Hispanic, and more recently has become Asian. The church thus continues to serve a classic American function: to be a bridge between the old world and the new.

At the same time, diversity within Christianity must ultimately be subordinated to unity, not least because the Creed still recited in most churches affirms faith in *one* holy, catholic, and apostolic church, the "one" being the only term that has not been subject to debate. The most prominent symbol of that unity is the Eucharist, and in the last decades of the twentieth century, important decrees have established full communion—the right to receive the Eucharist—among a number of churches: Episcopalians, Lutherans, and Catholics being the leading parties in the movement. There are still exceptions and obstacles, for as soon as an agreement is signed, a dissident party emerges to argue against it. But progress toward a more unified Christianity seems to be keeping pace with the cultural diversification of individual communities.

New Business

S. McCurry, *Praise the Lord Heritage Village Church*, New Charlotte, North Carolina, 1998.

A preacher is shown theatrically addressing his audience in person and via television.

If the current ecumenical and interreligious dialogues are a continuation of old business, the Christian Church also faces much new business at the dawn of a new millennium. If religious thought and practice continue to be shaped by the world around them, we can expect a number of dramatic developments in coming decades.

The global expansion of Christianity reflects a seismic shift which will be mirrored in a number of organizational changes. The majority of Christians now live south of the equator, and the "third world" nations are the fastest growing Christian populations. The image of Christianity as a European religion, transplanted to North America and then introduced by missionaries to the rest of the world, is no longer accurate. Christianity is already the mainstream religion in many coun-

The Cathedral of Notre Dame de La Paix, Yamoussoukro, Ivory Coast, 2000.

Architecture suggestive of earlier European culture is transplanted in 2000 to Africa, thereby signaling the universal message of Christianity.

tries that were only missionary fields a century ago. Leaders such as Jaime Lachica Sin (b. 1928) in the Philippines and Desmond Tutu (b. 1931) of South Africa have brought "post-colonial" Christianity to the attention of the European and North American churches. A pope from beyond Europe is a distinct possibility; and other hierarchies are likely to diversify as well.

Addressing social concerns, and taking a progressive role among institutional custodians of cultural values, should continue to occupy church leadership and laity in the twenty-first century. Themes that originated with liberation theology, such as a policy of preference for the poor and a recognition of the pastoral needs of base communities, are being applied in other cultures where Christianity may still be on the rise while poverty and injustice dominate. Within countries where the church is already firmly established, many churches are demonstrating increased commitment to social concerns, particularly on behalf of the poor and marginalized.

However, taking steps to alleviate obvious human misery is an easy call for the church. Other issues require discernment and judgments that have as much potential to divide communities as to unite them. For example, attitudes toward homosexuality, in general and within the clergy in particular, have been at the forefront of a number of mainline Protestant and Catholic denominations' deliberations, and have proven to be tests of the liberalism of these churches. Does a policy of inclusiveness on the grounds of Christian charity extend to those unions that are thought by some to violate the divine ordering of sexuality? Or are biblical accounts of creation and New Testament prohibitions of non-heterosexual behavior so much ancient taboo, to be abandoned in the interest of progress? Similarly, the ordination of women, common in many churches for decades, is still decades away for some, and out of the question completely for others. Here

Anastasis, Kariye Camii church, Istanbul, 1320. Mural.

Within a medieval mural painting that advances dramatically to a future beyond our imaginings, Jesus is shown pulling Adam and Eve from their graves at the end of time.

too the issue is one of literalness in adhering to the biblical text, and of deciding whether differentiation of gender roles was something cultural when the biblical books were written (and thus optional in different historical settings) or written into the organization of the Christian community (and thus non-negotiable).

Medical science has made it possible to support and extend life in a manner inconceivable only a few decades ago; and here too, Christian communities must face potentially divisive issues. If all life is to be protected, is it therefore legitimate to apply all technological means to sustain it, even when one is no longer able to function in any meaningful way in society? Or is the medical profession playing God and intervening in the natural cycle of individuals' lives? If we say "yes" to this latter question, do we not also call into question all the now-standard organ transplants and operations for cancer? If a pregnant woman discovers that her fetus will die or be unable to live a normal life, does the perceived wrongness of abortion outweigh medical intervention to save her life? If such a child should be diagnosed with a genetic disease, are the parents justified in having another child, or cloning embryonic tissue in order to save the one sick child? These questions may not have sounded like religious matters a decade or two ago, but they do now, for they summon up the most elemental questions of religion: the definition of life and the beliefs and qualities that give it value.

Bibliography

Part One: The Emergence of Christianity

Sources

Cameron, Ron, ed. *The Other Gospels: Non-Canonical Gospel Texts*. Philadelphia, PA: Westminster Press, 1982. A fascinating and readable selection of the earliest "banned" books in Christianity.

Eusebius, *The History of the Church from Christ to Constantine*. London: Penguin Classics, 1946. The standard source for the first three centuries, but the persecutions are exaggerated and Constantine appears larger than life.

Lake, K., trans. *The Apostolic Fathers*. Cambridge, MA: Loeb Classical Library/Harvard University Press, 1912. The earliest theological works in the Christian tradition outside the New Testament.

Schaff, Philip, ed. *Ante-Nicene Fathers, Nicene and Post-Nicene Fathers*. The most extensive collection in English of early Christian writings, thirty-eight volumes in all. The Victorian translations offer peculiar reading at times, but the set is a treasure-trove of Patristic texts.

Studies

Alföldi, Andrew. *The Conversion of Constantine and Pagan Rome*, tr. H. Mattingly. Oxford, England: Oxford University Press, 1948. Background to the political developments of Constantine's reign.

Herrin, Judith. *The Formation of Christendom*. Princeton, NJ: Princeton University Press, 1987. More "late antiquity" than "early Church," but still valuable for insights into Christian culture.

Fredricksen, Paula. *Jesus of Nazareth, King of the Jews: A Jewish Life and the Emergence of Christianity*. New York: Knopf, 1999. This describes the context of the first Christian teachings.

Frend, W.H.C. *The Rise of Christianity*. Philadelphia, PA: Fortress Press, 1984. Comprehensive and readable. Strong on the social history of the early Church.

Kelly, J.N.D. *Early Christian Creeds*. London, England: Longman, 1972. The development of creeds up to the period of Charlemagne.

Kelly, J.N.D. *Early Christian Doctrines*. New York: Harper & Row, 1978. Clear and detailed study of Nicaea and its aftermath in Greek theology.

Koester, Helmut. *Introduction to the New Testament*, 2 vols. Philadelphia, PA: Fortress Press, 1982. The intellectual world and social context of the first Christians, meticulously detailed.

Lietzmann, Hans. *A History of the Early Church*, tr. B. L. Woolf, 4 vols. London, England: Lutterworth Press, 1937–51. As comprehensive as Frend's *The Rise of Christianity*, but stronger on doctrinal than social history.

Mattingly, Harold. *Christianity in the Roman Empire*. New York: W. W. Norton, 1967. The religious transformation of Roman culture as seen on coins and in official documents.

Parkes, James. *The Conflict of the Church and the Synagogue: A Study in the Origins of Antisemitism*. New York: Athenaeum, 1979. Detailed and informative on Roman law as well as theology.

Pelikan, Jaroslav. *Christianity and Classical Culture*. New Haven, CT: Yale University Press, 1994. Essays on one of the most complex problems in early Church history: the dividing line between "pagan" and "Christian."

Perelman, Hayim Goren. *Siblings: Rabbinic Judaism and Early Christianity at their Beginnings*. New York: Paulist Press, 1989.

Films

The Gospel According to Saint Matthew (1964), directed by Pier Paolo Pasolini. Ordinary people playing the ordinary people from Matthew's Gospel, including Pasolini's own mother playing Mary.

The Greatest Story Ever Told (1965), directed by George Stevens. Detailed, but short on emotion.

The Last Temptation of Christ (1987), directed by Martin Scorsese. Realistic setting. Fantastic scenario in which Jesus has second thoughts about his mission on earth.

The Robe (1953), directed by Henry Koster The Passion seen through the eyes of a Roman centurion, who converts to the faith through the miraculous power of Jesus' garment.

Internet Resources

Early Church On-Line Encyclopedia (ECOLE). (http://cedar.evansville.edu/~ecoleweb/). Extensive and invaluable resource for students at all levels.

Novel

Sienkiewicz, Henryk. *Quo Vadis?* (1896). A hugely popular retelling of life under Roman persecutions, translated into many languages.

Part Two: The Christian Religion in Late Antiquity

Sources

Fry, Timothy, ed., et al. *The Rule of St. Benedict*. Collegeville, MN: Liturgical Press, 1981. Latin text and translation, with rich introductory material.

Sherley-Price, L., trans. *Bede's History of the English Church and People*. Harmondsworth, England: Penguin, 1955.

Webb, J.F. and D.H. Farmer, ed., trans. *The Age of Bede*. Harmondsworth, England: Penguin, 1965. Vignettes of seventh-century English religious life.

Studies

Bradshaw, Paul F. *The Search for the Origins of Christian Worship*. New York: Oxford University Press, 1992, 2002. A reconstruction of the beginnings of liturgy.

Bullough, D.A. *Carolingian Renewal: Sources and Heritage*. Manchester, England: Manchester University Press, 1991. Scholarly essays on various aspects of the ninth-century world.

Daniélou, Jean. *The Origins of Latin Christianity*. Philadelphia, PA: Westminster Press, 1977. A study by one of the leading French medievalists.

Dutton, Paul Edward. *The Politics of Dreaming in the Carolingian Empire*. Lincoln, NE: University of Nebraska Press, 1994. On dreams and their interpretations as imperial propaganda.

Fisher, Eugene J., ed. *The Jewish Roots of Christian Liturgy*. New York: Paulist Press, 1990.

Heer, Friedrich. *Charlemagne and his World*. New York: Macmillan, 1975. A lavish pictorial account of early medieval culture.

Herrin, Judith. *The Formation of Christendom*. Oxford, England: Blackwell, 1987. Detailed account of the formation of medieval culture; very good on Greek sources.

Hildebrandt, M.M. *The External School in Carolingian Society*. Leiden, Germany: Brill, 1992. A study of monasteries and their educational missions.

Leclercq, Jean, O.S.B. *The Love of Learning and the Desire for God: A Study of Monastic Culture*, trans. C. Misrahi. New York: Fordham University Press, 1982. The classic study of monastic theology.

Marenbon, John. *Early Medieval Philosophy (480–1150): An Introduction*. London and Boston: Routledge and Kegan Paul, 1983.

Stewart, Columba. *Cassian the Monk*. New York: Oxford University Press, 1998. A sympathetic and careful overview of John Cassian's work.

Sullivan, Richard E., ed. *"The Gentle Voices of Teachers": Aspects of Learning in the Carolingian Age*. Columbia, OH: Ohio State University Press, 1995. A study of aspects of the history of ideas.

Ullmann, Walter. *The Carolingian Renaissance and the Idea of Kingship*. London: Methuen, 1969. Lectures on political theory by a master historian.

Ullmann, Walter. *The Growth of Papal Government in the Middle Ages*. London: Methuen, 1970. A study of the development of centralized ecclesiastical authority.

Part Three: Medieval Western Christian Culture

Sources

Deane, S.N., trans. *Anselm: Basic Writings*. Chicago, IL: Open Court, 1966.

Fairweather, Eugene R., ed. *A Scholastic Miscellany: Anselm to Ockham*. Philadelphia, PA: Westminster, 1956.

Pegis, Anton, ed. *Thomas Aquinas: Basic Writings*, 2 vols. New York: Random House, 1945.

Tierney, Brian. *The Crisis of Church and State 1050–1300*. Toronto, Canada: Medieval Academy of America, 1988. A documentary history of Gregorian Reform and its aftermath.

Wippel, John F. and Allan B. Wolter. *Medieval Philosophy: From St. Augustine to Nicholas of Cusa*. New York: Free Press, 1969. A broad sampling of philosophical excerpts.

Studies

De Wulf, Maurice. *An Introduction to Scholastic Philosophy, Medieval and Modern*. New York: Dover, 1956. An introduction to the newly-rediscovered system of Thomism.

Evans, G.R. *Anselm and Talking about God*. Oxford: Clarendon Press, 1978.

Grundmann, Herbert. *Religious Movements in the Middle Ages*, tr. Steven Rowan. Notre Dame, IL: University of Notre Dame Press, 1995. The standard account, copiously documented.

Leff, Gordon. *Medieval Thought: Saint Augustine to Ockham*. Harmondsworth, England: Penguin, 1958. A condensed introduction to the philosophical tradition.

LeGoff, Jacques. *The Birth of Purgatory*. New York: Cambridge University Press, 1984. The rationale for and representations of an intermediate realm.

Marenbon, John. *Later Medieval Philosophy (1150–1350): An Introduction*. London and New York: Routledge and Kegan Paul, 1987.

Martin, C.J.F. *An Introduction to Medieval Philosophy*. Edinburgh, Scotland: Edinburgh University Press, 1996.

Maurer, Armand A. *Medieval Philosophy*. New York: Random House, 1962.

Murray, Alexander. *Reason and Society in the Middle Ages*. Oxford, England: Clarendon Press, 1985.

Pieper, Josef. *Scholasticism: Personalities and Problems of Medieval Philosophy*. New York: Pantheon Books, 1960. A graceful and appreciative essay on Scholastic theology.

Rickaby, Joseph. *Scholasticism*. New York: Dover, 1908. A defense of the tradition against modern attacks and neglect.

Southern, R.W. *The Making of the Middle Ages*. New Haven, CT: Yale University Press, 1953. One of the books that brought the medieval period to light in North America.

Ullmann, Walter. *A Short History of the Papacy in the Middle Ages*. London: Methuen, 1972. A lucid narrative by a leading papal historian.

CD

Hildegard von Bingen: Voice of the Blood. Deutsche Harmonia Mundi. The liturgy in settings by the great mystic.

Part Four: From Medieval to Modern, from One Church, Many

Sources

Bromiley, G.W., ed. *Zwingli and Bullinger*. Philadelphia, PA: G.W. Bromiley, 1953. Shorter works by Zwingli, with Bullinger's "Of the Holy Catholic Church."

Calvin, John. *Institutes of the Christian Religion*, ed. and tr. J.T. McNeill and F.L. Battles. Philadelphia, PA: Westminster, 1960. The classic foundation of Reformed theology.

Hillerbrand, Hans J., ed. *The Oxford Encyclopedia of the Reformation*, 4 vols. New York: Oxford University Press, 1996. A study of all the major themes and figures, with bibliographies.

Kretzmann, Norman, ed., et al. *The Cambridge History of Later Medieval and Renaissance Philosophy*. Cambridge, England: Cambridge University Press, 1982.

Lull, Timothy, ed. *Martin Luther's Basic Theological Writings*. Philadelphia, PA: Fortress Press, 1989. A selection of Luther's writings from the fifty-five-volume American Edition (Fortress Press, 1955–86).

Oberman, Heiko, ed. *Forerunners of the Reformation*. Philadelphia, PA: Fortress Press, 1981. Excerpts from the later Scholastics.

Olin, John, ed. *Catholic Reform*. New York: Fordham University Press, 1990.

Schmitt, Charles B., ed., et al. *The Cambridge History of Renaissance Philosophy*. Cambridge, England: Cambridge University Press, 1988.

Williams, G.H., ed. *Anabaptist and Spiritual Writers*. Philadelphia, PA: Westminster, 1963. A representative selection from the Radical tradition.

Studies

Brecht, Martin. *Martin Luther*. tr. James L. Schaaf, 3 vols. Minneapolis, MN: Fortress Press, 1993. A study of Luther's life and writings.

Edwards, Mark U. *Printing, Propaganda, and Martin Luther*. Berkeley, CA: University of California Press, 1994. Essays on the press as an instrument of religious reform.

Lindberg, Carter, ed. *Theologians of the Reformation*. Oxford, England: Blackwell, 2001. Essays on a number of influential thinkers of the period.

Muir, Edward. *Ritual in Early Modern Europe*. Cambridge, England: Cambridge University Press, 1997.

Muller, Richard A. *Post-Reformation Reformed Dogmatics*. Grand Rapids, MI: Baker Press, 1987–93. A summa from the Calvinist Summas.

Oberman, Heiko. *The Harvest of Medieval Theology: Gabriel Biel and Late Medieval Nominalism*. Cambridge, MA: Harvard University Press, 1963, and various reprints. A pathbreaking book, revealing relations between late Scholasticism and the early Reformation.

Sedgwick, Alexander. *Jansenism in Seventeenth-Century France*. Charlottesville, VA: University Press of Virginia, 1977.

Williams, George H. *The Radical Reformation*. Kirksville, MI: Jefferson University Press, 1993. A meticulously detailed survey of the Anabaptist movement.

CD

Junghans, Helmar. *Martin Luther 1583–1546*. CD-ROM. IBM Deutschland. The background and resources for appreciating Luther's work.

Part Five: From Enlightenment to Modernity

Sources

Descartes, René, *Philosophical Works*, 2 vols, trs. E.S. Haldane and G.R.T. Ross. Cambridge, England: Cambridge University Press, 1911.

Gaustad, Edwin S., ed. *A Documentary History of Religion in America*, 2 vols. Grand Rapids, MI: Eerdmans, 1983.

Heimert, Alan and Andrew Delbanco, eds. *The Puritans in America: A Narrative Anthology*. Cambridge, MA: Harvard University Press, 1985.

Hume, David. *Dialogues Concerning Natural Religion*, ed. Martin Bell. Harmondsworth, England: Penguin, 1990.

Smith, John E., Harry Stout, and Kenneth Minkema, eds. *A Jonathan Edwards Reader*. New Haven, CT: Yale University Press, 1995.

Studies

Bermejo, Luis. *Towards Christian Reunion: Vatican 1, Obstacles and Opportunities*. Lanham, MD: University Press of America, 1987.

Byrne, Peter. *Natural Religion and the Nature of Religion: The Legacy of Deism*. New York: Routledge, 1989. A study of the impersonal deity and its impact on Christian thought.

Chadwick, Owen. *The Victorian Church*. London: Black, 1967–70. A masterful look at religion in nineteenth-century England.

Clements, K.W. *Schleiermacher: Pioneer of Modern Theology*. London: Collins, 1987.

Collinson, Patrick. *English Puritanism*. London: Historical Association, 1983. A careful introduction by a leading historian of the Puritan movement.

Delbanco, Andrew. *The Puritan Ordeal*. Cambridge, MA: Harvard University Press, 1984.

Dreyer, Frederick. *The Genesis of Methodism*. Bethlehem, PA: Lehigh University Press, 1999.

Engell, James. *The Creative Imagination: Enlightenment to Romanticism*. Cambridge, MA: Harvard University Press, 1981.

Foulkes, Richard. *Church and State in Victorian England*. Cambridge, England: Cambridge University Press, 1997.

Gaukroger, Stephen. *Descartes: An Intellectual Biography*. Oxford, England: Clarendon Press, 1995. The philosopher's thought taken as a whole and set into its context.

Gould, Philip. *Covenant and Republic: Historical Romance and the Politics of Puritanism*. Cambridge, England: Cambridge University Press, 1996.

Hampson, Norman. *A Cultural History of the Enlightenment*. New York: Pantheon Books, 1968.

Harlan, David. *The Clergy and the Great Awakening in New England*. Ann Arbor, MI: UMI Research Press, 1980.

Harris, Harriet. *Fundamentalism and Evangelicals*. Oxford, England: Clarendon Press, 1998. The reemergence of conservative Protestantism.

Harrison, R.K. *Biblical Criticism: Historical, Literary, and Textual*. Grand Rapids, MI: Zondervan, 1978. The critical revolution in biblical study, critically assessed.

Lambert, Frank. *Pedlar in Divinity: George Whitefield and the Transatlantic Revivals*. Princeton, NJ: Princeton University Press, 1994. A study of the beginnings of Methodism in the American colonies.

Miller, Perry. *Jonathan Edwards*. Amherst, MA: University of Massachusetts Press, 1981. A reprint of the 1949 classic that brought much of Edwards' thought to light.

Noll, Mark A. *American Evangelical Christianity: An Introduction*. Oxford, England: Blackwell Publishing, 2001.

Pelikan, Jaroslav. *Bach and the Theologians*. New Haven, CT: Yale University Press, 1986.

Pottmeyer, Hermann. *Towards a Papacy in Communion: Perspectives from Vatican Councils I and II*. New York: Crossroad, 1998.

Ryme, Peter. *Natural Religion and the Nature of Religion: The Legacy of Deism*. New York: Routledge, 1989.

Schmidt, Martin. *John Wesley: A Theological Biography*. New York: Abingdron Press, 1962.

Smith, John E. *Jonathan Edwards: Puritan, Preacher, Philosopher*. Notre Dame, IN: University of Notre Dame Press, 1992. A sympathetic assessment by a formidable philosopher of religion.

Welch, Claude. *Protestant Thought in the Nineteenth Century*, 2 vols. New Haven, CT: Yale University Press, 1972–85. A study of the main lines and many of the subtleties of a theological renaissance.

Part Six: The Twentieth Century and Beyond

Sources

Catechism of the Catholic Church. Vatican City, Rome: Libreria Editrice Vaticana, 1994.

Flannery, Austin P., ed. *Documents of Vatican II*. Grand Rapids, MI: Eerdmans, 1975.

Flannery, Austin P., ed. *Vatican Council II: More Postconciliar Documents*, 3 vols. Boston, MA: St. Paul Editions, 1982.

McLaughlin, Terence P., ed. *The Church and Reconstruction of the Modern World: The Social Encyclicals of Pius XI*. Garden City, NY: Image Books, 1957.

Studies

Alberigo, Giuseppe, ed. *History of Vatican II*. Maryknoll, NY: Orbis Books, 1995.

Brackley, Dean. *Divine Revelation: Salvation and Liberation in Catholic Thought*. Maryknoll, NY: Orbis Books, 1996.

Cadorette, Curt. *From the Heart of the People: The Theology of Gustavo Gutiérrez*. Oak Park, IL: Meyer Stone Books, 1988.

Costa, Ruy O. and Lorine M. Getz. *Struggles for Solidarity: Liberation Theologies in Tension*. Minneapolis, MN: Fortress Press, 1992. Unity and diversity in the liberation movement.

Ferm, Dean William. *Contemporary American Theologies: A Critical Survey*. San Francisco, CA: Harper & Row, 1990.

Ferm, Dean William. *Third World Liberation Theologies: An Introductory Survey*. Maryknoll, NY: Orbis Books, 1986. Both of Ferm's surveys are precise and informative.

Gorrell, Donald K. *The Age of Social Responsibility*. Macon, GA: Mercer University Press, 1988.

Haddad, Yvonne. *Daughters of Abraham: Feminist Thought in Judaism, Christianity, and Islam*. Gainesville, FL: University Press of Florida, 2001. A bold venture in comparative feminist studies.

Hopkins, Charles H. *The Rise of the Social Gospel in American Protestantism*. New Haven, CT: Yale University Press, 1940. A study of Walter Rauschenbusch and his contemporaries in context.

Irvin, Dale T. *Hearing Many Voices: Dialogue and Diversity in the Ecumenical Movement*. Lanham, MD: University Press of America, 1994.

Isherwood, Lisa. *Introducing Feminist Theology*. Sheffield, England: Sheffield Academic Press, 1993.

Rouse, Ruth and Stephen Neill, eds. *A History of the Ecumenical Movement, 1517–1948*. London: SPCK, 1967.

Ruether, Rosemary R. *Religion and Sexism*. New York: Simon and Schuster, 1974.

Till, Barry. *The Churches Search for Unity*. Harmondsworth, England: Penguin, 1972.

Van der Brent, A.J., ed. *Major Studies and Themes in the Ecumenical Movement*. Geneva, Switzerland: World Council of Churches, 1981. A study of the progress of the ecumenical movement, measured at its peak.

Wiles, Maurice. *Christian Theology and Inter-Religious Dialogue*. Philadelphia, PA: Trinity Press International, 1992.

CDs

Profeta Salvadoreño. Horizontes. Salvadoran music of the liberation movement, some celebrating the martyr Romero.

Guillermo Cuéllar, Misa Mesoamericana; Exceso de Eqipaje. Fundación Monseñor Oscar A. Romero. The complete Mass, cast in lively Latin-American form.

Literary Credits

Every effort has been made to trace or contact all copyright holders. The publishers would be pleased to rectify any omissions brought to their notice at the earliest opportunity.

Baker Book House: from *Writings of James Arminius* by James Arminius, translated by James Nichols (Grand Rapids, MI: Baker Book House, 1956); **Cambridge University Press**: from *The New English Bible: New Testament* (Cambridge, UK: Cambridge University Press/Oxford: Oxford University Press, 1961), © Oxford University Press and Cambridge University Press 1961, 1970, reprinted by permission of the publishers; **T & T Clark**: from *Church Dogmatics*, Volume 2 by Karl Barth (Edinburgh, Scotland: T & T Clark, 1957), reprinted by permission of the publisher; **Columbia University Press**: from *The Letters of St. Boniface*, translated by Ephraim Emerton (New York: Columbia University Press, 1940), © 1940 Columbia University Press, reprinted by permission of the publisher; **Continuum International Publishing**: from *Complete Works of St John of the Cross*, edited by E. A. Peers, translated by P. Silverio de Santa Teresa (London: Burns, Oates & Washburn, 1934), reprinted by permission of the publisher; **Sutton Courtnay Press**: from *Life, Early Letters, and Eucharistic Writings of Peter Martyr*, edited by J. C. McLelland and G. E. Duffield (Montreal: Sutton Courtenay Press, 1989); **Doubleday Broadway Publishing Group**: from *The Fire of Love and the Mending of Life* by Richard Rolle, translated by M. L. del Mastro (Garden City, New York: Image Books, 1981), © M. L. del Mastro, used by permission of Doubleday, a division of Random House, Inc.; **Garrett Green**: from *Critique of all Revelation* by Johann Gottlieb Fichte, translated by Garrett Green (New York: Cambridge University Press, 1978); **HarperCollins Publishers**: from *On Religion: Speeches to its Cultural Despisers* by Friedrich Schleiermacher, translated by John Owen (New York: Harper & Row, 1958), © 1958 by Harper & Row Publishers, Inc., © renewed 1986 by Harper & Row Publishers, Inc., reprinted by permission of the publisher; from *Theology and the Church* by Juan Luis Segundo, translated by John W. Diercksmeier (New York: Harper & Row, 1987), © 1985 by Juan Luis Segundo, reprinted by permission of the publisher; from *A Rauschenbusch Reader* by Walter Rauschenbusch, edited by Benson Y. Landis (New York: Harper & Row, 1957); **Liverpool University Press**: from *Donatist Martyr Stories*, edited by Maureen Tilley (Liverpool, UK: Liverpool University Press, 1986), reprinted by permission of the publisher; **Edwin Mellen Press**: from *On Virginity and Against Remarriage* by John Chrysostom, translated by Sally Riegershoe (New York: Edwin Mellen Press, 1983); **Orbis Books**: from *A Theology of Liberation* by Gustavo Gutiérrez, translated/edited by Sister Caridad Inda and John Eagleson (Maryknoll, New York: Orbis Books, 1988), translation © 1988 Orbis Books, reprinted by permission of the publisher; **Oxford University Press**: from *The Major Works* by Anselm of Canterbury, edited by Brian Davies and G. R. Evans (Oxford, UK: Oxford University Press, 1998), © Janet Fairweather, 1998, reprinted by permission of the publisher; from *Epistle to the Romans* by Karl Barth, translated by Edwyn C. Hoskyns (Oxford, UK: Oxford University Press, 1933), reprinted by permission of the publisher; from *The Praise of Folly* by Erasmus, translated by John Wilson, edited by P. S. Allen (Oxford, UK: Oxford University Press, 1913), reprinted by permission of the publisher; from *Documents of the Christian Church*, selected and edited by Henry Bettenson (Oxford, UK: Oxford University Press, 1947), reprinted by permission of the publisher; **Paulist Press**: from *The Institutes* by John Cassian, translated by Boniface Ramsey (New York: Newman Press, 2000); from *The Life of St Francis* by St. Bonaventure, translated by Ewert Cousins (New York: Paulist Press); from *Francis and Clare: The Complete Works*, translated by Regis Armstrong and Ignatius C. Brady (New York: Paulist Press, 1982), from *Pietists: Selected Writings*, edited by Peter C. Erb (New York: Paulist Press, 1983); **Penguin Books**: from *The Book of Margery Kempe* by Margery Kempe, translated by B. A. Windeatt (London: Penguin Classics, 1965), © B. A. Windeatt, 1965, reprinted by permission of the publisher; from *Lives of the Saints*, translated by J. F. Webb (London: Penguin Classics, 1965), © J. F. Webb, 1965, reprinted by permission of the publisher; **Tim Reuter**: from *Ninth-century Histories: Volume 2. Annals of Fulda*, translated by Timothy Reuter (Manchester, UK: Manchester University Press, 1992), reprinted by permission of Tim Reuter; **John K. Ryan**: from *Introduction to the Devout Life* by St. Francis de Sales, translated by John K. Ryan (New York: Harper & Row, 1966); **Sheed & Ward**: from *Complete Works of St. Teresa of Jesus* by St. Teresa of Avila, edited by E. A. Peers, translated by P. Silverio de Santa Teresa (London: Sheed & Ward, 1946); **Simon & Schuster**: from *A Scholastic Miscellany: Anselm to Ockham*, edited/translated by Eugene R. Fairweather (New York: Macmillan, 1970); **SPCK Publishing**: from *Hildegard of Bingen: Mystical Writings* by Hildegard of Bingen, edited by Fiona

Bowie and Oliver Davies, new translations by Robert Carver (New York: Crossroad, 1990), reprinted by permission of the publisher; from *New Eusebius: Documents Illustrating the History of the Church to A.D. 337*, edited by James Stevenson (London: SPCK, 1987), reprinted by permission of the publisher; **SUNY Press**: from *The Ages of the World* by Friedrich von Schelling, translated by Jason Wirth (New York: SUNY Press, 2000); **Craig R. Thompson**: from *Colloquies of Erasmus*, translated by Craig R. Thompson (Chicago, IL: University of Chicago Press, 1965); **Trinity Press International**: from *A Reinhold Niebuhr Reader* by Reinhold Niebuhr, edited by Charles C. Brown (Philadelphia, PA: Trinity Press International, 1992); **University Press of Kansas**: from *The Earliest Life of Gregory the Great*, translated by Bertram Colgrave (Lawrence, KS: University Press of Kansas, 1968), reprinted by permission of the publisher; **John Wolters**: from *Revelation of Divine Love* by Julian of Norwich, translated by Clifton Wolters (London: Penguin Books, 1966), reprinted by permission of John Wolters.

Picture Credits

The author and publisher wish to acknowledge, with thanks, the following photographic sources. Every effort has been made to trace or contact all copyright holders. The publisher would be pleased to rectify any omissions brought to their notice at the earliest opportunity.

©Inigo Bujedo Aguirre, London: page 332
AKG London: pages 32, 55, 71, 121, 135, 139, 161, 185, 192, 200, 205, 230, 283, 286, 293, 308, 363
Andes Press Agency: page 382
The Art Archive: pages 196, 219, 386
Bridgeman Art Library: pages 49, 81, 97, 100, 108, 134, 147, 151, 157, 166, 170, 175, 249, 253, 259, 323
Mary Evans Picture Library: pages 47, 62, 64, 180, 190, 216, 242, 278, 292, 296, 298, 303, 305, 329, 351

Sonia Halliday: pages 92, 93
Robert Harding Picture Library: pages 28, 385
R. Higginson, London: page 76
Hulton Getty: pages 51, 105, 120, 221, 228, 232, 245, 282, 313, 326, 337
© Peter Kent, London: page 60
David King Collection, London: page 346
Peter Newark's American Pictures: pages 267, 269
Panos Pictures: page 381
Photo Oikoumene: page 360
Rex Features: page 364
Scala: pages 104, 130, 183
Henri & Anne Stierlin, Geneva: page 72

Index